CONNECTING KIDS

AND THE

INTERNET

a handbook for librarians, teachers, and parents

SECOND EDITION

Allen C. Benson and Linda M. Fodemski

NEAL-SCHUMAN NETGUIDE SERIES

Neal-Schuman Publishers, Inc.
New York   London

In addition to acknowledgments made elsewhere in this book, the authors and publisher are grateful to the following corporations for permission to reproduce the indicated figures:

Figs. 4–1, 4–2, 4–3 — Copyright 1999 Netscape Communications Corporation. All rights reserved.

Fig. 5–12 — Crayola, Chevron, and Serpentine designs are registered trademarks; Rainbow/Swash is a trademark of Binney & Smith, used with permission.

Fig. 5–19 — Schoolhouse Rock is a registered trademark and service mark of American Broadcasting Companies, Inc. All rights reserved.

Fig. 6–3 — Tramline, Inc.

Fig. 6–7 — Image provided courtesy of the JASON Foundation for Education.

Figs. 7–3 and 10–2 — Copyright © Houghton Mifflin Company. Reprinted by permission of Houghton Mifflin Company. All rights reserved.

Fig. 10–7 — Reprinted with permission of the International Telementor Center

Published by Neal-Schuman Publishers, Inc.
100 Varick Street
New York, NY 10013

Printed and bound in the United States of America.

Library of Congress Cataloging-in-Publication Data

Benson, Allen C.
    Connecting kids and the Internet : a handbook for librarians, teachers, and parents / by Allen C. Benson and Linda M. Fodemski. — 2nd ed.
        p.   cm.—(Neal-Schuman NetGuide series)
    Includes bibliographical references and index.
    ISBN 1-55570-348-8
    1. Internet (Computer network) in education Handbooks, manuals, etc.   2. Internet (Computer network)—Study and teaching Handbooks, manuals, etc.   3. Education—Computer network resources.
I. Fodemski, Linda.   II. Title   III. Series: Neal-Schuman net-guide series.
LB1044.87.B87   1999
025.06'37—dc21   99-16424
                                                          CIP

Contents

Figures

Tables

Preface

Both in school and at home, we all want the children in our care to have the best opportunities to learn, share, grow, and enrich their lives. The Internet offers kids remarkable opportunities. It enables them to access information that will help them with their homework and school papers—information that sometimes is unavailable anywhere else. The Net also opens up nearly boundless ways to make the most of free time by exploring hobbies online, playing games alone or with others, and sharing thoughts with friends around the world.

This second edition of *Connecting Kids and The Internet* will help teachers, librarians, parents, and anyone else who wants or needs to introduce children to the Internet. It was written with the understanding that many adults who read it might find terms like search engines, electronic archives, and global networks—and the vast array of the Web daunting. To help soften the transition, the book was designed as both a resource tool and a tutorial for self-teaching.

Since the first edition of *Connecting Kids and the Internet* was published in 1996, the Internet has grown and evolved so rapidly that there is little semblance between the Internet we described in 1996 and the Internet of today.

Requiring no prior experience, the current edition explains in easy-to-understand terms what the Internet is, how you can connect to it, what services are available, which tools you can use to access free resources, and how you can introduce these resources to children so they can put them to practical use.

If you are not yet connected to the Internet, we will show you how to do it yourself. Starting at the beginning, we define basic computer terminology and explain the hardware and software you will need. Then we explore a wide range of connection methods, explaining each in terms a novice can understand.

Tools and resources are thoroughly explained in non-technical terms. We present a wide variety of practical and creative ideas for using these tools with children. Also included are lesson plans that can be used as-is at home or in the classroom. They can also be used as templates for creating lesson plans yourself.

The CD-ROM, with a "Link Farm" and lesson plans, is a new feature of the second edition. The Link Farm enables the reader to link to fun, safe sites on the Internet directly from the CD-ROM. We have chosen both planning sites for adults and exciting sites for kids to explore. The CD-ROM also has 14 lesson plans that provide a wide variety of practical and creative ideas for using these Internet tools with children.

Teachers in both public and private schools who want to integrate the Internet into their traditional classroom activities will find this book useful because it offers unique lesson plans that teach kids how to utilize the Internet as a communication and resource discovery tool.

School library media specialists will find *Connecting Kids and the Internet* valuable as they may be the only individuals in their school who have an Internet connection. They can learn to access the Internet with this book, which will enable them to provide Internet resources along with traditional resources when teachers request materials to supplement classroom projects.

Training sessions for teachers could be set up using *Connecting Kids and the Internet* or the library media specialist could work through Parts IV and V with an entire class, teacher and all! Youth Services librarians in public libraries could reach the older children with Internet Day, selecting various ideas from this book as "topics of the day."

Parents who homeschool and parents in general can use this book to help their kids use the Internet safely and productively.

Elementary and secondary education professors as well as Internet trainers will also find this handbook a valuable tool for helping teachers and anyone else assisting children with the Internet.

WHAT IS THE SCOPE OF *CONNECTING KIDS AND THE INTERNET?*

Any book on the Internet could easily run into dozens of volumes, especially if it tried to list every resource and explain every application and operating system available. We have tried to focus on the best resources that are available for free, and the most practical, up-to-date, and popular systems running on the Internet.

Connecting Kids and the Internet, Second Edition, is organized in six parts:

Part 1, "Essential Information for Parents, Teachers, and Librarians," covers the basics: What the Internet is all about, how kids and teachers use the Internet, and why they do so. A glossary of terms and information on where to find online help and Internet-related news will help the reader become more comfortable using the Internet. Part I also covers Internet etiquette, safety, rules, and security.

Part II, "The World Wide Web for Younger Kids," talks about the software kids use to explore the Web. We start at the beginning with the basics. Once a firm footing in how to use Web browsers is established, special Web resources for kids are introduced. We show you some of our favorite sites, introduce you to online field trips, and suggest online entertainment for kids.

Part III, "Talking It Up: Fun Internet Activities for All Ages," introduces basic e-mail services—what e-mail software is and how to use it. This section covers mailing lists and how kids can find other individuals with similar interests. Part III closes with step-by-step instructions kids can follow to build their own Web pages.

Part IV, "Nose to the Grindstone: Learning Activities for All Ages," presents the nuts and bolts of finding and retrieving online information using search engines and subject trees. This section provides extensive search strategies for using full text resources, including newspapers, magazines, and books. We show you how to help kids find online libraries and tap into online bookstores. Chapter 15, which is completely new, presents self-study guides on a wide variety of topics, from how to use screen-capture programs for writing help sheets to how to find, install, and run telnet programs on the Internet. Part IV closes with what we think are "super surfing sites"—free resources that offer quality information in full text or abstract format.

Part V, "The Internet for Teens," will help you show older kids a side of the Net that goes beyond simple Web surfing. Chapter 16 explains what UNIX shell accounts are, how to get them, and why they are useful. The remaining chapters introduce kids to the world's largest bulletin board system and two of the most popular, early Internet applications: telnet and FTP.

Part VI, "Ready-to-Go Lesson Plans" reproduces the core of the 14 lesson plans discussed below. They are included in the book to facilitate easy browsing.

WHAT'S ON THE CD-ROM?

The CD-ROM located on the inside back cover is an exciting new complement to this edition of *Connecting Kids and Internet*. It contains two sections.

The first of these contains links—with annotations—to not only all of the Internet sites discussed in the book but to other carefully selected sites as well. Each of these links includes the name of the site, its URL (address), and a short annotation describing its purpose or it's potential use for educators.

You'll find hundreds of Web sites organized according to subject categories ranging from astronomy to zoology. Categories are listed separately so you can easily jump to a particular subject area. In selecting Internet sites for inclusion, we adhered to the same selection criteria we used in selecting the sites included in the book's lesson plans and activities:

1. the site's content is relevant to kids, parents, and/or educators;
2. material on the site supports the K–12 curriculum; or
3. the site is of high quality and was created by an authoritative individual or organization.

The second section on the CD-ROM is the lesson plans, which can be used as is so that a class can be planned with a minimum of lead-time. These lessons can also be customized to meet your own kids' needs or used as templates for other lessons.

When we were children, many of us were lucky enough to have special parents, teachers, coaches, librarians or other adults in the community who believed in us, encouraged a special talent, or communicated their love for something in a way that made us love it too. From games of catch in the backyard and encouragement in spite of missed notes at piano recitals, taking the extra time to make sure we really understood that geometry theorem, or recommending the next great book to take home from the library, these people helped us develop the confidence and direction we needed to shape our own adult lives.

With the help of such a concerned adult, we believe the Internet can give children the same kind of confidence and direction. We've seen the Internet energize and inspire kids to share and explore ideas, learn more about an activity or area of interest, or even test their abilities against those of their peers—while all along developing a comfort level with the technology that many believe will define our future.

Connecting Kids and the Internet contains all the information you need to make this happen with the children you work with. Turn the page and let's get started. They'll thank you for it later.

Conventions Used in This Book

This book applies the following conventions relating to typography, special word meanings, and formats for displaying certain types of data:

Characters that you type—commands or statements—are shown in boldface and the computer response is plain text. The following example shows that when you enter the command **type libraries.txt**, the computer responds with the text, *The document you tried to retrieve . . .*

```
$ type libraries.txt
The document you tried to retrieve has undergone many changes. Please read
the following:
The Gopher links are located at the following equivalent sites:
Name=Internet-accessible library catalogs
Type=1
Host=yaleinfo.yale.edu
Port=7000
Path=1/Libraries
```

Unless stated otherwise, pay careful attention to upper- and lowercase letters when entering data.

Special keys such as SHIFT, CTRL, ENTER, ALT, TAB, SPACE and ESC are shown in uppercase letters.

When you read the phrase "enter the command . . ." you should type whatever expression follows and then press the ENTER or RETURN key.

In specifying the form of a command, words enclosed in angle brackets (<>) indicate variables. In other words, you are to insert your own input in place of the bracketed information. For example, if you are asked to enter the command **get <filename>**, you supply the name of the file. If the file name were *net.bib.txt*, you would enter **get net.bib.txt**. If you are asked to type **subscribe <your name>**, you would type **subscribe John Doe** (assuming your name is John Doe).

For ease of reading, computer addresses and user names are printed in lowercase *italic* type. For example, *abenson3@ua1vm.ua.edu* and *cse.ogc.edu*. When an Internet address comes at the end of a sentence, please note that the last dot is a period, not part of the address.

File names and directory names also are printed in *italic* type. For example, you may be told to go to the */pub/history/doc* directory and retrieve a file called *constitution.txt*.

New terms are also in *italic* type. These are terms being introduced and defined for the first time.

By convention, the computer system you connect to is referred to as the *host* system. If it is your dial-up host (that is, the computer you dial-up to as your link to the Internet) it is referred to as a *local host*. If it is a host you springboard to from the local host (that is, reach by means of the local host), it is referred to as a *remote host*.

The terms *local* and *remote* have no significant meaning in geographic terms. The local host may be in the same room as you and the remote host may be on the other side of the globe, or your local host may be in another city and the remote host you use may be in the building adjoining your library.

Depending on the host to which you connect, the prompt you see on-screen will vary. A *prompt* is a symbol, word, or phrase that appears on the screen for the purpose of informing the user that the computer is ready to accept input. Common prompts are $ and %, but they may also consist of names or parts of Internet addresses such as *CRCINET 9>*. The terms *system prompt* or *host prompt* refer to the prompt used on a local or remote computer, a computer other than your own personal computer.

Command prompts are prompts that appear when you run a particular program on a host computer. Examples of typical command prompts you'll see include *FTP> MAIL>* and *TELNET>*, and so forth. When these and other prompts such as *help>* prompts are included in the text, they are printed in *italic* type.

Three address formats are used in this book:

Electronic mail (e-mail) addresses, whether they are e-mail addresses for individuals or pieces of software running on a computer, consist of two parts separated by an at sign (@), as in the following example:

> username@domain.com
> listserv@domain.edu
> info-server@domain.gov

Domain name and IP (Internet Protocol) addresses are computer addresses on the Internet, such as

> dra.com
> sklib.usask.ca
> 128.174.252.1
> 127.154.200.34

Web addresses start with a reference to a protocol such as *http://*, *gopher://*, *ftp://*, or *telnet://*, etc., followed by a domain name address such as *www.yahoo.com*, which may in turn be followed by a path name and file name such as */business/magazines/time.html*. This book uses the short-cut method of writing Web addresses that begin with *http://*; we drop the http://. For example, *www.star-host.com* is used instead of *http://www.star-host.com*. You can enter this short-cut address in our browser's **Location:** box. On your own, you can further shorten any URLs you find that begin with *www.* and end with *.com*. For example, for *www.star-host.com* you can enter only *star-host*.

Many terms used in this book are synonymous with the word *computer*. These include *remote host*, *local host*, *machine*, *personal computer*, *server*, and *system*.

The word *site* refers to a computer's location or address. For example, to say that a file is available at site *netcom.com* means that the file resides on a computer whose address is *netcom.com*.

Note: Throughout the book a number of Internet addresses for FTP sites, Web pages, and other directories are given. Be aware that many of these will change over time, especially Web pages and the location of files in FTP archives.

PART I

ESSENTIAL INFORMATION FOR PARENTS, TEACHERS, AND LIBRARIANS

Part I introduces the basics. In Chapter 1 you will learn what the Internet is, who uses it, and why. We specifically discuss ways educators and kids can use the Internet to learn new skills, locate information, have fun, and expand horizons. We also provide you with a glossary of terms and pointers on where to get help since the Internet is so big and changing so rapidly. In Chapter 2 we discuss issues relating to safety, rules, etiquette, and security. In Chapter 3 we point you toward resources that will help you keep up with the latest news about the Internet and find Internet-related news online.

Chapter 1

Finding Your Way through the Maze

Chapter 1 begins by defining some of the terms used in this book, listed alphabetically. With this list, you can create a spelling list or photocopy the entire section to post near your computer.

We explain who uses the Internet and why, including the key benefits it offers children using it today. Using this information, you can start discussions with your students about what they think the Internet is and why people use it, especially what they think kids might get out of it. You can use the discussion to springboard into mathematical concepts making estimates, figuring percentages, and constructing graphs and charts, depending on the age and grade of the children. You could then post their work in the room or on the main bulletin board for the rest of the school, send it home in a newsletter, or even submit it to the school or local paper.

We describe which organizations are in charge of shaping the Internet's technologies and we explain the Internet addressing system so you understand how e-mail addresses and Web addresses are constructed. We close out the chapter with tips on where to find help online.

BASIC INTERNET TERMINOLOGY

This section introduces you to terms that are used throughout this book.

AOL—*AOL* stands for *America Online*. This is a commercial online service that provides Internet access to local dial-up customers. It offers its subscribers exclusive access to shopping, events, travel information, news, and other information. To learn more, visit *www.aol.com*.

Archie—*Archie* is a collection of computers distributed around the world, called *Archie servers*. Each Archie server, independent of the others, collects and stores data on where files are located at thousands of FTP sites around the world. You use Archie when you want to find out where a particular file is located. You can use Archie to search through tens of thousands of files in seconds for the location of specific software applications or text files.

BBS—*BBS* stands for *bulletin board system*. This is a program that runs on a personal computer and enables others to call in through modems to download files, leave messages, or talk with others in real time. Real-time conversations online are conversations that take place in the present moment—response times are immediate, or at least measurable in milli- or microseconds.

Browsers—*Browsers* are Internet applications that enable you to see, listen to, and interact with various Internet resources and services. Two well-known browsers are Internet Explorer and Netscape Navigator.

CompuServe—*CompuServe* is a commercial online service that offers Internet access and memberships. When you join, you are given exclusive access to hundreds of forums, financial information, and advanced search capabilities. To learn more, visit *www.compuserve.com*.

E-mail—*E-mail*, short for *electronic mail*, is a service that enables people to exchange electronic messages much as they would conventional mail, but with many added conveniences like speed. E-mail can be used to communicate locally on a small network within a single library, or it can be used to communicate globally on the Internet.

Free-Net—*Free-Nets* are computerized community information systems. Most are linked to the Internet, and, as their name implies, there is no charge for connecting.

FTP—*FTP* stands for *File Transfer Protocol*. FTP is one of the most frequently used Internet services, enabling you to copy files from over a thousand different archives around the world. You'll use FTP to download software, images, and text files from all corners of the globe.

Gopher—*Gopher* is a service that enables you to find, retrieve, and publish information on the Internet. When you use Gopher, you are navigating through a system of menus. With Gopher, you can access things like the complete works of Shakespeare or the Federalist Papers or search over 5,000 computers around the world for Gopher items on a certain subject.

HTTP—*HTTP* stands for *HyperText Transfer Protocol*. This is the protocol that tells servers what to send to clients so the clients can view Web pages.

Internet—Also known as *the Net* for short. A system of interconnected computer networks spanning the globe that communicate with each other using a common communications protocol called TCP/IP.

IRC—*IRC* stands for *Internet Relay Chat*. This service enables participants to use their keyboards to "talk" with one another in real time in virtual rooms or "channels."

Mailing list—A *mailing list* (also called a *discussion list*) is a group or "list" of people with e-mail addresses. A message from one person on the list can be sent to everyone else on the list. Members of a list can join together to discuss a topic of mutual interest.

pathname or "path"—A *path* is the description of a sequence of menu items in Gopher or subdirectories in an FTP archive through which a program searches in order to find the files you specify.

TCP/IP—*TCP/IP* stands for *Transmission Control Protocol/Internet Protocol*. TCP/IP is the glue that binds the entire Internet together. It is the common language spoken by all systems *internetworking* around the globe. TCP/IP specifies two protocols, but is more often used to describe an entire suite of communications protocols that connect hosts on the Internet.

telnet—*Telnet* is a service that enables you to login to remote computer systems. For example, you use telnet to look at various library catalogs which are stored on university computers around the world.

URL—*URL* stands for *Uniform Resource Locator*, an addressing format used for cataloging items on the Internet. A URL can point to a document, a Web server, a Gopher server, an FTP server, a graphical image, or just about any other resource on the Internet.

Usenet—*Usenet* is a large collection of computers carrying something called *Usenet news*—distributed conferencing system consisting of thousands of discussion groups called *newsgroups*.

World Wide Web—The *World Wide Web* is also called *the Web* or *WWW*. The Web is an interactive service for disseminating and retrieving *hypermedia* documents. These are documents that include some combination of graphics, text, and audio information. Various words, phrases, or graphics contained in these documents form links to related items which may be located anywhere on the Internet.

WHAT IS THE INTERNET?

The Internet is one huge network of smaller computer networks all linked together. A *network* is one or more computers connected together in such a way that they can communicate with one another. There are many different kinds of networks. A *local area network,* or *LAN,* consists of computers in the same room or building. A *wide area network*, or *WAN,* consists of computers spread out over a much larger geographic area (e.g., a college campus or city- or countywide library system). On a larger scale, there are regional, state, national, and international backbone networks connected to the Internet. A backbone network is a network that acts as a conduit for information being transferred between other networks.

The Internet is worldwide in scope and connects millions of people into a single communication system. When your computer is connected to the Internet, you can access vast amounts of information, as well as games and other forms of entertainment, and people.

The thousands of networks that make up the Internet are interlinked with each other through high-speed circuits. Some people connect to the Internet through their workplace, school, library, or local government Free-Net. Others gain access to the Internet by going through commercial services.

Who Uses the Internet—and Why?

In the beginning, the Internet was mostly populated by computer scientists, academics, graduate students, and engineers. As the Internet grew, access became easier and a more diverse group of people across the world became involved. Now people from all walks of life, both children and adults, log on to the Internet daily.

Support for the lines that interconnect Internet sites comes from private industry and from state and federally funded research and educational organizations in the form of membership dues and service fees. In other parts of the world, infrastructure support comes from national research organizations and international cooperatives. Under no circumstances is the Internet free. At times it may appear to be a free service, but in reality someone has to pay for all of the hardware, software, and personnel expenses associated with the Internet. Some of these expenses are paid for by publicly funded government entities. Other expenses are covered by the private sector.

WHAT CAN EDUCATORS DO WITH THE INTERNET?

The following list describes many of the Internet resources and services that are available to educators:

- access a variety of resources not readily available elsewhere
- obtain hundreds of ready-to-use lesson plans
- get copies of software applications for such things as grading, tutoring, and skill building, including games that teach and applications that allow you to create such things as customized maps
- obtain documents, reports, and articles to help in lesson planning, classroom management, discipline, and more
- log on at your convenience to the local public or university library to reserve books or do research
- find information about special projects and opportunities available locally on a local community network or bring a distant community into your classroom or home
- share ideas and resources with peers and experts from a much broader group than the local community or state concerning administration, technology planning, or classroom projects
- gain support from other homeschoolers, counselors, or school librarians facing the same issues and difficulties as yourself
- work with others as a tutor or mentor or on research and development

projects that you wouldn't be able to otherwise afford or attend due to fi-
nances or location

- replace current classroom activities with Internet resources. Instead of your
classroom noticing when the monarch butterflies are migrating, participate
in the Internet Monarch Butterfly Project where kids actually send in data
from their locality producing a "live" map. This information is then used by
researchers studying monarch migration.

WHAT CAN KIDS DO WITH THE INTERNET?

There are many opportunities for kids on the Internet that aren't available elsewhere. Here are just a few:

- access a variety of resources that would otherwise be unavailable to them,
such as touring online a Smithsonian history exhibit or following along with
a frog dissection at their own pace
- get copies of software applications such as games for entertainment purposes
as well as math and science programs for help with their class assignments
and research papers
- discover that they will be valued by what they say and how well they say it
rather than their age, appearance, dialect, ethnic background, race, gender,
or physical differences
- learn more about favorite hobbies and special interests from juggling and
origami, to numerology and rocketry; connect with others who share similar interests
- ask experts questions and work with people of all ages, including adults across
the globe, to tutor or participate in research and development; or join the
online staff of a kids-only publication
- log on to the local public and university libraries to check whether an item
is available and to do research
- find information about their community or special interest through local or
distant community information networks, locating festivals or events pertaining to a particular family interest or finding an online field trip for the class
to go on, overcoming distance and financial obstacles
- talk in real time as fast as they can type with kids on different continents
simultaneously
- learn to use and benefit from the Net whether they are gifted and talented
or learning disabled
- research topics for homework assignments and school reports

WHO'S IN CHARGE?

No one single entity "owns" the Internet. NSFNET is currently being funded under the High Performance Computing Act (1991). Other national backbones like NASA's NSI and the U.S. Department of Energy's ESNET provide additional backbone services.

In Europe, international backbone services are provided by networks such as EBONE. Various smaller networks have formed alliances with each other and support the Internet on a regional level.

Although the Internet is not a centralized establishment and on the whole is self-governing, there are certain organizations that do exert influence over the Internet and coordinate many of the Internet's activities. The following list introduces organizations and explains their basic functions:

- **Center for Networked Information Discovery and Retrieval (CNIDR)** *www.cnidr.org/*. CNIDR was established in 1992 as a support center for the development of wide-area information retrieval tools such as the World Wide Web. With so many information resources available on the Internet, resource discovery or information discovery has become a critical issue. CNIDR provides a repository for such systems. Its home page is an excellent source of information providing free access to U.S. and International Patents.
- **The Electronic Frontier Foundation, Inc. (EFF)** *www.eff.org/*. The Electronic Frontier Foundation was established to make the new telecommunications technology useful and available not just to the technically elite, but to everyone. In keeping with the belief that the individual's constitutional rights should be preserved, the society places a high priority on maintaining the free and open flow of information and communications. The Electronic Frontier Foundation's home page is an excellent resource for archived information relating to everything from civil liberties issues to Net culture.
- **The Federation of American Research Networks (FARNET)** *www. farnet.org/*. Established in 1987 as a nonprofit corporation, FARNET's mission is to promote research and education in a computer network environment. Among other things, they offer members educational programs and assistance in improving information services. FARNET publishes a weekly online newsletter called *FARNET's Washington Update* that covers legislative, executive branch, and other policy events of interest to FARNET and its members. You can find *FARNET's Washington Update* along with other information at *www.farnet.org/contents/update/*.
- **The Internet Architecture Board (IAB)** *www.isi.edu/iab/*. Back in the early 1980s when this organization was first formed, it was known as the Internet Activities Board, or IAB. Its goals were to "coordinate research and development of the TCP/IP protocols and to give other research advice to the Internet community." Today, the IAB is technical advisory group for the

Internet Society and is responsible for overseeing the architecture of the rules and procedures used by the Internet.

- **Internet Assigned Numbers Authority (IANA)** *www.iana.org/*. This group provides a standardized way for systems to refer to network resources. Operated by the University of Southern California Information Sciences Institute, IANA maintains a registry of identifiers associated with Internet protocols. This enables systems to apply some standards when referring to network resources.

- **Internet Engineering Task Force (IETF)** *www.ietf.org/*. This group specializes in the development and approval of specifications that become Internet Standards. The IETF is made up of individuals with many different interests: network designers, operators, vendors, and researchers.

- **The Internet Research Task Force (IRTF)** *www.isi.edu/irtf/*. This is a research wing of the Internet Architecture Board. The IRTF concentrates on developing technologies that may be needed in the future, such as resource discovery, privacy, security, and library use of the Internet.

- **The Internet Society (ISOC)** *www.isoc.org/*. The Internet Society is a non-profit organization whose purpose is to facilitate and support the technical evolution of the Internet as a research and education tool. The Internet Society publishes *OnTheInternet* magazine bimonthly for all of its members. Selected articles from this magazine are archived on ISOC's Web site. Click on the links labeled **Members Only/Publications**.

- **The University Corporation for Advanced Internet Development (UCAID)** *www.ucaid.edu/international/*. The University Corporation for Advanced Internet Development (UCAID) is a nonprofit consortium made up of universities, private industry, and federal agencies all working together to build a new network called Internet 2. They are well on their way to meeting goals of creating and sustaining a new high-speed research network and creating new applications and development tools that can take advantage of the Internet 2's advanced network services. Children will benefit when new services resulting from Internet 2 are made available to every level of education and to the Internet community at large. To keep up-to-date on the latest news relating to Internet 2, check out *www.internet2.edu*.

THE INTERNET ADDRESSING SYSTEM

Every computer (referred to as a *host* on the Internet) has its own unique address, and every person that sends and receives e-mail has his or her own unique address. Two addressing systems are used concurrently on the Internet. One system is the IP address (Internet Protocol address) and the other is the Domain Name System.

IP Address

Every host on the Internet is assigned a unique IP address. The *IP address* is a numerical address consisting of four numbers separated by periods. An IP address looks like this: 128.86.8.7 and is read as "128 dot 86 dot 8 dot 7."

Domain Name System

Domain names consist of a series of subnames separated by periods. A domain name looks like this: *kids.ccit.duq.edu*. Domain names exist because they are easier to remember than IP addresses, which consist of numbers. For this reason, you are more apt to use domain names than IP addresses for addressing hosts and people. Computer systems actually only use the numerical address. The translation process from domain name to numerical IP address is done behind the scenes by software.

Each domain name has a corresponding IP address and you can use either one when contacting other hosts. For example, the home page for St. Leo the Great School can be reached with either the domain name *www.stleos.pvt. k12.ca.us/* or with its IP address, 206.40.36.4.

Understanding Domain Name Addresses

When you read domain name addresses from left to right, the subnames go from most specific to most general. The address *opac.sfsu.edu* tells you that there is a computer named *opac* located at San Francisco State University (*sfsu*), which is an educational institution (*edu*).

Other top-level domain names look like these:

edu:	educational institutions
com:	commercial businesses and for-profit organizations
gov:	U.S. government organizations
int:	international organizations
mil:	U.S. military organizations
net:	Networking organizations
org:	nonprofit organizations

There are top-level domains that describe countries, too. Here the country's two-letter international standard abbreviation is used. For example, the domain name *hydra.uwo.ca* has as its top-level domain *ca*, which stands for Canada. Great Britain has two codes: *uk* (United Kingdom) and *gb* (Great Britain). Examples of other geographical top-level domains include these:

ar	Argentina (Argentine Republic)
aq	Antarctica
au	Australia

be	Belgium
cl	Chile (Republic of)
fi	Finland (Republic of)
de	Germany (Federal Republic of)
us	United States

Domain name addresses will be easier to use as you become more familiar with the logic used to construct them. You can soon guess the location of a system by decoding its address. The address *ua1vm.ua.edu*, for example, consists of a series of three subdomains separated by periods or "dots." Starting at the far right, *edu* is the top-level domain. It tells you something very general about the computer's address. In this case, the *edu* tells you it's located at an educational institution.

The next subdomain to the left of *.edu* is more specific. In our example *.ua* refers to the University of Alabama. The next subdomain to the left is the computer's name, which in this example is *ua1vm*. Many university computer's names end in *vm* because they are IBM mainframes running an operating system called Virtual Machine, or *vm* for short.

Some domain names include codes for states, such as fl.us (Florida), ny.us (New York), and ca.us (California). Kids are sure to see the K12 domain on some of their travels. For example, *www.nsbsd.k12.ak.us/* is the address for the North Slope Borough School District in Alaska, and *bvsd.k12.co.us/* points you to the Boulder Valley School District in Boulder, Colorado. Several new domain name extensions have been proposed, including:

.arts for cultural and entertainment entities
.firm for businesses, or firms
.info for information services
.nom for those wishing personal nomenclature
.rec for recreation and entertainment entities
.store for businesses offering goods for sale
.web for entities related to the WWW

Internet addresses will make more sense as you begin using your Web browser and e-mail programs. The Web addressing system is explained in more detail in Chapter 4, "Browser Basics for Beginners," and e-mail addressing is explained in Chapter 8, "Simon Says, 'Get, Send, Forward!'"

WHERE TO GET ASSISTANCE

You will have many questions as you explore the Internet. The kids you are working with will have many more. In this section, we introduce popular glossaries you can find on the Internet and show you where to find online manuals, distance learning resources, and answer sheets called FAQs (Frequently Asked Questions).

You can use the information presented in this section to create your own ready reference collection—resources close at hand that help you answer fact-finding questions. The best place to store pointers to these resources is in your bookmark list. Bookmarks are explained in more detail in Chapter 4.

You don't need to do all the work yourself collecting resources. Use one of the suggestions in the Lesson Plan section to have the kids retrieve documents or find definitions themselves!

Whether you know a little or a lot about the Internet, you'll need help just because the Internet changes frequently. Embedded in all the examples are more resources than we describe. Explore these on your own or let your kids adventure around. Keep a notepad near your computer to write down addresses or sites you want to explore later because almost every excursion on the Net will yield a discovery or pique your curiosity about something new.

STARTING THE HUNT

WARNING! It is not a good idea to join a mailing list or Usenet newsgroup, send a message saying you are new, and then ask if anyone can tell you where to go for help. Your mailbox will fill with "flames" (harsh comments) coming from people who have heard that same question asked many, many times by new subscribers.

To avoid aggravating others and possibly getting your feelings hurt, here are some better ways to find help online—plus you can have fun while you are doing it!

Yahoo! Beginner's Luck and Zen

There's a Web site set up for Internet newbies where you'll find *Beginner's Luck*, a Web page with links to lots of interesting starting points like *Genie's Fingertip Guide to the Internet*, *A Beginner's Guide to Effective Email*, *Beginner's Guide to Life and the Internet*, and *Internet Fact Sheets & Tutorials*. You'll also find information on publishing your own Web page, reference materials, online computer magazines, information on establishing Internet connections, full-text guides, tutorials like *Zen and the Art of the Internet*, and access to a virtual library. All of this and more can be found at Yahoo's special *Beginner's Guides* Web page at *www.yahoo.com/Computers_and_Internet/Internet/Information_and_Documentation/Beginner_s_Guides/*.

Ask the Doctor!

Ask Dr. Internet is an online guide that features newsletters where people ask Dr. Internet their questions about using the Internet. This is a good source of information, although somewhat dated. (The last newsletter was distributed November/December 1996.) To view issues of *Ask Dr. Internet* on the Web, point your browser to *promo.net/drnet/*.

If the doctor isn't in and you need assistance with computer-related problems, try going to Free Help at *free-help.com/*. This site offers free access to over 30 consultants, and questions are usually answered within two or three days. When you submit a question you are asked to assign it a subject category. You can choose from any one of the following:

- Newbie
- Macintosh
- Windows
- Windows 95
- Dos
- Desktop Publishing
- HTML
- Microsoft Frontpage
- Perl
- Java
- Graphics
- Hardware
- Modem
- CD-ROMs
- Memory
- Netscape Navigator
- Internet Explorer
- MS Office
- Games
- Other software

Kind's Glossary

When you begin reading about the Internet or computers in general, you are bound to run into lots of acronyms and technical terms that need explaining. To help you with terms that we didn't include in our own glossary at the beginning of this chapter, consult Kind's Glossary. Irving Kind of Baltimore, Maryland, maintains an online glossary called *Babel: A Glossary of Computer Oriented Abbreviations and Acronyms. Babel* can be accessed several different ways:

- To view this glossary on the Web, point your browser to *www.access. digex.net/~ikind/babel.html*.
- For your own copy, connect to Temple University's FTP server at *ftp.temple.edu*, change directories to */pub/info/help-net*, and download the file *babel.txt*, or the most recent version. (FTP is covered in detail in Chapter 19.)

- To view this file through your Web browser, connect to *ftp://ftp.temple.edu/pub/info/help-net/babel.txt*.

Howe's Dictionary

Denis Howe's *The Free On-line Dictionary of Computing* (FOLDOC) contains over 11,000 computer-related terms, jargon, and acronyms. The easiest way to access it is on the Web at *wombat.doc.ic.ac.uk/foldoc/contents.html*. You can get your own copy of the dictionary for use off line by downloading the whole dictionary as a text file (4.1MB). You can find this file and a zipped version (compressed into a smaller file of 1.68MB) at *wombat.doc.ic.ac.uk/foldoc/source.html*.

GENERAL COMPUTER INFORMATION

A good place to look for answers to questions relating to computers is with the *TechWeb Technology Encyclopedia*. This encyclopedia includes over 10,000 definitions to technology terms and concepts taken from TechWeb's *The Computer Desktop Encyclopedia*. To get there, point your browser to *www.techweb.com/encyclopedia/defineterm.cgi*. Once you arrive, you can launch any keyword search you like. If you search on the term Macintosh, for example, you are presented with details about the Mac's history, the various models that are available, and the Mac interface. At the end of the article there are hyperlinks to other closely related terms, such as *Macintosh clone*, *Macintosh extension*, and *Macintosh Toolbox*.

Colleges and Universities

If you can't find the answers you need at TechWeb, try the UCS Knowledge Base. This Indiana University database, which can be accessed at *kb.indiana.edu/*, contains about 4,500 answers to questions about computing.

Many colleges and universities across the United States maintain online information systems. Some started out as bulletin board systems and others as Gopher menu systems. Today, many have switched over to Web home pages. No matter what the format, universities provide a wealth of online information for the beginning user. Some universities, such as the University of Arkansas at Fayetteville (*www.uark.edu*), work with the communities to provide cities with the physical computer space and training assistance.

For example, the University of Arkansas, Fayetteville, with support from the Bank of Fayetteville, provides community members with free training to maintain a community information network for Northwest Arkansas called *Aladdin*. You can visit the Aladdin home page at *www.uark.edu/community/comnet.html*.

Indiana University (*www.indiana.edu/~ucspubs/d023/*) offers more than 100 online help guides that assist students with everything from naming data objects to using Excel for Windows and Macintosh. A community college or university in your area may be doing the same thing. Check it out! There may be free courses offered monthly on services like e-mail, Gopher, and writing your own home page on the Web.

Even if these personal services aren't available in your area, you can still tap into online help and information services. Most colleges and universities offer online, locally produced help guides written for the novice. There's a list of over 3,000 college and university home pages worldwide, maintained by Christina DeMello at MIT. To view through the Web, connect to *www.mit.edu/people/ cdemello/univ.html*. Your kids will have fun exploring university home pages at Greg Davis's *The University Pages*. This complete, up-to-date list of universities on the Web can be accessed by clicking on a colorful imagemap of the United States.

TEACHING YOURSELF ONLINE

Some other good sources to go to for technology-related help are subject trees. These are Web sites that organize other Web sites according to subject categories. They often include a search engine that enables you to search their collection of links by keyword. If you are looking for online help and documentation, begin searches using the broader term "computers" (or "Internet") and then proceed down the path to see whether there are more specific subjects, such as Computing Dictionaries, Computing Questions, Online Courses, Technical Support, and so on.

The Internet is becoming a rich resource for distance education opportunities, many of them free. If you were to begin browsing at Yahoo! (*www.yahoo.com/*), for example, you could begin down a path that starts with **Computers and Internet**, and then proceed to **Information and Documentation**. The next screen lists dozens of resources ranging from collections of online computer manuals at *Help-Site Computer Manuals* (*help-site.com*) to something called *PC Lube and Tune Exit Ramp* (*pclt.cis.yale.edu/pclt/default.htm*), which provides tutorials and education on technical subjects, such as PC hardware, how to install operating systems, communication ports, and TCP/IP—a communications protocol used on the Internet.

Computer Lessons for Kids and Small Adults provides easy-to-understand lessons on how computers work, the DOS operating system, and files. This is part of a larger project run by Don Sleeth of Ottawa, Canada. When you visit his Web site at *www.kidsandcomputers.com/SiteToc.cfm* you will find him hard at work teaching his two daughters, ages 11 and 5, how to program computers using a programming language originally designed for children called Logo. Be sure to check out his newest link, *Kids Can Program!*, at *www.kidscanprogram.com/*.

For additional links to online educational opportunities, explore Yahoo!'s *www.yahoo.com/Education/* Web page.

FAQs (Frequently Asked Questions)

FAQs, pronounced "facts," are documents typically maintained by Usenet newsgroups. FAQs originally started out as lists of answers to commonly asked questions by newcomers to Usenet newsgroups. They also explained the newsgroup's purpose, permitted discussions, and prohibited discussions. Today, FAQs are used by thousands of online organizations, not just newsgroups. They still center around a specific topic or subject area and their intent is to inform the reader through a question-and-answer format.

One of the largest collections of Usenet-related FAQs is located at Ohio State's Web site at *www.cis.ohio-state.edu/hypertext/faq/usenet/FAQ-List.html*. Another great way for kids to find all sorts of FAQs originating from newsgroups, mailing lists, and other Internet organizations is to search Yahoo! by keyword. For example, if someone is interested in learning all about German Shepherds, go to *www.yahoo.com* and enter **german shepherd faq** as a keyword search. A broader search on the keywords **dog faq** will bring up links to FAQs on topics such as dog agility, dog breeds, and dog rescue.

To find FAQs related to computers and the Internet, browse Yahoo!'s subject tree following this path: *Computers & Internet/*. At the next screen search on the keyword **faq** and direct your search to "just this category" (Computers & Internet). When we did this search we found 42 categories and 710 sites for **faq**.

LESSON PLAN IDEAS

Kids will need to know some basic terms to better understand what they are doing on the Internet. They'll also be curious to know what many other terms mean. Linda Fodemski's 14-year-old son, Nick, wants to know what the extension *.GRP* stands for, and her six-year-old daughter, Rebecca, just asked her, "Momma, what is the Internet?"

Linda told her daughter that the Internet was a bunch of people all over the world using a bunch of computers to do a bunch of business, have a bunch of fun, and learn about a bunch of things! Then Rebecca asked how she could use the Internet. Linda told her she had to learn the language first. Linda and Rebecca created a "spelling list" of computer terms including: file, open, exit, close, quit, stop, and cancel. You too can create spelling lists appropriate for your particular age or grade level and situation.

Here are some suggestions to get your creative juices flowing!

For anyone:

- Download and print a copy of one of the previous dictionaries or guides to keep in class or at home.

For teachers:

- Put bonus questions at the end of any test, asking for a definition of an Internet term.

For school library media specialists:

- Post an Internet term or acronym of the month or week. You can do several things with this idea:
  1. Make it a contest, asking for the definition and source where that definition can be found.
  2. Simply post the term, its definition, and source as a service to children.
  3. Post the term, definition, and source but also request that students go to that source and find a new term along with its definition and submit it to the librarian to post the following week or month.

For any educator or community member (homeschoolers, listen up!): Enable the children themselves to be trainers. Administrators, teachers, or individual community members can get something like this going, either independently or in cooperation with the school system. Recruit one child from each class, or grade level, or each school, or homeschool, to be an "Internet Helper." Children can collaborate among themselves to provide Internet information for their class, grade level, school, or for the entire community.

This project would involve keeping a log of places where help can be found, assisting others looking for help, and writing articles for their class or school newspaper. More energetic students can submit articles to their local community newspaper. An incentive for public school students could be getting grade credits for their work. Homeschoolers are likely to be motivated by, and find satisfaction in, the collaborative aspects and production of a useful and valuable service.

RESOURCES

For background information on the Internet and how it has evolved, point your Web browser to the Timeline from the PBS series Life on the Internet *www.pbs.org/uti/*. While there, be sure to check out their Internet trivia quiz with multiple choice questions rated as easy, medium, and hard.

To learn more about the history of the Web, check out "The World-Wide Web: Origins and Beyond" by Lenny Zeltser at *www.seas.upenn.edu/~lzeltser/WWW/*. "A Brief History of the Internet from the Internet Society" is available at *www.isoc.org/internet/*.

For an up-to-date copy of *Hobbe's Internet Timeline* (now in version 3.3), visit *info.isoc.org/guest/zakon/Internet/History/HIT.html*.

For a complete list of country codes used in domain names, consult the Internet Society's Web site at *www.isoc.org/internet/infrastructure/connectivity/*.

For a fun online beginner's guides to the Internet, try pointing your kids to Newbie-U at *www.newbie-u.com/*.

Chapter 2

Safety@the.keyboard

Teaching children safe online computing practices is as important as teaching them keyboarding skills and techniques for finding information online. When you are *on* the Internet, you are interacting with people, ideas and belief systems, software, graphics and text files, and you have access to myriad products and services. Just as you follow certain protocols when you get into your car and drive across town to the mall, there are rules you follow when going online. Just as you choose which businesses to patronize and which ones to stay away from, you are faced with similar choices when you surf the Web.

In Chapter 2 we explain passwords and virus protection—basic concepts in computer security that are comparable to making sure your car tires are aired up and your brakes are working before going out on the freeway. We explain filtering software, monitoring software, and rating systems—services that claim to help guide your kids to *safe* Web sites much like you guide them to *safe* stores downtown. Netiquette refers to the rules governing proper behavior when communicating with others on the Net. This topic is thoroughly covered in Chapter 8 when e-mail is introduced. Acceptable Use Polices—rules that apply to using a system, such as your school's network or a private Internet service provider's system—are covered in this chapter. We also offer simple sets of rules and guidelines for you and your kids to follow to help ensure a safe and enjoyable online experience. Many of these rules can be copied and used as handouts in schools and libraries.

WORKING WITH PASSWORDS

Passwords are important to Internet users because of the multiuser nature of the system. Without passwords, it would be easy for others who are sharing the system to access information in your account or someone else's account. The strength of your password will be directly related to how secret it remains, so be very careful about the whole process of creating and changing passwords.

Choosing Passwords

When your kids dial-up to an Internet service provider, they'll need a user ID and password to log into their account. Choose passwords carefully. Here are a few basic rules to go over with kids:

- Never share passwords with others.
- Avoid writing passwords on slips of paper. If you do, hide them in a secret location. Don't leave them lying around the computer.
- If you are assigned a password by your Internet service provider, change it as soon as you begin using your account.
- Your password should be at least eight characters long.
- Include mixed case, punctuation, and numbers in passwords.
- Some passwords are easier to guess than others. Avoid using acronyms, phone numbers, names or modified names of pets, trees, streets, animals, towns, rivers, lakes, states, TV stars, cartoon characters, and family members. In fact, avoid any words that exist in an English or foreign dictionary.
- Do not use passwords that consist entirely of numbers or all one letter.
- The best passwords are easy to remember, but hard to crack. One way to create such a password is by taking the first letter of each word in a quote or favorite line of poetry. For example, *Roses are red, violets are blue* would end up being **rarvab**. Adding a number and some upper-case letters (**2RarVarb**)would make it even harder to crack, but still easy to remember.

Changing Passwords

A good rule of thumb is to have your kids change their passwords often, at least every six months. The procedure for accomplishing this will vary greatly depending on the system your kids use. If they are computing in a network environment at school, the system administrator is usually in charge of implementing password policies and procedures.

PROTECTION AGAINST VIRUSES AND MALICIOUS SOFTWARE

Viruses are small programs that infect computer applications and system files. In the case of macro viruses, your data files can be infected, most notably Microsoft Word and Excel documents. Some viruses remain dormant for an undisclosed period of time while others become immediately active. An important feature of any virus is that it replicates itself, usually by attaching itself to program files. The presence of a virus in your system may do little more than display a message on your screen, or make a soft ticking sound, or it may destroy data and delete files. A little time and money spent up front in putting some basic security measures in place can save you and your kids from having to spend a lot of time repairing or replacing corrupted data sometime down the road.

In addition to protecting your computer from virus attacks, you can also take steps to protect it from dangers associated with Java, ActiveX, and e-mail attachments. Look for anti-virus software that looks for viruses in e-mail messages you receive over the Internet and over school or company e-mail systems such as cc:Mail and Microsoft Exchange. Also look for filters that seek out hostile Java classes or ActiveX controls whenever you visit Web sites or download files from the Internet. Some anti-virus software even enable you to block access to potentially dangerous Web sites.

Avoiding Infection

The best defense against viruses is running anti-virus software. Look for products that offer these features:

- Periodic updates
- Signature-based scanning (detects most known viruses before they activate)
- Heuristics-based scanning (checks for virus-like code)
- Memory-resident monitoring (detects viruses residing in memory)
- Integrity checking (periodically checks status of files to see if changes have taken place)
- ICSA (International Computer Security Association) certification (Visit *www.ncsa. com/avpdcert.html* for a list of certified anti-virus software.)

To help prevent the spread of viruses, make kids aware of these potential sources of infection:

1. Floppy disks, including demo programs, disks brought home from school and borrowed from friends, floppy disks used by service technicians and network administrators, and floppy disks employees bring from home
2. Programs downloaded from online services including bulletin board systems and the Internet
3. E-mail attachments, which may either be executable files or data files, especially Microwoft Word documents.

Taking Action

If you suspect a virus has infected your PC, follow these general procedures:

1. Stop whatever you are doing and close out all applications that are open.

2. Shut the computer down and turn it off and leave it off for a moment. (Do not press the reset button or reboot the computer by pressing CTRL+ALT+DEL.)
3. Insert a write-protected emergency startup disk in the floppy disk drive and then turn your PC back on.
4. When the system finishes booting up, scan the hard drive (usually C:\) for viruses according to the instructions that came along with your anti-virus software. If all goes well, your software advises you on what steps to take if it detects the presence of a virus. After the virus has been removed, shut down your PC and then restart it. (When a virus is detected, your scanning software usually "fixes" the infected file by removing the virus. For additional tips on how to remove a particular virus, refer to the online virus databases maintained by McAfee at *www.mcafee.com/support/* and the U.S. Department of Energy at *ciac.llnl.gov/ciac/CIACVirusDatabase.html.*)
5. Scan all floppy disks you may have been using to prevent re-infecting the hard disk.
6. Lastly, if the scanning software does not successfully remove a virus from an infected file, you must take the necessary steps to remove the infected file itself by deleting it. (Refer to the instructions included with your anti-virus software for properly deleting infected files.)

Macintosh Virus Information

Symantec Corporation, the developer of Norton AntiVirus, has set up a Web page filled with Macintosh virus information along with basic information on what viruses are and how they spread. They also cover trojan horses, Hypercard viruses, SAM, and Mac virus updates. You can reach them at *www.symantec.com/techsupp/ index.html.* When you arrive at this site, search **Support options by product**, selecting Norton AntiVirus for Macintosh.

Sources of Virus Information

Even if you think you may not have anything on your personal computer worth protecting, you should consider the safety of others using your computer. When your computer is left unprotected, you have a greater chance of passing malicious software on to your friends and the friends of your children.

In this section we list software virus information sites with the tools you need to keep your computer secure from attacks. Here are some of the better known virus information sites on the Net. They provide information on anti-virus software, virus alerts, and how to remove viruses.

Virus Information Site	Web Address
Aladdin Knowledge Systems LTD	*www.esafe.com/*
DataFellows	*www.datafellows.com/*
Dr. Solomon's Virus Central	*www.drsolomon.com/*
IBM Antivirus Online	*www.av.ibm.com/*
McAfee Virus Page	*www.mcafee.com/*
Symantec	*www.symantec.com/us.index.html*
Thunderbyte	*www.thunderbyte.com/*

The Stiller Research home page at *www.stiller.com* offers information on how viruses work and how to protect your PC, myths regarding viruses, descriptions of common viruses, plus background information on their anti-virus product *Integrity Master*.

ACCEPTABLE USE POLICIES AND OPERATING RULES

Networks and Internet hosts have developed rules that are called *Acceptable Use Policies*. These are statements that outline an organization's core principles and explain what it considers to be acceptable and unacceptable use of its services.

When you set up your Internet account with a service provider, you'll be asked to agree to abide by the service provider's operating rules or "terms of service." In the case of educational institutions, there may already be schoolwide or districtwide policies in place. Go over these rules with your kids and help them understand their meaning and why it's important to adhere to them.

For further information on the subjects of security, ethics, and the Internet's place in an educational setting, refer to FYI22 (For Your Information No. 22) by J. Sellers and J. Robichaux, *Frequently Asked Questions for Schools* (May 1996). This text file can be found using your Web browser to contact *ftp://ftp.ridder.no/ .02/rfc/fyi22.txt*. If you don't find it there, try using Archie (described in Chapter 19) to search it out in other locations on the Net.

CHILD SAFETY ON THE NET

When the Internet was first designed, it was done in such a way that it had no centralized communications system. This made it less vulnerable to destruction by intercontinental missiles. There wasn't a single authority governing its operations nor was there anything that could be considered a central headquarters that exercised control over the Net's activities.

Today the Internet is not only being used by the government and the military, but it's also being used to conduct business, educate children, transfer e-mail between people from all walks of life, and much more. The Internet also carries a wide range of textual material and images that some may find offensive.

This same decentralized system that was built to withstand nuclear attack has also made it technically impossible to limit what takes place on the Internet today—to "censor" what some people may deem objectionable.

Intellectual Freedom: "Freedom of the Mind"

Arguing whether a particular piece of material on the Internet is "good" presents an interesting problem, but in the framework of intellectual freedom, it has little to do with whether the material should be banned from the Net. The crucial issue is whether one individual should be given the right to force his or her concept of morality on another. In order for an individual to even act morally or immorally, he or she must have the freedom to choose.

Yes, the presence of kids being on the Internet presents a special problem in this regard, but it is no different than what has existed in the world with books and telephones for years. When children go to the public library or local bookstore, who controls what they read? Who teaches children what to say when they take a phone call and are asked whether they are home alone?

In cyberspace, just as in libraries and bookstores, parents have the right and responsibility to control the flow of information to their children and only their children. If your kids are on the Internet, there is the potential that they'll be exposed to materials or conversations that are questionable. Teach them in advance how to respond to these situations.

WHAT PARENTS AND TEACHERS SHOULD KNOW

Just as you might teach your child to be street smart before sending them off to college, teach them to be Internet smart before cutting them loose unsupervised on the Net. Presented in this section is a list of ideas that you can build on—things that are relevant to online life. Listed are general guidelines concerning just what a child might be exposed to online, suggestions for talking to your kids about what they are accessing, and a list of rules that can help keep online experiences safe.

Things kids should watch out for:

1. Kids will have access to text and image files that may be violent or sexual in nature. They can also link up with live conversations in "chat rooms" or read advertisements that are violent or sexual in nature.
2. There are people using the Internet who might try to arrange a face-to-face encounter with a child that could be dangerous to the child or the child's family.
3. Children might receive e-mail that is upsetting to them because of the rude or inflammatory tone in which it is written.

Safeguards for parents and teachers:

1. Spend time with your children while they are online. Inform them of what services they are using and what information is being made available by that service. Some commercial online services like America Online allow you to block a child's access to certain areas on their system.
2. Teenagers will require more privacy, but still need supervision and commonsense advice about what they are doing.

Rules for kids:

1. Kids should never give out personal information such as telephone numbers, addresses, school names or last names, in e-mail messages or in public online forums. Be very cautious about this, unless both you and your child know with whom it is you are communicating.
2. Encourage your kids to confide in you. If something doesn't seem right— for example, they are being asked to respond to something in an e-mail message that makes them feel uncomfortable—ask them to bring it to your attention.
3. Kids should never arrange to meet with someone in person without adult permission. If your child does become friends with someone on the Internet and would like to meet them in person, go with them and arrange the meeting in a public place.
4. Point out that they cannot believe everything they read on the Net.
5. They should never send photographs of themselves to e-mail buddies without checking with you first.
6. Point out to your kids that some people may portray themselves to be someone they're not.
7. Set up rules about what time of day your kids can go online, how much time they can spend online, and which services they can access.

Filtering Kids' Access to the Internet

The development of *filtering* software began in 1995 when concern over pornography on the Internet became a national concern. *Time* magazine's cover story on July 3rd, 1995, "Cyberporn," contributed to bringing this issue to the forefront. The most recent development resulting from what Mike Godwin calls the "cyberporn panic" (see *Cyber Rights: Defending Free Speech in the Digital Age*, Time Books, 1998) is the Children's Internet Protection Act. Under this act, introduced by Rep. Bob Franks of New Jersey and Sen. John McCain of Arizona, public schools and libraries receiving federal tax dollars for Internet access would be required to install and use software filters on their computers.

The percentage of pornographic material available on the Internet is extremely small when you compare it with all of the hundreds of thousands of nonpornographic images and text files that are also available. However, for parents and educators who are concerned about what information their children will have access to, there are software products available that are designed just for screening Internet materials. Unfortunately, most filtering tools can be outwitted and are less than 100 percent effective. Those that can't be gotten around are so restrictive they prevent a child from getting the most out of their Internet experience. In the end, parents are still the best filtering mechanism. We recommend supervising kids online just as you supervise them during other activities. If you are a parent and you can't copilot your kid's online activities, then you might consider filtering software.

How Filtering Works

Filtering software attempts to restrict a child from accessing particular sites and materials. When a child tries to access a blocked site, a message appears on the screen stating that it is blocked. Some software is preset, which means that the sites the software will block have been predetermined based on subjective evaluations by the software producer. Other filtering tools use keyword blocking, which prevents access to sites using objectionable words and phrases. What is considered objectionable varies from one program to the next, but all vendors consistently include sexual material in this category. Other areas of concern that are addressed to varying degrees include violence, nudity, religion, and politics.

One program called *Net Nanny* allows you to disable keyword blocking and it permits you to edit the blocked sites list. Features like this enable you to customize your filtering practices to better match the maturity level of your children.

Filtering Features to Look for

When you choose an application, look for these features:

- Does the software producer provide updating services and is there a cost for this service? Sometimes updated site lists can be downloaded automatically rather than manually.
- Does the software allow you to limit access by time of day?
- Are blocked sites fixed or changeable?
- Can you override the system should you choose to?

Types of Filtering Applications

The two most popular kinds of filtering systems are clients and proxy servers. For individual users at home, client software is the best solution. *Client-based* software is installed and runs on a single computer. Examples include Cybersitter (*www.solidoak.com*), Cyber Patrol (*www.microsys.com*), and Surfwatch (*www.surfwatch.com*).

Filters that run on proxy servers make more sense for libraries and schools. A *proxy server* works like this: every time a user sends information to or receives information from an Internet server, it must first pass through a proxy server. The proxy server (a combination of hardware and software) can either be in-house or running at a remote location. The server is configured with different preferences or "profiles" depending on an organization's concerns and beliefs. *To configure preferences* means to set parameters on the proxy server so the server screens the sites your children request with their Web browser (Netscape Navigator and Microsoft Internet Explorer, etc.). The choices you are given usually enable you to block Web sites that contain material pertaining to sex, hatred, violence, or drug abuse.

Further granularity in control can be set by choosing different levels of access within each profile. For example, you may allow access to all violence or no violence. Then again, you may decide hitting with no blood is okay, but torture and death is not.

You obtain remote proxy services by paying a subscription fee to a company that owns a proxy server. BESS offers both onsite and remote proxy services. You can receive additional information by calling them at 800–971–2622 or by visiting their Web site at *www.n2h2.com*.

There are several filtering programs that help parents, teachers, and librarians block offensive or inappropriate Web site content. Some of these programs are described in the section that follows. For a thorough evaluation of filtering software, see Karen G. Schneider's *A Practical Guide to Internet Filters*, (Neal-Schuman Publishers, 1997). Schneider also maintains a Web site at *www.bluehighways.com/* where you can access the summary report of The Internet Filter Assessment Project, which is a librarian's view of Internet filters. Schneider's Web site also offers online updates to her book on Internet filters.

SurfWatch

SurfWatch, which runs on Win3.x, Win95, and Macintosh computers, enables parents to restrict kids' access to materials covering four main categories: sexually explicit material, violence and hate speech, gambling, and illicit drugs and alcohol. SurfWatch offers a service called ChatBlock that automatically blocks access to chat sites on the Net. Their Yahooligans feature limits children's access to *www.yahooligans.com* and the links originating from this domain. Sites deemed objectionable are done so based on company standards and by using context-based pattern matching. SurfWatch claims that checking the context of objectionable words is always done accurately.

Other filtering options enable you to turn the filtering off completely, block

Figure 2–1 SurfWatch blocks access to over 100,000 sites with explicit sex, violence, drugs, or gambling, including chat sites.

access using SurfWatch filters, or block access to the entire Net except for the sites you allow. If you're curious what SurfWatch filters block, visit their home page and test a site against SurfWatch filters by entering any Web site address you wish.

To purchase SurfWatch online, connect to their Web site *www.surfwatch*.com shown in Figure 2–1. You can also order by calling (800)458–6600. For additional information, contact *sales@surfwatch.com*.

PlanetView Parental Control

PlanetView Parental Control is a filtering system that uses age-specific profile settings to limit what kids under 18 years old can access. Each profile specifies how it will handle 13 different areas of concern, ranging from advertising to violence. For example, the producers claim that kids 0–5 years old are prevented from seeing any violence, and kids 10–13 are allowed to see extreme violence presented for informational or educational purposes. You can go in and customize the default settings of your profile at any time.

On the technical side, PlanetView operates using a client/server solution. The client is a PlanetView Web browser. You must use a PlanetView browser to register, change your profile settings, or update account information. Your browser communicates with the PlanetView server, which maintains all of the information about which sites should be blocked. Any updates to the list of blocked sites is done on the server. You don't have to worry about updating your personal computer.

When you first register with PlanetView's Parental Control, you are assigned a standard profile. There are four to choose from based on age.

PlanetView runs on various platforms, including Sega Saturn® and Net Link™. Sega (*www.sega.com*) is a manufacturer of video game hardware and software. PlanetView does not work with AOL, CompuServe, or Prodigy. To learn more about PlanetView, visit PlanetWeb's Web site at *www.newview.com*.

Surf Monkey

Surf Monkey operates on a principle similar to PlanetView. Surf Monkey uses its own proprietary Web browser with parental control and other safety mechanisms built right in. The Surf Monkey browser offers a colorful interface that enables kids to *slime*, or *shatter* sites with which they get bored. A free copy of the browser can be downloaded from Surf Monkey's Web site at *www.surfmonkey.com/*, or you can order a free CD-ROM by filling out an online form. Surf Monkey promotes many features of its browser including:

- *Starsites Directory*—a list of hand-selected sites
- *Blocking service*—When kids enter a Web address, Surf Monkey checks the address against a blacklist provided by SurfWatch which is updated daily. Links to newsgroups are disabled. Downloading any .exe files is blocked.
- *E-mail control*—Surf Monkey uses a password-protected Buddy List. This contains the names and e-mail addresses of buddies you say are safe to correspond with and locks out strangers. Messages coming in from "unknowns" are locked. You can access all locked mail and either delete it or add the sender to the Buddy List. Profanity in e-mail messages is blocked out. Web sites that offer free, unfiltered e-mail services are added to the SurfWatch blacklist. E-mail can be blocked entirely.
- *Chat room control*—Surf Monkey sponsors its own chat rooms which are monitored by Surf Monkey staff. Bad words are filtered out before they appear in a chat room. Kids are blocked from accessing any non-Surf Monkey chat rooms. Surf Monkey can block all chat if that's desired.

Net Nanny

Parents have the ability to add and edit watchwords or phrases in Net Nanny's dictionary. If, for example, you would like to restrict your child from giving out their name, address, and phone number online, you'd simply add that information to the dictionary. If you program the word "sex" or phrases like "where do you live?," Net Nanny will always see it and, under one configuration, shut the com-

©1994-1998 NetNanny Software International, Inc.

Figure 2–2 Net Nanny's Web site offers information on their filtering services plus links to safe sites for kids. (Reprinted by permission of Net Nanny Software International Inc. 1999.)

puter down when these words or phrases are detected by the software. To protect your credit card numbers and telephone numbers, add them to Net Nanny's screening lists. If shutting down the system is too drastic, you can configure Net Nanny to simply monitor activity.

NetNanny can also restrict access to Internet sites, including USENET newsgroups like *alt.sex*. The blocked sites list is free and updates can be downloaded from Net Nanny's Web site at anytime. Users can customize and edit this list to meet their own needs.

At the time of this writing, Net Nanny could run on Windows 3.x/95, but there wasn't a version for Macintosh. Net Nanny works with AOL, Prodigy, MSN, and other commercial online services. To purchase Net Nanny online, connect to their Web site *www.netnanny*.com shown in Figure 2–2. You can also order by calling (800) 340–7177. For additional information, contact *netnanny@netnanny.com*.

Before Buying a Filter

If you decide to buy a filter for your home, school, or library computer, consider the following tips from Karen Schneider's *A Practical Guide to Internet Filters* (Neal-Schuman, 1997). Ideally, a useful and appropriate filter will:

- Block what you want it to—and only what, where, and when you want it to,
- Let you see what's blocked,
- Let you change what's blocked,
- Not create extra work or much with your computer system.

Schneider also suggests an eight-step selection process for choosing a filter:

1. Identify operating environment
2. Decide what you want the filter to do
3. Identify current products
4. Contact potential vendors
5. Design filter tests
6. Test filters
7. Make decision
8. Begin deployment

What Other Alternatives Are There?

If you are not so concerned with blocking access to objectionable sites, but you are interested in tracking where your children go, you might consider monitoring software. Net Nanny, described earlier, supports this feature. Cyber Snoop from Pearl Software, Inc. also shows you which sites your children visit by monitoring their online activity. You can download Cyber Snoop by going to *www.peralsw.com*.

vImpact's product, The Library Channel, offers a solution that gives libraries an opportunity to manage which Internet sites their patrons can access. The Library Channel is a software package that presents a simple, easily understood, graphical interface to both Internet resources and local resources. Librarians can use the software to help organize their CD-ROM products, Web pages preselected by librarians, local community information, and their online catalog.

The Library Channel organizes information based on a hierarchical menu system. The main menu screen has 18 different *topic worlds* ranging from Arts and Entertainment to Travel and Geography. Kids will be interested in Kids and Teens World. When kids click on this menu item they are transported to the Kids and Teens World level-one screen. This screen contains a list of topics related to kids and teens created by librarians, and it can be modified by librarians.

When kids choose an item on the level-one screen—for example, History—they are then presented with a level-two screen that lists several subtopics relating to history for kids and teens. When one of those subtopics is selected, The Library Channel takes the kids to the *Cybershelves*—a screen filled with numerous Internet links and other digital resources indexed by librarians. When kids select a link from the Cybershelves, The Library Channel opens a Web browser and connects to the chosen site.

The Library Channel offers some customization of Web browser features. Librarians can enable/disable direct URL entry from the keyboard, customize button bars, modify the functionality of menu choices such as Save and Print, and so forth. Security features enable you to enable/disable accessing resources outside selected and cataloged sites and disable accessing URLs in a library-managed "unacceptable list." To learn more about all of the features The Library Channel has to offer, check out its Web site at *www.vimpact.net/vimpact/*.

Rating Systems

PICS™ (*www.w3.org/PICS/*), which stands for *Platform for Internet Content Selection*, is a set of technical specifications that makes it possible to design rating systems by using metadata in Web pages. *Metadata* is data about data. Metadata provides information about other information. PICS helps to coordinate the efforts between rating services, such as RSACI (Recreational Software Advisory Council on the Internet at *www.rsac.org*) and software companies, such as Cyber Patrol (*www.microsys.com*).

To limit access to the Internet using PICS, Web authors must embed metadata in their HTML source code. Then you must use a Web browser or filtering software that is PICS-compliant and understands the rating system being used. Microsoft's Internet Explorer and most filtering software is PICS-compliant.

Net Shepherd (*www.shepherd.net*) uses its own PICS rating system instead of keyword blocking. Be careful about limiting your browser's settings or Net Shepherd's settings so that you can't connect to unrated Web pages. Most Web pages do not yet include PICS labels in their HTML code, so you are likely to get a lot of "denied access" messages. Both blocked sites and unrated sites can produce this message in filtering software and browsers.

Cyber Patrol (*www.microsys.com*) can be set to recognize either RSACI or SafeSurf PICS settings. The SafeSurf Rating Standard (*www.safesurf.com*) is a very detailed, voluntary rating system that was developed with input from parents worldwide. SafeSurf, shown in Figure 2–3, attempts to describe content objectively.

One of the challenging aspects of implementing PICS is that it requires every Web site to be rated. PICS-compliant rating systems also use several dozen possible ratings when rating Web sites. A simpler alternative to the PICS rating system is the VCR system. In 1996, Solid Oak Software (*www.solidoak.com/vcr.htm*) started the VCR (Voluntary Content Rating) Web page rating system. The VCR system, which is supported by CYBERsitter, enables publishers to insert a line of code in their page that alerts others of objectionable content. It uses a simple rating system with two basic categories: "adult" sites are for individuals 18 and older, and "mature" sites are not suitable for kids under 13.

Figure 2–3 SafeSurf helps make the Internet safe for children through its development of the SafeSurf rating standard.

Shopping Online

Another issue that is relevant to life online and a potential concern for parents and educators is shopping online. The method of transacting business is a concern if a question of security exists.

The Net has received a lot of negative publicity about the safety of using credit cards online. There is a perception that sending credit card information out onto the Net is a bad idea. No transaction is tamperproof, including purchases you make in stores and restaurants. If you are concerned, you are usually given the option to supply your credit card number by calling an 800 number.

If you question the issue of security when using your credit card to make purchases online, check out David Kline's opinions in an article titled, "False Alarm: Credit Card Security," available at Web site *http://www.hotwired.com/market/95/43/index1a.html*.

RESOURCES

Filtering Facts is a nonprofit organization that promotes the use of filtering software to protect children from online pornography. Filtering Facts' Web site *filteringfacts.org* provides a list of anti-filter sites including American Library Association, American Civil Liberties Union, and Student Association for Free Expression of Massachusetts Institute of Technology (MIT S.A.F.E.)

If you'd like to keep up to date on issues relating to computer viruses, consider joining the discussion list called VIRUS-L. To subscribe, send an e-mail message to *listserv@lehigh.edu*. In the body of the message, type **sub VIRSU-L <your name>**.

If your Internet service provider offers access to USENET newsgroups, check out *comp.virus* for current information on virus-related issues. The VIRUS-L discussion group and the *comp.virus* newsgroup maintain a FAQ on viruses that can be downloaded from site *ftp://rtfm.mit.edu//pub/usenet-by-hierarchy/comp/virus/* or *ftp://ftp.cert.org//pub/virus–l/virus-l.README*.

BugNet boasts that it is "the global authority on PC bugs and fixes." You can search all of BugNet's free materials at *www.bugnet.com* and discover why your PC whines and sneezes and dies. *PC World's Bugs and Fixes Tips* at *www.pcworld. com/resources/hereshow/bugs_and_fixes.html* is another interesting site to visit if your PC is wheezing.

The Parental Control Page, at *www.worldvillage.com/wv/school/html/ control.htm*, believes that the best approach to dealing with objectionable material on the Net is through education and parental control, not government controls. Their home page offers a list of links to sites that are involved with kid's safety on the Internet.

JuniorNet is a monthly online subscription service for kids aged 3–12. It combines CD-ROM technology with the Internet. Kids use a CD-ROM to interact with JuniorNet online service. The JuniorNet technology prevents kids from accessing the wider Internet. Much of the content offered by JuniorNet is adapted from well-known children's publications including *Highlights for Children*, *WeeklyReader*, and *Ranger Rick*. At the time of this writing, JuniorNet was offering a special introductory rate of $9.95/month. For more details, contact *www.juniornet.com*.

PBS takes a creative approach to teaching kids how to judge Web sites. *PBS Kids:techknow* gives kids an opportunity to pass an interactive quiz and receive an official PBS Kids Web license. Point your kids to *www.pbs.org/kids/techknow/*, "the cool cyberliteracy site for kids!"

The Telecommunications Act of 1996 contained the Communications Decency Act (CDA), which made posting "indecent" and "patently offensive" material on the Internet a crime, provided the material was available to minors. Shortly after President Clinton's signing of this bill into law, the ACLU and 19 other plaintiffs challenged the constitutionality of the law. On June 26, 1997, the U.S. Supreme Court found the Communications Decency Act unconstitutional. To learn more about matters relating to this issue, visit the Citizens Internet Empowerment Coalition Web site at *www.ciec.org/*, the Center for Democracy and Technology at *www.cdt.org/cda.html*, and Three Rivers Free-Net at *trfn.pgh.pa.us/Internet/ Policy/decency.html*.

Chapter 3

Keeping Up with What's New

The Internet is a very dynamic environment in which to work. With each passing day, new sites are coming into existence on the Internet while others are disappearing. Resources and services are changing daily, too. Just as teachers like to keep up with the latest resources that are available in print, they will also find it relevant and necessary to keep up with the newest digital resources. Some Internet resources you can find immediate use for and others serve as reference resources—only to be used if needed.

Kids will find some of these specialized services interesting because they will help keep them informed of the newest fads and "what's hot" on the Net. Some kids will really take off with this new technology and want to keep up-to-date with the newest products and services and track what is happening in terms of Internet growth.

In this chapter, we discuss how you and your kids can keep up with the latest changes in network technology and all the new Internet resources that are coming online daily. We'll point you to Net sites that provide up-to-date statistics on Internet usage and growth. We offer a list of magazines and newsletters with complete subscription information and pointers to online electronic journals that will help keep you informed about what's new.

If you're not familiar with the various Internet applications like FTP, Gopher, e-mail, and so on, read through those chapters first and learn how those programs work. If you're already a veteran *Internaut*, the resources listed in this chapter will serve a more immediate purpose.

RESOURCES FOR KIDS, TEACHERS, AND PARENTS

Here is a list of resources that will help keep you and your kids up-to-date on the latest Internet happenings. We've divided this section into eight parts:

- E-mail
- Etext
- Government
- Web Sites
- News and Information
- Software
- Technology
- Online Magazines

For your convenience, you can also access a hyperlinked version of this resource section on the CD-ROM that accompanies this book. First establish your Internet connection. Then, find the subject heading **What's New** in our CD-ROM "link farm." When you find a resource that looks interesting and you want to explore it further, simply click on the resource name highlighted in blue and you will automatically connect.

E-mail

In this section we show you how to stay up-to-date on new discussion lists that are becoming available. (Discussion lists are described in more detail in Chapter 9.)

NEW-LIST

To help keep you informed about the newest discussion lists that become available, subscribe to NEW-LIST, an automated mailer that is delivered right to your e-mail box. To subscribe, send **sub new-list <your firstname and lastname>** in the body of an e-mail message to *listserv@hypatia.cs.wisc.edu*.

Etext

The resources presented in this section relate to newly published electronic texts, or *etexts*.

NEW ELECTRONIC JOURNALS

Keep up-to-date on new or soon-to-appear electronic journals and newsletters by subscribing to the NEWJOUR mailing list. You can easily subscribe on the Web by going to *gort.ucsd.edu/newjour/subscribe.html* and filling out an online subscription form. The complete NEWJOUR archive can be browsed or searched on the Web at *gort.ucsd.edu/newjour/*.

Government

These sources keep you up-to-date on legislation affecting the Internet.

TELECOM-POST

TELECOM-POST is a newsletter focusing on congressional action on telecommunications; ot pulls relevant articles and posts off other Net sources as well as print publications. To subscribe, send an e-mail message to *listserv@cpsr.org*. In the body of the message enter: **subscribe telecom-post <firstname_lastname>** (substitute your own name).

THE COOK REPORT ON INTERNET

The Cook Report on Internet (*cookreport.com/*) is a monthly newsletter concerned with the National Information Infrastructure; Federal Policy toward the commercialization and privatization of the Internet; and issues affecting school, library, and community network access.

There is a subscription fee, but some services are offered free of charge, such as special reports, index to past issues, and summaries of current issues.

Web Sites

In this section we show you how to keep up with what's new on the Web.

WHAT'S NEW TOO!

What's New Too! (*newtoo.manifest.com/*) service is maintained by Manifest Information Services. What's New Too! claims to post an average of over 500 announcements per day within 36 hours of submission. On their front page they offer a dialog box for entering keyword searches on all of their current listings. If you want to run a more refined search, look for a link to their **Search Page**.

INTERNET RESOURCES NEWSLETTER

The Internet Resources Newsletter (*www.hw.ac.uk/libWWW/irn/irn.html*) is a monthly newsletter edited by the Heriot-Watt University Library staff and published by Heriot-Watt University Internet Resource Centre. The purpose of the newsletter is to keep readers informed about new Internet resources, especially those that are relevant to the research interests at Heriot-Watt University.

WHAT'S NEW

What's New (*www.whatsnu.com/*) is one of the largest directories of new sites on the Web. What's New allows you to search or browse by category. The What's New index covers new submissions for the last seven days. Older listings are archived. You can search phrases by placing your search terms in quotes. You also have the option of running what they call "partial word matches" (tradition-ally called substring searches). This means that when you search on **house** you will get hits containing **house**, **houses**, **lighthouse**, **schoolhouse**, **dollhouse**, **in-house**, etc. Your search terms are highlighted in your search results.

THE SCOUT REPORT

Originating at the University of Wisconsin-Madison, *The Scout Report* (*scout.cs.wisc.edu/scout/report/*) is a publication of the Internet Scout Project, a project funded by the National Science Foundation. The report is a selective, annotated weekly listing of newly discovered sites and network tools. To receive the electronic mail version of *The Scout Report*, subscribe to the *scout-report* mailing list. Subscribing to the *scout-report list* can be done at *scout.cs.wisc.edu/scout/lists/*.

YAHOOLIGANS!

One way kids can keep up with what's new on the Web is by checking out the "New" area of Yahooligans! home page. To connect, point your Web browser to *www.yahooligans.com/*. Once you arrive, look for an icon at the top of the page labeled "New." Clicking here will link you to a Web page listing recent additions from the past week. The last time we checked the recent additions link, we found a new book review site, an online story suitable for young readers called "Mr. Flibby," audio clips from Mr. Potato Head from the movie, articles about bears, information on BMX racing, and more.

Many kids like using Yahooligans! as their "default" home page—the home page their Web browser connects to as soon as they start up their browser. It offers an alphabetical list of broad subject areas ranging from Around the World (Coun-tries, Politics, History, etc.) to The Scoop (Comics, Weather, Events, etc.).

While you are at Yahooligans!, click on the button labeled **Net Events** to learn about live events taking place on the Net weekly. Kids will find announcements about live chat sessions with famous sports figures or be introduced to ongoing special programs, such as reading about day-to-day experiences of sailing solo around the world.

KIDS Report

Looking for an annotated list of resources selected by K–12 students? KIDS Report is the place to go. This online publication is produced by two classrooms in Madison, Wisconsin, Madison Metropolitan School District; and two classrooms in Boulder, Colorado, Boulder Valley School District. By pointing your browser to *scout.cs.wisc.edu/scout/KIDS/index.html*, you can start exploring KIDS Report by either browsing current and past issues, or by searching their archives.

Net-happenings

One of the single best sources for keeping up with what's new is a mailing list called Net-happenings. Gleason Sackman produces and edits Net-happenings as a service of the Internet Scout Project in the Computer Sciences Department at the University of Wisconsin, Madison. Net-happenings points you to a dozen or more new Internet resources every day including Web sites, corporate information, new Internet books and software, mailing lists, and more. If you know someone who is looking for new resources and enjoys finding things by serendipitous discovery, point them in this direction.

You can view Net-happenings on the Web or via USENET newsgroup *comp.internet.net.net-happenings*. For Web access, point your browser to *scout.cs.wisc.edu/scout/net-hap/*.

News and Information

In this section we introduce you to resources that help you stay current on Internet- and computer-related news and information.

Internet Research Group's Monthly Reports

These papers are technical in nature and would be of interest to anyone wanting to know more about the inner workings of the Internet. These reports contain articles from regional networks, the Internet Architecture Board, some Internet engineering reports, and a calendar of events. They also list newly published RFCs and usage reports from organizations such as InterNIC. You can access the Internet Monthly Reports via FTP by pointing your browser to *ftp://nis.nsf.net/internet/newsletters/internet.monthly.report*.

Request for Comments (RFC) and For Your Information (FYI)

Internet documentation called RFCs and FYIs provide background information on various technical details relating to the Internet. RFC documents, also known as Request for Comments, can be retrieved from numerous sites and by various means. The easiest method is to go to the FTP server *nic.ddn.mil* and look in the directory /rfc. Here you find all of the RFC files listed with file names *rfc*.txt* (the asterisk * is a variable that should be replaced with one of the RFC numbers listed in that directory). There are hundreds of files in the /rfc directory, so be prepared if you enter the **ls**, **ls -l**, or **dir** command when using a UNIX shell account. (More on this in Chapters 16 and 19.) You may want to create a capture file. To connect to this FTP server via the Web, simply point your browser to *ftp://nic.ddn.mil/rfc/*. Before you begin exploring, first read the *fyi-index.html* file.

Some of the RFCs may be of particular interest to educators. For example, the file *rfc1709.txt* offers an introduction to how the Internet can be applied in K–12 education along with technical information on building a data communications service. There are other RFCs that offer general introductions to the Internet and how it can be used. Here are a few examples:

> *rfc1392.txt* "Internet Users' Glossary" (also FYI 18)
> *rfc1432.txt* "Recent Internet Books"
> *rfc1462.txt* "What is the Internet" (also FYI 20)
> *rfc1463.txt* "Introducing the Internet—A Short Bibliograpy of Introductory Internetworking on Readings for the Network Novice" (also FYI 19)

If you prefer using the Web, go to *www.cis.ohio-state.edu/hypertext/information/rfc.html* for a complete list of RFCs. Look for the link labeled **index** which links you to all RFCs listed by number, with titles and authors. This, too, is a very long list and will take a while to load in your browser.

THE INTERNET SOCIETY

The Internet Society's Web server offers two categories of What's New Information: Headlines and Events. To connect to this site, point your browser to *www.isoc.org*. Since this information relates to Internet policy issues and standards, it will be more interesting to adults than kids. If you click on **All About the Internet**, you come to a list of other links including one labeled **Internet News**. Click on this and you can browse through dozens of articles relating to such topics as E-commerce, Vice President Gore's announcement of Internet 2 development, Communications Decency Act rulings, and more.

MECKLERMEDIA

Mecklermedia Corporation is a major player in the Internet media world. Along with publishing books and magazines like *Internet World* and *WebWorld*, they also have their own Web site called *Mecklermedia's internet.com*. To connect, point your Web browser to *www.internet.com* and to *www.internetnews.com*.

At *internet.com*, you can keep up with what's new by signing up for free e-mail newsletters covering a variety of topics. For example, if your kids are interested in Internet-related stocks, and Web industry mergers and acquisitions, they might enjoy the *Internet Stock Report* newsletter. *Internet World Daily* is for those interested in news stories about Internet technology. You can learn about the newest terms added to PCWebopaedia by subscribing to *PCWebopaedia News*, a bimonthly newsletter with hyperlinks to resources. Other newsletters cover Internet software, advertising, service providers, shopping, search engines, servers, and Web devlopment.

Mecklermedia's newswire can be accessed at *www.internetnews.com*. Here you find news stories on electronic commerce, products, legislation, business, and more.

Software

Software developers are always coming out with new applications and revisions to existing ones. The best places to go for updates on what's new are file libraries—Web sites that specialize in archiving software. In this section we show you where some of the biggest and best are located.

Consummate Winsock Apps

Forrest Stroud writes for *Boardwatch* magazine and reviews Internet software each month in his column, "Consummate Winsock Apps." (You can read Stroud's column online each month at *www.boardwatch.com*.) Go to Stroud's Web site at *cws.internet.com/* and click on the icon labeled **What's New** to find out about the latest software releases.

Not all shareware libraries offer a **What's New** department, but clnet's shareware.com offers that and more. When you visit their site at *www.shareware.com/* you are given the choice of either searching or browsing their shareware database containing over 250,000 files. You can focus on "new arrivals" by running searches by platform type (Windows, Mac, etc.) and when the software was added to the system: The last 10 days, 30 days, or 60 days.

FILEZ at *www.filez.com* doesn't archive files. It searches over 7,000 other file archives all around the world every week and creates a catalog of their holdings. This catalog is then made searchable, giving you access to more than 75 million files. Look on their front page for a "List of filez the last 2 days," and a link to **New Last 20 Days.**

Technology

The Nando Times online newspaper at *www.nando.net/* offers a link on their home page called **Techserver**, which links to several news articles relating to information technology. This service is updated daily.

Edupage offers a collection of article summaries on issues relating to information technology, telecommunications, and higher education. To read Edupage online, visit their home page on the Web at *educom.edu*. Click on **Publications** and then click on **Edupage**.

Infobits is a service provided by the University of North Carolina at Chapel Hill's Center for Instructional Technology. Each month the center sends out brief notes on a number of information technology and instruction technology Internet resources that come to the group's attention. You can stay in touch by viewing Infobits online at *www.iat.unc.edu/infobits/infobits.html* or you can subscribe to their mailing list. To subscribe, send the message **subscribe infobits <your name>** in the body of an e-mail message to *listproc@listserv.oit.unc.edu*.

The transition from government-supported backbones to a totally privatized system in the United States has led to the development of a new system of backbones called Internet 2, the Next Generation Internet. To stay up-to-date on I2's latest developments, check out Greg Wood's Internet 2 Web page at *www.internet2.edu/*.

Check out Ziff-Davis Publishing Company's home page for reviews of the latest software and hardware. Either click on the link marked **What's New** or run full-text searches on any one or all of ZDNet's 13 computer-related magazines available at *www.zdnet.com/*.

Online Magazines

While print magazines may not be as up-to-date as their online counterparts, they do offer other advantages, such as portability. All of the magazines and newsletters listed below have sites on the Web and some have counterparts in the print world. The electronic editions of print magazines offer a variety of features only available online including access to back-issue archives, "favorite" Web sites, searching capabilities, and more.

Boardwatch Magazine *www.boardwatch.com*
CD-ROM Online *www.nsiweb.com/cdrom/default.html*
cnet online *www.cnet.com*
The Cook Report on the Internet *cookreport.com/*
FamilyPC *www1.zdnet.com/familypc/*
HotWired *www.hotwired.com*
Inside the Internet *www.cobb.com/int/index.htm*
Internet Research *www.mcb.co.uk/cgi-bin/journal3/intr*
Internet World *www.internetworld.com*
ISP Business News Service *www.ispbusinessnews.com/*
Mecklermedia's iWorld *www.internet.com/*
NetGuide *techweb.cmp.com/ng/home/*

Netsurfer Digest *www.netsurf.com/nsd/*
Online MacinStuff Times *www.informedusa.com/t/mactimes.html*
Online Magazine *www.online-magazine.com/index.htm*
TechWeb *techweb.cmp.com/*
WEBsmith *www.ssc.com/websmith/smith.html*
WWWsmith section in *LINUX Journal www.ssc.com/lj/*
Wired *www.hotwired.com/wired/*
WizzyWygs *www.wizzywygs.com/*

RESOURCES

The Internet Traffic Report at *www.InternetTrafficReport.com/* is a feature of the Andover News Network. This report monitors the flow of data around the world. Graphs display network speeds and levels of reliability over the last 24 hours. Andover News Network's home page also offers links to the latest news stories relating to AOL, cable, E-commerce, hardware, Internet, software, and other technology-related issues.

PART II

THE WORLD WIDE WEB FOR YOUNGER KIDS

The most exciting and innovative part of the Internet right now is the World Wide Web. Unlike all of its predecessors, including Gopher, Veronica, Archie, and WAIS, the Web offers a user-friendly, multimedia window to the Internet.

The Web is evolving continuously. As you read more about the various online educational activities in this part, you'll discover how the Internet is blurring the lines of many types of traditional educational activities. Typical learning activities for children, such as penpal exchanges and field trips, can be taken to new levels and become broader in scope on the Internet than was possible before. A search for a penpal can turn into classrooms across the globe collaborating on a science project. It may take months to book a field trip to a nearby museum but online you can explore the inside of a cave or volcano anytime. A search for information about how the brain works may take you to a site that offers a "tour" of the brain, discussion lists for kids to get in touch with other kids, and games!

You'll find businesses and organizations of all sizes that offer educational field trips or entertaining places for kids to enjoy. There are government organizations sponsoring projects for youth and university students offering online newspaper authoring for students.

The Web brings freedom of the press right into your home. When A.J. Liebling wrote, "Freedom of the press belongs to anyone that owns one," it took a big bank account and control of a magazine or newspaper to enjoy freedom of the press. The Web has changed all this. Children publishing their poetry, stories, and artwork is as common as professors publishing their musings on genetic algorithms in computing.

The popularity of the Web can be attributed to its scope and ease of use. The Web doesn't require that you learn a lot of cryptic commands. You use a program called a *browser* to navigate the Web by pointing-and-clicking to link to sites all around the globe.

In Chapter 4, we explain how the Web works and introduce the software you'll need to browse the Web.

Chapter 5 offers a Web sampler that demonstrates the diversity of sites for children and people involved in educating children.

In Chapter 6, we explain the idea of virtual field trips and describe many virtual field trips and online activity sites.

Chapter 7 is the section to turn to on rainy days—places for kids to explore and just have fun. We also cover special resources just for homeschoolers, too.

Chapter 4

Browser Basics
for Beginners

The World Wide Web is just one part of the Internet, but it is probably the part that you'll find kids using the most. You'll use software called a browser to view Web sites and discover how the WWW makes it possible to access more information, pictures, sound, or explanations, without necessarily having to reach for a dictionary or open an atlas. The HTML language used to create Web pages is quite a remarkable way to present a multimedia presentation of any subject.

WHAT IS THE WORLD WIDE WEB?

The *World Wide Web* is also referred to as *the Web*. It was developed in 1989 at the CERN research center in Geneva, Switzerland, and introduced on the Internet in 1991. Since then it has experienced phenomenal growth.

As with other Internet services, the Web is built on a client/server model. The user utilizes a program called a *Web browser* (the client), which in turn connects to computers that serve up Web pages (the servers). The clients communicate with servers on the Web using a standard protocol called *HTTP* (*Hypertext Transfer Protocol*). HTTP is a set of rules used for transferring information on the Web, and it enables Web clients and servers to communicate with each other.

The Link Farm on the CD-ROM found in the back of this book has even more information about Web browsers, safety on the Internet, and pointers for newbies. Click on these folders: **Internet Safety** and **Web Design.**

HOW THE WEB WORKS

HyperText is a system of managing textual information by creating associations between different documents. A hypertext system is made up of several documents. One or more words in a document or the entire document itself is linked to other words or groups of words in other documents. This linking enables you to move easily back and forth from the original document to the linked document. Hypertext documents on the Web are called *Web pages* or *Web sites* and may be linked to other Web pages located on the same computer or to Web pages located on computers thousands of miles away.

Here's an example of how all this works: There's a Web page called *Not Just for Kids* and on this Web page there's the phrase "Rosie's Rhubarb Review." When you click on these words you are hyperlinked to a page with subject headings for different sites that Rosie has reviewed. This link is on the same computer as *Not Just for Kids*. When you click on one of these subjects headings, for example, **Animals**, you are hyperlinked to a page listing sites on the Web about animals that Rosie has written a review about. These sites are maintained on computers other than the *Not Just For Kids* site. *Not Just for Kids: www.night.net/kids*

THE WEB ADDRESSING SYSTEM

WWW addresses are commonly referred to as *URLs* (*Uniform Resource Locators*). URLs identify the location of a resource anywhere on the Internet. A URL is a string of text that includes information on the type of resource (WWW, Gopher, FTP, etc.), the machine's Internet address, and where the item is located on that machine.

The address for a document called *My Virtual Reference Desk* is *http://www.refdesk.com/index.html*. The part of the URL before the colon identifies the protocol being used by the server providing the file. In this example, it is *http*, which stands for *HyperText Transport Protocol*. This means that the resource being described is a hypertext document. The second part of the URL (the part after the two forward slashes) gives the Internet address as *www.refdesk.com*, the host where the item is located. The third and fourth parts provide the directory path or file name. There is not a special directory for the item in this example, so only the file name *index.html*, is listed.

You will also occasionally see Web addresses beginning with other protocols, such as *Gopher://* (for Gopher servers) *and FTP://* (File Transfer Protocol). The URL *ftp://ftp.unt.edu/pub/misc/startrek.txt* tells us that the Internet service being used is FTP (File Transfer Protocol) and that the document resides at *unt* (University of North Texas)—an educational (*edu*) institution—and that we are viewing a text (*txt*) file called *startrek* in the directory */pub/misc/*.

The URL format for a Gopher server's root menu is **gopher://host address**. For example, if you want to connect to the Fun and Games section of the Gopher server at the University of Minnesota, you'd point your Web browser to *gopher://spinaltap.micro.umn.edu:70/11/fun.*

Several university and other libraries are listed on the CD-ROM in The Link Farm, such as webCATS—a site designed just to keep you connected with all of the Web-based libraries in the world.

When a URL is listed without this first reference, the HTTP:// protocol is assumed. If you know the name of a company or organization and you have their domain name, you can usually find their home page by inserting a *www* in front of the address. For example, the University of Arkansas at Little Rock has the domain name *ualr.edu*. Their home page on the Web is *www.ualr.edu*.

BEGIN BY BROWSING

You'll really start to understand what hypertext is all about when you begin using it. A Web browser is software that interprets and displays on your screen the hypertext data sent to you by the host server. Browsers enable you to easily view and navigate the chaos of the Internet.

Browsers come in two flavors: character-based and graphical. Character-based browsers only display characters, no images. Lynx is a popular UNIX-based Web browser that displays only characters. Lynx has also been ported to MS-DOS, which enables you to run a character-based Web browser on your PC. If you happen to view a page that contains graphics while running Lynx, the image is replaced by the word [LINK] in square brackets. When you access the Internet through a shell account as described in Chapter 16, you may be able to run Lynx by typing **lynx** at your system prompt. Not all Internet service providers offering shell accounts support Lynx.

Graphical browsers can display images and text, or just text. As you move around the Net, you are often given the option to view pages with graphics or view pages in text-only mode. Using a graphical browser to view pages in text-only mode speeds up the downloading process because Web pages with text-only mode require much less memory than the same pages when they include images. Some graphical browsers are designed just for kids, like the ones we describe later in this chapter and those introduced in Chapter 2.

COOKIES

Cookies are text files that reside on your computer and are maintained by your Web browser. Web servers store information about you in the *cookies.txt* file—usually demographic and advertising information, but it can also be information about your surfing habits and experiences.

Cookies are not programs that can be run. Cookies can't destroy files on your hard drive and most only last until you close down your browser. They can't do anything malicious to your computer. One server might store information about you that you consider private, such as user IDs and passwords that you enter as you browse, and another invasive server may come along and steal that information.

Persistent cookies are stored on your hard drive until a specific date and then they expire. These can track your browsing habits. Internet Explorer (IE) stores persistent cookies in separate files named with the user's name and the domain name of the site that sent the cookie, for example, *anyuser@microsoft.txt*. The file is stored in the */Windows/Cookies* subdirectory.

You can't avoid these problems by deleting the cookies.txt file. Navigator and IE will create a new one the first time a server transfers a cookie to your browser.

You could go in and delete the cookies you don't want or delete all of the contents. Note that blocking your browser so it doesn't accept cookies can prevent some online services from working. Cookies may be needed by the server to help you access different pages on the site. If this is the case you will have to turn cookies back on.

Netscape stores the *cookies.txt* file in the Netscape directory. You can also set your browser so it alerts you when a server attempts to download a cookie to your hard drive, or you can stop your browser from accepting cookies altogether. Asking to be alerted whenever a server tries to pass a cookie to your browser will become tiring because you will continually be closing the warning dialog box.

You enable cookie security in Netscape 3.0 by clicking on **Options|Network Preferences**. In Navigator 4.0 click on **Edit|Preferences|Advanced**. In IE you can prevent any cookies from being sent to your browser by clicking on View|Internet Options and then click on the **Advanced** tab and click on the **Disable All Cookie Use** option.

You can also use a utility program specifically designed to control cookies. *PGPcookie.cutter* can be downloaded from Pretty Good Privacy, Inc.'s site at *www.pgp.com* and sells for $19.95. Other cookie controllers can be found on Web sites featuring cookie software, such as Cookie Central at *www.cookiecentral.com/* and JunkBusters at *www.junkbusters.com/ht/en/links.hml#nsclean*.

THINK LIKE A THESAURUS

An important thing to remember about Web browsers is that they basically do the same thing, even though some have more bells and whistles and special features than others do. We describe two very different browsers in this chapter; however, you can use this information to help you operate any Web browser. They all are going to have the same basic features, but they'll be called something different and be located in a different place on each browser.

The trick to this is to think like a thesaurus! What is it that you want to do? Send mail? It might be listed as *send mail* or it could be listed as *send message*.

Almost every software program includes pop-up or dialog boxes. You have to make a choice or change a setting and then close the box. The button to do this might be called *OK*, *CLOSE*, or *OPEN*. If children can be taught to look for a term similar to what they want to do, rather than the exact word, they'll have an easier time switching from one program to another.

For example, Web browsers offer a special file to store URLs and the site name for that URL. You go to this file and click on the name to connect to that site and you don't have to type in the whole address or scramble around for the piece of paper where you wrote it down. Netscape calls this file *Bookmarks* and Internet Explorer calls it *Favorites*. Web browsers also have a box where you can type in or cut and paste in a URL. It might be labeled *Location* or *URL* or *Address*. The RELOAD button on one program means the same as the REFRESH button on another.

Also, if you don't see a button to click on to perform the function you want, try looking under the different menu options. These options are listed by more than one word and often show the shortcut key or key combination available to perform the function.

Allow kids to spend some time getting to know the program you will be using. Drag your cursor slowly over icons or let it rest there a moment because often you'll be able to access an information balloon that describes what the icon does. Look for small down arrows that will indicate hidden information. Watch your cursor as you move it over different elements in the window. A change in the cursor indicates other options you have, such as resizing a window or moving a toolbar or activating a link or Help file.

WHAT IS NETSCAPE?

Netscape Communicator is a multipurpose Internet tool that enables you to do many things, including browsing the Web and sending and receiving e-mail. Each component in this suite of tools has its own name. For example, the Web browser is called *Netscape Navigator* and the e-mail program is called *Netscape Messenger*. You can customize this program to open only the parts of the program you want to use.

Netscape Navigator is a powerful graphical Web browser, created by the same people who created Mosaic, and now owned by America Online. Netscape Communicator is available for free download from the Netscape Web site: *home.netscape.com*.

Navigating with Netscape

At the top of the Netscape screen is the menu bar, pictured in Figure 4–1. Clicking any of these menu names displays a pull-down menu with several choices. For example, when you choose the menu item File, a pull-down menu appears giving you options such as mailing a document, opening a file, saving a file, and quitting the program. Options followed by ellipses (…) lead you to another pull-down menu with additional choices.

Figure 4–1 Netscape Navigator's menu toolbar.

Just below the menu bar is the navigation toolbar, shown in Figure 4–2, which consists of icons and/or words that you can click to perform some of the tasks in the pull-down menus. In other words, the navigation toolbar icons are shortcuts. These are functions you will use often or repeatedly. The Back icon takes you to the previous link, the Forward icon takes you one link forward, and the Home icon takes you to the page you have designated as your opening screen when you start Navigator.

Figure 4–2 Navigation toolbar icons are shortcuts to frequently used functions.

Below the navigation toolbar is the location toolbar. The dialog box here shows the address for the site to which you're currently linked. You can click once in the location dialog box to highlight the text and type in any URL you want to go to. In Figure 4–3, we entered *www.si.edu/*, the URL (Web address) for the Smithsonian Institution. After you type in a URL, press ENTER to retrieve that page.

> You'll find dozens of science and institutions online exhibit sites in The Link Farm on the CD-ROM. There is also a section of sites to help you keep up with what's new on the net!

Figure 4–3 The location toolbar displays the URL of the page you are currently viewing.

While at the Smithsonian home page we chose Events & Activities by clicking on those words with the mouse. This took us to another page and the URL listed in the location dialog box changed to *www.si.edu/activity/start.htm*. Again we clicked on an item, this time called What's New. The URL listed in the box changed to *www.si.edu/whatsnew/start.htm*. Listed here are items added to this site for the past two years. Items added within the last two months are listed individually and described. That is how we found Kid's Castle (*www.kidscastle. si.edu/*), shown in Figure 4–4.

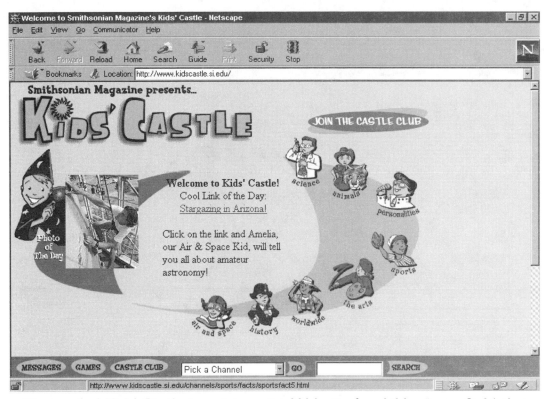

Figure 4–4 Kids' Castle is an interactive Web site for children ages 8–16 that you'll want to explore more.

You can hide both the navigation toolbar and the location toolbar using the tiny arrows on the left of each line. Click once on the tiny arrow and the line will disappear, leaving a narrow bar with an arrow. Click on the arrow again and you can view that line again. Both lines can be hidden independently of each other. The menu bar always remains in view and cannot be hidden. Figure 4–5 demonstrates what the screen looks like with these toolbars hidden while viewing the high graphics version of the Eisenhower National Clearinghouse for Math and Science Web site. The URL for this site is *www.enc.org/fr_index.htm*.

Figure 4–5 Eisenhower National Clearinghouse for Math and Science
home page, high graphics version.

Other items that can be turned off are the image-loading feature and Java script capabilities. If you don't have a particularly fast computer or you are not interested in all of the graphics, you can change the settings for these items by choosing **Edit | Preferences | Advanced |** and then clicking on the boxes with check marks for **Automatically load images** and **Enable Java** and **Enable Javascript**. Netscape will now only display an icon in place of where the images would be, and pages with Javascript will not load. Figure 4–6 shows what the Browser Boulevard page, located at the Browser Watch home page (*http://browserwatch.internet.com/browsers/browsers-big.html*), looks like with the graphics turned off. We also decreased the font on this page to be able to capture the full screen. You may choose to decrease the font when the text runs off the screen. It is easier to decrease the font that use the horizontal adjustment bar at the bottom of the page to move the screen left and right to read all the text.

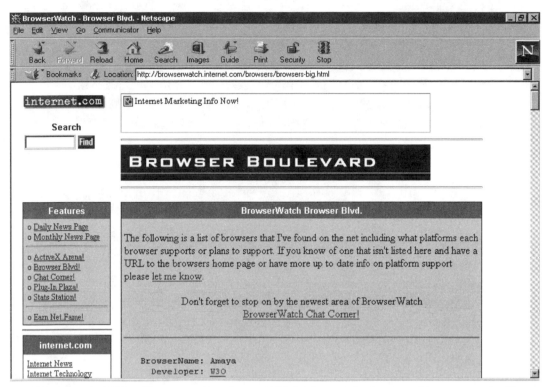

Figure 4–6 The Browser Boulevard Web site with the graphics turned off.

THE BUSINESS OF BOOKMARKS

As you navigate the Net, you will find Web pages you'll want to return to and sites that you just don't have the time to explore right at the moment, so you use the bookmark feature to easily return to them at a later time.

Let's say that a student serendipitously discovered the *Interactive Frog Dissection* site located at URL: *http://curry.edschool.Virginia.EDU/go/frog/*. Choose **Bookmark|Add Bookmark** from the menu bar at the top of the page. Your bookmark is now set! The default insertion point for added bookmarks is at the end of the list. There are different ways to manipulate your bookmark list.

1. You can connect to any item in your list by clicking on the title.
2. You can view your bookmark list as a separate page and manipulate the arrangement of the bookmarks or add a new folder anytime. For example, to set up a folder for your class or for each member of your family, choose **Bookmark|Edit Bookmarks**. The bookmark list will now be displayed as a separate page. At the top of this page choose **File|New Folder**. A *Bookmark Properties* Box will appear. In the name field, type your class name, such as "Mrs. Safely's Third Grade" or an individual child's name, such as "Alex." Click the OK button to set this folder in your bookmark file. You will then see a new folder icon added to your bookmark list with the name you typed next to it.

An Extension Activity

Create a list of all the shortcut keys for the various functions. Experiment from there! Is it quicker to use the mouse or keyboard? Take a survey, asking adults and kids, then chart the results. Is there a difference between adults and kids and who uses the mouse or the keyboard more?

---

3. You can send your bookmark file to another location, such as your hard drive, as an HTML file that can then be imported into another browser or editor. Some people familiar with HTML find it easier to write a bookmark file in HTML, then import or bring the file into Netscape again.

PUT THE GLUE STICKS AWAY

Perhaps you want to create a list of Web addresses to post in the school library or you find a list of keypals you want to hand out to your students. Kids might want a copy of a joke, or the instructions for a science project that they found. Use the mouse to click-and-drag across the item to highlight it. Release the mouse button and choose **Edit|Copy**. Now leave Netscape and open a word processor or clipboard file, choosing **Edit|Paste** from its menu bar. That's all there is to it! Remember to position the cursor in your text before pasting the new text. Also, save the word processor or clipboard file before closing it.

WHAT IS SURF MONKEY?

Surf Monkey is the first Web browser designed just for kids. The Surf Monkey browser looks like the control panel of a rocketship. The engine inside this rocketship is Microsoft's Internet Explorer 4.0 browser.

The Surf Monkey character is animated and even talks to the kids, acting as guide, helper, and buddy! He sympathizes with them when downloading a page seems to take forever. He'll entertain them with wisecracking comments and amusing actions. And he gets help from Cyberspace Control to block access to unsuitable Internet content and language.

Kids will love the gadgets that explode, squash, or slime a Web page they find yucky or boring and may find reassurance with the multilevel blocking available with the use of this program. The Surf Monkey Web site, shown in Figure 4–7, claims it's "way more fun than a barrel of regular monkeys."

Figure 4–7 You can download the Surf Monkey browser from their home page located at *www.surfmonkey.com/banner.html.*

How to Use Surf Monkey

Surf Monkey guides you through the setup process from download to install. After starting the browser, kids are connected to the Surf Monkey home page where they can launch their voyage from a colorful cockpit full of buttons and switches to experiment with. The home page includes a directory with links to fun sites, with censored sites automatically blocked by daily updates.

The Web site also offers chat rooms, blocking access to chat rooms outside of the Surf Monkey network. Cybot Surf Monkey from Cyberspace Control will actually automatically throw someone out of a chat room if inappropriate language is used. Surf Monkey filtering options are controlled using Surf-watch filtering software. This software provides multiple layers of supervisor controls built into the product and is described in detail in Chapter 2.

Surf Monkey has multimedia e-mail capability and the animated character will even read your e-mail to you out loud! And yes, Cybot will block out bad words from your e-mail too. Surf Monkey e-mail accounts are available by becoming a Surf Monkey member. The Surf Monkey club membership fee is $29.95. Included in this price are software upgrades and enhancements. The Rocketship browser is available for free download or you can have it mailed to you on CD-ROM.

Surf Monkey System Requirements

You will need IE 4.0 on a PC to run Surf Monkey. Your PC should have Windows with 32 Mb Ram and multimedia capabilities. The site offers extensive technical support, including a system configuration checkout for a full rundown. Surf Monkey works with any Internet service provider.

WHAT'S HOT AND WHAT'S COOL

The Web changes every day and some sites keep track of new sites coming online. Many sites offer items that are new to their site, new to the Internet, or pertinent to the subject matter covered by that site. You'll find links to these often presented as **What's Hot**, **What's New**, and **What's Cool** buttons on the home page.

> Chapter 3 offers more details about sites that keep up with what's new. In The Link Farm on the CD-ROM you'll find all the resources from Chapter 3 plus many others, such as **Kathy Schrock's** *Guide to the Internet*.

LESSON PLAN IDEAS

The resources and projects accessible on the Web can keep your students busy for months. One of the best tips for using the Web with kids is to use search engines to locate sites containing the information you are interested in.

Remember that it's easy to lose track of time while browsing and your students may do just that while surfing the Web. An alarm clock or kitchen timer may be helpful in monitoring this situation.

You can use your bookmarks as a source for ideas when planning lessons just as you use the library and books in your personal collection.

RESOURCES

K–12 Schools on the Web

Hundreds of schools, ranging from elementary through high school, are publishing on the Web. To begin exploring who's doing what, point your Web browser to *www.yahoo.com/Education/K_12/*. Here is a sampling of some of the links you'll find:

> Academic Competitions
> Alternative
> Distance Learning
> Gifted Youth
> Home Schooling
> Institutes
> Parental Involvement

Web Browsers

> Netscape
> Download from: *www.netscape.com/download/index.html*
>
> Internet Explorer
> Download beta versions from: *www.microsoft.com/msdownload/*
>
> Surf Monkey
> Download from: *www.surfmonkey.com/banner.html*
>
> Lynx
> Download from: *http://sol.slcc.edu/lynx/current/*

The ICYouSee Guide to the World Wide Web (*www.ithaca.edu/library/Training/ICYouSee.html*) is a project of the Ithaca College Library designed to serve as a self-guided training page and tour of the World Wide Web. Its primary purpose is to provide an introduction to the World Wide Web by addressing seven basic questions. It also offers a survey of interesting and useful places on the Web, including a useful guide for determining the quality and value of any Web site, teaching children how to think more about a site rather than react to its graphics, bells, and whistles.

Chapter 5

A Few of Our Favorite Things

In this chapter we offer a Web site sampler. Here we list Web pages that we think are especially interesting or demonstrate the diversity of sites on the Internet for children and people involved in educating children. Browsing through this chapter will help you understand that some sites only offer information about one particular subject, such as the B-eye page, and how other sites can lead to many more fun and educational places for kids, such as Yahooligans!

Some sites are purely educational, such as the Science Museum of Minnesota's Maya Adventure pages, while others are purely fun, offering activities for children or discussion forums for them to connect with other kids, such as KidsCom. Some sites are more serious, such as the White House home page and others are more lighthearted, such as the Yuckiest Site on the Web.

Browse through here and visit these sites to broaden your understanding of what is available online for children and you'll find at least this many more new places to discover with your own students or children.

Figure 5–1 The Butterfly WebSite

Address: *mgfx.com/butterflies/*

What's there: How do you attract butterflies to your garden? The Butterfly WebSite (Figure 5–1) will tell you how to attract butterflies, raise butterflies, and much more!

The **Science Museum of Minnesota** presents **Maya Adventure**, a World-Wide Web site that highlights science activities and information related to ancient and modern Maya culture.

Maya Adventure includes images from the Science Museum's anthropological collections and activities developed by the Science Museum's education division. Featured in the project is information from two exhibits about the Maya developed by the Science Museum of Minnesota, **Cenote of Sacrifice** and **Flowers, Saints and Toads**.

(Click here if you are using a text-based browser.)

Figure 5–2 Maya Adventure

Address: *www.smm.org/sln/ma/*

What's there: At the Science Museum of Minnesota (Figure 5–2), explore the ancient Maya culture through online exhibits, science activities, and other resources in the exhibit halls. Also check out their sister site, the Thinking Fountain, at *www.sci.mus.mn.us/sln/* for more creative science activities.

Figure 5–3 A Guide to Virtual Slovenia

Address: *www.ijs.si/slo*
What's there: Join a Slovenian newsgroup (Figure 5–3), study the language or gather statistics at the Slovene pages. You'll find recipes, currency information, and even a Slovene-English, English-Slovene dictionary.

Figure 5–4 Welcome to the White House

Address: *www.whitehouse.gov/WH/Welcome.html*
What's there: Visit the White House Web page (Figure 5‑4) and send an e-mail message to the President, take an online tour of the First Lady's garden, read the current press releases, and access information about other government agencies.

Figure 5–5
Virtual Tourist

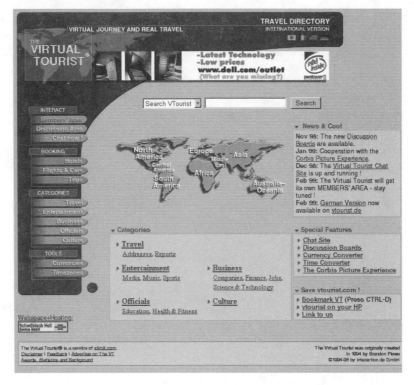

Address: *www.vtourist.com/*
What's there: Find out about the culture, currencies, and cost of traveling in different parts of the world (Figure 5–5).

Figure 5–6
The Yuckiest Site on the Internet

Address: *www.yucky.com*
What's there: Billing itself as "Yuckiest Site on the Internet!," at this site (Figure 5–6) you'll find out what roaches eat, how to get rid of them, a multimedia library, and more.

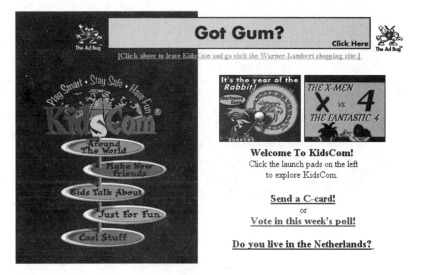

Figure 5–7 KidsCom

Address: *www.kidscom.com/*

What's there: KidsCom (Figure 5–7) is an educational and entertaining electronic playground for kids 4 to 15, but parents will have fun here, too! Kids can find keypals, enter contests, and play games, plus there is a link just for parents and teachers.

See the world through the eyes of a honey bee

Welcome to the B-EYE pages! Have you ever wondered how other creatures see the world? Here you can find out. Well, at least you can find out how HONEY BEES see the world. Well, let's say you can find out what we THINK the world looks like to a bee. Well, not the WHOLE world, really, but a subset of the world, namely a number of greyscale pictures. But, still, I'm sure you will find it an interesting experience...

Figure 5–8 B-eye

Address: *cvs.anu.edu.au/andy/beye/beyehome.html*

What's there: See the world from a different perspective at the B-eye page (Figure 5–8). A neuroscientist offers a tool here that allows you to view a gallery of "b-eye" images, or choose a picture and run the program.

Figure 5–9
Calvin and
Hobbes

Address: *www.uexpress.com/ups/comics/ch/*

What's there: The official site for *Calvin and Hobbes* cartoon lovers (Figure 5–9). Contains an archive of all the comics plus background information about the characters of this strip.

In The Link Farm on the CD-ROM you'll find links to more online magazines and E-zines for kids.

Figure 5–10
MidLink

Address: *longwood.cs.ucf.edu/~MidLink/*

What's there: Midlink is an online magazine (Figure 5–10) for those middle people in your life, generally kids ages 10–15. Articles explore topics like Native American Geometry and Monu-MENTAL history. Join the Haiku Exchange or point older students to the Secondary Roads page to explore topics such as interactive 3–D models of chemical compounds.

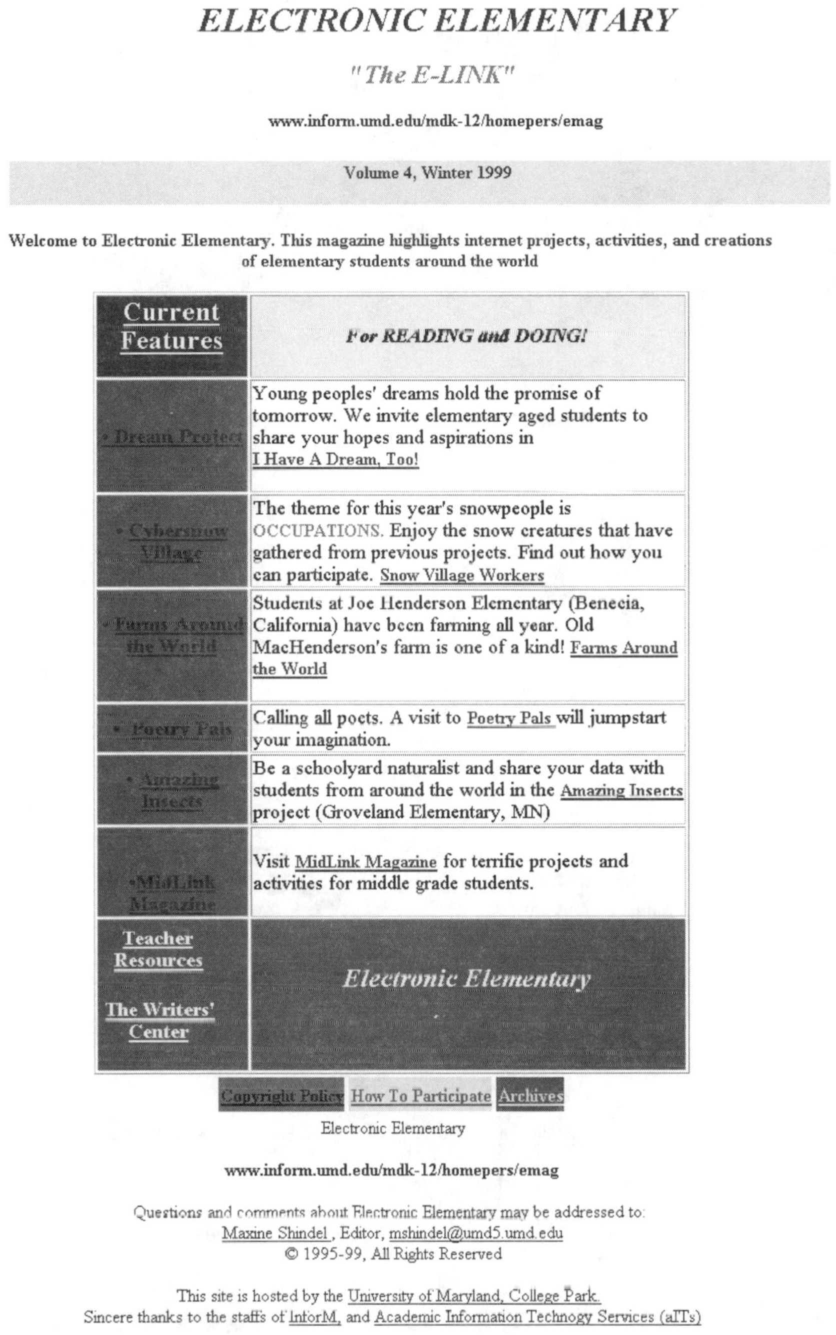

ELECTRONIC ELEMENTARY

"The E-LINK"

www.inform.umd.edu/mdk-12/homepers/emag

Volume 4, Winter 1999

Welcome to Electronic Elementary. This magazine highlights internet projects, activities, and creations of elementary students around the world

Current Features	For READING and DOING!
• Dream Project	Young peoples' dreams hold the promise of tomorrow. We invite elementary aged students to share your hopes and aspirations in I Have A Dream, Too!
• Cybersnow Village	The theme for this year's snowpeople is OCCUPATIONS. Enjoy the snow creatures that have gathered from previous projects. Find out how you can participate. Snow Village Workers
• Farms Around the World	Students at Joe Henderson Elementary (Benecia, California) have been farming all year. Old MacHenderson's farm is one of a kind! Farms Around the World
• Poetry Pals	Calling all poets. A visit to Poetry Pals will jumpstart your imagination.
• Amazing Insects	Be a schoolyard naturalist and share your data with students from around the world in the Amazing Insects project (Groveland Elementary, MN)
• MidLink Magazine	Visit MidLink Magazine for terrific projects and activities for middle grade students.
Teacher Resources The Writers' Center	*Electronic Elementary*

Copyright Policy How To Participate Archives

Electronic Elementary

www.inform.umd.edu/mdk-12/homepers/emag

Questions and comments about Electronic Elementary may be addressed to:
Maxine Shindel , Editor, mshindel@umd5.umd.edu
© 1995-99, All Rights Reserved

This site is hosted by the University of Maryland, College Park.
Sincere thanks to the staffs of InforM, and Academic Information Technogy Services (aITs)

Figure 5–11 Electronic Elementary

Address: *www.inform.umd.edu/MDK-12/homepers/emag*

What's there: The Electronic Elementary magazine (Figure 5–11) highlights Internet projects, activities, and creations of elementary students around the world. Make Poetry Pals, read about students farming, become a naturalist and share data in the Amazing Insect Project, or create a "snowperson" for the Cybersnow Village!

Figure 5–12 Crayola Saturday

Address: *www.crayola.com/index.html/*

What's there: So what are crayons made of and what is the most popular color? The Crayola page (Figure 5–12) has answers to these questions and more crayon trivia and history. Color online or check out their new craft project each week. Also visit the Crayola Art Education pages at *www.education.crayola.com*.

> There are dozens of other resources for teachers listed in the Teaching Resources section of The Link Farm on the CD-ROM, such as **The Chalk Board: A Classroom Corporate Connection.**

Latest Revision: January 5, 1999

Named by NetGuide Magazine as One of the 50 Best Places to Go Online!

WELCOME TO EDWEB, written and produced by Andy Carvin. The purpose of this hyperbook is to explore the worlds of educational reform and information technology. With EdWeb, you can hunt down on-line educational resources around the world, learn about trends in education policy and information infrastructure development, examine success stories of computers in the classroom, and much, much more. EdWeb is a dynamic work-in-progress, and numerous changes and additions occur on a regular basis.

To begin, please enter the EdWeb Home Room. To speed up your access, please select the Home Room nearest you:

EdWeb @ Global SchoolNet

Figure 5–13 Edweb

Address: *edweb.gsn.org*

What's there: A must-see site (Figure 5–13) for educators new to the Internet. Explores the worlds of educational reform and information technology. Access the WWWEDU (pronounced "Wedo") discussion list that explores the role of the WWW in education and hunt down online educational resources around the world.

Figure 5–14
Daily Almanac

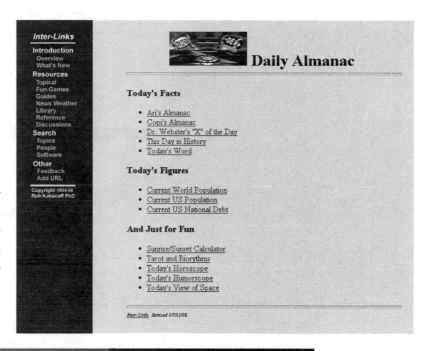

Address: *alabanza.com/ kabacoff/Inter-Links/fun/ almanac.html*

What's there: What is the current U.S. national debt and how much of it is each citizen responsible for? Find out this fact and others, such as the current U.S. population, and discover fun stuff like your "humorscope" at the Daily Almanac page (Figure 5–14).

Figure 5–15
West's Legal
Directory

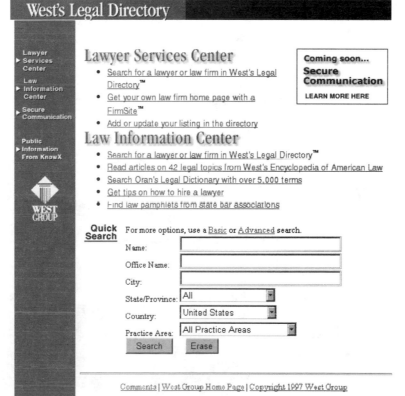

Address: *www1. wld.com/wld.htm*

What's there:

West's Legal Directory (Figure 5–15) is a serious site that can be used with older students or to demonstrate to younger kids how adults use the Internet. You can search for lawyers or law firms, get tips on how to hire a lawyer, or look up terms in the legal dictionary.

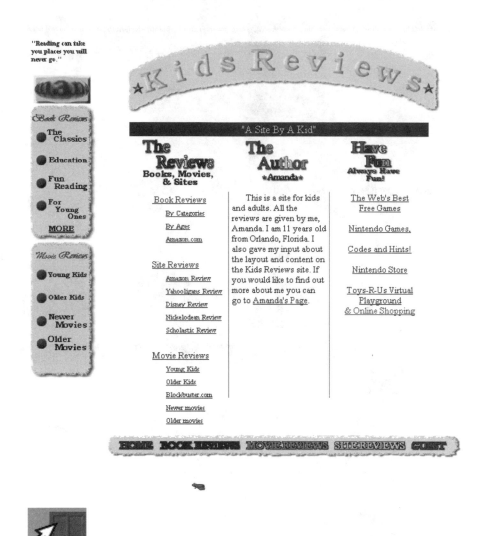

Figure 5–16 Kids Reviews

Address: *www.kidsreviews.com/*
What's there: Read movie and book reviews for young kids and older kids from 11-year-old Amanda (Figure 5–16)! She provides links to the favorites, like Disney, Nickelodeon, and Yahooligans!, plus Nintendo game codes and hints.

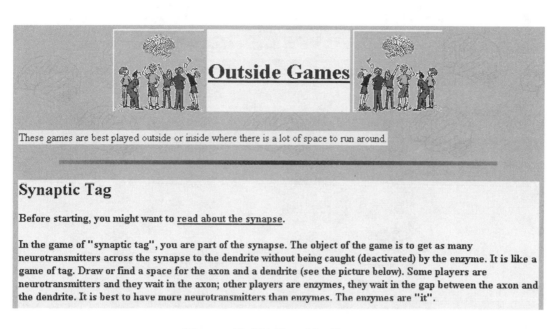

Figure 5–17 Outside Games

Explore how the brain works with kids in the most imaginative ways (Figure 5–17), such as this "synapses" game (*faculty.washington.edu/~chudler/neurok.html*).

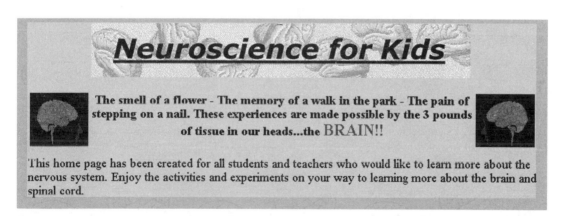

Figure 5–17a Neuroscience for Kids

The Neuroscience for Kids home page offers dozens of games, lesson plans, and other activities to get kids thinking about their brains.
Address: *weber.u.washington.edu/~chudler/outside.html*
What's there: Play outside games to teach kids about how the brain works; if it's raining, check out the rest of the Neuroscience for Kids site (Figure 5–17a). There is so much here, you'll need to come back again and again!

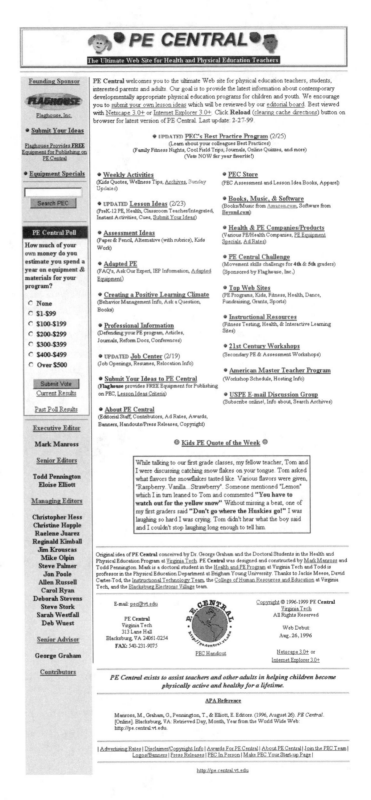

Figure 5–18
PE Central

Address: *pe.central.vt.edu/*
What's there: PE Central is the ultimate Web site (Figure 5–18) for health and physical education teachers.

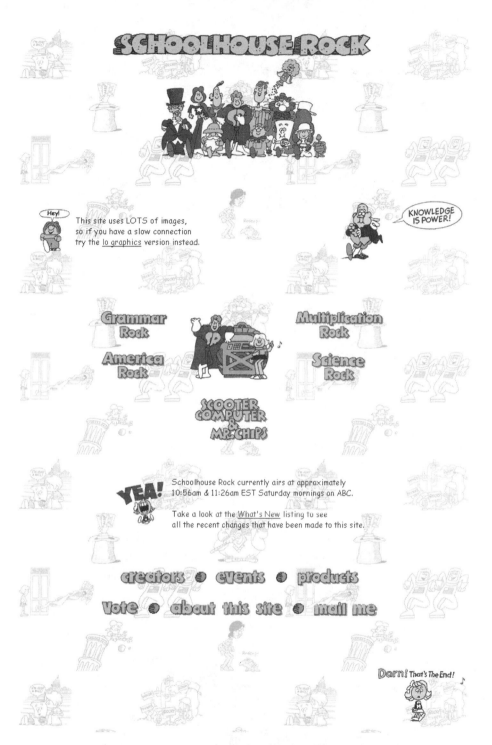

Figure 5–19 Schoolhouse Rock

Address: *genxtvland.simplenet.com/SchoolHouseRock/index-hi.shtml*
What's there: Created and maintained as a personal hobby, Schoolhouse Rock offers the songs, lyrics, and videos from this series (Figure 5–19) for free download, plus trivia.

Welcome!

www.4Kids.org is a weekly feature published in newspapers all over North America. It is designed for kids (and their parents) to find fun, educational, and safe spots to visit on the World Wide Web. That's our vision. Each week the 4Kids staff searches out cool places to go so that kids can spend their online time having fun learning rather than searching. Check out our map to see if a newspaper near you carries this week's current issue. Also, you can view our back issues or browse our database of cool spots. If you have a favorite site just "4Kids" nominate it!

Find K-12 Resources handpicked for **you** with the **Interests Finder**.

Send us some mail if you like, we would love to hear from you! Copyright ©1998, www.4Kids.org. All rights reserved.

Figure 5–20 www.4kids

Address: *www.4kids.org/*

What's there: This site (Figure 5–20) is designed to be a unique and valuable resource for youngsters as well as parents, teachers, and librarians. Each week fun, educational, and safe spots to visit on the WWW are featured in newspapers all over North America. Check out the map online to see if a newspaper near you carries this week's current issue.

Figure 5–21 Yahooligans!

Address: *www.yahooligans.com*

What's there: A searchable, browsable index (Figure 5–21) of the Internet designed for Web surfers ages 7 to 12. Features cool sites, new sites, and a random link button when you're in the mood for a surprise!

All the sites listed here—plus many others—are included in The Link Farm on the CD-ROM. There are graphics sites for the younger set and Web page design tutorials for older students. Check The Link Farm for resources to share with the kids in the classroom or at home or to point to when they are online alone.

Chapter 6

All Aboard for
Field Trips

In this chapter we introduce you to the idea of virtual field trips. Virtual field trips enable children and young adults to explore many areas of the world without the expense of having to leave their school or home or town. Many different types of groups are putting together expeditions, adventures, museum exhibits, and other types of online tours and projects. There are literally hundreds of them for you and your students to explore.

Virtual field trips offer you the opportunity to take your kids on a tour of the White House or the Port of Seattle without leaving town. There are virtual field trip exhibits to the Smithsonian Institution, the Galapagos Islands, aquariums, and NASA missions. We'll explain how you can use a virtual field trip site in your class, library, or home and give you a description of several sites to get you started.

LEAVE THE HASSLE BEHIND

A virtual field trip is similar to a regular trip without the cost and hassle of organizing anyone. It is different from a regular field trip because so many more resources can be utilized. Some field trip adventures are designed to describe a particular topic, such as how light travels, and others explore a particular subject, such as microbiology at the Microbial Zoo (*commtechlab.msu.edu/sites/dlc-me/zoo/*).

Many sites are quite like a traditional field trip with a guided and narrated tour of Web sites that have been selected by educators or professionals and arranged in a series so students can follow with the click of a single button. These types of virtual field trips assemble the most important sites that tell a story or follow a theme. They often provide a narration window with text that explains the site at the grade level it is intended for.

Figure 6–1 The Microbial Zoo home page.

Other sites present exhibits similar to what you'd find when walking into a museum, viewing the directory, and then deciding which section you'd like to explore. Still other sites offer detailed projects, extensive exhibits with links to many other resources, tours, and chat rooms, or discussion lists for collaborating with other kids and professionals.

Bad Weather? Don't Worry!

As teachers and parents, we know that field trips motivate and educate our kids. As teachers we know they are time-consuming, difficult to organize, and often affected by the weather. As parents we know that schedule and finance conflicts make field trips difficult and infrequent. In many cases, the places we would most like to visit aren't nearby or aren't open at the time we are covering them in the curriculum. The next best thing to a real field trip is a virtual field trip (see Figure 6–1). Virtual field trips can take you places you truly couldn't go otherwise, for example, inside a volcano or deep under the ocean. And they are open all the time!

> You'll find dozens of virtual field trip sites, such as the **Honolulu College Dinosaur Exhibit**, listed in The Link Farm on the CD-ROM.

The Benefits of Virtual Field Trips

- Virtual field trips give students room to move at their own pace and explore things as deeply as they choose.
- Virtual field trips can include global and off-planet destinations, taking you to places you otherwise would not or could not go.
- Virtual field trips are safe and free of hazards.
- Virtual field trips can tap into many types of expert resources on a single topic, enriching the learning experience.
- Virtual field trips can be repeated over and over again.

How To Use Virtual Field Trips

There are many ways to use a virtual field trip site, whether in a public library setting, a classroom, or the living room of your home. Libraries and schools can encourage kids to go on virtual field trips with their families at home and give presentations or share adventures at a special family night. Families can use these sites as part of a birthday party or to gather information on a place they will actually be traveling or where one family member will be going.

In the school, an entire class can visit the site together with the use of an overhead projector and LCD panel.

Students might be offered extra credit for creating a virtual field trip presentation for a local senior citizen center, church youth group, or library. A student could also be given the option of using a virtual field trip or online exhibit for an element in a report or presentation.

A library could attract youth or high school students to the library with a Virtual Field Trip Day each month, forming a youth group that meets at the library. A display of holdings from the library pertaining to the country or place or subject the field trip describes could be set up.

At home these field trips can be used to supplement a topic the children are studying or to enable them to find out more about a subject they find very interesting beyond what is offered in the class or after the class project has ended. Families can use online exhibits to enrich their children's lives when traveling is not possible. Virtual field trips present a wonderful opportunity for children to relate to and engage in a mutually enjoyable activity with grandparents or other family members who are unable to travel much.

Most virtual field trip sites have additional resources available for teachers; however, these resources can be used by a librarian, parent, or motivated student. Additional resources can include posters, field trip outlines, challenge questions, puzzles, question-and-answer databases, ask-an-expert forums, collaborative science experiments, learning centers, interactive lessons, and links to archived material.

FIELD TRIP SITES

Educational Web Adventures LLP

Educational Web Adventures (*www.eduweb.com/adventure.html*) believes that learning should be a journey of exploration and discovery (Figure 6–2). It develops interactive Web sites, learning modules, and Web adventures for clients that include Colonial Williamsburg, the Weisman Art Museum, the JASON Project, and the Bell Museum of Natural History. These sites are offered online free of charge. The American Library Association has recommended this site that challenges visitors to explore a subject critically and work toward a rewarding resolution.

Each site is designed to have a sense of fun about it and offers a clear navigation system and appealing design. Their Web sites range from small learning modules to elaborate adventures involving simulations and games. Games and simulations use the lure of an interactive story to draw visitors into a new situation in which they must answer questions and problems in order to finish the game successfully. In some cases, players assume a new identity such as an art detective or an undercover wildlife officer to learn more about the subject in an exciting way. Simulations may employ branching story lines and multiple resolutions to reveal the consequences of the players' choices.

Educational Web Adventures

Home

Services & Rates

At the Helm

Contact Us

Our Adventures and Web Sites

Discover the world of art, science, nature and social studies with our online adventures and Web sites! Learn more by clicking on a category title, or go straight to the adventures.

Art and Art History

- **NEW! Building Surprises: The Architecture of the Weisman Art Museum.** Explore this unusual building and think about architecture in a new way! (Fourth grade to adult)
- **ArtEdventure! Color Theory vs. Dr. Gray and his Dechromatizer.** Learn about color theory to defeat a villain who drains the color from fine art. (Fourth grade to adult)
- **A. Pintura: Art Detective.** Art history disguised as a noir mystery. (Fourth grade to adult)
- **Inside Art.** Explore a painting from the inside out. (Fifth grade to adult)
- **Prang's Fun Pro soybean crayons.** Animations and information about the first crayon made from a renewable resource.

Science and Nature

- **The Watershed Game.** Manage a watershed to preserve water quality. (Fifth grade to adult)
- **Who's Out There? A Space Science Adventure.** How to lead a search for other life in the universe. (Fifth grade to adult)
- **Digital Lab: Observing a Coral Reef.** Dive into Bermuda's coral reef to examine corals and analyze environmental change. Demo only. (Sixth grade to adult)
- **Be a Spacecraft Engineer.** Design a new spacecraft based on the STARDUST comet-sampling craft. (Fourth grade to adult)
- **Catesby's Web.** An online adventure about a colonial naturalist and his scientific legacy. Developed for Colonial Williamsburg's Electronic Field Trip program.
- **Tiger Adventures and Activities**
  - **The Tiger Talks Back.** A cartoon tiger answers questions about tiger behavior and biology. (Second grade to adult)
  - **Tracking The Tiger Trade.** Go undercover to Asia to expose the illegal trade in tiger parts. (Sixth grade to adult)
  - **Tiger on the Loose!** Help the police track and identify a runaway tiger. (Sixth grade to adult)
  - **Zoo Tiger.** Design a safe, healthy zoo exhibit for the runaway tiger. (Sixth grade to adult)
  - **Save the Tiger!** Breed a captive tiger to help save the species. (Sixth grade to adult)
  - **Survive!** Select a habitat and try your luck at hunting. (Fourth grade to adult)
  - **The Tiger Handbook.** An interactive handbook about tiger ecology, endangerment and conservation. (Sixth grade to adult. Also third to fifth grade version)
- **Amazon Interactive.** Learn about the people and geography of the Ecuadorian Amazon. Try running a community-based ecotourism project. (Fourth grade to adult)

Social Studies

- **Amazon Interactive.** Learn about the people and geography of the Ecuadorian Amazon. Try running a community-based ecotourism project. (Fourth grade to adult)
- **Catesby's Web.** An online adventure about a colonial naturalist and his scientific legacy. Developed for Colonial Williamsburg's Electronic Field Trip program.
- **Enslaved.** Research the slave trade using original documents and images. Developed for Colonial Williamsburg's Electronic Field Trip program.
- **A Day in the Life.** Spend a day as three young people in eighteenth-century Williamsburg. Developed for Colonial Williamsburg's Electronic Field Trip program.
- **Loyalty or Liberty?** Gather secrets for both Loyalists and Patriots in revolutionary Virginia, then decide where your own loyalties lie. Developed for Colonial Williamsburg's Electronic Field Trip program.
- **Tracking The Tiger Trade.** Go undercover to Asia to expose the illegal trade in tiger parts. (Sixth grade to adult)
- **The Watershed Game.** Manage human activities in a watershed to preserve water quality. (Fifth grade to adult)
- **Coming Soon! Trouble at the Fur Post: A Minnesota History Mystery.**

Web Sites

- **Bell Museum of Natural History**
- **Minnesota Department of Children, Families & Learning**
- **Minnesota IDEALS**
- **Mississippi Market Natural Foods Co-op**
- **Tiger Information Center**

Read what Web surfers and reviewers saying about our Web adventures!

Figure 6–2 Educational Web Adventures lists their adventures by subject category.

The Virtual School Bus

The Virtual Field Trips Web site (*www.field-guides.com/*) is devoted to providing online field trips that take you to places you could only dream about going. Each field trip (Figure 6–3) covers a specific topic, such as salt marshes or volcanoes, with sites selected by experts on the subject the field trip covers. These sites have been arranged in sequential order to build a story for you to follow. Every field trip has a set of prepared documents that you can print out for each person on the trip, including brief teacher's guides and other selected Web sites that provide background or curriculum guidance.

The Virtual Field Trip site enables you to increase the speed of a trip by allowing you to *pre-cache* the sites to be visited. Pre-caching automatically downloads every site used in the field trip. Once this process has been completed, all of the pages are stored on your local system and you can move from one page to another as fast as your system allows.

Figure 6–3 The Virtual Field Trips home page.

You can even have audio prepared by the field trip's expert. They also offer the *Field Guide* authoring tool to easily customize the text that is displayed in the narration window or to add and delete stops to the tour.

Also offered are ideas for teachers about using this site, such as curriculum supplements, an introduction to teaching online and a library. One of the distinctive features of this site is the help available for anyone interested in creating their own virtual Web tour or field trip.

Possible field trips you can take from this site are:

- Deserts
- Deserts K–8 (a modified version of the desert field trip aimed at a younger age group)
- Hurricanes
- Natural Wonders of the World
- Oceans K–6
- Salt Marshes
- Sharks
- Volcanoes

Terra Quest

TerraQuest (*www.terraquest.com/*) offers three in-depth field trip expeditions:

Virtual Antarctica—A team of polar explorers go in pursuit of the perfect penguin, with digital photography and satellite uplinks (Figure 6–4).

Figure 6–4 Virtual Antarctica's navigation bar.

Virtual Galápagos—Join a shipload of wired adventurers (Figure 6–5) on their sail through this living laboratory of evolution. Includes dispatches from the field.

Figure 6–5 Virtual Galápagos offers a gallery of digital images.

Yosemite National Park—Noted adventurer Erik Weihenmayer (Figure 6–6) makes his inspirational ascent climbing three thousand feet of solid rock, straight up the face of El Capitan.

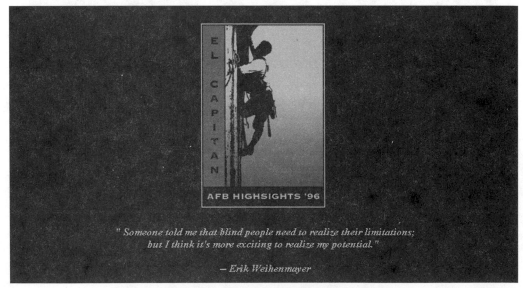

Figure 6–6 Presented in association with the American Foundation for the Blind.

JASON Projects

Most teachers are already familiar with the JASON projects (*www.jasonproject. org/*); however, it is also a useful online resource for librarians and parents. Dr. Robert Ballard, discoverer of the wreck of the RMS *Titanic*, founded the JA-SON Project after receiving thousands of letters from students around the world wanting to go with him on his next expedition. The JASON projects (Figure 6–7) bring the thrill of discovery to millions of students worldwide with year-round scientific expeditions designed to excite and engage students in science and technology and to motivate and provide professional development for teachers.

The JASON Project offers live satellite and Internet broadcasts to watch the expedition and interact with scientists. Teacher development materials and resources prepare students and teachers for participation in these projects and the scientific principles they'll encounter during the live broadcasts. Some courses are offered for professional credit.

JASON Online Systems gives students and teachers news and discussion groups to communicate with peers. The Online Systems is an integral part of the interdisciplinary curriculum, providing data-gathering and sharing exercises. The Web site provides graphics, video and sound clips, and interactive exercises on current and past projects. The JASON Project Web site also contains photo scrapbooks of recent expeditions, journal entries of students involved in the project, online chat sessions with JASON scientists and ways to get involved with the project. Statewide/regional networks are designed to reach every middle-school student in the area.

To learn more about JASON and how to participate in the project, go to the Get Involved section of the Web site or call 1–888–JASON-00 (1–888–527–6600).

Figure 6–7 The current expedition, *JASON X: Rainforests—A Wet & Wild Adventure!*

Wet & Wild Adventure! travels to the Amazon Center for Environmental Education and Research (ACEER), located in the Peruvian Amazon rainforest with "mini-expeditions" visiting the temperate rainforests of Washington State and the fossil rainforest remains in Colorado.

Past expeditions were:

JASON VIII: *Journey from the Center of the Earth* focused on gushing geysers, frozen glaciers, boiling mudpots, and volcanic activity as students explored two of the most exotic locations on the planet, Iceland and Yellowstone.

JASON VII: *Adapting to a Changing Sea* explored how life adapts to a changing sea, climate changes affecting coral reefs, sharks sensing water both shallow and deep, and the biomechanics and behavior of crocodiles in two expeditions to the Florida Keys.

JASON VI: *Island Earth* focused on the Big Island of Hawaii witnessing the largest surface lava flow in that area for 25 years, looked for evidence of volcanic activity elsewhere in the solar system through NASA's infrared telescope, and studied the unique biology of Hawaii.

JASON V: *Planet Earth* traveled to the Central American country of Belize to study the health of our planet and the effect people have on it. Scientists explored life in the canopy of a rainforest and the Western Hemisphere's largest barrier reef.

JASON IV: *Baja California Sur* went to two sites along Mexico's Baja California Peninsula and examined tubeworms and other organisms living off hydrothermal vents in the Guaymas Basin in the Sea of Cortez and studied migrating gray whales in the Pacific Coast's San Ignacio Lagoon.

JASON III: *The Galapagos Islands* followed in the footsteps of Charles Darwin to explore several land and marine sites and examine animal, bird, and marine species that are found nowhere else on earth.

JASON II: *The Great Lakes* undertook a comprehensive examination of two War of 1812 schooners on the bottom of Lake Ontario. For the first time, students were able to drive JASON, the Remotely Operated Vehicle (ROV), via two-way satellite link.

JASON I: *The Mediterranean Sea* discovered the first hydrothermal vents in the Mediterranean Sea, examined an ancient Roman shipwreck, and retrieved artifacts from under 2,100 feet of water.

Voyages of the Mimi

Voyages of the Mimi (*www.lmsd.k12.pa.us/mimi/98/index.htm*) is a place to explore the archive of records from the past five years' expeditions of the Mimi. The purpose of the project (Figure 6–8) was to enable "land-locked" fans of the *Voyage of the Mimi* multimedia program to vicariously join in when the actual sailing vessel *Mimi* and her captain left port. These archives allow students and visitors to learn all about these interdisciplinary scientific expeditions using a multimedia approach. Videos are available to tell the story of the First Voyage of the Mimi, a scientific expedition to study whales, and the Second Voyage of the Mimi, telling the story of archaeologists in search of a lost Maya city. Science and math themes are explored as students are introduced to scientists and others who employ science and math in everyday life.

Figure 6–8 Mimi incorporates the use of lesson plans, hands-on activities, and projects to integrate the program into the classroom and extend concepts in every voyage.

Mister G's Virtual Field Trips

Mister G's Virtual Field Trips (*www.bess.net/~garyg/trips.htm*) explore the Puget Sound area (Figure 6–9). See shipping ports, the Pacific Science Center, boats, forts, and museums, and visit links to hundreds of sites. Mr. G is Mr. Gillespie, a sixth grade teacher at Mirror Lake Elementary School. This school has an Internet Club of fifth and sixth grade students that meet once a week after school to build these online field trips. Mr. G helps them get organized, write code, scan, learn the Apple QuickTime camera, and save it all so it opens in Netscape. This club would love to hear from other students who are doing the same thing!

FIELD TRIPS · LESSON PLANS · CLASSROOM LINKS · E-MAIL · GIFT SHOP

Figure 6–9 Explore the Puget Sound area at Mr. G's Field Trips site.

Field trips currently offered include:

Pacific Science Center
The Chittenden Locks
Fort Nisqually
The Port of Seattle
Center for Wooden Boats
Camp 6 Lumber Camp
Northwest Recycling Center
Washington History Museum
Tacoma Fire Boat
Camp Thunderbird

Figure 6–9a Students learn such applications as Apple Quick Time camera to build virtual field trips.

The Franklin Institute

The Franklin Institute (*sln.fi.edu/*) offers a huge listing of exhibits and interactive online projects for children to foster the development of a scientifically and technologically literate society (Figure 6–10).

Founded in 1824, the Franklin Institute of the State of Pennsylvania for the Promotion of the Mechanic Arts had a twofold purpose: to educate and foster science and technology literacy among a new generation of mechanics, and to support and promote local manufacturers. For the next half century, the Franklin Institute became the nation's most important institution for the organization and dissemination of technical information and knowledge on new technologies and in the promotion of science-based industries.

In 1934, the Franklin Institute opened the Science Museum—called the *Wonderland of Science*, the museum advocated a "hands-on" approach to learning and demonstrated the institute's continued interest in popular education.

Figure 6–10 The Franklin Institute offers over a hundred projects.

At this site you'll find Hotlists and Exhibits. Hotlists are organized lists of resources on the Internet that science educators and other science enthusiasts may find useful. The sites have been screened for their educational appropriateness. To be listed, each resource needs to stimulate creative thinking and learning about science. You'll find the online exhibits by following the link *Educational Hotlists* from their home page and then choosing *Online Exhibits* or use the URL *sln.fi.edu/tfi/jump.html*.

Some examples of online exhibits are:

Legendary Lighthouses	Splendors of Egypt
The Renaissance	The Microbial Zoo
Early Motion Pictures	The Brainium
Blazing a Genetic Trail	The Telegarden
The Face of the Moon	

Anyplace Wild®

Anyplace Wild® (*www.pbs.org/anyplacewild/*) is presented by PBS as a supplement to their half-hour television series that explores a new wilderness area. Each week they travel to some of the world's most spectacular places and offer information online about each week's guests and each area's natural history, wildlife, geology, flora and fauna, and human history.

Around the World Journal

Around the World Journal (*russell.webtravel.org/atwj/*) documents what an individual might see and discover while traveling around the world (Figure 6–11). Russell Gilbert asks the question: Ever think about quitting your job and hitting the road? He did and he kept a journal along the way. Along the way he also took more than 120 photos! The Table of Contents offers links to specific countries, a photo album, world maps, a breakdown of expenses per country, and comments from readers. He also provides links to other resources on the Internet.

Around-the-World Journal
(A 9-month trip through 26 countries)

by Russell Gilbert

Figure 6–11 Around the World Journal will appeal to high school age youth.

The journal includes the following sections:

Introduction (Start here)
September, 1991 (Dallas, Hawaii, Fiji)
October (Fiji, New Zealand, Australia)
November (Australia)
December (Australia, Hong Kong, Singapore)
January 1992 (Malaysia, Thailand)
February (Thailand, Nepal)
March (India, England, Wales, Scotland, Greece)
April (Greece, Ireland, Northern Ireland)
May, 1st Half (France, Switzerland, Italy)
May, 2nd Half (Italy, Austria, Germany, Czechoslovakia, Poland)
June (Germany, Sweden, Denmark, The Netherlands, Belgium)

World Surfari

World Surfari (*www.supersurf.com/*) was created in 1996 by 12-year-old Brian Giacoppo. Brian is still offering a different virtual adventure every month in a manner that will appeal to elementary or middle-school-aged students (Figure 6–12).

 習う Want to learn Japanese? <u>Go Here!</u>

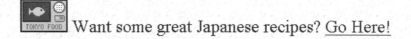 Make a Jumping Frog Origami. <u>Go Here!</u>

Want some great Japanese recipes? <u>Go Here!</u>

Figure 6–12 Recipes and activities from one of Brian's page about Japan.

World Surfari takes a look at the people who live, work, and play in each country visited. Brian presents textual information gathered from sources such as the *CIA World Fact Book* into summaries about each country's geography, economy, government, environment, and transportation. Surfari also offers fun recipes, jokes, and links to interesting Web sites that have something to do with the featured country.

ONLINE EXHIBITS AND MUSEUMS

Scientific American

Scientific American (*www.sciam.com/explorations/*) offers online exhibitions and an Ask-the-Expert section. Most suitable for high school students, the online exhibits contain articles with hyperlinks to new terms and more information. A list of related resources is offered at the end of each article (Figure 6–13).

Figure 6–13 Scientific American online exhibits offer in-depth study of subjects at the high school and older age level.

Sample Online exhibits are:
Dinosaur Theory February 01, 1999
Come Closer, My NEAR January 18, 1999
The Laser at (About) 40 January 04, 1999
Recipe for a Worm December 21, 1998
Hello, La Niña December 14, 1998
Simulating Sol November 16, 1998
Captain Kirk, Meet HAL November 02, 1998
Jove's Thunder October 26, 1998
Soap Opera August 31, 1998
Solar Flyer August 17, 1998
Mini Molecular Rotor July 27, 1998
Bond Beware July 20, 1998
Welcome to the Neighborhood June 29, 1998
Slices of the Past June 22, 1998
Tiny Trampoline May 04, 1998
Brightening the Microworld April 20, 1998
Slow Ride to the Red Planet March 30, 1998
Mapping the White Continent November 11, 1997
A Turn of the Gear April 28, 1997
Europa: Wet and Wild April 14, 1997
The Trail of Hale-Bopp March 31, 1997
Great Balls of Ice! August 19, 1996
Electric Collections June 3, 1996
Molecular Machines May 27, 1996

Saturn Close Up May 5, 1996
Cities Over Time April 28, 1996

The Ask-the-Experts section will appeal to a broader age and grade range. Questions and answers are archived under the categories of astronomy, biology, chemistry, computers, environment, geology, math, medicine, and physics.
Some questions are:

- How do large trees, such as redwoods, get water from their roots to the leaves?
- What is Godel's Theorem?
- What is Thalassemia?
- When a massive object—such as a star—spins, how is its gravitational field affected?

The Exploratorium

The Exploratorium (*www.exploratorium.edu/general/fact_sheet.html*) is a museum of science, art, and human perception founded in 1969 by physicist Frank Oppenheimer (Figure 6–14). The Exploratorium's mission is to create a culture of learning through innovative environments, programs, and tools that help people nurture their curiosity about the world around them.

Online since December 1993, The Exploratorium's net presence is called ExploraNet. Here you'll find electronic versions of their famous hands-on exhibits, such as how to dissect a cow's eye.

expl⬤ratorium
online exhibits

ENGLISH ESPAÑOL FRANÇAIS

NEW! The Temple Illusion - This ancient temple holds a secret...can you reveal the mystery?

NEW! Which embryo is human?-Can you tell the difference between a chicken and a human?
Try the Cool Flash Version

NEW! Changing Illusions -Tease your brain with five interactive illusions. You won't believe your eyes. Requires Shockwave.

CLASSIC! Fading Dot - If you stare at this dot, for few moments it disappears.

FastBall Reaction Time - Can you hit a 90 m.p.h fastball? Requires Shockwave.

Scientific Slugger -See what makes a Home Run. Requires Shockwave.

Disappearing Act -An animal that blends in with its environment is much easier to see when it's moving than when it's still. Requires Shockwave.

Droodles --What's a droodle, its a riddle and a doodle all rolled up in one. Requires Shockwave.

Figure 6–14 The Exploratorium is physically located in the Palace of Fine Arts in the Marina district of San Francisco.

ONLINE TOURS & PROJECTS

The White House (*www.whitehouse.gov/WH/Welcome.html*)

NASA's Quest Project (*quest.arc.nasa.gov/index.html*) offers grant information, ideas for using technology in the classroom, and a guide to NASA online reources.

Volcano World (*volcano.und.nodak.edu/*) is an extensive source of volcano information featuring pictures, movies, games, and more.

Views of the Solar System (*spaceart.com/solar/eng/homepage.htm*) is a multimedia adventure unfolding the splendor of the Sun, planets, moons, comets, asteroids, and more. Discover the latest scientific information or study the history of space exploration, rocketry, early astronauts, space missions, and spaccraft through a vast archive of photographs, scientific facts, text, graphics, and videos.

The Nine Planets—A Multimedia Tour of the Solar System (*www.ex.ac.uk/Mirrors/nineplanets/*) offers an overview of the history, mythology, and current scientific knowledge of each of the planets and moons in our solar system. Each page has text and images; some pages have sounds and movies; most provide references to additional related information.

ExplorA-Pond (*www.uen.org/utahlink/pond/*) is a pond ecology Web site that offers an outdoor classroom in which to design and build a pond, to put your local pond online, and to find pond math and pond science ideas.

In The Link Farm **Science** category on the CD-ROM there are links to biology, weather, environment, geography, and physics Web sites!

Global School House Project (*www.globalschoolhouse.org/site/visitors.html*) is a nonprofit, public service organization that has focused on using communications technologies to support learning for the past 15 years. You'll love this site if you want to connect with other classrooms around the world to find interesting global learning projects to build, promote, and join.

Their Kids and Teens area spotlights projects that the Global School House manages or supports, such as ThinkQuest, Africa Quest, Community Share, International Schools CyberFair, Newsday, GeoGame, and the Ambassador Program. They also archive "Stuff You Missed," which documents projects that have already taken place. Visit the page at *www.gsn.org/project/index.html* for a list of available projects.

Projects start and end at different times throughout the school year and cover activities for all ages and grade levels. The Teachers and Parents section is a treasury of valuable educational resources, including articles concerning the use of technology in an educational setting, contests and educational competitions, mailing-list information for the educational community, and links to valuable educational Web sites.

RESOURCES

- Museums and Aquariums Index (*zlinks.com/museums.html*)—A large listing of museums and aquariums on the Internet, ranging from the California Museum of Photography to the Museum of Fine Art in New York City.
- Sites Alive (*www.sitesalive.com/*)—A commercial site offering virtual field trips for students in grades three through nine. The creators of the site founded the School for Field Studies in 1980 to provide students with real-life experience in studying and performing research on environmental issues. Participating students experience and learn through travel journals, photos, questions and answers, and audio from student researchers who travel around the world. Current expeditions are:
  1. Rainforest Live—understanding the last remaining rainforest of Australia.
  2. Oceans Live—exploring the coral reefs of the Caribbean Sea.
  3. Class Afloat Live—a voyage around the world on board the ship Concordia.

  Classes of 30 students are enrolled at each site for both fall and spring semesters (13 weeks), and smaller classes for shorter summer programs. Current costs as of spring 1999 are: $350—half-year enrollment—entire school with fewer than 500 students; $299—full year, all programs—license for classroom with 30 students or less; $49.95—full year, all programs—family access.
- A list of field trip sites is available at *kendaco.telebyte.com/billband/Trips-scientist.html*.
- Pages and pages of links to sites with virtual field trips, online tours, and exhibits can be found at Fantastic Voyages from 4Kids.Org (*www.4kids.org/coolspots/fantasticvoyages/page1.shtml*). Just a few of their listings are:

Kyoto National Museum in Japan
University of Oregon's Historical and Cultural Atlas
National Geographic's Pirates World Wide Web
Blue Angels—jump into the cockpit of an F/A 18 Hornet
The Virtual Cave—become a cyber-spelunker.

Chapter 7

That's Entertainment

In this chapter we take a look at the Web from the perspective of pure enjoyment and how opening up that aspect of it to kids will help them learn also. We try to point out that there are many types of sites that can offer kids a learning experience.

We've divided the sites up into roughly K–6 and 7–12 grades; you'll notice, however, that some fall into the 4–10 grade range, so experiment. In the descriptions for some sites, we also offer ideas and suggestions on how to use the site for a particular learning activity.

Anyone involved with homeschooling families will want to take note of this chapter, also, as there are many resources directed just for the homeschooler.

Click on **Misc.** in the Link Farm on the CD-ROM for more fun sites kids can explore!

LET THE WEB ENTERTAIN THEM

If nothing else you can use this chapter for rainy days, as a reward or privilege to be earned, or when you must use a substitute in the classroom. A few ways entertainment sites can be educational are:

- Many sites have a **What's New** button or link—kids can keep up-to-date with new ideas being displayed on the Web. A new idea may even ignite kids' curiosity to explore something beyond what they find online or at a particular site.
- Children are bound to find a word or two that they don't know, but the Web

makes it very easy to look up a definition. Linda has discovered that questions her own children ask about jargon terms they've read while roaming around online lead to quite interesting discussions as her children searched for the root meaning behind these terms.

- Some kids will be inspired by what they see in the way of graphics and animations, which will lead them to explore how to do it themselves.
- Children are often so enthusiastic over something they've discovered online that they share it with their friends. What better way is there to understand something yourself than to try to teach it to someone else? Kids teaching kids helps them figure out where the gaps are in their own knowledge.
- While surfing, children are practicing Web navigational skills and searching techniques. These skills will help them use their time efficiently when doing research online.

Entertainment Hotspots: Grades K–6

Site Name: Kids Web—The Digital Library for K-12 Students
URL: *www.npac.syr.edu/textbook/kidsweb/Misc/funstuff.html*
Description: A large collection of sites for children, organized by subject and separated into two grade levels: K–6 and 7–12.

Site Name: Making Friends and Other Crafts for Kids
URL: *www.makingfriends.com/*
Description: Lots and lots and lots of craft ideas here! Placemats, holiday crafts, uses for recycled items, messy things and things with yarn—it is the craft central idea place from a graphic designer of 20 years.

Site Name: Me Too—The Network Only for Kids
URL: *www.metoo.net/entertainment/*
Description: Coloring pages, games such as Hangman and Concentration (Figure 7–1), contests, and trivia! There are no ads here and site contents are rated "G" in movie terms. They send out birthday cards and encourage feedback from parents and educators.

Figure 7–1 Me Too monitors site contents throughout the day.

Site Name: mamamedia.com

URL: *www.mamamedia.com/home/superdoorway/home.html*

Description: A megasite (Figure 7–2) with audio, bright colors, and fun for kids! Don't let this fool you, though. All activities are grounded in 15 years of research at Harvard and MIT on how kids learn best—but you don't need to tell the kids that! Offers detailed articles for educators and parents, such as how fourth graders built software programs, but that is all in the grown-ups section. For kids there are over 2,000 safe Web sites, almost 100 replayable activities in the digital sandbox, and online tools to meet the creative needs kids have.

Figure 7–2 All the fun at mamamedia.com is backed with the intention to nurture kids' natural love for learning.

Site Name: Looney Tunes Karaoke Song Book

URL: *www.kids.warnerbros.com/karaoke/cmp/list.htm*

Description: For kids who love to sing. You'll need to have a Real Audio Player for this site. (See the resource section of this chapter.)

Site Name: Wacky Web Tales

URL: *www.eduplace.com/tales/*

Description: Do you know someone that loves to write stories or makes them up all the time? Send them here (Figure 7–3). Choose a story title, fill in the blanks for the parts of speech and let the program finish it. Don't forget to print it to send to Grandma or a penpal!

Figure 7–3 Pick from a variety of story ideas such as "Lessons Aesop Never Taught" and "The Great Dough Disaster" at the Wacky Web Tales site.

Site Name: Disney Clip Art
URL: *www.disneyclipart.com/Coloring_Pages/*
Description: Download coloring pages with Disney characters (Figure 7–4) or movie scenes—then print and color! Could be used to create signs for home, classroom, or club.

Figure 7–4 Free coloring pages with Disney characters or theme parks to download.

Site Name: ZooNet Image Archives
URL: *www.mindspring.com/~zoonet/gallery.html*
Description: A large assortment of photos of animals you'd see in a zoo to download for your personal use (Figure 7–5). The site's copyright statement would be a great starting place to discuss copyright issues.

Figure 7–5 ZooNet Image Archives

Figure 7–6 The Disney site will keep them busy and entertained for hours if you don't watch out!

Site Name: Disney
URL: *disney.go.com/*
Description: Any kid directed to this site (Figure 7–6) should have a timer nearby to get them offline! Described as "A whole bunch of cool games!" from a nine-year-old who's been there.

Site Name: World Village Kidz
URL: *www.worldvillage.com/kidz/*
Description: Send postcards to friends, play games and puzzles, chat, and play with online toys—check these out!

Site Name: Skylight's Kids Graphics
URL: *members.xoom.com/Sky_Light/*
Description: Free graphics (Figure 7–7) for kids to download, includes tile backgrounds for Web pages plus ABCs, borders, and pets. Kids can use these graphics to create interesting newsletters, signs or art.

Figure 7–7 Free graphics for kids to download and use.

Site Name: The Refrigerator
URL: *www.artcontest.com/*
Description: Each week, the producers of The Refrigerator (Figure 7–8) Art Contest pick five pictures to display in "The Competition." Viewers send in votes and the lucky winner is posted on the home page for a week where everyone can see it.

Figure 7–8 The Refrigerator

Entertainment Hotspots: Grades 7–12

Site Name: NASA's Jet Propulsion Laboratory
URL: *www.jpl.nasa.gov/*
Description: Information for the young engineer or space enthusiast about past, present, and future NASA missions; plenty of photos!

Site Name: The Ultimate Band/Radio List
URL: *ubl.com/radio/*
Description: Lists hundreds of bands and artists, with links to other Web sites with information about the performers. Offers a music store, listening room, charts, e-zines, and concert information. The Radio List offers geographically categorized lists of radio stations on the Internet for the United States, Canada, and Europe. A teenager's heaven!

Site Name: ESPN Online
URL: *espn.go.com/*
Description: Sports enthusiasts—here is your place for sports headlines, news, and information.

Site Name: The Student Center
URL: *studentcenter.infomall.org/comics.html*
Description: The Comic links are just one page on this site created by teens for teens. Offers chat and discussion on just about any topic a teen thinks about. Also visit the **games** link at: *studentcenter.infomall.org/games.html.*

Connect to **The Scout Report** and **KIDS Report** from The Link Farm on the CD-ROM. Both these sites list new sites to check out—and the KIDS Report is written by students!

Site Name: Lycos Games Guide
URL: *www.lycos.com/resources/games/index.html*
Description: Dozens of games, from action and adventure to cards and puzzles, presented here according to genre.

Site Name: Web Diner Inc.
URL: *www.webdiner.com/*
Description: A fun site and great resource for any budding Webmaster, complete with Web page templates and graphics (Figure 7–9).

Drive Thru Pickup Window
for Web Page Templates

Figure 7–9 The place for kids to have fun designing Web pages for friends and family.

Site Name: The 1999 HML Virtual Calendar
URL: *www.humvee.net/cal99/*
Description: What adolescent young man doesn't want to own a Hummer automobile? At this site (Figure 7–10) he can create a calendar with a picture of one of these much-more-than-a-jeep automobiles and dream on!

Figure 7–10 Need a present for a Hummer enthusiast? How about a Hummer calendar? The site is also full of statistics on these cars.

Site Name: Game Cafe
URL: *www.girltech.com/HTMLworksheets/GC_menu.html*
Description: Scavenger hunts, mad scientist experiments, palindromes, chat, advice, women in history, sports, film reviews, a bow-tique and more to explore at the Game Café! Creates a world of fun for the adventurous spirit. Club Girl Tech features eight entertaining and educational areas for girls as well. There is a Parents' Area with girl-development research and a Teachers' Area with lesson plans and other helpful information.

Site Name: The Internet Movie Database (IMDb)
URL: *www.imdb.com/*
Description: IMDb is the ultimate movie reference source (Figure 7–11) and covers everything you could ever possibly want to know about movies. It's fully hyperlinked both within the database and to thousands of external sites and is updated continuously.

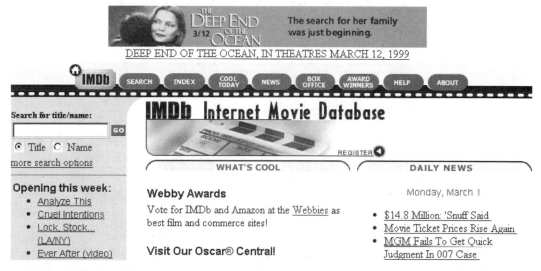

Figure 7–11 Internet Movie Database currently covers over 170,479 titles.

Site Name: Web Chess
URL: *www.june29.com/Chess/*
Description: This site allows two individuals to play chess over the Web (Figure 7–12). Join in a game, wait for an opponent, or just watch the other games being played!

Welcome to WebChess

Figure 7–12 Is there a chess enthusiast in your life looking for an opponent?

THERE'S NO PLACE LIKE HOME

This book is for anyone in the position of helping kids learn about the Internet, regardless of where they do it or why, and that includes homeschoolers. Librarians and parents of homeschoolers may want to note the resources listed in the following section. There are many resources to help meet the needs of the homeschooling family. This section could also be useful for librarians putting together a Quick Guide or handout list of online resources for homeschoolers. Teachers may want to check out some of these sites for creative ideas to use in class.

Debra Bell, director of the Home School Resource Center in Palmyra, Pennsylvania, and publisher of the *Home School Resource Catalogue*, said, "Home schooling is the face of American education in the future. And I think technology and computer-based learning are only going to foster home-based learning" (Bella Stander, "Staying Close to Home." *Publishers Weekly*, 17 July 1995: 142–144). Publishers who are making an effort to reach out to this loosely defined community are finding that homeschoolers are actually linked together through many networks, including the Internet.

Several sites on the Web cater exclusively to homeschoolers. Other sites are produced by families and include children's resources and activities. Still other sites promote alternative educational philosophies. The following list is a sample of what you'll find. If you want more, start your search engines and try terms such as *alternative education* and *home-based learning*, or the name of a particular philosophy or curriculum, such as Waldorf or Oak Meadow or Conclara.

HOMESCHOOLING RESOURCES

- The Oregon Home Education Network (OHEN) (*www.teleport.com/~ohen/*) is a nonprofit statewide organization that supports Oregon's homeschooling families, providing local, state, and national homeschooling activities and resources, including opportunities to network with other homeschoolers. Their Web site offers books, publishers information, and homeschooling FAQs.
- Growing without Schooling (*www.holtgws.com/*)—Holt Associates is a clearinghouse for information about homeschooling and the work of John Holt. He founded *Growing without Schooling* magazine in 1977 as a way to support homeschooling families and to provide a forum for them to communicate with one another. Emphasis is placed on children's ability to learn without a formal curriculum and without mimicking school in the home.
- Home School Legal Defense Association (HSLDA) (*www.hslda.org/*) provides legal help to homeschoolers nationwide.
- Teacher Link (*http://teacherlink.ed.usu.edu/resources/homeschool/index.html*) offers a listing of homeschool online resources.
- Jon's Homeschool Resource Page (*www.midnightbeach.com/hs/*) links to online and community-based resources for homeschoolers.
- Mindfull—Exploring Old Ideas in New Ways (*rethinkingeducation.com/*) presents their annual conference every Memorial Day weekend. Founded in 1994 by two mothers, Mindfull produces the Rethinking Education conference series and Mothering Weekend Retreats. They believe that education is a mutual endeavor; a lifelong cooperative process of questioning and discovery...a true exploration of self, society, the large world.

You'll find an extensive listing of Internet search engines and directories in The Link Farm on the CD-ROM, including a category called **Search Engines Just for Kids**.

- Yahoo!
  Check out the sites listed at Yahoo!. Look under **education|k12|home schooling**. Be sure you have plenty of time, there are many sites listed here. Also, browse through the subhead Alternative for more links.
- Real Audio Player
  Download the software from *www.real.com/*.

PART III

TALKING IT UP: FUN INTERNET ACTIVITIES FOR ALL AGES

People have always had the desire to communicate with each other quickly and easily. As technology becomes part of our everyday lives it is essential to understand the various ways to do this on the Internet. There are many tools for communicating on the Internet and it is vital that the children of today learn how to use them. These new methods of communication will provide opportunities for the kids of today to be more entrenched with communities near and far.

In Chapter 8 we introduce *electronic mail*, or *e-mail*, one of the most popular uses of the Internet. We cover basic mail concepts and discuss how it is used to send messages and files from one person to another. Two popular mail programs are explained and resources for others are given at the end of the chapter.

Chapter 9 introduces a service called *mailing lists*, which is simply a group of people with e-mail addresses sharing messages in a managed way. Messages are sent from one person on the list to everyone else on the list. Mailing lists provide a unique way to communicate with others interested in the same subject as you.

Chapter 10 explores the world of online *penpals* or *keypals*. There are many Internet resources for connecting kids with similar interests so they can correspond as individuals or as groups or classrooms with other classes—across the country or across the globe!

Chapter 11 explains the medium of *HTML (Hypertext Markup Language)*, which is used to write Web pages. Web sites have become a major publishing activity and method for communicating on the Internet. Many young people are writing their own Web pages or creating Web pages for a classroom or extracurricular activity, such as Odyssey of the Mind teams.

Chapter 8

Simon Says,
"Get, Send, Forward!"

Electronic mail, or *e-mail*, is one of the Internet's most popular services. E-mail gives kids the means to send and receive messages to and from just about anyone anywhere. In this chapter, we cover basic mail activities including sending and receiving mail, and attaching files to your mail, and e-mail jargon and netiquette. We also describe two popular mail programs, Eudora Light and Netscape's Messenger (the latter is included with the Netscape Navigator browser).

THE E-MAIL ADVANTAGE

E-mail is electronic messages that are transferred automatically between computers. Transfers may take place over telephone lines using modems or over computer networks. One of the more notable conveniences is the speed with which e-mail travels. E-mail messages travel on high-speed networks and usually arrive at their destination within minutes of being sent. As a result, Internet users have come to refer to the regular postal service as *snail-mail* when comparing it to the speed at which e-mail travels. Usually an e-mail message will take a couple of minutes to reach its destination. Sometimes, however, it can take up to a couple of days, which usually indicates some type of problem. The thing to remember is that e-mail is not designed for immediacy, it's designed for convenience.

E-mail messages can be stored on the computer and viewed in a word processor for editing. One e-mail message can easily be directed to multiple recipients, without photocopying, stuffing envelopes, or postage costs.

Simon Says: "Get a Mail Program"

The process of sending and receiving e-mail is fairly simple. You use software called a *mail program* to compose, read, and send messages. These programs vary from simple stand-alone programs to more sophisticated programs that help you manage a large amount of e-mail. Mail programs send your e-mail to the remote host to which you addressed the message. The message is received and stored in a file system until the recipient starts his or her mail program to retrieve and send e-mail. The file system where messages are stored is called the user's *mailbox*. If you send a message to a user who doesn't have a mailbox at the Internet address you specify, a special program running at that address creates an error report and sends the message back to you, often with a description of why the e-mail could not be successfully delivered. When this happens, your mail is described as having been *bounced back*.

There are many varieties of mail programs to choose from and various ways to get them. Some Web browsers, such as Netscape Navigator and Microsoft Internet Explorer, come with e-mail programs. Commercial online services such as America Online and CompuServe give you e-mail capability using a proprietary mail program. E-mail programs are also sold separately. These programs can be purchased at computer stores or through catalogs or online. Some companies offer a trial version of their software or a free version that you can download from their Web site.

There are also free e-mail services, supported by advertising, that you can get by filling out a registration form that provides some demographic information advertisers use. Another type of free e-mail is Web-based e-mail services, such as Hotmail and Yahoo!, which permit you to send and receive your mail from just about any computer or terminal that has a local connection to the World Wide Web. You don't have to worry about hardware or ISP settings. Simply go to the service's address on the World Wide Web and type in your user name and password. Some services have popular features such as a spellchecker and filters to sort your e-mail. Web-based e-mail is supported by advertising, also.

Regardless of which type of mail program you use, you will be able to compose and read messages without being online the entire time. It is more economical to log off your account after you have checked for new mail. Once you are offline, your mail program can still be running and you can then read new mail, write replies, and compose new messages. All messages you write when offline will be stored in queue until you log on again or instruct the program to send messages in the queue.

Most mail programs provide some type of filing system so that you can keep track of your messages. E-mail messages can be printed, stored in another folder, saved to a separate file, or deleted completely.

ANATOMY OF AN E-MAIL MESSAGE

E-mail messages contain lines of text that follow a certain format. The opening section of an e-mail message is called the *header* and contains field names. The message header is followed by another section called *the body of the message*.

This is where the person composing the message enters the actual text. E-mail messages can also contain a signature or attachments.

In the header section of an e-mail message, each field name is followed by a colon and one or more items of information. Message headers can be long and contain many fields or they can contain only a few fields as in the example below. You don't need to understand what every field in the header means before you can use the Internet mail system effectively. Many e-mail programs enable you to choose how you want to view the message header—simple or detailed.

Here is a sample of the header fields on an e-mail message:

> From: JGitshaw@mercury.world.us
> To: Acbenson@host.yab.com
> Cc: lfodemsk@foo.bar.edu
> Subject: San Antonio

The following brief descriptions provide basic definitions of the different header fields:

- The "From" field describes the person who sent the message.
- The "Return-Path" field provides information about the address of the person who originated the message.
- The "Received" field tells when the message was received by a particular computer, the path that the message took, and which mail programs were being used. Depending on how many computers handled your message along the way, your message header may show one or more of these Received fields.
- The "Date" field shows the time and date the message was sent. After the Date field there is another From field which is different from the first From field. This second From field gives the real name of the person who sent the message.
- The "Subject" field is specified by the sender and summarizes what the message is about.
- The "To" field gives the names of all the people who are to receive copies of the message. If the message is sent only to you, only your address appears here.
- The "Message-id" field is meaningless to us humans, but it does contain a unique identifier that computers find interesting.
- The "CC" (carbon copy) field shows the address of anyone who has received a copy of the message.

The body of the message is separated from the header. You do not see the header as part of the message when you compose it. The header is attached automatically when you send your message.

> Find more information about online safey and security issues in The Link Farm on the CD. All the sites from Chapter 2—Safety@the.keyboard are listed in the section Internet Safety, plus other sites concerning security issues.

Your Signature, Please!

A *signature* is a few lines of information about the sender at the end of an e-mail message. This is an optional feature on your mail program. Many adults include their postal mailing address, phone number, and FAX. For the most part, children should not give out their last name, phone number, or mailing address. Just as in everyday life, children must learn to exercise caution when giving out personal information in the form of a signature file. Their families' or schools' Web site might be appropriate for some e-mail they send and not suitable at all for others.

Many people use the signature block to express their creativity by including small pictures they have drawn with keyboard characters and famous quotes from their favorite authors. People who include extravagant drawings along with 10 or 15 lines of text are considered annoying.

If you choose to use the signature option on your mail program, the signature is automatically included at the end of every e-mail message you send. You can create this file using any text editor or word processor. Some mail programs enable you to create the file from within the mail program itself. If not, you'll create a next-text document, include no more than four of five lines of text about yourself, and save the file with the name *sig.txt*. Save the file in the directory of your mail program. Using a signature file reduces the chance of making a mistake when typing contact information and it also prevents you from forgetting to include this information with your message.

Two important rules for kids to follow when creating their signatures are:

1. Include information that will help a reader respond to your e-mail, such as your first name, e-mail address, and Web home page address, if there is one. Do not give out your last name, phone number, or mailing address.
2. Keep the signature polite and brief. As a rule-of-thumb, signatures should be no longer than four or five lines. Your signature should not be longer than your message.

A typical signature looks something like this:

```
************************************************************************************
Allen C. Benson                                    /(-)(-)\Does the name Pavlov
acbenson@host.yab.com                                        ring a bell?
************************************************************************************
```

Simon Says: "Attach"

The *Attchmnt:* line in the header is where you indicate whether you want to attach one or more files to the message. To attach a file to an e-mail message you will need to know two things: 1) where the file is located and 2) what the file is named. Attached files preserve system information. For example, you can attach a file created in another program, such as a Microsoft Word file, WordPerfect file, or Excel spreadsheet, and the person you send it to can open the attached file using the same program on their computer. Attachments must be formatted so that they can be exchanged between different mail systems. Formats are *ASCII, binary*, or *MIME*. There is a setting in your mail program to designate which format the mail program should use. ASCII is plain text, and binary is used for non-text files, such as executable programs, spreadsheets, and databases. MIME (Multipurpose Internet Mail Extensions) is *multimedia*, meaning it has the ability to include graphics, video, and sound in a message. MIME is a very flexible format. It enables you to include virtually any type of file or document in an e-mail message—text, images, audio, video, and other application-specific data. The following is an excerpt of a header from an e-mail message sent with an attachment using the MIME format. The attached file is an image of a fish named Sparky.

> To: *grandma@house.in.woods.org*
> Attchmnt: My Fish Sparky
> Subject: Got an A in science today!

Want to know more about Internet addressing issues? Check out the section **Internet Help Guides** in The Link Farm on the CD!

E-MAIL ADDRESSING SYSTEM

E-mail addresses are usually shown as *userid@domain-name*. The address consists of two parts separated by an @ sign. The part before the @ sign is the user's ID (the person to whom you are sending your message). The part after the @ sign is the person's Internet address, usually in the form of a domain name. For example: *acbenson@brook.asumh.edu*. This address tells us that the user's ID is *acbenson* (in this case, an abbreviation of Allen C. Benson), and that his electronic mailbox resides on a computer named *brook* at an *edu* (educational institution) named *asumh* (Arkansas State University Mountain Home).

When you set up a new e-mail account, the system administrator will either assign a user ID to you, or you will be asked to make up your own. Your service provider always determines the domain name, whether it is a school, library, or business. For example, if you open an account with AOL, your e-mail address will end with *aol.com* as in *acbenson@aol.com*. If your daughter enrolls at

Northwestern University, her e-mail address would look something like *rebecca@nwu.edu*.

Other Systems' Addresses

You can send mail to people who have their accounts with services that aren't directly on the Internet.

- For users with accounts on Delphi, follow the format *<userid>@delphi.com*
- For users with accounts on AT&T Mail, follow the format *<userid>@attmail.com*
- For users with accounts on America Online, follow the format *<userid>@aol.com*
- A CompuServe user ID is a nine- or ten-digit number with a comma inserted in the middle. To send mail to CompuServe users, replace the comma with a period and add *@compuserve.com* at the end. For example, user id 76543,2105 becomes *76543.2105@compuserve.com*.
- Users with MCI accounts are given numbers that look like phone numbers. Simply remove the hyphen and add *@mcimail.com* at the end. For example, 555–1234 becomes *5551234@mcimail.com*.

Troubleshooting Address Problems

Here are a few pointers to help ensure that your e-mail addressing is done properly:

1. With most computer systems, it doesn't matter whether you address e-mail to users in uppercase or lowercase. With other systems, though, if you send mail with the address in uppercase, the mail may be undeliverable, even if everything else about the address is entered correctly. In general, if you're not sure whether the computer to which you are sending mail is case-sensitive, type the address in lowercase.
2. Make sure you specify the full address.
3. If mail is returned to you, look for error messages that may explain why.
4. Check to make sure you have spelled everything correctly in the address.

Finding E-Mail Addresses

A good place for information on locating e-mail addresses is a FAQ called "How to find people's e-mail address FAQ" maintained by David Alex Lamb. View David's FAQ at: *www.cs.queensu.ca/FAQs/email/finding.html*. Lamb suggests that the best way to find someone's e-mail address is to contact the person directly and ask. If that is not an option, try one of the many search services on the Web.

Lamb's FAQ lists many common search tools, such as MESA (MetaEmail SearchAgent), which allows you to submit a single query to multiple search engines, and Four11, a commercial online directory service with over 10 million listings.

Also try the services listed on Allen Benson's "The Librarians Guide to the Internet" Web site at *www.star-host.com/library/index.htm*. Benson maintains a list of current "people locator services" in the section LOOKING FOR PEOPLE. One service listed is Switchboard, the leading white and yellow pages directory on the Web used by America Online for its more than 10 million members.

POPULAR MAIL PROGRAMS: EUDORA LIGHT AND NETSCAPE MESSENGER

Providing complete documentation for every available mail program is impractical and beyond the scope of this book. Instead, we have covered two common mail programs—a stand-alone e-mail client called *Eudora Light* and the mail program packaged with the Netscape Navigator browser called *Netscape Messenger*. The Microsoft browser, Internet Explorer, is very similar to Netscape, so if you learn one you can easily switch to the other. They offer the same features but use different terminology for some functions. See Chapter 4, "Browser Basics for Beginners" for more information.

Using Eudora Light

One of the best products for accessing e-mail with a SLIP/PPP connection is Eudora Light by Qualcomm. This is a free, watered-down version of Qualcomm's *Eudora Pro*, which costs around $65.00. The freeware version is available for download from their Web site: *www.qualcomm.com*. Versions are available for both Mac and Windows.

The first time you start Eudora after installing, it will display options. This is where you'll enter the required e-mail account information to be able to send and receive e-mail messages. Now you're ready to send an e-mail message to someone!

When starting Eudora after this, the left side of the screen displays a list of your mailboxes, such as IN, OUT, and TRASH. Remember that mailboxes are the same as file folders—just a way to organize your messages. You can create custom mailboxes to sort your mail. Any custom mailboxes you create will appear here, also. The right side of the screen will appear blank until you open one or more mailboxes. Open a mailbox by double clicking on its name. More than one mailbox can be opened at a time (see Figure 8-1). The mailbox screens can be arranged to cascade or you can tile them horizontally or vertically, for easier viewing.

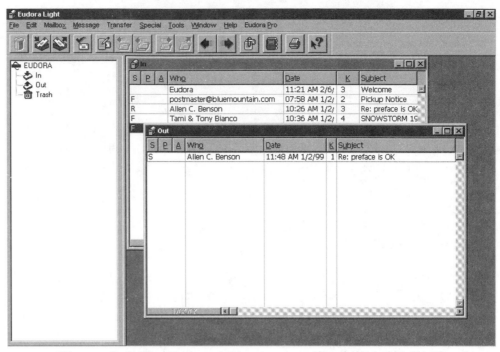

Figure 8–1 The Eudora Light screen with the IN and OUT
mailboxes open in a cascade view, so they overlap.

Each mailbox screen displays a list of e-mail messages stored there. You will simply click on a message to view it. Individual messages can be displayed to cascade or tile alongside a mailbox window, as in Figure 8–2.

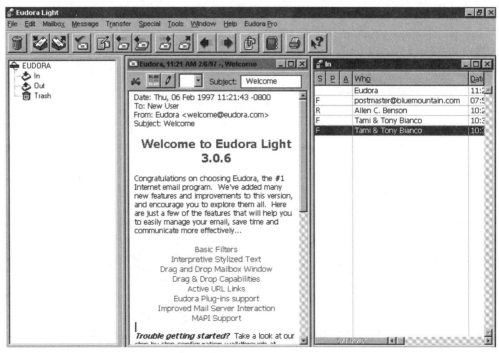

Figure 8–2 The IN mailbox with one mail message is open
in the Eudora Light mail program.

EUDORA: SENDING AND RECEIVING MESSAGES

To compose a new message, click on the icon with a tablet and pencil, or choose **Message | New Message** from the menu bar. A new message screen will appear on the right side of the Eudora window. The header fields are included, so just type in the information next to each field name. As you type information into these fields, notice that the status bar at the top of the new message window changes to reflect the name of the recipient and the subject of the e-mail. The header is separated from the body of the message, so you can easily tell where to start typing your text.

If you choose to use a signature file, the signature will appear in the body of the message. Pressing ENTER several times will move the signature down on the page and make room for you to type text. There are several additional settings and composition tools available in the New Message window. One decision you have to make is which type of file transfer protocol to use. The default setting is for MIME.

The last and largest button on this menu bar is the SEND button. It can also read QUEUE, depending on your settings. When the button reads QUEUE, any message you compose will be saved to a folder to be sent later. When the button reads SEND the program will attempt to send the message immediately. If you are not online at the time, you will see a message stating that the mail could not be delivered. The program then stores unsent messages in the OUT folder and marks them with a "Q" to designate that these messages have not been sent.

To retrieve new mail, click on the icon with a check mark and envelope, or choose **File | Check Mail** from the menu bar. A dialog box will prompt you for your password if you are not logged on to your Internet account. Another dialog box will appear showing the progress of the download and how many messages are being retrieved. Eudora will also automatically send any messages you have queued without prompting or giving you a chance to change your mind and not send a particular message. Any new messages you have are displayed as a list in the IN mailbox. Just click on any message to open it and read it.

One of the great advantages of e-mail is that you can easily *forward* a message you received to someone else or several other people. When viewing a message, notice that some of the icons at the top of the Eudora window that used to be gray now have colors. Full-color icons are active and can perform a function. Two icons have arrows pointing to the left and two icons have arrows pointing to the right. The icons with left arrows help you to reply to either just the sender of that message or everyone the message was sent to. The icons with right arrows help you to forward or *redirect* the message. Forwarding sends the message to another person with you as the sender. Redirecting sends the message to another person with the original sender listed as the sender by-way-of-you.

Eudora: Attaching Files

In Eudora you attach a file to a new message or message you are forwarding by clicking on the icon with the paper clip. From the menu bar you can also choose: **Message | Attach File**. A browse box opens and enables you to move through directories and drives until you locate the file you want to attach. Once you locate the file you want to attach, click once on it and the name of that file will appear in the file name box near the bottom of the browse box. Then click on the OPEN button. You will return to your composition. As a check, look at the *attachment* field in the header to see if the file name is listed there. If not, repeat these steps. You can attach more than one file to a single e-mail message.

Table 8–1 E-mail Shorthand
aamof—As a matter of fact
bfn or **bbf**—Bye (bye) for now
brb—Be right back
btw—By the way
bykt—But you knew that
cmiiw—Correct me if I'm wrong
cul—See you later
eol—End of lecture
fitb—Fill in the blank
ga—Go ahead
gmta—Great minds think alike
iac—In any case
imho—In my humble opinion
jic—Just in case
lol—Laughing out loud
otoh—On the other hand
<g>—Tells the reader you're grinning
<l>—Tells the reader you're laughing
<s>—Tells the reader you're smiling
<j>—Tells the listener you're joking

Using Netscape Communicator

Netscape Communicator is a multipurpose Internet tool that enables you to do many things, including browsing the Web and sending and receiving e-mail. Each component in this suite of tools has its own name. For example, the Web browser is called Netscape Navigator and the e-mail program is called Netscape Messenger. You can customize this program to open only the parts of the program you want to use. Netscape Messenger offers an easy-to-use interface to send and receive e-mail, including the ability to attach HTML documents and more to your e-mail messages. Netscape Communicator is available for free download from the Netscape web site: *home.netscape.com*.

You will need to designate the name of your mail server and enter information to configure the mail program to do what you want. Contact your service provider to find out what your SMTP and POP3 mail server addresses are. Options in other panels include setting up an automatic carbon copy to someone, personal information about yourself or organization, whether you will use a signature file, and designating that your mail is sorted by date, subject, or sender.

THE NETSCAPE SCREEN

If you do not have Navigator configured to automatically start Messenger (the e-mail program), click on the mailbox icon in the lower right of the window or choose **Communicator | Messenger Mailbox** from the menu bar (Figure 8–3). This will start the e-mail program. Each program will run independent of the other.

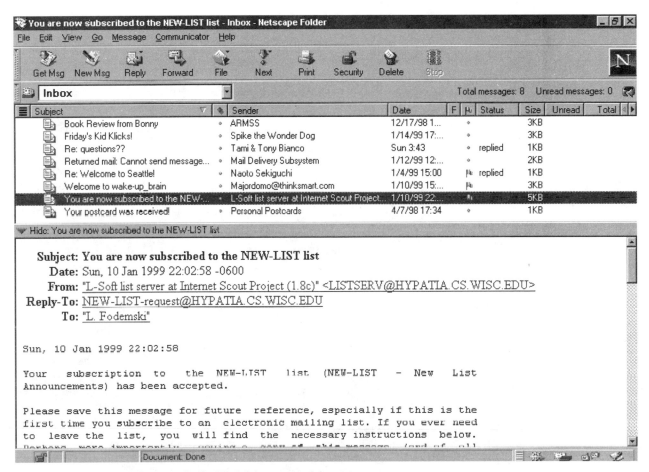

Figure 8–3 The Netscape Messenger screen.

At the top of this window is the menu bar, pictured in Figure 8–4. Clicking any of these menu names displays a pull-down menu with several choices. For example, when you choose the menu item **File**, a pull-down menu appears, giving you options such as mailing a document, opening a file, saving a file, and quitting the program. Options followed by ellipses (. . .) lead you to another pull-down menu with additional choices.

Figure 8–4 Netscape Messenger menu bar.

Just below the menu bar is the toolbar, shown in Figure 8–5, which consists of icons that you can click to perform some of the tasks in the pull-down menus. In other words, the toolbar icons are shortcuts. These are functions you will use often or repeatedly. These can be configured to be icons or just text or an icon with text.

Figure 8–5 Netscape Messenger toolbar.

Below the toolbar is the Location dialog box. This box lists the name of the current folder or mailbox that you are viewing (see Figure 8–6) The down arrow at the right end of this box enables you to view a full list of all your mailboxes and select another one to view. Highlight and click on another mailbox to open it and view the messages in it.

Figure 8–6 Netscape Messenger Location dialog box. Notice the down arrow to the left that enables you to collapse or hide this feature. On the far right you can easily see how many total messages you have and how many are unread.

You can hide both the toolbar and the line with the Location dialog box using the tiny arrows on the left of each line. Click once on the tiny arrow and the line will disappear, leaving a narrow bar with an arrow. Click on the arrow again and you can view that line again. Both lines can be hidden independently of each other. You may want to hide them to create more screen space for viewing messages. The menu bar always remains in view and cannot be hidden.

NETSCAPE: COMPOSING AND SENDING MESSAGES AND ATTACHMENTS

To write a new message, click on the New Message icon. This will open a composition window. The header fields are marked with icons. If you point the cursor to any of these icons, an *information balloon* appears, describing what that icon does. Clicking on one of these icons makes it active and provides fields for you to enter information or choose other options. For example, if you want to attach a file to your message, click on the paper clip icon. This will make the attachment feature active. Now click anywhere in the blank box to the right of the icon or you can choose **File | Attach | File**. A browse box opens and enables you to move through directories and drives until you locate the file you want to attach. Once you locate the file you want to attach, click once on it and the name of that file will appear in the file name box near the bottom of the browse box. Then click on the OPEN button. You will return to your composition, and the name of your file will appear in the box to the right of the paper clip icon.

The lower half of the screen is where you'll enter the text of your message. If you point your cursor to the SEND button, an information balloon will either state **send now** or **send later**. **Send Now** and **Send Later** also appear in a popdown menu from the menu bar item File.

USING FILTERS IN NETSCAPE

Netscape's Messenger has many features, including the ability to format fonts and colors and to filter your e-mail. Formatting enables you to make your e-mail pretty by using different fonts and colors and even inserting images. Filtering is a way to manage your mail automatically by selecting criteria for the filter to look for and designating where the message should be filed if it meets those criteria. Filters can be used to trash junk mail or mail received from an unwanted source. You can also use filters to sort mail coming into one account for various users or people—such as a class. If 15 kids in a class are using the same account for 15 different projects, each kid can have a folder in Netscape. Each student would then require all correspondents to specify a unique word in the subject line of any e-mail sent to them. Then set the mail filter to sort mail into the various folders as it comes in automatically. Mail filters can be set in a variety of ways that can be as complex as you need.

NETIQUETTE FOR NEWBIES

Newbies are new users just joining the Internet. Here are some basic rules, safety tips, and commonsense practices newbies should follow relating to e-mail ethics:

- Be courteous. When choosing words, keep in mind that e-mail is somewhat impersonal.
- Be brief. Don't include a lot of material that has nothing to do with the topic that's being discussed.
- Be clear. State what you have to say clearly and concisely.
- Include a salutation, just as you would when composing an "ink and paper" letter. If you are not clear about how to address someone, consider how you'd address him or her in person. Always opt for a more formal salutation if you aren't sure.
- Use proper grammar and punctuation. There is no need to *over*-punctuate, either.
- Include a signature or your e-mail address at the end of your message. It is often easier to locate a return e-mail address in a signature than to find it in the message header. (Some mail programs drop this portion of the message.)
- When you're responding to someone's messages, include the portion of text you're responding to.
- Never create a mailing list of thousands of Internet users and then mail them all something that they haven't asked for, especially an advertisement. This practice is called *spamming* and is considered to be very rude. People that spam can lose their accounts and get *mail-bombed*—have thousands of pieces of junk mail sent right back at them.
- Give out personal information cautiously, just as in everyday life. According to the Parents Guide to the Internet, published by the U.S. Department of Education (*www.ed.gov/pubs/parents/internet*), children should never use their real names when choosing e-mail addresses, in order to make it difficult for strangers to contact them and other family members by phone or in person.
- Think before you send. Remember that e-mail can be copied and disseminated with incredible ease. Once you have sent an e-mail message, the recipient could conceivably forward it to a huge number of people, or to the one person you wouldn't want to see it.
- It is not a good idea to open attachments from people you don't know. Attachments can carry viruses, including "macro" viruses, which could infect your computer. Hot links to URLs that appear in e-mail messages have also surfaced as potential security risks.
- Notify an adult if you receive a *chain letter* or *virus warning* message. Chain letters are messages asking you to forward that particular message to as many

people as you can. Far more common than viruses are hoax virus warnings. These are widespread and make the rounds for years. Popular names for these hoax viruses are *Good Times* and *Join the Crew*.

RESOURCES

- For more information about Eudora, contact:
  Qualcomm Inc.
  6455 Lusk Blvd.
  San Diego, CA 92121–2772
  Telephone: (619) 597–5113
  (*www.qualcomm.com/quest/QuestMain.html*)
- For more information on e-mail messages warning of viruses, visit *www.kumite.com/myths/home.htm*, a site devoted entirely to Internet virus hoaxes and myths. You'll also find information at the National Computer Security Association (NCSA) Web site (*www.ncsa.com/wordvir1.html*).
- For help and information on—as the site name states—"Everything E-Mail," visit *everythinge-mail.net/e-mailtips.htm* by Mary Houten-Kemp.
- Another extensive source for e-mail information can be found at *www.e-mailhelp.com*. One main resource offered is an instructional video entitled E-mail For Everyone™, called a "superb teaching tool" by *School Library Journal*. The video can also be seen on many public television stations in the United States.
- Information about various types of e-mail programs and applications, including reviews, ratings, and pricing, can be found at Tucows E-mail Clients (*tucows.planetstl.com/mail95.html*).

> Also use one of the search engines listed in The Link Farm on the CD-ROM. Check the section **Search Engines** to search for reviews about particular e-mail programs.

- Inter-Links (*www.alabanza.com/kabacoff/Inter-Links/e-mail/e-mail.html*) is an Internet navigator, resource locator, and tutorial which directs you to other sites on the Internet relating to e-mail usage.

Chapter 9

Mailing-List
Mania

Electronic mailing lists offer a highly efficient way to disseminate information to large groups and hold long-distance discussions among many people. Discussion lists are a critical component of scholarly collaboration. Many colleges and universities use them to facilitate faculty-student communication, enhance classroom education, and conduct group business. In this chapter we describe how mailing lists work, how to join, quit, and manage the messages, and we introduce the four common mailing-list managers. We also point out lists that may be of interest to students and educators.

MAILING LIST COMMUNITIES

An electronic mailing list is a community of people who have come together to discuss a topic of interest via e-mail. A message from one person on the list can be sent to everyone else on the list. The person sending the message has only to send one message rather than a lot of individual messages to a whole bunch of people. To post a message to other list members, a member sends e-mail to the list address. A copy of the message is then automatically mailed to each of the list's subscribers.

Lists are organized around topics, so you can find a list that deals with a particular interest or field of study. Using this tool, a group of students can share ideas or information about a particular subject without having to write letters or make phone calls to several other people. For just about any topic you can think of there is a mailing list to discuss it! Some lists offer a Web interface that enables users and list managers to interact within an intuitive graphical environment. The Web interface is a crucial step in making mailing lists more readily available to users of all experience levels.

THREE COMPONENTS TO SIMPLIFY THE CHAOS

Mailing lists are made up of three components:

1. Listowner—a person who put the idea together and got the software that is used to manage the list and distribute the messages running.
2. Mailing-List Manager—software designed just for managing mailing lists. This specialized software manages every piece of e-mail coming in and going out each day—a number that can reach into the thousands.
3. Subscribers—a list of the e-mail addresses of all the folks who subscribed, or joined, that list. The group as a whole is called a *list* and they have a name called a *listname*.

It is important that you understand the functions of these three components when using a mailing list because you'll need to use a different address for each component.

You'll only send an e-mail message to a listowner if you are having a problem with the list, such as problems joining (subscribing) or leaving (unsubscribing). You'll also contact the listowner if you have problems with people discussing something other than the list topic. The listowner's e-mail address will be posted in the first mailing you receive from the list after joining.

You'll send commands to the Mailing-List Manager software when you want to subscribe or unsubscribe or suspend your subsciption for a period of time, such as when you are on vacation. You'll also send commands to the software to get information, such as a list of discussion lists. The address for the software is called the *subscription address* and will typically start with "listserv" or "majordomo" or "listproc" or "<listname>-request." For a complete list of available commands, send the word help in the body of an e-mail message addressed to the subscription address.

You'll communicate with other subscribers when you want to add something to the discussion or ask a question of others on the list. The address to send messages to other members of that list is called the *list address* and will typically begin with the name of the list, such as *childrens-voice@schoolnet.carelton.ca*.

Check out **Keypals** in The Link Farm on the CD-ROM for sites that have their own mailing lists for newsletters and online projects.

NOTA BENE!

When you first subscribe to a list, you are sent a general information sheet that includes the listowner's name and e-mail address. It is similar to a welcome message and very important. You should always keep this first message. It will explain how to unsubscribe and give you other important information about that particular list. The number of members of any given list may vary from less than a hundred to thousands.

The listname attempts to describe the topic of the list. In Table 9–1 we've listed a few samples to show you what we mean. Note the two different addresses given for each mailing list: a list address and a subscription address. The list address is where you e-mail your messages when you want to communicate with all of the subscribers on the list. The subscription address is used to send commands to the Mailing-List Manager software.

Table 9–1	Sample mailing-list names, topics, and addresses		
Listname	**Topic of discussion**	**List Address**	**Subscription Address**
STAMPS	Stamp Collecting	stamps@cunyvm.cuny.cdu	listserv@cunyvm.cuny.edu
GAMES-L	Computer Games	games-l@brownvm.brown.edu	listserv@brownvm.brown.edu
ORIGAMI-L	Origami	origami-L@nstn.ns.ca	listserv@ nstn.ns.ca
SWIM-L	Swimming	swim-l@uafsysb.uark.edu	listserv@uafsysb.uark.edu
UNICYCLING	Unicycling	unicycling@mcs.kent.edu	unicycling-request@psuvm.psu.edu
CHILDRENS-VOICE	Singing	childrens-voice@schoolnet. carleton.ca	listproc@ schoolnet.carleton.ca
KITES	Kites	kites@harvard.harvard.edu	kites-request@harvard.harvard.edu
FERRET	Ferrets as pets	ferret@cunyvm.cuny.edu	listserv@cunyvm.cuny.edu
BIRDCHAT	Wild birds	birdchat@arizvm1.ccit.	listserv@arizvm1.ccit.arizona.edu

MAILING-LIST MANAGERS

There are various mailing-list managers available and each one does basically the same thing—it manages e-mail for the listowner. You'll need to know which one you're working with because the commands for each may vary slightly. The four mailing-list manager applications discussed here are LISTSERV, ListProc, Majordomo, and <listname>-Request.

LISTSERV

LISTSERV is currently available for VM, VMS, unix (13 brands), Windows NT, and Windows 95. It is also being ported to the Macintosh and to MPE (HP3000).

Mailing lists managed by this software use LISTSERV as the first word in the address. In Table 9–1 you'll notice that many of the subscription addresses begin with *listserv*. If Linda wanted to subscribe to the list called SPROUTAGE-L to find more resources about gardening, art, and outdoor play with children, she'd send an e-mail message with the following command to *listserv@listserv.net*: **subscribe SPROUTAGE-L Linda Fodemski**. She would write to others on this same list using a different address: *Sproutage-L@home.ease.LSOFT.com*.

> Find more resources for gardening with children in The Link Farm on the CD-ROM!

ListProc

ListProc (short for Listprocessor) is a mailing-list manager that is unique because of its FAX command. When using this command, ListProc will send an archived file to your FAX machine. It is common, but not always the case, that ListProc mailing lists use addresses that begin with *listproc.* as in *listproc@cern.org*.

Table 9–2 MathMagic lists using Majordomo	
List Address	**Subscription Address**
mathmagic-k-3–open@forum.swarthmore.edu	majordomo@forum.swarthmore.edu
mathmagic-4–6–open@forum.swarthmore.edu	majordomo@forum.swarthmore.edu
mathmagic-7–9–open@forum.swarthmore.edu	majordomo@forum.swarthmore.edu
mathmagic-10–12–open@forum.swarthmore.edu	majordomo@forum.swarthmore.edu
mathmagic-general-open@forum.swarthmore.edu	majordomo@ forum.swarthmore.edu

Majordomo

Majordomo is another mailing-list manager that uses its own name as the first word in subscription addresses. There are sets of Majordomo mailing lists called MathMagic where students team up with each other to solve difficult math problems. These lists are presented in Table 9–2.

<listname>-Request

Another type of mailing-list manager uses the word *request* in its address. The subscription e-mail address usually follows the format *<listname>-request@host.address*. It's safe to say that you'll be dealing with a human being when sending requests to these addresses. Two examples of the request addresses are included in Table 9–1.

JOINING THE FRENZY

To subscribe to a mailing list, send an e-mail message to the subscription address (the one that begins with listserv, listproc, majordomo, or <listname>-request). Leave the subject line empty. In the body of the message, type the command **subscribe <listname> <your name>**. When writing to <listname>-Request addresses, just type out your request using plain English. If you end up getting a response from a machine, follow whatever instructions it gives you and try again.

You'll receive a message notifying you when your subscription has been accepted. Notification may come in a few minutes, or it make take several hours, and it will come in the form of an e-mail message sent to your e-mail address. When you join a list, be sure to save a copy of the introductory e-mail you get from the list administrator—this almost always contains instructions on how the list is run, how to post messages, and how to remove yourself from the list at a future date.

Making Your Fingers Fly

Once you're on the list, you'll receive all the e-mail that is sent to the list by other members. When you want to write a message to everyone else on the list, send your e-mail to the list address. For example, if your name is Nick Rosser and you're interested in joining the mailing list called STAMPS that talks about collecting stamps, you would type: **subscribe stamps Nick Rosser** and send it to *listserv@cumyvm.cuny.edu*. To write to others on this list, use the address *stamps@cumyvm.cuny.edu*.

When It's Time to Say Good-bye

Remember to always save your initial message from the list since it contains the exact form of the unsubscribe command for that list. Some lists require the command **unsub** and others require **unsubscribe**. Basically, when you want to leave a list, send the command **unsubscribe <listname> <your name>** in the body of an e-mail message to the subscription address. If you were a member of the STAMPS mailing list, you'd send the command **unsubscribe stamps Nick Rosser** to *listserv@cunyvm.cuny.edu*.

Help! I'm Drowning!

Some mailing lists send lots of mail every day. It is a good idea to check your e-mail everyday for the first couple days after joining a list to get an idea of how much mail you'll receive daily from the list. It is easier to read, file, or delete a few messages every day than to go through more than a dozen once a week. You may also find that you get an enormous amount of mail from a particular list. You may want to unsubscribe or get the messages in *digest* format.

A digest is a compilation of a day's or week's worth of mail sent to you in a single e-mail message. It's easier to manage a lot of mail if you receive it in digest format. Here are the commands for accomplishing this:

- Majordomo: Send the command **subscribe <listname>-digest**
- ListProc: Send the command **set <listname> mail digest**
- LISTSERV: Send the command **set <listname> digest**

To cancel the digest command and once again receive all correspondence as separate mailings, send these commands:

- Majordomo: Send the command **unsubscribe <listname>-digest**
- ListProc: Send the command **set <listname> ack**
- LISTSERV: Send the command **set <listname> mail**

Leaving on Vacation?

If you plan on leaving for a vacation, but don't want to go through the trouble of unsubscribing and then subscribing again when you return, suspend service with these commands:

- ListProc: Send the command **set <listname> mail postpone**
- LISTSERV: Send the command **set <listname> nomail**

Majordomo doesn't support this service.

When you get back from vacation, resume service with these commands:

- ListProc: Send the command **set <listname> mail ack**
- LISTSERV: Send the command **set <listname> mail**

COMMON TERMS, MISCELLANEOUS COMMANDS, AND ETIQUETTE

This section provides you with a list of other common commands and terms that you'll need to become familiar with when using mailing lists. If you'd like a complete list of commands for each of the mailing-list managers, send the command **help** in the body of an e-mail message to any Majordomo, LISTSERV, or ListProc address. Remember to send the command to the subscription address, not the list address.

Common Terms

Flaming: posting an e-mail message intended to insult, provoke, or threaten

Post: sending a message to a mailing list or newsgroup

Spam: flooding a mailing list with inappropriate, irrelevant, or obnoxious messages

Subscribe/Unsubscribe: joining and unjoining a mailing list

Thread: a series of messages pertaining to a single topic or responding to a particular posting

---

Find online dictionaries and dictionaries of computer terms, such as The Free Online Dictionary of Computing, listed in the **Internet Help Guides** section of The Link Farm on the CD-ROM.

Miscellaneous Commands

Obtaining a list of subscribers:

- Majordomo: Send the command **who <listname>**
- ListProc: Send the command **recipients <listname>**
- LISTSERV: Send the command **review <listname> f=mail**

Obtaining a list of stored messages:

- Majordomo: Send the command **index <listname>**
- ListProc: Send the command **index <listname>**
- LISTSERV: Send the command **index <listname>**

Retrieving a stored file listed in the above index:

- Majordomo: Send the command **get <listname> <file name>**
- ListProc: Send the command **get <listname> <file name>**
- LISTSERV: Send the command **get <file name> <filetype> <listname> f=mail**

Etiquette

After kids join a mailing list, they should learn about any rules or customs the list may have and abide by them. These rules may vary from one group to the next. Kids can use the following general guidelines for any mailing list they might join:

- Save the first information file or message for future reference.

- Never send mailing-list manager commands to the list address.
- Avoid flaming (launching personal attacks).
- Before responding to a message, take a moment to think about whether it would be more appropriate to respond privately to the individual who posted the message.
- Check your e-mail daily. Delete any unwanted messages and transfer to disk messages you want to save.
- When you first subscribe to a list, *lurk* for a while before posting your thoughts or questions. Lurking is when you read incoming messages for a couple days to understand the audience and determine whether you're interested in what the subscribers are talking about. You will also become aware of any customs or practices that are particular to that list.

MAILING LISTS FOR TEACHERS AND PARENTS

KIDLINK

This list provides announcements for KIDLINK projects. To subscribe, send the following message to *listserv@nodak.edu*: **subscribe kidlink <your name>**

KIDFORUM

The KIDFORUM list was started to promote interest in monthly discussions between classrooms of students. Topics are selected in advance. To subscribe, send the following message to *listserv@nodak.edu*: **subscribe kidforum <your name>**

KIDPROJ

The KIDPROJ list promotes the exchange of curriculum ideas and projects for kids between the ages of 10 and 15. To subscribe, send the following message to *listserv@nodak.edu*: **subscribe kidproj <your name>**

Gifted & Talented Teachers

The GT-TEACH list is for those persons working with children in gifted and talented programs. To subscribe, send the following message to *listserv@GT-TEACH.k12.ar.us*: **subscribe GT-TEACH <your name>**

CACI

Children Accessing Controversial Information is a discussion group that addresses problems and issues relating to kids using the Internet. To subscribe, send the following message to *caci-request@cygnus.com*: **subscribe caci <your name>**

Web Talk

The WebTalk Mailing List is an unmoderated forum for posting and answering questions and passing along news, comments, and observations related to integrating the World Wide Web into teaching curricula. To subscribe, send the following message to *list@mail.lr.k12.nj.us*: **subscribe k12–webdev <your name>**

PUBYAC

PUBlic libraries, Young Adults, and Children list is concerned with the practical aspects of children and young adult services in public libraries. It focuses on programming ideas, outreach and literacy programs for children and caregivers, censorship and policy issues, collection development, administrative considerations, puppetry, and professional development. To subscribe, visit their Web site at *www.pallasinc.com/pubyac/*

LM_NET

LM_NET is the Internet discussion group serving the worldwide school library media community, with more than 8,000 members from the United States, Canada, and other countries in Europe, Asia, and the Americas. To subscribe, send the following message to listserv@*listserv.sur.edu*: **subscribe LM_NET <your name>**

MAILING LISTS FOR KIDS

KIDCAFE

The KIDCAFE is a place for kids 10–15 years old to meet and talk—no adults allowed! To subscribe, have your kids send the following message to *listserv@nodak. edu*: **subscribe kidcafe-topics <your name>**

Kids' Literature Forum

Kids' Literature Forum is primarily for students age 9 to 18 interested in discussing any form of literature. Teachers, media specialists, and other professionals are also invited. To subscribe, have your kids send the following message to *majordomo@riverdale.k12.or.us*: **subscribe kidlit <your name>**

The **Language** section of The Link Farm on the CD-ROM offers many other links to language resources on the Web.

GAKUSEI-L

GAKUSEI-L and its associated lists are forums for students of Japanese to "talk" with each other throughout the world. The Gakusei lists (*gakusei-l@Edu. Hawaii.uhcc.uhunix*) at the University of Hawaii are organized into three separate lists according to the student's level of Japanese. Students are encouraged to lurk for a while before submitting a simple self-introduction. The main aim is to encourage communication using Japanese, and no corrections are made to individual postings. Lists of this type are useful to learners of all languages. The list owner is Laura Kimoto, University of Hawaii at Hilo, USA, (*kimotol@uhunix.uhcc.hawaii.edu*). To subscribe, send the following message to *listproc@uhunix.uhcc.hawaii.edu*: **subscribe GAKUSEI-L <your name>**

FINDING MAILING LISTS TO JOIN

There are mailing lists for anyone's interest and if you can't find one for your topic, there is always the opportunity to start your own. In this section we list several resources to help you find a list about art or cats or ferrets or weather forecasting or wagons or where to get the software to start your own list!

To search all of the LISTSERV discussion lists for those relating to a particular subject, send an e-mail message to any major LISTSERV using the following syntax: **list global/<keyword>**, where <keyword> is the subject or topic for which you are looking. For example, you can get a list of mailing lists on gardening by sending the command **list global/gardening** to *listserv@ubvm.cc. buffalo.edu* (any LISTSERV address will do). Using this command will limit the report you receive to just those LISTSERV lists that have the word or text string you specified. (Using the "list global" command by itself without using the <keyword> modifier would result in a huge report listing thousands of mailing lists!)

Subscribe to New-List to keep informed about newly created mailing lists. To subscribe, send the following message to *listserv@hypatia.cs.wisc.edu*: **subscribe new-list <your name>**

Pitsco

Pitsco (*www.pitsco.com/p/Respages/listinfo.html*) sells hands-on educational products for teaching science and technology in the classroom. On their Web site they offer a list of the major databases to search for particular listservs and information on how to e-mail for lists of lists.

Liszt

Liszt (*www.liszt.com/*) is a Web site that has received recognition from Web sites such as Yahoo! and Excite and is included as part of the Internet Scout Report Toolkit. This site offers a huge directory of mailing lists, helpful advice about how to find mailing lists that interest you, and information about how to join and use mailing lists.

Other Mailing-List Sources

A list of publicly accessible mailing lists can be found at the Publicly Accessible Mailing Lists site (*www.neosoft.com/internet/paml/indexes.html*).

Download mailing-list manager software from the following Web sites:

- For Listserv software visit L-Soft's site (*www.lsoft.com/listserv.stm#WHAT*)
- For Majordomo software visit Great Circle Associates site (*www.greatcircle. com/majordomo/*)

Visit Swarthmore College Web site (*http://forum.swarthmore.edu/discussions*), host to the MathMagic mailing lists, for an extensive listing of math-related discussions lists.

Chapter 10

Finding Friends in
Faraway Places

Communicating with others using the Internet can take a variety of forms, such as global classrooms, electronic "appearances," mentoring, and keypals. Regardless which type of activity children participate in, these online collaborations foster communication, cultural awareness, and learning. The various forms for children to communicate with others using the Internet are excellent ways for kids to understand more about any subject, whether it is language arts, history, geography, social studies, or science. In this chapter we'll demonstrate the range of activities keypals projects can take. You can start as simple as finding another student with similar interests to correspond with, or jump right into a global classroom project that lasts for several weeks.

THE MEANING OF KEYPALS

Keypals are like penpals and then some. All the different keypals projects described in this chapter have the basic element of kids communicating with others using the Internet. The exact configuration of who is meeting whom and what they are doing together is so much more than two friends hand-writing letters to each other.

The telecomputing projects available offer one-student to one-student exchanges, many-students to many-students exchanges, and a variety of possibilities in between that typically involve the third element of a professional. There are many terms to describe these various situations, such as *global classrooms* and *electronic mentors*.

Most keypals use a keyboard and e-mail to write to each other; however, the International Penfriend resource (described later) is one Web site devoted to keeping the art of traditional letter writing alive using the Internet to put "penfriends" in touch with each other. There are other resources that help connect entire classrooms as they explore a particular topic. This may mean two classrooms from towns with the same name learning the origin of both city names as they study the culture and history of that particular area. It could also be as complex as students from a high school in Texas communicating with students from South Africa, Norway, Finland, Denmark, Peru, Russia, Estonia, Chile, Mexico, England, Iceland, Germany, and Canada. In this real-life project called "The World at Our Fingertips," students exchanged information about their experiences living in the 14 different countries.

There are keypals projects and opportunities for children of all ages. Linda's daughter has corresponded with cousins and friends online since she was three years old. Sitting on Mom's lap, Rebecca dictated and Linda typed the letters, attaching photos and drawings that were either scanned in or created in a paint program. Rebecca became familiar with the components of an e-mail message and the keyboard. Linda began by having Rebecca find the letters of her name on the keyboard and having her always typing her own name. It progressed from there to typing simple words until Rebecca was able to type her own messages.

The process helped Rebecca become familiar with electronic correspondence and using a computer. Even at age three, she was thrilled with real-time communication using the computer when participating in a chat session or online project. It was not something that took up hours or was done every day. This was an activity that Linda and Rebecca shared two or three times a week together. Generally, teachers and librarians will not have the time to devote attention to a small child in this manner; however, it is definitely possible in the home environment. A teacher might offer one-on-one time with students who may have to stay in from recess or some other out-of-class activity because of a health condition or injury.

Once children are able to write and type, activities for them can range from simply finding and writing to a friend their own age to activities where they collaborate on a story or solve a problem. For older children there are specific keypal clubs for kids with special interests or needs or concerns to highly elaborate and detailed projects for junior high and high school students. A few examples of these are described later in this chapter.

Check out the resources in The Link Farm on the CD-ROM under the **History** category to find out more about a penpal's country!

FRIENDSHIP AND LEARNING GO HAND IN HAND

Keypals projects were the first educational telecomputing activities to be tested online. Foreign language students can sharpen their reading and writing skills by actually communicating with native speakers about things they have in common. Geography studies come alive when a child knows someone living in a distant land. Integrated keypals projects give students and teachers a sense of what everyday life is like in a foreign country. Students pay greater attention to the spelling and punctuation and grammar of their native language as they participate in these projects that often involve a professional or expert in the field.

GLOBAL CLASSROOMS DEFINED

Currently, the most popular types of educational telecomputing projects are global classroom projects. These are often more topically focused than keypals projects and involve groups of students rather than individual students. Group-to-group exchanges can evolve into fascinating collaborative explorations. For example, a technology specialist from Amarillo, Texas, organized a collaborative exploration of local nuclear facilities among a half-dozen upper elementary classes.

Some global classroom projects are quite complex and can involve students for one or more school semesters. The "Desert and Desertification" project, coordinated by Hannah Sivan, David Lloyd, and Oded Bar from Sde-Boker, Israel, was a year-long, four-stage interdisciplinary project for students from around the world who were interested in studying about deserts in the past, present, and future. It included a rich array of activities, involving participants in discussion, online and offline data collection and organization, sound and image collection and transmission, film viewing, subject matter expert interviews, literary analysis, desert field trips, simulations, role-plays, and environmental forecasting.

A similarly rich and varied project was "The S.S. Central America—A Shipwreck to Remember." This year-long project with historical and meteorological emphases was coordinated by Jamie Wilkerson of Rosewood Elementary School in Rock Hill, South Carolina. In this project, students electronically explored the voyage and sinking of a 272-foot wooden steamship, along with the weather conditions that led to its demise. Electronically they consulted with members of the Columbus-America Discovery Group, the team of scientists and historians who worked to salvage the Central America's history and treasures.

THE KIND OF PEOPLE YOU'LL MEET

Still another variation of the keypal idea is *electronic appearances* and *electronic mentoring*. Electronic appearances are when a locally, nationally, or internationally known person is available online for a short period of time to answer questions. You can watch for these occurrences and have the class sit in on a discussion, even if you don't participate. These events could also be posted at a particular spot in the library or listed in the newspaper with other library happenings.

Electronic mentoring is usually more structured and is often a collaborative project involving a teacher or parent. Electronic mentors can be subject-matter specialists from universities, businesses, government, or other schools. For example, later in this chapter we describe the HP Telementor Program.

Somewhere in between these two structures are the *Ask-An-Expert* services. These services are called Ask-A-Geologist or Ask-Dr. Math, and they tend to come and go, as one person leaves the position of expert and another takes his or her place. Questions are submitted via e-mail concerning whatever subject matter the expert discusses and then answers are sent back to the sender or posted in an archive. The expert may be a professional in his field or a graduate student.

> Encourage kids to share the sites listed in The Link Farm on the CD-ROM with their penpals.

A PLACE TO START LOOKING

North Dakota's Educational Network, SENDIT, (*www.sendit.nodak.edu/sendit2/ keypals.html*), is a great place to start your search for keypals. This site offers The Keypals Database. With this one link you can access four major keypals resources: ePALS Classroom Exchange (Figure 10–1), Key Pals and Correspondents Exchange, KeyPals Club, and the IECC (Intercultural E-Mail Classroom Connections). Each resource is described fully later in this chapter and can assist students and educators in finding Internet penpals.

The following resources fall into three categories: Keypals Sites, Mailing Lists for Keypals, and Other Telecomputing Keypal Projects. At the end of many of these listings is a section called *Also Check Out* that points you to one or more particular areas of a Web site that will also be very interesting to kids or useful in the learning environment.

Keypals Sites

Figure 10–1 ePALS Classroom Exchange home page claims to be the world's largest classroom keypal network.

ePALS

ePALS (*www.epals.com/*) can connect your classroom with classrooms from 90 countries speaking 87 languages—10,486 classrooms, representing more than 750,000 students. Founded in 1996, ePALS' objective is to provide students with a teacher-monitored opportunity to meet and correspond with other classrooms from around the world. Search their database for a classroom or project or add your classroom profile to the database.

Also Check Out

At the ePALS Resources link (*www.epals.com/resource/*) you'll find :

- College Bound (*www.collegebound.com/*)—A site that helps U.S. and international students in college search, selection, and financial aid eligibility.
- E-Tutor (*www.e-tutor.com/*)—An online curriculum for K–12 students. Teaches basic skills of reading, writing, mathematics, science, and social studies.
- Highwired.Net (*www.highwired.net/home/*)—Award-winning online newspaper service for schools that allows free Web-based publishing for school newspapers.
- Weekly Reader Galaxy (*www.weeklyreader.com/*)—For prekindergarten to grade 10, activities, contests, games, online field trips, and much more!

KEY PALS AND CORRESPONDENTS EXCHANGE

If you'd like to find or share collaborative classroom projects for use over the Internet, then this is the section for you!

The Project Center is updated each week with projects from other teachers like you. These projects come from a variety of online sources, such as the Classroom Connect mailing list. You can publicize your online project here by filling in the Project Submission Form or by sending an e-mail description to projects@hmco.com. Check back each week and get your classroom involved in projects from all over the world!

Figure 10–2 Houghton Mifflin Project Center can help you find or share collaborative classroom projects over the Internet.

Key Pals and Correspondents Exchange (*www.eduplace.com/projects/*) is a Houghton Mifflin Company endeavor to help you find or share collaborative classroom projects for use over the Internet. The Project Center (Figure 10–2) is updated each week with projects from other teachers. This site also offers the Creating Online Projects page with tips to help you and your students launch your own online project, including hints for more effective project postings and links to sites related to designing online projects.

A partial listing of current online projects:

- Postcard Geography (All grades)
- Our Hundredth Day (Grades K–2)
- Geography: A Local and Global Study (Grades 6–8)
- Ollie Online Weather Project (Grades K–3)
- E-mail Down Under (Grades 2–4)
- Canada Project (Grades 2–4)
- Pen Pals in a Bag (Grade 6)
- Backpack Buddies (Grades K–8)
- Olympic TeleConnection (Grades K–12)
- FreeZone EPALS (All grades)

KEYPALS CLUB

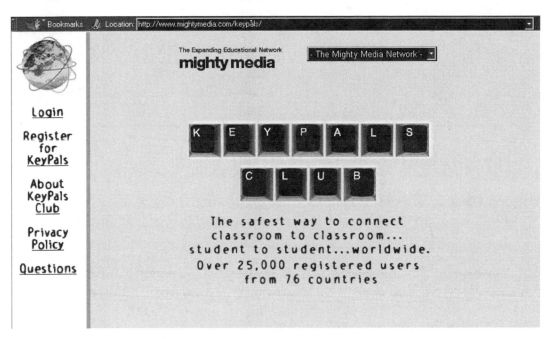

Figure 10–3 The Expanding Educational Network's Mighty Media site offers much more for kids and teens besides their Keypals Club.

Mighty Media, creators of the Youth in Action Network and Teacher Talk, offers the KeyPals Club (*www.mightymedia.com/keypals/*). This is a place for young people to locate and correspond with other youth and students around the world (Figure 10–3). The service provides an easy-to-use interface plus a database to help locate a student or contact a class from anywhere in the world. Users must register to use the service with a valid, working e-mail address.

Also Check Out

Check out the Summit Action Youth page for interesting activities, such as, the official Youth Voice Web site for the President's Summit for America's Future, Planet Youth, which offers free home pages to student groups who want to effect positive change in schools and communities, and the Kindness & Justice Challenge.

INTERNATIONAL PENPALS

International Penfriends (IPF)

Figure 10–4 International Penpals Web site promotes traditional penpal correspondence right down to offering a used stamp exchange link on their site.

This is the site to find traditional penpals! International Penfriends (IPF) (*www.ozemail.com.au/~penpals/*) was established in April 1967 and has now grown to be the world's largest penfriend club, with over 300,000 members worldwide aged from 8 to 80 years (Figure 10–4).

IPF does not match penfriends via the Internet. The main objective of the club is to keep the art of letter writing alive and to use this form of communication to encourage worldwide friendship.

You can join as an individual or as part of a school class or youth group. Each member is provided with a personal list of penpals who have been individually matched according to age group, hobbies, and interests. Each member's name is also given to 14 other members of the club. This system enables members to start writing to their penfriend right away and to receive surprise introductory letters from other members.

Also Check Out

IPF offers a used stamp exchange division and an international magazine called *People & Places*. They welcome contributions to the magazine and award a prize of $200 for the best article in each edition. They also sell a booklet on letter writing and penfriend hints.

> Use resources found in The Link Farm on the CD-ROM, such as **MapQuest**, to generate maps of where penpals live.

Cyberpals

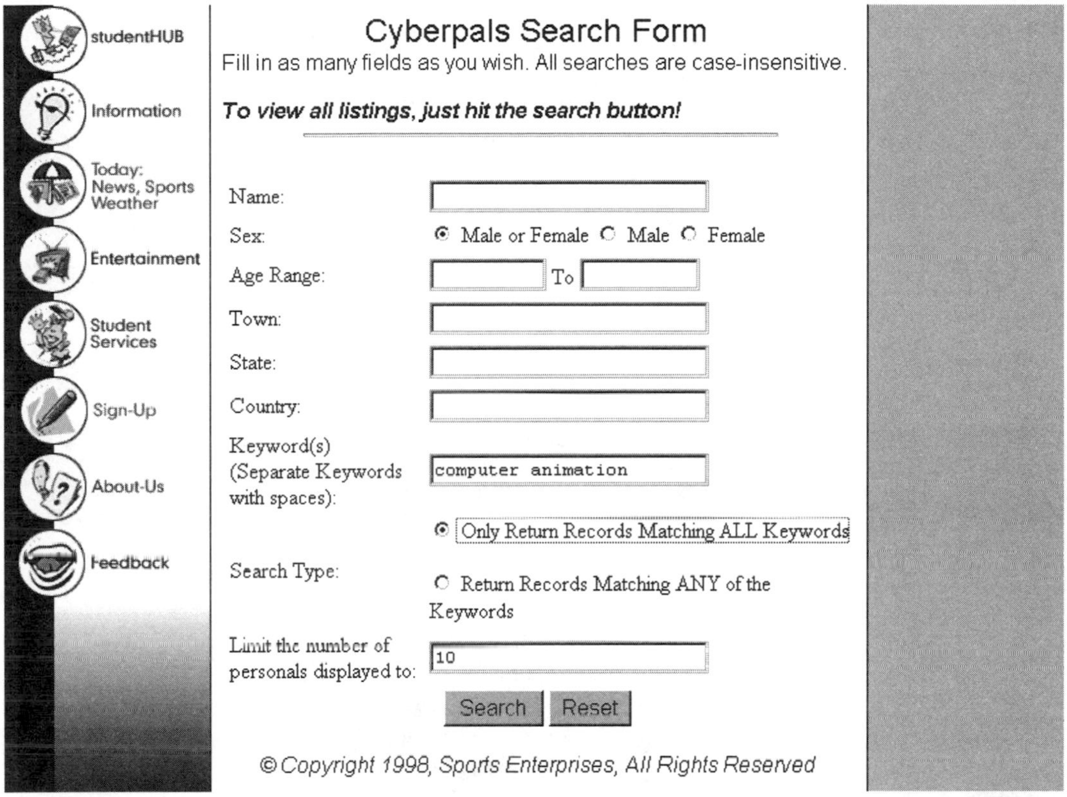
studentHUB
Information
Today: News, Sports Weather
Entertainment
Student Services
Sign-Up
About-Us
Feedback
Cyberpals Search Form
Fill in as many fields as you wish. All searches are case-insensitive.
To view all listings, just hit the search button!
Name:
Sex:
Male or Female
Male
Female
Age Range:
To
Town:
State:
Country:
Keyword(s) (Separate Keywords with spaces):
computer animation
Only Return Records Matching ALL Keywords
Search Type:
Return Records Matching ANY of the Keywords
Limit the number of personals displayed to:
10
Search
Reset
© Copyright 1998, Sports Enterprises, All Rights Reserved

Figure 10–5 Cyberpals search form enables kids to look for a keypal in their hometown or another kid with their same interest, regardless of location.

Cyberpals (*studentcenter.infomall.org/cyberpals.html*) is a Web community for students—specifically college students, high school students, and teenagers. It's based on a simple idea that students are surfing around to different sites on the Web, preferring to hang out with other students (Figure 10–5). The Student Center claims, "you can be pretty confident that just about everybody here is a fellow student. And we do promise you that everything in here is FOR fellow students." This site attempts to provide helpful information but mostly it wants to be the place that young people turn to for entertainment and fun.

Also Check Out

The Student Center features chat, free Web-based e-mail, discussion forums, the Digital Postcards Center, free home pages and the school home page directory.

SIGNAL

According to SIGNAL's Web page, it is "one of the world's largest and oldest mail advertising publications for penpals, collectors, correspondence clubs, mail traders." At the SIGNAL Worldwide Penpal Directory (*www.saunalahti.fi/~signal/*) you'll find the Internet version of their quarterly magazine that was established in 1960. Each issue contains 500–1,000 ads for penpals, with photos, from 50–90 countries. *Teachers and parents may want to check this site out first before aiming students or children there. May be more suitable for high school students or to be used to find a keypal for a student.*

KIDSCOM

Figure 10–6 Kidscom's "Find A Keypal" page gives kids an idea of the zany creatures they'll discover at this site while searching for a keypal.

Kidscom (*www.kidscom.com/orakc/Friends/newfriends.html*) is a Web site devoted to helping kids find friends online (Figure 10–6). This site requires parental permission for kids to join the program and they offer Iggey & Rasper's Internet Safety Tips to ensure kids are communicating safely online.

U.S.–N.I.S Pen Pal Programs

The U.S.–N.I.S. Pen Pal Programs (*www.friends- partners.org/oldfriends/ccsi/penhome.htm*) is offered by the Center for Civil Society International. CCSI is an information clearinghouse focused on American voluntary organizations, nonprofits, and independent associations. Incorporated in the state of Washington, it operates as a private, nonpartisan educational organization. The list of links can help individuals or classrooms find penpals. Some groups specialize in exchanges between the United States and Russia, Ukraine, or other former Soviet countries, while some of the organizations will arrange exchanges among people of any nationality. You'll find penpal programs for individuals, environmental youth groups, Moscow high school students, and the Russian Orphans Pen Pal Program.

Mailing Lists For Keypals

IECC

Intercultural E-Mail Classroom Connections (*www.stolaf.edu/network/iecc/*) mailing lists are provided by St. Olaf College as a free service to help teachers and classes link with partners in other countries and cultures for e-mail classroom penpal and project exchanges. Since its creation in 1992, IECC has distributed over 19,000 requests for e-mail partnerships. IECC offers many other forums for students (and teachers) to post requests for assistance on projects, surveys, and questionnaires or for help with specific classroom projects involving intercultural activities

Internet Foreign Language Partners

The Internet Foreign Language Partners site (*http://138.87.135.33/fl/main.htm*) uses an interactive database to match up students who are studying the same language, are at about the same level, and want to use the same Internet resources.

Also Check Out

Their list of related links: *www.ling.lancs.ac.uk/staff/visitors/kenji/keypal.htm#student*.

Other Telecomputing Keypals Projects

HP E-MAIL MENTOR PROGRAM

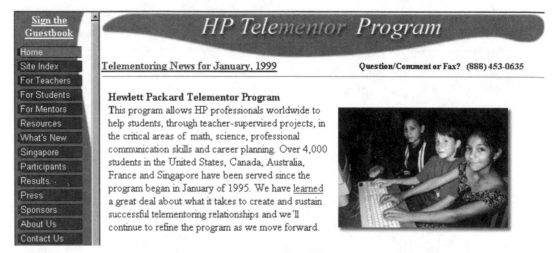

Figure 10–7 One of the functions of the HP Telementor Program mentors is to help 5th–12th grade students develop career plans.

The HP E-mail Program (*www.telementor.org/hp/*) is a structured, project-based program where HP employees worldwide volunteer to telementor 5th–12th grade students in unique one-to-one electronic relationships (Figure 10–7). The focus of the HP E-mail Mentor Program is to help students excel in math, science, and professional communication skills and develop solid education and career plans for life beyond high school. Participation in the Hewlett Packard E-mail Mentor Program is a collaboration between teacher, mentor, and student. The basis for the telementor relationships is regular classroom activities where each participating student collaborates with his or her mentor under the direction and supervision of the accepted program teacher.

Also Check Out

Great Telementoring Project Starting Places: *www.telementor.org/hp/info/links.html.*

JUDI HARRIS'S NETWORK-BASED EDUCATIONAL ACTIVITY COLLECTION

Access Judi Harris's collection from the University of Illinois College of Education Learning Resource Server (LRS) (*lrs.ed.uiuc.edu/Activity-Structures/*). The goal of LRS is to provide resources that help learners move from surfing to serving, with links to some of the most exciting uses of technologies for learning on the Internet. Judi Harris's collection consists of columns she's written for *The Computing Teacher/Learning and Leading with Technology* and an archive of telecomputing projects. The articles archived range from 1992–1995. Projects archived are from 1995 to 1997 and are a valuable resource for ideas and topics.

Here is a selection of Judi Harris's columns from *The Computing Teacher/ Learning and Leading with Technology*:

- August–September 1992: Electronic Treasures by Electronic Mail
- February 1994: People-to-People Projects on the Internet
- April 1994: "Opportunities in Work Clothes": Online Problem Solving Project Structures
- August–September 1994: The Electronic Emissary: Bringing Together Students, Teachers, and Subject Matter Experts
- March 1995: Educational Telecomputing Projects: Interpersonal Exchanges

A selection of topics from Judi Harris's 1997 Curriculum-Based K–12 Educational Telecomputing Projects organized by Activity Structures is presented below. *Please note that some of these projects have ended.* In these cases you'll often find an archive site that enables you and your students to follow along with a project as if it were happening in real time. Sometimes you'll be referred to a different site that is now handling the project or presenting it in a different form. In either case, you'll get plenty of ideas of the types of projects possible, including valuable curriculum and lesson plan resources.

Activity Structure: Keypals

How People Live in Europe and the Middle East
Math Pen Pals: Communication Through Numbers Project
Northwest Territories—Hawaii Chat Page
Penpals from Holland

Activity Structure: Global Classrooms

Animal Farm
Desert and Desertification Project
Developing Sustainable Energy for the Future
Earth's Crust and Plate Tectonics Project
Reduce, Reuse, Recycle, Revise, Respond
Transatlantic Classroom

Activity Structure: Electronic "Appearances"

> Adopt-a-Student Online
> "Ask-the-Scientist" CU-SeeMe Videoconference Schedule

The following are from various activity structures:

> Earth to Mars Chats
> Women of NASA
> NASA K–12 Virtual Conferences
> The Telegarden
> Teen Court

Browse the **Miscellaneous** section of The Link Farm on the CD-ROM for more interesting places to point kids, such as **Co-Ops for Kids**—a site devoted to teaching kids the principles of cooperative business.

THE ODYSSEY

Figure 10–8 Teachers, students, and parents will love the adventures and interaction available via The Odyssey. This site alone would make a great afterschool program for any library.

The Odyssey: World Trek for Service and Education (*www.worldtrek.org/odyssey/teachers/index.html*) is an "interactive world trek" that will link students in classrooms with volunteers traveling around the world for two years learning about different cultures and volunteering with local grassroots organizations (Figure 10–8). The World Trek and its interactive, multimedia use of the Web will capture and maintain students' interest as they learn important computer skills, interact with a diversity of cultures, and learn of some of the practical and inspirational ways that people throughout the world struggle to overcome poverty and oppression. Students will also participate in service learning activities in conjunction with The Odyssey and learn how to support each other's activities via the Web. Follow the trek as it unfolds or use the archived version to highlight a particular course of study in your classroom.

TCET

The Texas Center for Educational Technology (*www.tcet.unt.edu/*) offers technology information resources such as publications and project descriptions, and links to educational organizations and educational resources on the Web, including Internet projects and consortium sites.

Chapter 11

Launching Your
Own Home Page

If your kids enjoy going online and feel comfortable with the Internet as a communication medium, one day they might also like to explore publishing on the Internet. Creating a Web page is not only fun but also a great way to share information cheaply.

This chapter takes a look at what kids can do as publishers on the Internet. It also explores what others are already doing, not only in the area of publishing, but as bookstore and newsstand operators.

BLAZING TRAILS WITH THE WEB

The most likely medium kids will choose for making their mark on the world—by sharing their stories, artwork, sound bytes, and secret online "finds"—is the World Wide Web.

The Web is already one of the world's most important publishing mediums. With an Internet audience numbering in the millions, the potential for exposure is great. Many kids have already jumped in with both feet and are publishing class papers, picture books, school newspapers, and more.

WHAT'S THE CATCH?

Publishing on the Web isn't as simple as typing up a document and then mailing it off to someone for publication. You need to connect with an Internet Service Provider (ISP) that will *launch* or *host* your Web page for you. These terms mean that the provider provide space on their computers for you to store the files that make up your web pages. Most ISPs offer free personal Web pages when you sign up for an e-mail account; however, there are some ISPs that charge for this and others that don't offer it at all. A personal Web page is a site that is not selling anything. Ask your ISP about the cost and availability of hosting your personal Web page, or go to their home page to find this information.

> Visit the clip art sites listed under the category **Clip Art** in The Link Farm on the CD-ROM. Almost all these sites provide copyright and use statements or policies, which would provide a good starting point to discuss these issues. Plus the kids will get to collect a few images as they go!

PUBLISHERS' RIGHTS

It's important for kids to understand their rights and the rights of others publishing on the Web. The Web is always changing and what may be considered right today may be considered wrong next year. This section explains some basic principles that apply today.

Publishers on the Internet own the copyright to any original text they create. They also own the copyright to any original images they create. If kids want to use graphics from someone else's home page, they should ask for permission.

Kids should also be made aware that these rights could possibly extend into the design of the home page itself. This is especially true where a Web publisher combines graphics and text to form original designs.

Collectors of Pointers

One issue that is less clear concerns the rights to links. A *link* is just an address pointing to another site on the Web. Some publishers on the Web do nothing more than assemble collections of pointers that serve as a table of contents to other sites on the Web. If kids build a link to another piece of information on the Web, they should try to make it clear that the user will be linking to something created by someone else—another publisher.

Some Web publishers have gone as far as suggesting that others should agree to a license before linking to their page. In time, we may see some publishers charging users for the right to link to their home page.

If publishers add value to their collection of links by organizing and structuring the collection in a special way, adding their own information to it, and then offering it to others, they may deserve some protection against copying by other Web publishers. This does not mean that their rights as compilers would supersede those of the individuals who provide the original information to which they're linking.

What's OK to Use?

Kids can legally use anything they created to construct their page. This includes any pictures they've painted, photographs they've taken, stories they've written, drawings they've sketched, and so forth. They can also use any information that's in the public domain, such as older things no longer covered by copyright. (Note that just because a work doesn't bear a copyright notice doesn't mean it isn't protected under copyright law.)

Figure 11–1 The Copyright Website offers tips on copyright fundamentals, copyright registration, and more.

For additional information on copyright issues, check out The Copyright Website (*www.benedict.com/index.html*). Figure 11–1 shows the opening screen from this site.

HTML: A CODE FOR KIDS

If a child you know is ready to start contributing to the great flow of information on the Internet, the first thing for him or her to do is learn about *HTML* (*HyperText Markup Language*). HTML is a code, or language, used by Web browsers such as Netscape Navigator and Microsoft's Internet Explorer to transfer things like text and images to the screen.

We only cover the basics here, but there are many advanced features for creating Web pages for kids to explore, such as forms, sound, video, frames, image maps, and more. Everything they need to know in terms of "how-to" information is available online free of charge.

Do-It-Yourself Online Help

As their interests expand, kids can find out more by asking questions and sharing ideas in any one of many NUGgies (Netscape User Groups) such as *comp.infosystems.www.authoring.html*. This particular newsgroup is the place to pose basic questions on how to do something. Other *comp.infosystems.www* newsgroups cover issues related to forms, image maps, transparent gifs (graphics interchange format), and more. Find out more about newsgroups in Chapter 18.

Using a search engine like Lycos or Webcrawler to run a keyword search on *HTML* or *Web Publishing* should bring up several interesting links to helpful information, too.

Use the resources listed in the **Internet Help Guides** section of The Link Farm on the CD-ROM for more sites that offer help to newbies, such as **Newbie-U** and **TechKnow**. Also see the section **Web Design** for pointers to sites for beginning and advanced Webmasters.

Learning Your HTML ABCs

All Web pages have a code embedded in them. This code is what the browsers read to present images and text on your computer screen. You can type these codes by using any text editor, or you can use an *HTML editor*. HTML editors are text editors designed specifically for placing HTML code within your document. First we'll explain some of the basic codes and usage of these codes, then we'll tell you more about HTML editors.

TAGS ARE THE TOOLS

HTML code consists of *tags*. A tag is one or more letters or words enclosed in brackets, for example: **<HR>**. This is the Horizontal Rule tag. This tag places a line or rule on your page. Case does not matter when typing the tags; however, you may want to use all caps to differentiate the tags from the text you want to appear to the viewer.

Many tags must be used in pairs. That means you must have one tag at the beginning of an element in your document and one tag at the end of that element. An element may be the whole document, an image, a sentence, a word, or table. For example, if you want a word to appear in boldface type, you would use the tag **<B>** before the word and the tag **</B>** at the end of the word you wanted to appear in bold.

Many of the tags are easy enough to remember, such as in the previous example you use "B" for bold. Also notice that the tag at the end of the word contains a forward slash. This is true of all tags that come in pairs.

You'll actually only need to learn one code or letter or word to define a tag and then add a forward slash to it for the second tag in the pair. It might help to think of the forward slash as an "end" or "stop sign" for the tag, because it turns the tag off at that point.

<Basic> HTML <Tags>

There are two basic ways to write an HTML document. One way is to place all your text and graphics and then go back and add in all the codes or tags. The other way is to write in the tags as you go. You may find that it is easiest to do a little of both.

All HTML documents must contain a few basic tags before you insert any of your text or graphics. You may want to create a template for writing Web pages that already has these tags. These basic tags tell the Web browser that it is an HTML document, where the document begins and ends, and what the document is called. Every Web page will have the following tags:

```
<HTML>
<HEAD>
<TITLE></TITLE>
</HEAD>
<BODY></BODY>
</HTML>
```

Notice that some of the tags are nested within other tags and all the tags and elements are nested within the basic tags **<HTML>** and **</HTML>**. Nesting tags is common. When you begin using more tags you'll have to pay attention to the order of nesting—it can make all the difference between a Web page that appears the way you want and one that doesn't!

Even though this list above is all the required tags for an HTML document, nothing would appear on the screen if you tried to view it on the WWW because it is ONLY tags—there is no text and no other elements. Take a look at the code again in Table 1 after we added some basic text. Notice where the text is placed.

Table 11–1 Basic HTML tags to use in all Web pages
<HTML> <HEAD> <TITLE> The Name of My Web Page Goes Here </TITLE> </HEAD> <BODY> Text or pictures go here. </BODY> </HTML>

Figure 11–2 Viewing the page in Table 1 using Aardvark Pro HTML editor.

Now we'll add some real text and titles to this document and actually make a document someone might publish. For example, if your name is Rebecca and you have a recipe for apple dumplings that you'd like to publish, you'd go through the following steps to create your HTML document.

1. Start with a blank page and type in the tags shown in Table 1.
2. Type the title of your document in between the **<TITLE>** and **</TITLE>** tags. For this example, we've typed in **Rebecca's Internet Kitchen**.
3. Now type the actual recipe between the **<BODY>** and **</BODY>** tags. If the recipe is already saved in a file, you can open that file and cut and paste the recipe into this section.
4. To make the name of the recipe bigger than the rest of the text, type in *heading tags*. In this case we've used a level one heading. This is the largest heading tag available. HTML defines six levels of headings, ranging from one to six. Each heading tag consists of the letter "H" and a number from one to six. You'll use heading tags to define the structure of your document much like writing an outline. It is common to use the **<H1>** and **</H1>** tags for the first level heading at the top of your page, often times duplicating the text you placed in between the title tags.
5. To separate the ingredients list from the instructions, insert the paragraph tags **<P>** and **</P>**. Type **<P>** just before the first ingredient and just before the first word in the recipe instructions. Then type **</P>** after the last ingredient and after the last word in the instructions. This will add a double

space between the two sections. The paragraph tag is a paired tag; however, the ending tag **</P>** is optional.

6. The last tag we'll use is the line break tag **
**. This is not a paired tag. This tag inserts a line break without any extra spacing. Insert one of these tags after every ingredient. If we don't do this, all of the ingredients will run together in one long sentence rather than being broken up into one ingredient per line.

7. Now save the file. Remember, using a text editor or word processor, you must choose Save AS and save the document as text only. When choosing from a list of formats to save your document as, choose Text Only, Text Only with Line Breaks, or DOS Text. All HTML files must have the extension .htm or .html. Use the following guidelines when saving and naming HTML files.

- Use small, simple names for your HTML files
- Don't use special characters in the file names
- Use the extension .html (or .htm for DOS and Windows systems).

Remember to make a note of where you saved the file on your hard drive or to label the disk, if you saved the file to a floppy disk. For example, you may want to call the file we just created *REBECCA.HTM* and save it in a directory on your hard drive called *WEBPAGES*. The path to find this document again would be: *C:\WEBPAGES\REBECCA.HTM*.

The finished document looks like this:

```
<HTML>
<HEAD>
<TITLE> Rebecca's Internet Kitchen </TITLE>
</HEAD>
<BODY>
<H1>Apple Dumplings</H1>
<P>
2 cups sugar <BR>
2 cups flour<BR>
2 cups water <BR>
1 teas salt<BR>
1/4 teas cinnamon <BR>
2 teas baking powder<BR>
1/4 teas nutmeg <BR>
3/4 cup shortening<BR>
1/4 cup butter<BR>
3/4 cup milk<BR>
6 apples<BR>
</P>
```

```
<P>
Combine sugar, water, cinnamon, and nutmeg in a
medium saucepan. Heat over medium heat until mix-
ture becomes syrup; add butter. Pare and core
apples; cut into fourths. Sift flour, salt, bak-
ing powder into bowl. Cut in shortening with a
pastry knife (or a regular table knife) until mix-
ture becomes crumbly. Add milk all at once and
stir just until moistened. Roll dough out to 1/4
inch thickness. Cut dough into six 5-inch squares.
Arrange four pieces of apple on each square and
sprinkle with additional sugar, cinnamon. Fold cor-
ners to center of each square and pinch edges to-
gether to seal dumplings (make sure they are sealed
tightly and no apple is sticking out!). Place dump-
lings in buttered baking dish. Pour syrup over dump-
lings. Baste dumplings with the syrup once or twice
while baking. Bake: 375F for 35 minutes. </P>
</BODY>
</HTML>
```

To preview this Web page to see what it would look like online you can start your Web browser without going online. Just click on the icon or filename that starts your Web browser. After it is open, type the pathname for the file in the location box near the top of the browser screen. Using the example above, type: **C:\WEBPAGES\REBECCA.HTM**. This box may be called Locator or URL or GO TO depending on the browser you are using and the version of that browser. Your Web home page will now appear in your Web browser's window. You can also view Web pages with some HTML editors, such as Figures 11–2 and 11–3.

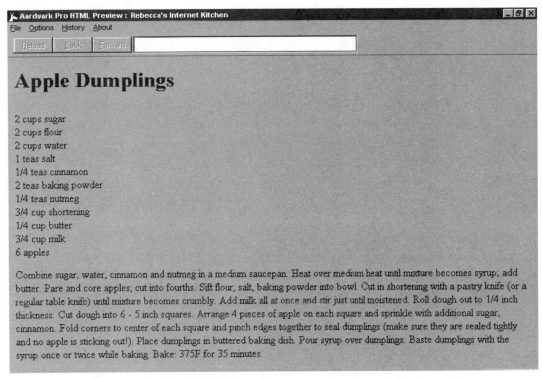

Figure 11–3 Rebecca's home page recipe for apple dumplings
viewed with Aardvark Pro HTML editor.

This exercise mentions only the absolute basics of HTML. There are many, many other tags for things like italics, bold, different types of lists, and images, to name just a few. There are more tags to define things such as the centering or placement of elements on the page and to describe the background color of the page itself. In fact, there is so much more that entire books have been written about HTML. To really explore all that can be done with the HTML code, a budding Webmaster should obtain one of these books from the library or check any of the hundreds of documents online that describe this code. With the basics we've given here, plus a few more codes described next, any child can put together interesting Web pages.

Visit some of the sites listed under the What's New category in The Link Farm on the CD and view the source code for these sites to see how people are creating interesting elements on their Web pages.

ADDITIONAL HTML TAGS

Lists

There are several different tags to organize lists in various ways. A couple of the most common list tags are called Ordered Lists (numbered lists), Unordered Lists (bulleted lists), and Menu and Directory Lists (lists without numbers or bullets that only use indents). Each type of list has its own beginning and ending tag; however, all the lists use the same tag to denote each element in the list. This tag is **<LI>**.

For an Ordered List:

```
<OL>
<LI> Make the pie
<LI> Bake the pie
<LI> Eat the pie
</OL>
```

For an Unordered List:

```
<UL>
<LI> First Grade: Mrs. Miller
<LI> Second Grade: Mr. Ball
<LI> Third Grade: Miss Prothlett
<LI> Fourth Grade: Mr. Hadley
</UL>
```

For a Menu List:

```
<MENU>
<LI> Trigonometry
<LI> Physics
<LI> Photography
<LI> Band
<LI> Medieval History
<LI> Creative Writing
</MENU>
```

For a Directory List:

```
<DIR>
<LI> Texas Instruments B.E.S.T. Robotics Sign-up
<LI> Odyssey of the Mind Problem Descriptions
<LI> Teen Court Introductory Meeting
<LI> Basketball Tryouts Dates
<LI> Regional Youth Group Activities for March
</DIR>
```

Comments

The Comments tag **<!— This is a comment—>** is used to insert information into your document for your use only—information that you don't want anyone else to see. You might use this tag to "hide" text or an element, such as a picture, that you don't use all the time. For example, maybe your Web site lists book reviews or sources for computer-game hints and you want to include a special image file next to items that are new. If one week you didn't read any new books or find any new game hints, you could mark your image tag with a comment. This way, the old items won't have the "new" image next to them and you won't have to retype the tag once you do have new items to add. You can simply delete the Comment tag and the image will again show up in your document. Here are some other examples:

<!— The Smithsonian website: get the address—>
<!— Update this section April 5th—>
<!— IMG SRC="images/new.gif"—>

Backgrounds and Images

Backgrounds are fun to use and can really add a lot, or take away a lot, from your Web page. Backgrounds can be just a color or they can be an image file. Background colors are described using the "#" sign and a six-character code. The Background Color tag is placed inside the **<BODY>** tag. There isn't an ending tag for this tag. For example, the code for one shade of blue is #0000FF. (NOTE: these are zeros, not letter O's.) To use this color for the background of your Web page, type the following code:

<BODY BGCOLOR="#0000FF">

You can also change the color of your text with this tag. For example, to have a black background with white text, use the tag:

<BODY BGCOLOR="#000000" TEXT="#FFFFFF">

As you experiment with different colors and combinations of background colors and text colors, you'll discover that some colors overpower your content and other colors make it difficult to read the text. Many Internet service providers offer HTML help documents at their Web sites, including charts or lists of the color codes. For example, the ColorIndex (*www.infi.net/wwwimages/colorindex.html*) is available at the site of InfiNet, a business that offers Internet access and provides online publishing solutions for newspapers.

To use an image file instead of a color for your background, you'll use this tag: **<BODY BACKGROUND="name of your file">**. Using an image file for a background can be trickier because the image will be tiled, or repeated, instead of just showing up once. For example, if your image file contains the words Alex's Game Place, these words will be repeated to cover the entire background of your page. Many times an image file such as the one just described will make it difficult, if not impossible, to read any text on your page—so be careful and preview your page before putting it online.

Images are also fun to include on your Web site, but like the background tag, you should be careful when using it. Images take longer to download, or appear, in the browser window. Most people are used to the Internet moving at the speed of light and may just move on past your Web site if they have to wait a couple minutes for images to appear. The image tag **<IMAGE SRC="the name of your image file goes here">** does not have an ending tag, however, there are many tags available to help you modify the placement of your image. These advanced tags enable you to set an image flush with the right margin or align text so that it appears next to the image and starts at the same level as the image.

Links

When you start adding links to your Web pages you'll need to learn a little more about HTML code than we can cover here, but we wanted to at least mention it. The link tag **<A>** and **</A>** is a paired tag.

> *Notice that paired tags must have both parts in the document or your document will not appear as you thought it would. This holds true for the brackets and quotation marks used in some of the tags. Just try leaving one quotation mark or one bracket out and view your page and you'll understand how important they are!*

It may help to know that the letter "A" in the link tag stands for *Anchor*. You'll use this tag whenever you want to make a link to something else. The different variables for this tag enable you to link to another place in the same page, to another page you wrote, to an image, or to someone else's Web site!

Link, or anchor, tags must contain the address or path that describes to the browser how to get to the place you want to take viewers. It must also have a word that will show up on your Web page as a *hyperlink*. Hyperlinks are words, phrases, or images that enable you to view another document or picture when you click on them with a mouse. When viewing Web pages you'll notice that links are often highlighted in blue or underlined.

Using the directory list we created previously for an example, if you wanted to link the list item *Odyssey of the Mind Problem Descriptions* to the Web site that has this information, you'd add the following tags and address to this entry and it would look like this:

**<LI> <A HREF="http://www.odyssey.org/problems/index.html">
Odyssey of the Mind Problems Descriptions</A>**

Notice what was added and where it was added. We left the <LI> tag outside of
the link/anchor tag because we did not want that tag to appear on our Web page.
We also included the address for the Web site that has the problem descriptions
listed. We used the original entry, *Odyssey of the Mind Problem Descriptions*,
for the words that will appear in our document as a link.

USING AN HTML EDITOR

HTML editors are basically text editors or word processors designed specifically
for placing HTML code within your document. Often they offer you the ability
to view your Web page without having to start your Web browser.

With some HTML editors, you just select text and then click on the button
that represents the type of tag you want to insert. This would embed the proper
HTML tags just where they needed to be. Other HTML editors are
WYSIWYG—What You See Is What You Get! You don't even see the codes being embedded; you just see the document as it will look online.

There are a lot of different HTML editors to choose from. Some are simple
and basically make it easy to insert tags; they provide a viewer to preview pages
without using the Web browser. Others are quite complex, offering such functions as the ability to view the connections among all your pages, a feature that
checks whether your links are all working, or a selection of special templates with
themes. One big plus for using an HTML editor is when you get into more advanced elements like forms, tables, and style sheets. These elements require quite
a lot of coding, and some editors offer wizards that walk you through the creation of something like a table or form. These wizards can save you a lot of time
and frustration.

Linda has used a shareware editor called Aardvark Pro for a few years now. It
is simple enough that she didn't have to buy a book just to learn how to use it,
yet it still offered advanced features like forms and tables. Aardvark Pro was used
to create the demonstration pages for Rebecca's Internet Kitchen. Once Linda
began designing Web sites for companies and organizations, she tackled the job
of learning Microsoft's Front Page Editor. It is a powerful Web page creation
tool that she did have to buy a book about; she also had to visit Microsoft's Help
pages online to help her understand how to use the program effectively. She felt
the effort was worth it once the Web pages she was designing became more complex.

We recommend that you create a few Web pages manually first to get familiar
with the tags and have fun. Once you decide to create a Web site with several
pages and you know what type of material you want to post, then you can take a
look at some HTML editors and see which one will best suit your needs. Many
of them offer trial versions or demos that you can download and use for a time

before deciding to purchase it. Some are free and some are shareware. You can find an extensive listing of HTML editors, along with ratings and contact information, at Mac's Big List of HTML Editors *union.ncsa.uiuc.edu/HyperNews/get/ www/html/editors.html.* Here is what Mac's site had to say about both Aardvark Pro and Front Page.

Aardvark Pro

Author: Functional Business Systems
Availability: Shareware, $75
Current version: 2.4.2
Home page: *www.tmgnet.com/aardvark/index.html*
Description: (Kevin Read says:) Aardvark has to be simply the best HTML editor available today. You'll find Wizards and shortcuts to make even the most complex pages a breeze. Aardvark keeps track of URLs and Images so you can insert links into your document with just a click. Aardvark's in-built preview function has to be seen to be believed, no need to launch those memory hungry browsers—do it all in Aardvark.

FrontPage

Author: Microsoft
Availability: Commercial, $149
Current version: 1.1
Home page: *www.microsoft.com/msoffice/frontpage/default.htm*
Description: A visual client/server Web publishing environment. Editor provides WYSIWYG editing, built-in spell checking, easy creation of links and clickable images, forms creation, image type conversion, and more. The editor is only one small component of this environment. Free trial download at *www.microsoft.com/msdownload/sbn/0700.htm.*

Design Pointers

Rebecca's home page wouldn't win a design award, that's for sure. It is just a study in how to construct a basic home page. Your students can create simple Web pages like Rebecca's all day long. If you are going to put the energy into a Web site for your class, school, library, or individual interests, it is worth taking the time to create a storyboard for your Web site. Design is important. One good way to learn something about Web page design is to view what other people are doing. When you see a page you like, you can study the HTML tags used to create that page by clicking Netscape's **View** menu and then choosing **Source**. Keep in mind that Web pages look different to different users. This happens because various browsers display HTML tags differently. For example, what users see while viewing a home page through Lynx, a text-based browser, will be quite different from what they see when viewing it through a graphical browser like Netscape. The same page can even look different when viewing it in Netscape Navigator or Microsoft's Internet Explorer, even though both are graphical browsers.

KIDS PUBLISHING ON THE NET

Now that we've explained the "how-to" of publishing information on the Web, let's take a look at some of the ways in which kids are putting these skills to practice. This section lists a number of avenues for kids interested in self-publishing.

Global Show-n-Tell

Figure 11–4 Online exhibits like Global Show-n-Tell offer kids an opportunity to exhibit their artwork online.

Global Show-n-Tell, shown in Figure 11–4, is an online exhibition sponsored by Telenaut Communications that lets children of all ages publish their artwork online. To enter your own artwork, contact them via e-mail at *show-n-tell@telenaut.com* or visit their exhibit online *www.telenaut.com/gst/*.

International Kids' Space

Figure 11–5 International Kids' Space assists kids in writing their stories online.

Kids' Space (*www.kids-space.org*) was launched in March 1995 as the personal home page of an individual. It is now sponsored by NTT (Nippon Telegraph and Telephone Corporation), one of the largest world telecommunication companies located in Japan. Kids' Space offers kids a chance to link to other kids' sites, to post and exchange their ideas and questions with kids all around the world, and to publish their creative writing, pictures, and music on the Web (see Figure 11–5). To submit stories, visit *www.kids-space.org/forms/formS.html*. Kids' Space has many young readers and maintains a strict policy regarding violent or inappropriate words that might offend or give the wrong image to very young children.

Crayon

Create Your Own Newspaper
Your Personalized Internet News Service

http://crayon.net/

New to CRAYON?
Join over **200,000** people and **CReAte** Your **FREE** Newspaper or test-surf an **example** CRAYON newspaper.

CRAYON Subscribers
Click right this way to **read** your newspaper. You can also **modify** your paper, **update** your e-mail address, or **delete** your paper.

Fig 11–6 Crayon: CReAte Your Own Newspaper.

Crayon (*www.crayon.net*) helps kids create their own online newspaper. This site (Figure 11–6) was developed and is maintained by two Bucknell University graduates, Jeff Boulter and Dave Maher. There is an online help section that describes the process of creating an online newspaper. Then, just follow their directions, answer questions about the design, layout, and content of your paper—and you're a Web publisher of your own newspaper! Crayon also provides links to several other sites with online publications covering topics such as business, entertainment, sports, comics, weather, and more. Their listing of news sources (*www.crayon.net/using/links.html*) is a great resource itself and is frequently updated.

Find more online newspapers for and by kids under the heading **Online Newspaper** in The Link Farm on the CD-ROM, including **K–12 Newspapers,** one of the best listings for newspapers for kids on the Internet!

WRITING CONTESTS

Real Kids, Real Adventures

Figure 11–7 Real Kids, Real Adventures site encourages and helps kids who want to become "real" writers.

Any young adult that is a writer or wants to be a writer should visit Real Kids, Real Adventures (*www.realkids.com/club.shtml*). Deborah Morris, author of the "clubhouse," offers a relaxed and inviting atmosphere at this Web site (Figure 11–7) with the philosophy "Don't let anybody tell you it's impossible. Reach for the stars!" She offers stories about real-life kid authors for those students who can't quite believe it is true and lots and lots of tips about what a kid can do to get his or her writing career started. Her regularly sponsored writing contests may be just the thing some kids need to get motivated to write. A recent contest is to write a true story—either yours or someone else's—that will include the following specific elements: main character, ONE point of view (POV), dialogue, and exciting action. Deborah offers much assistance and lots of help and tips. The contests are open worldwide to any child between the ages of 8 and 17 at the time of their submission. They do not accept electronic entries and all entries must be in English. The first-place winners receive an award certificate, $50 (U.S.) check, and an autographed copy of the Real Kids, Real Adventures volume of his/her choice.

Canadian Student and Chapbook Writing Competitions

1998–1999 Canadian Student and Chapbook Writing Competitions (*home.ican.net/~susioan/contests.html*) lists several student writing competition sites with information about submission deadlines and contest rules.

RESOURCES

Commercial Resources

- Gini's Over the Rainbow Graphics (*www.fishnet.net/~gini/cool*), a worthwhile, inexpensive commercial site, offers a combination of free and for-sale graphics. It is a vast collection of all types of Web graphics, fonts, and other graphics-related resources. At Gini's Rare and Vintage Graphics collection you'll find dozens of clip art collections available for download on the honor system. These sets are available for reasonable fees ranging from $1.95 to $9.95 or you can become a member for a one-time fee of $29 and download it all! Includes links to such things as public graphics archives, culture-specific graphic Web sites, and graphic maps and globes, just to name a few.
- Art Today (*www.arttoday.com/PD-0025129*) is a megasite, reasonably priced, offering 750,000 files for you to download, including 2,150 fonts! For a $29.95 yearly fee you have access to download drawings, icons, woodcuts, cartoons, photos, etchings, animations, and fonts. This includes EPS (encapsulated postscript), WMF (Window Metafile), JPG (Joint Photographic Experts Group), and GIF (Graphics Interchange Format) files and both TrueType and PostScript fonts for either Macintosh or Windows—all keyworded, cross-referenced, and categorized.

Free HTML Resources

- Looking for dots, flowers, stars, arrows, pointers, icons, or various other gizmos and gadgets to use in your home page? Check out UNCG (*www.uncg.edu:80/~bucknall/uncg/icons/*).
- Free Art Graphics for HTML (*www.mcs.net/~wallach/freeart/buttons.html*)• Jeffrey Zeldman—Pardon My Icons (*www.zeldman.com/icon1.html*)—large collection of faces.
- Web Clip Art from The Mining Co. (*webclipart.miningco.com*)—free icons and graphics.

How-to Manuals for HTML

- A good Web-based beginner's manual on how to create HTML documents can be found at (*www.ncsa.uiuc.edu/General/Internet/WWW/HTMLPrimer.html*).

Join an HTML Club

- Join the HTML Writers Guild (*www.synet.net/hwg/*) for help. Over 70,000 members, ranging from professional Web page designers to newbies just starting out, find support and educational and informational assistance in this guild, which offers online classes and a collection of useful sites such as Design Resources, WWW/HTML Related Online Journals, HTML Resources for tables, frames, and style sheets, and NewTech Resources for Java, Shockwave, VRML, RealAudio, and whatever comes along next week.

PART IV

NOSE TO THE GRINDSTONE: LEARNING ACTIVITIES FOR ALL AGES

The Internet provides a variety of opportunities for learning. Courses are being offered on the Web that offer hypertext textbooks and learning environments for communications and interaction. For example, the History of Western Civilization course (*history.idbsu.edu/westciv/*) at Boise State University is entirely virtual. The course materials are presented online, assignments are presented via e-mail, and class discussions are carried on asynchronously via discussion lists. Students who take Art Appreciation Online offered by Southern Utah University at *www.suu.edu* are taken on virtual field trips researching art and artists on the Web.

In other settings, you find sites acting as clearinghouses for distance education opportunities. Well-established projects like the Globewide Network Academy (GNA) at *uu-gna.mit.edu:8001/uu-gna/* use the Internet to publish information about traditional distance education courses ranging from kindergarten to doctoral programs. GNA's catalog lists programs that are delivered through traditional means, such as videotape or snail-mail. CASO's College Course Catalog at *www.caso.com/iu/courses.html* focuses on distance learning on the Internet, but specializes in cataloging programs that are offered on the Web and/or via e-mail.

In yet another Internet-based learning environment kids can point-and-click their way around the globe browsing by subject. For example, kids who like history might consider starting at a site called the *Trenches* at *www.worldwar1.com/* where they can explore the history of World War I. They can take a theme-based guided tour, or browse through collections of maps, artwork, photos, or even listen to audio files. Kids visiting Kids Web at *www.npac.syr.edu/textbook/kidsweb/*

will find similar opportunities for browsing, but over a broader range of subjects including art, science, social studies, sports, and more.

And finally, there is a category of learning on the Web that is self-directed and requires special searching skills. Kids will have specific questions and want to know just where to go for answers. Where should they start digging for answers? Where are the electronic bookstores, virtual libraries, newsstands, and magazine racks? How do kids tap into the human resources that are accessible on the Net? Part IV answers these questions. Here we teach you the basics of online research and point you to some of the best Internet-based tools and resources available.

In Chapter 12, "Finding the Good Stuff," you'll be chasing down Web spiders and climbing Yahoo! subject trees looking for information. Here we show you what tools kids need in order to find information fast and efficiently. We explain how to plan a search, define topics, and help you become familiar with terms and concepts associated with computerized database searching.

In Chapter 13, "Discovering Libraries without Shelves," you'll be touring virtual libraries. You'll visit the Internet's first online public library at the University of Michigan and tour some of the biggest libraries in the world, including the Library of Congress.

In Chapter 14, "Browsing Virtual Bookstores," we introduce you to the world of e-zines and help you stake out some of the best bookstores and newsstands on the Net.

In Chapter 15, "Serious Research Sites," we point you toward *human* resources—individuals and organizations that can help you with your homework and other information needs. We also show you where to go for top-notch information resources that offer free access to full-text databases.

Chapter 12

Finding the Good Stuff

The Internet has a substantial amount of information that will be useful to kids, whether they are working on their own personal projects or homework assignments for school. What do we mean by "finding the good stuff"? In this chapter we place emphasis not only on the *finding* process, but also on the *quality* of resources found. We show you the best ways to search for information and point out the best sources for searching, including indexes, abstracts, and full-text magazine and newspaper articles databases.

IS THERE ANYTHING GOOD THAT'S FREE?

Commercial online services like Lexis-Nexis (*www.lexis-nexis.com*) have tremendous full-text reference libraries centrally located and easily searchable with one search screen. The Internet isn't this integrated, but it does offer some very good opportunities for information seekers. The Internet's free full-text resources are spread around the globe on hundreds of different computers and are accessed through various means, including Telnet, FTP, and the Web.

Another difference between commercial online services and the Internet at large exists in the quality of the resources. Commercial online services offer access to resources like up-to-date encyclopedias and almanacs. They offer daily updates of newspapers like the *Los Angeles Times* and *USA Today*. Kids aren't going to find this "pay as you go" information for free on the Internet. Still, there is a plethora of information available on the Net that is free and in some subject areas, like science and technology, the depth and breadth of information is astounding.

NAVIGATING THE INTERNET

Basically, there are only two ways to find information on the Net: You can run keyword searches or you can browse directories. When you *search*, you use the brute force of computers to dig up information. Computer applications designed to do this sort of work are called *search engines*. Northern Light (*www. northernlight.com*) is an example of a search engine and is described later in this chapter. You plug in a keyword or phrase, maybe some logical operators (AND, OR, NOT), press ENTER, and then wait for the search engine to do its thing. In only a matter of seconds, the search engine looks through thousands of indexed terms, pulls out any matches it finds, and then displays them on the screen in something called a *results list*.

Browsing directories or subject categories is when you do the searching yourself without the aid of a search engine. You can find answers to specific questions by browsing, but it may be more accidental than planned. This is because you can't always be certain where your journey will take you and that the answer you seek will be there waiting for you at the end of your journey. One day while in a musical mood we set out looking for a tool that would enable us to write music using a computer. We thought to ourselves, "Should we go down the **computer** path or the **music** path?" We tried both and after some serious browsing ended up scoring some hits going down the **Music|Software** path.

At other times, browsing has proven to be more effective than searching because of the terms used to describe a particular topic. We once started down a **Science and Nature** path at Yahooligans! (*www.yahooligans.com*) wondering if we would find something on acoustics. Within seconds of the start of our search we discovered a virtual reality Java piano created by Paul Flavin. This piano played pitches and displayed sound waves on an oscilloscope. What a great hands-on lesson in physical acoustics for kids. (If you would like to explore this resource further, go to *www.frontiernet.net/~imaging/play_a_piano.html*.)

After discovering the "Play a Piano" site, we went back to Yahooligans! and ran a keyword search on "physical acoustics" and "acoustics" and neither search brought up our "Play a Piano" site. Then we tried "sound" and got over 400 hits. The first page of hits didn't include any pointers to our "Play a Piano" site. Finally, when we searched on "sound waves" we got a hit pointing to the "Play a Piano" site. This example demonstrates one instance where browsing under a broad subject heading gave us better results than trying to pick a keyword that described our topic.

The best place to steer kids for subject category browsing is a *subject tree*. A subject tree is a list or directory of subject terms arranged in a hierarchical fashion. In other words, the subject terms start out very broad in scope (at the root of the tree) and as you travel up through the tree, the terms become narrower and narrower until finally you arrive at the tip of a twig—a document filled with text.

BROWSING VS. SEARCHING

Most directories are searchable, but that does *not* make them search engines. Searchable directories like Yahoo! do not store or present information in the same manner that search engines do. Directories have content and their content is structured. Information is selected and stored in categories and subcategories by humans. You don't know what a search engine like Northern Light can tell you about *wet-bottom shoo-fly pie* until you ask it the question. After a search engine performs its search and returns its results, you may have your answer, or you may have hundreds of irrelevant hits about **wet bottom** canoes, or the song "**Shoo Fly Pie** and Apple Pan Dowdy."

While directories employ people who organize information into categories, the scope of a directory's contents may not be as broad as what can be accessed by a search engine. Another drawback using directories is that you can't always figure out where to start. Would you have guessed that a recipe for wet-bottom shoo-fly pie was hiding down this path on Yahoo!: **Society and Culture|Food and Drink|Cooking|Recipes|Desserts|** and from there you must jump to Amy Gale's recipe archive and index of sweet pie recipes?

There really isn't a technique for browsing. It's just knowing which tree and which branches to climb first. Let's take a look at a few of the better known directories, and then we'll introduce you to search engines.

EXPLORING YAHOO! AND YAHOOLIGANS!

Yahoo! is a successful Web directory and search engine that was launched in 1994 by two Stanford University doctoral candidates, Jerry Yang and David Filo. To connect to Yahoo!, point your Web browser to *www.yahoo.com*. The opening screen for Yahoo! is the root of the subject tree. Older kids and adults will find this site to be an interesting place to begin any browsing adventure. It's built around 14 broad subject areas ranging from Arts & Humanities to Society & Culture.

Yahooligans!, Yahoo!'s sister site, is also a directory and search engine but it is designed just for kids ages 7–12. This is a fun and colorful place to send kids who don't have a particular topic in mind, but would just like to surf. Kids can start on the main page at *www.yahooligans.com*, choose a topic that interests them, and be on their way. The search engine is content-filtered and pulls up hits especially chosen for young surfers. What gets on Yahooligan's! reject list? According to their online help information, it's sites that are "sleazy, slimy, snarly, paranoid, hateful, hideous, harmful, pornographic, or prejudiced." Like Yahoo!, Yahooligans! is paid for by ads, and parents should be aware that young kids may not be able to distinguish between advertisements and features.

Both directories work the same. Find a topic that interests you, point and click and you'll link to another Web page with several subject headings, much narrower in scope. Select one of these and continue pointing and clicking, working your way up through the tree until you connect to a home page.

To show you how it works, let's start climbing the Yahoo! subject tree by grabbing onto the root called *Entertainment*. When you click on this term, you link to the following list of narrower terms:

Actors and Actresses (6131)
Advice (226)
Amusement and Theme Parks (262)
Audio/Visual Equipment (212)
Books and Literature@
Chat (21)
Comics and Animation (3321) [new]
Companies@
Contests, Surveys, and Polls (451)
Cool Links (1339)
Employment (294)
Events (189)
Food and Drink@
Gambling@
Games@
Humor, Jokes, and Fun (5083) [new]
Magic (149) [new]
Miscellaneous (159) [new]
Movies and Films (10606) [new]
Music (51458) [new]
Mystery (21) [new]
News and Media (660) [new]
Organizations (13) [new]
People@
Performing Arts@
Radio@
Reviews (22)
Science Fiction, Fantasy, and Horror (1661) [new]
Television@
Trivia (115)
Virtual Cards (700) [new]
Indices (31)
Usenet (13) [new]

Note some of the special features offered in the above listing:

- You can halt your browsing at this point and switch to a keyword search. At the top of the screen, there's a place to enter your keywords for searching either the Entertainment documents alone or all of Yahoo!.

- The numbers in parentheses after each subject term refer to the number of subject headings that are categorized under that term.
- When there is an @ sign after a term it means that term is indexed in other places in Yahoo!.

Let's continue down one of the branches of this subject tree by selecting the topic *Amusement and Theme Parks*. This selection links you to five pages listing the names of various theme parks and amusement parks. At the top of the page you also find links to narrower subject terms beginning with *Amusement Park Ride Physics*, *Boardwalks*, *Commercial Products and Services*, *Engineering*, *Haunted Houses*, *Merry-Go-Rounds*, and so on.

If you choose *Roller Coasters*, you pull up two pages of links to Web sites featuring information on coasters. At this point, you may think you're nearing the end of your climb, but as you will discover, the climb can go on much further depending on which branch you follow. The more time you spend at this Web site, the more you begin to realize just how big the Yahoo! subject tree really is!

FOR KIDS ONLY

Finding worthwhile directories organized just for kids can be a challenge. Sites like Yahoo! have lots of links to explore, but how do you know which sites are valuable? Fortunately, information organizers like the Association for Library Service to Children (ALSC) and the Ramapo Catskill Library System compile lists of recommended sites. In the section that follows we introduce you to some of the best.

700+ GREAT SITES

ALSC's recommended list, 700+ Great Sites at *www.ala.org/parentspage/ greatsites/amazing.html*, is for children from preschool through age 14. The Children and Technology Committee use selection criteria for determining which sites will be included. They pay close attention to who the site's creators are; the site's purpose; its design, organization, and usability; and the quality of its information content.

One of their subject categories is **Literature and Language**. When kids click on this link they are greeted with subtopics ranging from **Favorite Children's Stories** to **Writing by Children**. **Writing by Children** connects kids to 18 carefully selected sites. One site is *Writing Den* for kids in grades 6 through 12 who wish to improve their English reading, writing, and comprehension skills.

KidsClick!

KidsClick!, shown in Figure 12–1, is a search engine and Web guide for children developed by the Ramapo Catskill Library System. You can reach this site by pointing your browser to *sunsite.berkeley.edu/KidsClick!/*. It wouldn't be hard for kids to get lost for hours in this guide browsing through its 3,803 hand-selected records. The aim of the librarians who created this database was to begin "addressing concerns about the role of public libraries in guiding their young users to valuable and age appropriate web sites."

"Web Guide and Search Tool for Kids by Librarians"

Search word(s): [   ] [Search] - or, Advanced Search

Facts/Current Events
Encyclopedias, Dictionaries, Trivia, News, Holidays, Forecasts, more...

Science & Math
Animals, Natural Disasters, Space, Math, Experiments, Dinosaurs, more...

Fine Arts
Drawing, Theater, Photography, Dance, Architecture, Music, more...

Weird & Mysterious
Ghosts, ESP, UFOs, monsters, Aliens, Disappearances, more...

Health & Well-Being
Medicine, Disabilities, Family Life, AIDs, Exercise, Parenting, more...

Popular Entertainments
Rock Music, Movies, TV, Toys, Comic Books, Celebrities, more...

Religion & Mythology
Christianity, Judaism, Islam, Bible, Religion (General), Mythology, more...

Home & Household
Food, Pets, Hobbies, Crafts, Gardening, Babysitting, more...

Sports & Recreation
Team Sports, Games, Camping, Fishing, Olympics, Horsemanship, Martial Arts, more...

Society & Government
Law, Schools, Politics, Military, Business, Minorities, Organizations, more...

Machines & Transportation
Cars, Trucks, Spacecraft, Planes, Trains, Tools, more...

Literature
Stories, Poetry, Humor, Authors, Books, Jokes, Quotations, more...

Reading, Writing, Speaking
Grammar, Foreign Languages, Spelling, Composition, Vocabulary, Writing, more...

Computers/The Internet
Software, Programming, Internet, Key-Pals, Computer Games, Hardware, more...

Geography/History/Biography
Regions, Cities, Biography, States, History, Folklore, more...

Copyright © 1998, *All rights reserved.*
Document address http://sunsite.berkeley.edu/KidsClick!/
Created by a bunch of librarians. Read more about us! and also note our privacy policy.
This page updated August 19, 1998; database updated daily.
Direct problems, suggestions, and comments to jkuntz@rcls.org

KidsClick! was initiated under a Federal Library Services and Technology Act (LSTA) grant obtained by the Ramapo Catskill Library System. LSTA funds administered by the New York State Division of Library Development. Additional support provided by the Berkeley Digital Library SunSITE.

Figure 12–1 KidsClick! Makes searching and subject browsing available to children.

This site is fun to navigate, and without frame technology it's easy to explore full-screen views of subject lists. The front page on this site includes a simple search screen and a link to an advanced search screen. The scope of this site's coverage is wide—from Science & Math to Weird & Mysterious. As a special feature, advanced search windows are placed at the bottom of each page displaying submenus. The advanced search options include limiting results to *All reading levels*, *Up to grade 2*, *Grade 3–6*, and *Grade 7+*. Search results can also be limited to sites with *Some or no pictures*, *Some pictures*, or *Many pictures.*

Figure 12–2 illustrates two records taken from the KidsClick! database. Each entry begins with the site's title followed by its URL. Descriptions are geared for kids and is sure to grab their attention. Each record rates how many illustrations are included, the reading level, and under what subject heading the site is classified.

Figure 12–2 Sample records found in KidsClick!

Earth Day Coloring Pages —

http://earthday.wilderness.org/kidsstuff/colorindex.htm

The ancient forests need our help. As you read about and color these pictures of the ancient forest, you'll see why very old forests are so important. After all, without these trees there would be no forests for animals to live in or for people to visit when we want to remember just how old living things can be.

[Illustrations: many | Reading Level: 0–2 | Subject: Earth Day]

4-H Children's Garden —

http://commtechlab.msu.edu/sites/garden/index.html

Imagine a special garden created for children and the young at heart. This is the Michigan 4-H Children's Garden, a place where plants, children, and imaginations grow. As one of the horticultural gardens on the campus of Michigan State University, this garden features over 56 individual theme areas that create a place of wonder, enchantment and delight for people of any age.

[Illustrations: many | Reading Level: 7+ | Subject: Gardening]

DIG (DISNEY'S INTERNET GUIDE)

Maintained by Disney.com, Dig is intended to serve both kids and families. When kids visit Dig at *www.disney.com/dig/* they'll be met with the same, simple, easy-to-use interface most directories use. Subjects are organized under main topics and subcategories. The important feature to note is that every site at Dig has been reviewed by one of Disney's editors. Their goal is to keep materials out of their database that are inappropriate for kids.

Special attractions found at this site include specialized search engines and Web tours. One search engine enables kids to "dig locally." Kids can click on a pull-down menu and choose a state of their choice for local information hunting. Another search engine allows kids to search by "Activity"—for example, camping, learning, parties, crafts, holidays, and so on. These searches can be further limited to an age from 1 to 12 (or older).

Disney Web Tours are real-time tours—interactive tours that take place in the present moment. To take part, you need a Web browser that supports Java chat and frames. This would include Microsoft Internet Explorer 3.0 or higher, or Netscape Navigator 3.0 or higher. If kids miss one of these tours, they can always visit Disney's tour archive and explore American History, Space, Shareware, Dinosaurs, and more anytime they wish.

FOR EDUCATORS ONLY

Sponsored by American Fidelity Educational Services, Education World at *www.education-world.com/* lists more than 50,000 sites in its database. The front page lists weekly features, such as Lesson Planning, News/Eye on Schools, and Curriculum. At the top of the page you can run a search or link to their directory to browse by topic. This site's education links cover a broad range of topics including Continuing Education, Distance Education, K12 Schools Online, Special Education, Teachers' Resources, and more.

One of the more interesting features at Education World is the Grade Specific Resources category, which in turn leads you to two subcategories: Elementary and Secondary. The Elementary category is further broken down into K–2, Grades 3–5, and Grades 6–8. Each subcategory includes resources for both students and teachers. This site also features three mailing lists (site reviews, newsletter, and job listings) and the ability to add sites for inclusion. The ease with which sites can be added accounts for the large number of records included in this database.

WHICH SITES ARE WORTHWHILE AND WHICH ARE NOT?

As you can see, there are lots of places to explore on the Web and you may not have time to filter everything your kids view. How can you begin helping your kids learn how to determine what's good and what's not good? One answer is offered by PBS. PBS offers an interactive site called *techknow* that helps teach kids how to judge for themselves whether a Web site is good or not. Even if your kids aren't interested in learning these skills, they're sure to enjoy meeting their favorite PBS stars at *www.pbs.org/kids/*—Arthur, Charlie Horse, Kratts' Creatures, Mister Rogers, and more.

But for the more serious-minded kids, point their browser to *www.pbs.org/kids/techknow/* and click on the link labeled **you be the judge**. Here kids are asked to run a search on a "topic of the week" and then taught how to judge the quality of the sites they find. Kids have to think about different ways of measuring a site's value. They are given lots of guidance and have to consider many pertinent questions, all of which help them understand what to look for. Here are the criteria they are asked to consider, rating each one with a number from 0 (worst) to 10 (best):

- How easy or difficult was it to navigate the site?
- Did you like the site's design?
- How would you rate the site's content?
- Did you feel like you were part of a Web community?
- What was your overall impression of the site?

At the close, they are invited to write their own review and submit it to PBS kids.

Barbara J. Feldman, a syndicated newspaper columnist, offers her advice for parents, teachers, librarians, and others, on what's good. Feldman's home page, Surfing the Net WITH KIDS at *www.sufnetkids.com/*, reviews, rates, and organizes sites with educational content by topic. Her subject headings include:

- Arts, Crafts, Music
- Computers, Internet
- Games, Hobbies
- Geography
- Holidays, History
- Language Arts
- Math
- Science

Each week Feldmen reviews the best sites included in a particular topic, such as dinosaurs, virtual zoos, aquariums, ecology games, and robots.

START YOUR SEARCH ENGINES!

As we mentioned earlier, when you search the Internet for information, as opposed to browse, you use search engines that do most of the work for you. In the first edition of this book we spent a lot of time explaining how one search engine called Lycos worked. Dozens of new search engines have evolved since that time and each one has its own set of rules for digging out information.

In this edition of *Connecting Kids and the Internet* we decided to take a slightly different approach. Instead of studying one or two search engines in detail, we thought we'd teach you basic principles of searching that can be applied to most search engines on the Net. We point you to what we think are some of the best search engine sites, but that's all we do—point you in the right direction. It will be up to you and your kids to read the Help files (look for a button labeled **help** on the site's front page) to see what each individual site defines as their default search and what advanced search features are available. The balance of this chapter gives you all the background information you need to understand what others are talking about when they explain how to use *their* search engine.

HOW COMPUTER-BASED SEARCHING WORKS

For some kids, searching the Net for information is going to be a form of entertainment. It will be spontaneous, unplanned, and maybe a little experimental. These kids feed words and phrases into search engines, jump from topic to topic seeing what they can find. For other kids, searching the Net is serious business. These kids have a question and they need an answer. We wrote this section to help kids with the serious kind of searching.

The process of finding the information in these databases is called *searching*. When you start a search, you begin by describing the search topic and identifying key concepts. Next, you identify words and phrases that express each concept. Lastly, you use search features such as *truncation, logical operators, nesting, phrases*, and *proximity operators* to make search statements that describe the information you are trying to retrieve. We explain these concepts in greater detail as we guide you through the rest of this chapter.

Defining Your Topic

First you have to answer the question, "What is the topic?" In this example, let's say the topic is *lowering cholesterol levels through diet*. Defining your topic can sometimes be difficult, but it's an important first step. The next step in the search process is to choose which terms you plug in to your search engine.

Choosing Search Terms

To help you choose which words and phrases to search, answer the question, "What words must be in the article or report for it to be relevant to my topic?" As you can see in Table 12–1, you could base your search on just three words, but that would limit your results.

Table 12–1 Listing the different concepts contained in your search topic		
Concept 1	**Concept 2**	**Concept 3**
low	cholesterol	diets

Here are three things you can do to insure that you get all of the relevant articles in a database:

1. *Use synonyms and other related terms*. Write down all of the synonyms and related terms you can think of. This process is ongoing and you continue to develop your list even after you begin your searching. As you begin reading the materials that your search uncovers, you discover new words and phrases that define your topic. Examples for our sample search topic are presented in Table 12–2.

Table 12–2 Expanding on your main topics by adding synonyms and other related terms		
Concept 1	**Concept 2**	**Concept 3**
low	cholesterol	diets
decrease	high-cholesterol	nutrition
reduce		
eliminate		
control		

2. *Use truncation.* Truncate for various word endings. Truncating is like using "wildcards"—symbols that represent one or more letters. The general rule for truncating is place the truncation symbol immediately after the root of the word. Search engines vary, but usually the truncation symbol is an asterisk * or a "#" sign. Avoid truncating on three or less letters. Truncating **diet*** would search on

    diet
    diet**s**
    diet**ed**
    diet**ary**
    diet**ing**

Advanced search engines allow you to specify wildcards at the beginning, middle, or end of words.

3. *Avoid implied or unnecessary terms.* Remove unnecessary words that are implied by the database in which you are searching. For example, don't include the keyword **education** when you are searching a database that specializes in education-related research. Don't include the word **computer** when searching in a computer-related database.

Creating the Search Statement

The last step in preparing for online searching consists of creating search statements. As you create your search statements, you define relationships between words and search specific *fields* or *indexes* using

    I. Logical operators
   II. Proximity searching
  III. Nesting
  IV. Field searching

I. Use *logical operators* to define relationships between words.
    A. Do all words need to be in every record? If so, use the **and** operator. **And** narrows, or restricts, your search. Example: **cholesterol and restrict and diet** tells the search engine that all connected words are required. Every record must contain all terms. Some search engines use the "+" sign to designate that a word must be included, for example **+8mm +camcorder.** As an alternative, some services offer pull-down menus associated with a text box that say "must contain these words" or "all of these words." Both of these phrases are equivalent to using the **and** operator.
    B. Are there words you don't want in a record? If so, use the **not** operator. (Be careful using **not** because it can exclude relevant articles.) Example: **jazz not blues** retrieves records about jazz but excludes articles containing the word **blues.** Some search engines use the "–" sign to des-

ignate that a word must not be included, for example **+jazz–blues**. As an alternative, some search engines provide pull-down menus associated with a text box that say "must not contain these words" or "should not contain these words."

C. Are there words that are interchangeable? If so, use the **or** operator. **Or** widens, or expands, your search. Example: **lower or restrict or reduce** increases the number of items in the search results because you are allowing for alternate words. Some search engines provide pull-down menus associated with a text box that say "any of these words," "should contain these words," or "can contain these words."

II. Use *proximity operators* to specify distances between search terms. When you search on **low and cholesterol and diet** you retrieve some articles where these three terms occur close to each other, but you could also get articles where these terms are paragraphs apart. Proximity operators enable you to specify how close the search terms should be to one another. This is very important to apply when searching full-text databases where the search engine scans the text of an entire article looking for occurrences of your keywords. Each search engine will have its own way of representing proximity operators. Here we describe some of the most common methods used.

A. The word **near** or an **N** is used when searching for words next to each other but in any order. For example, **soybean n farm*** would find **soybean farm** and **farming soybeans.**

B. The word **with** or **W** is used when words have to be next to each other and in the exact order you have written them. When you search on **dairy farming, trout fishing, baseball cards, chocolate cream pie, ground zero,** or **low cholesterol diet**, you of course want these terms to be right next to each other and in the exact order they are written. These are considered *phrases*. Some databases treat a group of words as a phrase if all words are entered on one line. This is possible when multiple text entry boxes are provided. Other search engines will require an operator, such as **low (w) cholesterol (w) diet**. It is becoming more and more common on the Internet to place words within double quotes to designate a phrase, for example **"low cholesterol diet."**

C. You can also specify an exact number, for example, **within 3 words (3W).** Every database will do it a little bit differently. Some search engines allow you to search for terms within the same sentence (**w/s**), or within the same paragraph (**w/p**), too. Study each search engine's Help files to see if this feature is available.

Stopwords are commonly used words that are ignored by search engines. Some of the most common stopwords are:

a	had	or
an	have	that
are	he	this
as	her	to
at	his	was
be	in	which
but	is	with
by	it	you
for	of	&
from	on	

When stopwords must be made part of a phrase—for example, **search and destroy missions** or **cost of living**—see if you can use proximity operators and specify that a certain number of words may intervene. For example, **low cholesterol (3w) diet*** would retrieve: **low cholesterol diets**, **low-cholesterol and low-fat diet**, **low cholesterol high fiber diet**, etc. In the example **war and peace**, you might find that that entering **war w1 peace** or **war "and" peace** will get your desired results.

III. In more complex searches, use parentheses ( ) to specify precedence in your search statement. The terms you include, or "nest," in parentheses will be acted on first. Keep related terms grouped together and combine them with **AND**, **OR**, or proximity operators. For example, to search for documents that contain information about both car and auto racing, try this advanced query: **(car or auto) AND racing**.

IV. *Qualifiers* or *field searching* restrict a search to a specific field. For example, when searching some of the earlier text-based automated library catalogs (also called OPACs) you might use the qualifier **ti** to search the title index, **au** to search the author index, or **su** to search the subject index. For example, you enter **au=Sousa, John Philip** to search on the author named John Philip Sousa. Search engines such as AltaVista have an extensive list of qualifiers that enable you to search different areas of Web pages. For example, you could direct your search on the keyword **gardening** to the domain name addresses or the titles of documents. Different organizations use different terms for the same service. For example, Britannica Online calls this an "Informative Tag." Britannica enables you to search on the title of an article with the **title=** tag or you can search on the contents of an article with the **contents=** tag.

TIPS FOR SEARCHING THE WEB

As we close this section on searching strategies and techniques, here are some general tips to consider when hunting for information on the Web. These, combined with all of the information presented earlier on how to formulate effective search statements, should help you find what you are looking for.

1. Most services offer *simple* and *advanced* search modes. Advanced search modes are always more powerful and allow you to incorporate many of the features described in this chapter.
2. Use the **Help** files to learn what features are supported by a particular service.
3. Study one or two search engines in depth rather than being somewhat familiar with dozens.
4. Use only lowercase letters in your search statements unless you want your search to be case sensitive. (Not all search engines support upper- and lowercase, but a few do. Help files explain this.) If you can find a search engine that's case-sensitive, take advantage of it and separate the dollar *bills* from the President *Bills*.
5. Search engines usually process what is in parentheses first, and the entire search statement is usually searched from left to right.
6. One of the most important features to understand about any search engine is how *simple searches* handle two or more words entered into a text box. Some search engines treat them as a phrase and others combine words together with an implied Boolean **AND**. For example, the following statement: **Car racing or horse racing** may be treated as **(car and racing) or (horse and racing)** by some search engines, and others may drop the **or** and look at it as a phrase **car racing horse racing**. Naturally, you wouldn't get any hits if it were interpreted as a phrase.

EXPLORING SEARCH ENGINES ON THE WEB

There are dozens of search engines on the Internet that allow you access to a wide variety of resources including reference books, statistics, directories, business and financial data, general news, and government reports. The information has been collected and organized in digital format by many different organizations. The producers of the data determine how the content is formatted. Some data are presented as full-text articles or Web pages. Other data are presented as bibliographic citations, giving only author, title, publisher, and so on. And some data are presented in the form of abstracts or brief summaries.

Table 12–3 General Search Engines

Name of Service	Address
AltaVista	altavista.digital.com
Argus Clearinghouse	www.clearinghouse.net
Excite	www.excite.com
Galaxy	galaxy.tradewave.com/
Hotbot	www.hotbot.com
Infoseek	www.infoseek.com
Looksmart	www.looksmart.com
Lycos	www.lycos.com
Northern Light	www.northernlight.com
OneKey	www.onekey.com
Yahoo!	www.yahoo.com

Table 12–4 Search Engines Just for Kids

Name of Service	Address
AOL NetFind for Kids Only	www.aol.com/netfind/kids/
Ask Jeeves for Kids	www.ajkids.com/
Awesome Library	www.awesomelibrary.org/
Disney's Internet Guide DIG	www.disney.com/dig/today/
EdView Smart Zone	home.edview.com/search/
i-Explorer	www.i-explorer.com/
KidsClick!	Sunsite.berkeley.edu/ KidsClick!/
Librarian's Index to the Internet	sunsite.berkeley.edu/ InternetIndex/index.html
LycosSafetyNet	personal.lycos.com/safetynet/ safetynet.asp
Magellan Green Light Sites	www.mckinley.com/
PBS ZOOMsearch	www.pbs.org/wgbh/zoom/ home4.html
SafeSearch	www.safesearch.com
StudyWEB	www.studyweb.com/
Yahooligans!	www.yahooligans.com

Table 12–5 Multithreaded Search Engines

Name of Service	Address
Dogpile	www.dogpile.com
Inference	www.inference.com/infind/
Mamma	www.mamma.com
Metacrawler	www.metacrawler.com
MetaFind	www.metafind.com
Savvysearch	guaraldi.cs.colostate.edu

Table 12–6 Specialized Search Engines and Directories

Name of Service	Address
Bill Nye the Science Guy's Nye Labs Online	nyelabs.kcts.org/flash_go.html
Children's Software and More! (Look for the link labeled **Download**)	www.kidsdomain.com/
Classroom Connect	www.classroom.com/grades/
DejaNews (Searching Usenet Newsgroups)	www.dejanews.com/
Education World	www.education-world.com/
Fast FTP Search	ftpsearch.ntnu.no/
Searchopolis	www.searchopolis.com/
Smithsonian Search	web6.si.edu/
StudyWEB	www.studyweb.com/
Time for Kids	www.pathfinder.com/TFK/
ZooNet Animal Links	www.mindspring.com/~zoonet/ anilinks.html

Table 12–7 Meta Sites (sites listing many links to search engines)

Name of Service	Address
All-In-One	www.albany.net/allinone/
The Virtual Web Search Site	www.dreamscape.com/franvad/ search.html

Chapter 13

Discovering Libraries
without Shelves

Most kids know something about libraries. They start visiting libraries as toddlers, attend preschool story hours when they're three to five years old, and take part in the summer reading programs as they get older. They know their library opens at a certain time and closes at a certain time. Kids know something about librarians, too—individuals who read aloud to them, recommend titles, assist them with computers and other sundry hardware, and respond to their requests for help in finding information. The libraries we're talking about are built with wood, bricks, and mortar and are staffed by helpful people.

There is another kind of library that exists on the Internet called a *virtual library*. Kids will enjoy the freedom associated with virtual libraries. They are always open and kids don't have to wait for a ride into town to visit one. In fact, computers connected to the Internet enable kids to visit virtual libraries all around the world without ever leaving their homes!

WHAT IS A VIRTUAL LIBRARY?

Libraries that can be accessed on the Internet are called virtual libraries. Virtual libraries are not real libraries. In fact, they are not really "virtual" libraries in the truest sense, but that is what we call them.

Virtual reality is reality that's not real. By putting on some special devices, like a head-mounted display and sensory gloves, you are able to see images and experience the sensations of sound and touch. You think you are somewhere else, not here. A true virtual library would be one where you feel you are really there. You see images of books. You can reach out and touch them. You immerse yourself totally into this synthetic world.

Visiting Virtual Libraries on the Internet

The virtual libraries we introduce here are nothing more than online databases or card catalogs that can be viewed on a computer monitor. Kids won't see any real books, just text displayed on their screen, or maybe a graphical image of a book's spine. But that's pretty neat in itself.

These libraries are open 24 hours a day, every day of the year. Whether the library is right next door or on the other side of the globe, distance won't matter. Neither will it matter if the library is a major university library or a small public library. As long as your kids have an Internet connection, they can access a virtual library in just a few seconds.

There's a double bonus if your local public library or school library also happens to be a virtual library. Not only can kids view their library's collection from home, but they may also be able to place holds on books they'd like to reserve and pick up later, and place the holds any time of day whether the real library is open or not.

Land of Ten Thousand Lakes

If you're lucky enough to live in Anoka, Minnesota, you can view your library's holdings from home. Without leaving the house, kids can check to see whether their library has a book they're interested in and if it does, they can place a hold on it and pick it up later. In fact, they can tell the system from which branch they'd like to pick up their book. Kids can also check library hours, leave messages in a suggestion box, and even find out information about themselves, such as whether they have any outstanding fines.

The Anoka County Library System is easy to connect to from any point on the Internet and kids can do it by using their Web browser. Have them start by pointing their browser to *anoka.lib.mn.us/opener.html*. Once they connect, they will be in Minnesota—virtually speaking, that is. The opening screen is presented in Figure 13–1.

To activate any function, select the related option. For detailed instructions concerning this page, click here.

SEARCH THE CATALOG	SEARCH PERIODICALS	OTHER RESOURCES
ABOUT THE LIBRARY	ABOUT MY ACCOUNT	EVENTS /NEWS

Please send comments, suggestions, or bug reports to" webmaster"
Revised 29-OCT-1997 js

Figure 13–1 This is the opening screen you see when you stop in and visit the Anoka County Library in Minnesota.

"So," you and your kids might ask, "why should we go to the public library in Anoka, Minnesota, when we live here in Sylvia, North Carolina?" One reason might be that your local library can't be accessed on the Internet, so you do your research at a library that is connected. When you find the books you want, you can copy the citations and take them to your local library next time you visit it. Whatever your local library doesn't have in its holdings, you can order through interlibrary loan. Other research that kids could do while visiting Anoka includes verifying authors and titles, or running subject and keyword searches for a bibliography. These tasks, of course, can be performed at any one of hundreds of different online libraries.

Another practical reason for visiting remote systems would be because of their value-added services, such as the super *Homework Center* developed by Oregon's Multnomah County Library. This library also features *KidsPage for Kids to 8th Grade*, and *Outernet for Young Adults*. You can visit this outstanding Web site at *www.multnomah.lib.or.us/lib/homework/*. Other interesting sites are listed in the Resources section at the end of this chapter.

Whether your kids are interested in simple title/author verification, or exploring sites that offer special services, a good strategy is to point them to a meta site that lists many libraries. WebCATS, introduced on the next page, is just such a site and it organizes libraries by type. Of special interest to kids would be the

K–12 schools and public libraries. The Internet is a dynamic environment, so it pays to visit sites like webCATS often and explore individual libraries to see what new changes have taken place.

FINDING OTHER LIBRARIES

There is a great site on the Web designed just to keep you connected with all of the Web-based libraries in the world. The site is called webCATS and you can find it at *www.lights.com/webcats/*. WebCATS offers different ways of accessing libraries. You can browse a geographic index that organizes libraries by country. When you click on United States, the index is broken down into individual states. You can also use webCATS to find libraries of a certain type, such as Armed Forces, College and University, Government, or K–12 Schools.

WebCATS offers a link to Hytelnet, one of the first major sites for listing Internet-accessible libraries. You can connect directly by pointing your browser to *www.lights.com/hytelnet/*. Hytelnet has provided an invaluable service over the years, but as you will see when you connect, the site is no longer being supported and may soon be closing down. It is still an important resource because it lists library sites that rely on an older method of making their catalogs available to Internet users worldwide. The method used is called *telnet*, a service described in great detail in Chapter 17. (For fun, try telneting to the Anoka County Library and you will see how different it is. Chapter 17 will get you started. The telnet address for the Anoka County Library is *anoka.lib.mn.us*. At the *Username:* prompt, enter **LIBRARY**.)

WELCOME TO THE INTERNET PUBLIC LIBRARY (IPL)

IPL, the world's first virtual public library, is a storehouse of electronic reference books and services. Hosted by the University of Michigan's School of Information, IPL offers access to general reference tools like dictionaries, encyclopedias, and atlases; access to reference materials classified by subject like science, education, health, and nutrition; Youth Services and assistance with homework questions; and services to librarians and other information professionals.

There's too much to cover here in one section, so we'll only give you a brief introduction to some of their most popular services. To get started, point your Web browser to *ipl.sils.umich.edu/*. Two links that kids are sure to enjoy are the Teen and Youth links. The Teen Division offers links to carefully selected, annotated resources on fun topics like "Sports" and "Dating and Stuff," and more serious subjects like "Issues and Conflicts" and "Math and Science."

There are a lot of good links in the IPL Youth Division. Information covers subjects as diverse as picture books, poems, dinosaurs, transportation, physics, the ancient world, and hygiene. Links are annotated so there's no question about content.

The Reference Center is one of the most popular services IPL offers. To get to the IPL Reference Center, click the **Reference** button shown in the main screen and you arrive at an image map. The Reference Center is organized into 11 subject areas plus a service for answering reference questions. If you're viewing this Web page through a graphical browser, you can explore the reference collection by clicking on the "virtual books" laying around the "virtual librarian's office."

Subjects covered in the Reference Room include: Reference, Arts & Humanities, Business & Economics, Computers & Internet, Education, Entertainment & Leisure, Health & Medical Sciences, Law, Government & Political Science, Sciences & Technology, Social Sciences, and Associations.

The question-answering service can be accessed one of three ways:

1. By filling out a form online,
2. By sending an e-mail request, or
3. By visiting the MOO (Multi-user Object Oriented environment).

MOOs enable visitors to interact with IPL staff in "real time." Keep in mind that the reference-answering service is experimental and run by volunteers. They ask that you please limit your questions to those that are of some importance. Due to limited time and staff, answers tend to be brief—factual answers or pointers to other sources that may offer some assistance.

SEARCHING THE REFERENCE COLLECTION

When you first connect to the IPL, you'll notice a link labeled *Web Searching*. This will link you to eight popular search engines and archives, including AltaVista, The Argus Clearinghouse, DejaNews, Excite, HotBot, Magellan, Northern Light, and Yahoo!. These are designed for conducting searches Webwide. The IPL also offers a search service that hunts down information in their own Reference Library. You can link to this search service from either the Reference Center page, or directly at *www.ipl.org/ref/RR/search.html*.

Exploring the reference collection by pointing and clicking on virtual books that are sitting on virtual bookshelves is fine if you have a lot of time to browse, but if you're in a hurry to find out whether the IPL has anything relevant to your research, use the search form they offer. You also have the option of searching specialized collections, including Online Texts, Online Newspapers, Online Serials, Associations on the Net, and Teen Collection.

We tried a search on the words *Chernobyl, Russia*. The search engine looks for matches in five indexes including title, acronym, description, subject headings, and keywords. We landed one hit with a search on the term **Chernobyl, Russia**. The results from this search were displayed in the form of a brief abstract. By clicking on the underlined document title, you can link to the full-text document.

THE BIG WHEELS

In this section, we introduce you to two "real" libraries that can be accessed via the Internet. They are two of the bigger, well-known computerized library systems in the nation. Kids can access both on the Internet free of charge. They include: CARL Systems Library Catalogs and the Library of Congress in Washington, D.C. These services will be most appropriate for kids in their middle to late teens.

CARL

CARL Corporation was established in 1988 as CARL Systems to develop and market the library system used by the Colorado Alliance of Research Libraries. CARL Systems are used by very large, networked library systems, especially those in the Rocky Mountain region of the United States. CARL offers access to several databases, including online catalogs, periodical databases, and other library systems. Like many online information systems, CARL restricts access to certain fee-based databases. These are reserved for local library patrons and require passwords.

The easiest way to connect to CARL Systems is via the Web at *www.carl.org*. CARL's Web site is intuitive and easy to follow. Kids should have no problem exploring on their own.

You can also telnet to *pac.carl.org*, if you prefer this method of connection. (Telnet service is described in detail in Chapter 17.) Older kids that have never telneted might enjoy this change of pace. To get them started, if you're running Windows 95/98 have them enter this URL in the browsers location box: **telnet:/ /pac.carl.org**. (Remember that when an Internet address comes at the end of a sentence, the last dot is a period, *not* part of the address.)

At the *Enter Choice>* prompt, type **PAC** and press ENTER. The system will then ask you to identify your terminal type. At the *Select Line #:* prompt, type **5** (which is for vt100) and press ENTER. This brings you to CARL's opening menu. The two services that will be most useful to older teens include:

1. UnCover
2. CARL Systems Library Catalogs

Exploring the UnCover Database

UnCover is a periodical index and document delivery service that indexes over 20,000 journals and magazines in science, medicine, and technology, and to a lesser extent, the social sciences and the humanities. Over 6,000,000 articles are indexed and about 4,000 citations are being added each day.

Besides being one of the biggest journal article indexes, UnCover is also one of the most up-to-date. As soon as UnCover receives a journal from the publisher, they enter information from the journal's Table of Contents into the UnCover database.

Only under very special circumstances would kids make use of UnCover's document delivery system. If kids in high school or college absolutely need an article and they need it *now*, UnCover can deliver almost any article cited in their index to your FAX machine within 24 hours for a fee. Charges are assessed for each individual article. There is no cost for searching their index.

To use UnCover, type **1** at the main menu and press ENTER. You will be an *Open Access User*—a user who doesn't pay a fee, so press ENTER two more times. The system will then ask you if you want to create a PROFILE. A PROFILE contains personal information such as your name and e-mail address and is beneficial if you plan on ordering and paying for articles. If you don't plan on doing this, just press ENTER two more times. This brings you to the main UnCover screen. It is from this screen that kids may launch an author or word search. Have them type the appropriate letter (**w** for word search, **n** for name) and then press ENTER. Next, they'll be prompted to enter the search term(s). After UnCover completes its search and returns a list of numbered hits, kids enter the number of the citation they'd like to view and press ENTER.

To move back through previous screens, press **q** for quit. When kids find an article of interest, they can print the citation and take it to their school or public library. The article might be in a journal or magazine held locally or it may be obtainable through interlibrary loan.

The Browse by journal title feature enables kids to view all of the journals indexed in the UnCover collection in title order. Enter a letter of the alphabet or the title of a magazine or journal and press ENTER. When you see a journal title you're interested in, enter its line number and press ENTER to see the complete citation.

Accessing this same service via the Web is quite simple. Look for the link labeled **Search UnCover** on the main page at *www.carl.org*. On the next page, click on a similar button also labeled **Search UnCover**. On the third screen you come to, look for a button labeled **Search UnCover Now**. This brings you to the final search screen.

Exploring CARL Systems Library Catalogs

Kids can also access various online library systems from the main menu. The benefit of using CARL is that kids will be presented with the same automated library system at every site they visit. They won't need to learn a new search engine every time they switch to a different library. The Welcome screens will vary and each system will offer its own unique services, but when they connect to the library's online catalog, that will be the same everywhere.

To connect with a library's online catalog, kids should look for a menu item that reads something like *1. Library Catalog*. They can, of course, explore any other menu items they wish.

To access the CARL System Libraries via telnet, type **4** at the main menu and press ENTER.

To connect to libraries in the Eastern United States, for example, type **35** and press ENTER. The following list of libraries is displayed on the screen.

> 1. UnCover *** 2. Open Access Databases
> 　　3. Licensed Databases *** 4. CARL System Libraries *** 5. FAQ
> 　　　LIBRARY CATALOGS—EASTERN UNITED STATES
> 　　60.　Atlanta/Fulton County Public Library　(GA)
> 　　61.　Baltimore County Library (MD)
> 　　62.　Bibliomation (CT)
> 　　63.　Broward County Libraries (FL)
> 　　64.　C/W MARS (MA)
> 　　65.　Capitol Region Library Consortium (CT)
> 　　75.　Chicago Public Library (IL)
> 　　66.　Libraries of Middlesex (NJ)
> 　　67.　Maryland Interlibrary Consortium (MD)
> 　　68.　Montgomery County Department of Public Libraries (MD)
> 　　69.　Monroe County Library System (NY)
> 　　70.　Morgan State University (MD)
> 　　71.　Northeastern University (MA)
> 　　72.　Resource Sharing Alliance of Illinois (IL)
> 　　73.　University of Maryland System (MD)
> 　　74.　Westchester Library Systems (NY)
> You may enter //EXIT at any time to leave this system.
> Enter the NUMBER of your choice, and press the <RETURN> key >>

To visit any one of these libraries, kids enter the line number of choice and connect via telnet. While one system is trying to connect to another, they shouldn't be surprised by the odd characters that print to their screen like ^P++^P0^P++^P0. Tell them to be patient and wait for the library's Welcome Screen to appear.

CARL enables searchers to jump from one library to the next—Libraries of Middlesex in New Jersey to the Baltimore County Library in Maryland—with nothing but a keystroke. If at any time kids want to disconnect from one of these institutions, have them type **//exit** at the prompt and press ENTER. They should then get a message: You're now back at HOME. This will bring them back to the original site from which they started.

The search screen they'll be working with looks very similar to the one in UnCover. Kids will still use **n** for name searches and **w** for word searches. Here the browse feature, **b,** enables kids to browse by title, call number, or series name.

THE LIBRARY OF CONGRESS

In the fall of 1993, the Library of Congress announced the availability of a new online system called *LC MARVEL* (Library of Congress Machine-Assisted Realization of the Virtual Electronic Library). LC MARVEL made information about the library's activities and collections available free of charge to anyone with an Internet connection. LC MARVEL was built on a special Internet application called a *Gopher server*. This Gopher server still exists today, but it isn't kept up-to-date. If you'd like to explore this site and see what Gopher is all about, point your Web browser to *gopher://marvel.loc.gov/*.

The recommended method of connecting to the Library of Congress nowadays is via the Web. You can think of the home page as the main lobby of the Library of Congress. Imagine yourself standing in this main lobby looking around. You see doors leading to various rooms, each one with a sign above it telling you what's inside. One sign reads: *If you'd like to explore American Memory, enter here!* Another sign reads: *THOMAS: Legislative Information here!* And there are other signs that read: *Exhibitions, Library Services, What's New, General Information, Special Programs*, and *Research Tools*.

In this section, we briefly introduce you to some of the services beyond the main lobby. First, to get to the main lobby, point your browser to *lcweb.loc.gov*. The opening screen will look something like the one shown in Figure 13–2.

Figure 13–2 The Library of Congress Web Site

Services on the Library of Congress Web Site

The first room kids should visit is American Memory. The link to this service is located at the top of the home page. Here kids can find items relating to American history including documents, still images, sounds, and movies. If you would rather jump right to a special collection, you can click on one of the collections listed on the home page. On the day that we visited, there were Baseball Cards, 1887–1914; Buckaroos in Paradise: Folklife on a Nevada Cattle Ranch, 1945–1982; and more.

PUZZLE-SOLVING ADVENTURES

Another American Memory link, The Learning Page, may be of primary interest to parents and teachers, but there is one *Learning* link that kids are sure to enjoy. It's called *Historical Detective*. Kids (or adults!) are asked to solve a particular riddle or puzzle using resources and services provided by the Library of Congress online. Other links on The Learning Page include pathfinders for exploring the American Memory collections, links to the latest Feature Presentation, and an Educator's Page with lesson ideas.

THERE WERE 923,218 REQUESTS YESTERDAY!

A feature kids may find interesting under the General Information link is one called About the Library. When this page loads, look for a link labeled **The Library of Congress World Wide Web Site (LC Web)**. This is where usage statistics are stored. The Library of Congress tracks how many people connect to their system every day of the week and how many of their files are accessed. Then they list each file separately and tally how many times each file was accessed in a day. Another interesting feature is that the Library looks at the last two letters of each visitor's Internet address to see what country he or she is from. Then the library lists how many requests each country makes in a given period of time, from *ae* (United Arab Emirates) to *zw* (Zimbabwe).

Back when we wrote the first edition of this book in 1995, LC MARVEL had recorded about 38,000 files being downloaded on a single day. This time (1999) when we checked we were astounded to see that the average number of files being transmitted daily had risen to 923,218! Ask your kids what country they think logs the most visits to the Library of Congress and then ask them to come to this page to see if they were right.

WHEN IN THE COURSE OF HUMAN EVENTS . . .

In January 1995, under a directive of the 104th Congress, an online resource named Thomas came into existence. The first service it made available to the

Internet public was Bill Text. Since that time Thomas has grown to include all of the following services:

- Floor Activities in the House and Senate
- Latest House Floor Actions
- Bill Summary and Status
- Bill Text
- Votes
- Public Laws by Law Number
- Major Legislation
- Congressional Record Text and Index
- Resumes of Congressional Acitivity
- Committee Reports
- Committee Home Pages
- House Committees
- The Legislative Process and How Our Laws Are Made
- Enactment of a Law
- Historical documents collection that includes early congressional documents, *The Declaration of Independence*, *The Federalist Papers*, and *The Constitution*.

You can get to Thomas from the Library of Congress home page, or connect directly at *thomas.loc.gov*. Thomas enables you to search the text of Bills of the current Congress by bill number or by keyword and phrase.

Kids may continue browsing through the various rooms in the Library of Congress system, much in the same way they browsed the subject trees discussed in Chapter 12. There are so many choices, kids could easily spend months at this site alone. If kids are interested in exploring one of the Library's Internet resources pages, they will find links to Congressional Mega Sites, home pages for members of Congress, calendars, schedules, news and analysis, links to executive agencies and independent agencies, the judicial branch and law-related Internet sites, meta indexes for state and local government, and much more.

Library of Congress Information System

The earlier LC MARVEL system also provided a gateway for kids to connect with the Library of Congress Information System (LOCIS) using telnet. Starting at the original Gopher site *gopher://marvel.loc.gov/*, kids can still get to LOCIS by following the path: */Library of Congress Online Systems/Connect to LOCIS (Public Users—No Password Needed) <TEL>*. You can also telnet to LOCIS from the Library's home page on the Web. Click on the link called **Search the Catalogs**, and then find the link **Telnet to LOCIS**.

LOCIS represents more than 28 million records, including all books and other cataloged items, copyright files since 1978, federal bill statutes files, and public policy citations since 1976. The reference/retrieval system (SCORPIO) and the technical processing/cataloging system (MUMS) are also available. Searching hours are Monday-Friday, 24 hours a day; Saturday until 5:00 p.m.; and Sunday after 11:00 a.m.

While older kids may find it interesting to explore the catalog via telnet, younger kids won't find it as user-friendly as the research tools accessible via the Web site. When telneting in, the main menu appears as it is shown in Figure 13–3, and the Library of Congress Catalog menu appears as it is shown in Figure 13–4.

```
    L O C I S :  LIBRARY OF CONGRESS INFORMATION SYSTEM

       To make a choice: type a number, then press ENTER

 1   Library of Congress Catalog        4   Braille and Audio

 2   Federal Legislation                5   Foreign Law

 3   Copyright Information


 *    *    *    *    *    *    *    *    *    *    *    *

 7   Searching Hours and Basic Search Commands
 8   Documentation and Classes
 9   Library of Congress General Information
10   Library of Congress Fast Facts
11   * * Announcements * *

     The Organizations (NRCM) file is no longer created or supported by LC.
     It has been removed from LOCIS.

12   Comments and Logoff
     Choice:
```

Figure 13–3 Teleneting to the Library of Congress Information System Main Menu

```
1     BOOKS cataloged from 1898 to 1949                              LOC1
        (most older records are in PREM, option 4 below)
2     BOOKS cataloged from 1950 to 1974                              LOC2
3     BOOKS cataloged since 1975                                     LOC3

4     Older, incomplete, unedited BOOKS and SERIAL records for items PREM
        cataloged from 1898 to 1980.  These records are NOT repeated in
        LOC1, LOC2, LOC3 or LOCS.  This file also contains older records
        for maps, music, sound recordings and audiovisual materials.

5     SERIALS cataloged at LC & some other libraries                 LOCS
6     MAPS and other cartographic items                             LOCM
7     SUBJECT TERMS and cross-references from LC Subject Headings    LCXR

8     Multiple file search options  (except Sun-Fri, 9:30pm-6:30am US Eastern)
9     Multiple file search options  (Sun-Fri, 9:30pm-6:30am US Eastern)

To search LC's Music, AV, Manuscript, Computer Files & other catalog files,
sign on to any LOC file (choices 1-3, 5-6) and see HELP screens.

12    Return to LOCIS MENU screen
        Choice:
```

Figure 13–4 Telneting to the Library of Congress Catalog Menu

To search the Library of Congress catalog using the Web, go to the main page at *lcweb.loc.gov/* and click on the link called **Search the Catalogs**. Kids are then given the option of performing word searches and browse searches using the Web-based system. Again, the main purpose for kids accessing systems such as this is to search for items that they can later get from their local library or order through interlibrary loan.

RESOURCES

Listed here are several resources pointing you to online library catalogs and digital libraries.

- Library Information Servers via the WWW are listed at *sunsite.berkeley.edu/Libweb/*. Currently lists over 2,500 pages from libraries in over 70 countries.
- The New York Public Library's catalog is divided into two sections: CATNYP is the main catalog and LEO is the branch libraries' catalog. You can connect to both at *www.nypl.org/catalogs/catalogs.html*. Features catalogs, electronic resources, digital library collections, online bookstore, and links to events and exhibitions.
- Yahoo! maintains an alphabetical listing of university libraries ranging from Aalborg University (Denmark) to York University (UK); business libraries; digital libraries; health libraries; Native American libraries; science libraries; and many more. Check them out at *www.yahoo.com.* Follow the path */Reference/*Libraries/.
- Paul Coddington of Northeast Parallel Architectures Center at Syracuse University has put together a virtual library for kids called Kids Web: The Digital Library for K–12. You can access Kids Web at *www.npac.syr.edu/textbook/kidsweb/*.
- The Gopher Tree of Internet-Accessible Libraries, originally based on the data files from HYTELNET (*www.lights.com/hytelnet*), is a long list of library catalogs accessible on the Internet. Kids can either browse through menus where they see libraries arranged by geographical location, or they can locate specific libraries by searching a keyword index. To connect, to this Gopher site, type **gopher://libgopher.yale.edu** in your browser's location box.

The following list provides links to digital library projects.
- Victor is the online information system for the University of Maryland. It links to the catalog of the University of Maryland Libraries and other University System of Maryland libraries. You can reach this site at *www.lib.umd.edu/UMCP/*.
- The Yale University Library online catalog is made up of three systems, Orbis, Morris, and the Center for Research Libraries. You can connect by pointing your browser to *www.library.yale.edu/pubstation/workstat.html*.

- The Harvard Online Library Information System (HOLLIS) can be accessed via telnet. If you are running Windows 95, try typing **telnet:// hollis.harvard.edu** in your browser's location box. If this doesn't connect you, see Chapter 17 for assistance.
- The University of Texas online library catalog contains records for more than six million items. You can connect to their system named UTNetCAT via the Web at *www.lib.utexas.edu/utcat.html* or via telnet at *utcat.utexas.edu*.
- MIRLYN (Michigan Research LibrarY Network) is the online library catalog of the University of Michigan. Look for the Guest Signon button on their Web site at *mirlyn.web.lib.umich.edu:80/*. This links you to the library catalogs and index databases which include free access to ERIC, Africana, and RELICS (Renaissance Liturgical Imprints Census) indexes.
- Librarians Information Online Network (LION) is a source of information for K–12 school librarians. Resources are listed alphabetically and range from information on automation systems for school libraries to Young Adult Librarian's Help.

If your kids are interested in more than just author and title searching, try sending them to some library Web sites that have value-added services just for kids and teens. Here are a few to explore:

- The *Youth Page* and *YA Web* at the Canton Public Library, Canton, Michigan (*www.metronet.lib.mi.us/canton/*)
- Mt. Laurel Hartford School's Library without Walls (*www.voicenet.com/ ~srussell/student.html*)
- Naples High School Library Media Center (*www.se.mediaone.net/~nhslmc/*).
- Henderson Hall Library, St. Andrews School (*www.saint.andrews.pvt.k12. fl.us/lib/Newlib.htm*)
- Stetson Middle School Library (*www.voicenet.com/~bertland/index.html*.

Chapter 14

Browsing Virtual
Bookstores

Besides being a platform for publishing personal home pages and links organized by subject, the Internet is a great place for making electronic books, magazines, and newspapers available. Some are free, and some are available for a fee. Some are distributed as a single item by the author, and others are stocked in virtual bookstores, newsstands, and cyberlibraries.

In this chapter, we begin with a brief discussion on intellectual property rights and other matters relating to the dissemination of electronic documents. It is important for kids to begin thinking about intellectual property rights on the Internet and to be familiar with the exclusive rights held by copyright owners.

Kids writing research papers and reports need to know how to cite information that they find on the Internet. To assist kids in this area, we present a section on citing electronic resources according to the APA and MLA styles.

In the balance of the chapter we present several places where kids can go to browse electronic newspapers and magazines online, purchase their favorite books, and download electronic books for free.

THE IMPORTANCE OF INTELLECTUAL PROPERTY RIGHTS

Although most Internet users believe in the free flow of information, questions have been raised about the importance of copyright protection and how it applies in a network environment. For some people, producing information is a livelihood and they take risks and invest time and money to produce their information. If their intellectual property rights go unprotected on the Internet, they will be less likely to contribute. They believe that it's just as important in a network environment to preserve the protections that copyright affords as it is in a traditional print environment.

Many Internet users, especially in the field of education, make their information freely available and grant unlimited redistribution of their works over the Internet. Their main interest is in distributing their work and the personal recognition that results. Due to an increasing amount of unauthorized modifications and reproductions without proper credit, many of these authors are now attaching a notice to their electronic newsletters and magazines with the proviso that they be redistributed in full, without modification, and with proper credit given to the author.

Copyright Information

Under current copyright law, the moment a work is created, it is copyrighted even if it is distributed without a copyright notice. (Exceptions are works created by the Federal Government or when the owner of a work expressly states that it is dedicated to the public domain.) To prevent people from making a false assumption that a work is public domain, it makes sense for anyone claiming copyright protection to include the notice: *Copyright 1999 by <insert the copyright holder's name>*.

Exclusive Rights of Copyright Owners

To better understand the impact of computer and communications technology on the creation, reproduction, and distribution of copyrighted books, magazines, and newspapers in a network environment, it is important to understand the exclusive rights currently granted to copyright holders in Section 106 of the copyright law:

- to reproduce the copyrighted work in copies or phonorecords;
- to prepare derivative works based upon the copyrighted work;
- to distribute copies or phonorecords of the copyrighted work to the public by sale or other transfer of ownership, or by rental, lease, or lending;
- in the case of literary, musical, dramatic, and choreographic works, pantomimes, and motion pictures and other audiovisual works, to perform the copyrighted work publicly; and
- in the case of literary, musical, dramatic, and choreographic works, pantomimes, and pictorial, graphic, or sculptural works, including the individual images of a motion picture or other audiovisual work, to display the copyrighted work publicly.

When kids use computers to access electronic books and magazines and other online services, unless authorized or specifically exempt, infringement of the reproduction right can occur, for example, when

- a printed work is scanned into a digital file;

- a digital file is uploaded to a server or downloaded from a server;
- a digital file is transferred from one computer to another;
- an e-mail message posted to a mailing list is captured to a disk.

Online resources relating to copyright are listed at the end of this chapter.

CITING ELECTRONIC SOURCES

Citing sources found on the Internet differs greatly from citing print sources. Two of the better-known style manuals, APA and MLA, are adapting their citation examples to include electronic sources, but they face some interesting challenges. For example, how can kids cite e-mail they receive from a discussion list if the e-mail isn't collected and archived in a permanent location? How can a permanent citation be created for an online resource that changes its location and content? What about listing page numbers? When kids use the print version of magazines they can easily see page numbers. When they use full-text online resources, page numbers are not always included. These concerns should be addressed over time as citation methods evolve.

If teachers ask your kids to use MLA format when citing sources in their research papers, your kids should consult *MLA Handbook for Writers of Research Papers*, 4th edition, by Joseph Gibaldi. This manual covers citing electronic sources, portable and online, in section 4.9. The fifth edition of the *MLA Handbook* is scheduled for release in June 1999 and will include all of the latest recommendations for citing online sources. The only citation examples authorized by MLA that can be found on the Web are those found on MLA's Web site at *www.mla.org*. Look for the link labeled **MLA Style** for tips on citing sources your kids find on the Web. Nancy Crane at the University of Vermont offers additional examples of citing electronic sources in the MLA style at *www.uvm.edu/~ncrane/estyles/mla.html*.

If APA is your kids' style of choice, have them consult the *Publication Manual of the American Psychological Association*, 4th edition. This edition, published in 1994, may be somewhat dated with regard to citing electronic sources. In *Web Extension to American Psychological Association Style* (WEAPAS), T. Land presents some alternatives for citing online resources. While Land hasn't had time to create any specific examples on his Web page, you can learn something by reading through the references listed at the end of a proposed standard published at *www.beadsland.com/weapas/*.

The American Psychological Association offers examples of citing electronic sources on their Web site at *www.apa.org/journals/webref.html*. Nancy Crane also offers examples of APA style citations at *www.uvm.edu/~ncrane/estyles/apa.html*.

Andrew Harnack and Eugene Kepplinger, authors of *Online: A Reference Guide to Using Internet Sources*, took some of the information contained in their book and made it available online at *www.smpcollege.com/online-4styles~help/*.

This is a good source if you're looking for examples beyond MLA and APA. Harnack and Kepplinger include *The Chicago Manual of Style* and *The CBE Manual for Authors, Editors, and Publishers* published by the Council of Biology Editors in 1994. The *Chicago Manual* doesn't cover Internet-based resources, but Harnack and Kepplinger make recommendations on how to adapt the *Chicago Manual's* guidelines to Internet sources.

In the following section, we introduce you to examples of electronic publications that are available free of charge. If you or your kids would like to discover more, submit a search using one of the Web search engines listed in Chapter 12 (and keywords such as *newspaper*, *magazine*, *zine*, *ezine*, *ejournals*, *etext*, etc.).

THE NEWSPAPER BIZ

AJR NewsLink at *www.newslink.org/* is a comprehensive guide to more than 9,000 online newspapers, magazines, broadcasters, and news services worldwide. AJR NewsLink combines features from the *American Journalism Review* magazine with original content and publication lists of NewsLink Associates. Kids should go here if they want to read online U.S. dailies. Each state has at least one full-service daily that can be accessed from AJR NewsLink.

AJR NewsLink, pictured in Figure 14–1, also links to alternative newspapers—newspapers that write about the arts, counterculture, or non-mainstream news. They even link to specialty newspapers like the *Navajo Hopi Observer* out of Flagstaff, Arizona, and Delaware's *Delaware Beachcomber and Coast Press*. When you link to a newspaper called *Asian Pages*, you hear traditional Asian music in the background, assuming you have a sound card and speakers. From *Asian Pages* you can hopscotch to the Hmong Homepage or Asian Studies Virtual Library.

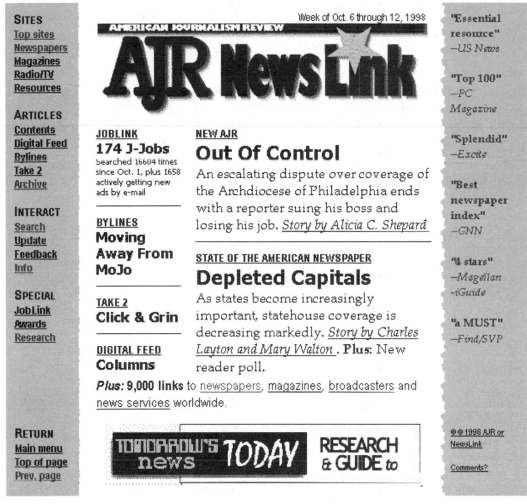

Figure 14–1 AJR NewsLink is a good source to go to for daily newspapers all around the United States. (Reprinted by permission of *American Journalism Review* and Newslink Associates.)

The last day we visited AJR NewsLink, readers had rated daily news that they thought deserved to be in a Top Ten list. These are the titles that were listed, along with their Web site addresses:

1. New York Times   *www.nytimes.com*
2. USA Today   *www.usatoday.com*
3. CNN Interactive   *www.cnn.com*
4. Washington Post   *www.washingtonpost.com*
5. Los Angeles Times   *www.latimes.com*
6. Jerusalem Post   *www.jpost.co.il/*
7. Times of London   *www.the-times.co.uk*
8. New Jersey Online   *www.njo.com*
9. Washington Times   *www.washtimes.com*
10. Philadelphia Inquirer *www.phillynews.com*

K–12 Newspapers on the Net

Students around the United States are publishing their school newspapers and student newsletters on the Web. One of the best listings for these publications is maintained by Yahoo! at *www.yahoo.com/*. Follow this path: **News** and **Media|Newspapers|K–12**. In our first edition we introduced you to *The Arrow*, the official newspaper of Flathead High School in Kalispell, Montana. It's still there, going strong. So is the *Chatterbox*, published by Walnut Hills High School in Cincinnati, Ohio, and the Berkeley High School *Jacket*, and many more. Yahoo! lists titles accompanied by short descriptions, so you have to dig deeper if you want to learn more about individual papers.

Searching Newspapers for Free

Electric Library, a product of Infonautics Corporation, doesn't let you access their full-text articles without paying, but you can search their indexes for free. If you point your browser to *www.elibrary.com* you'll see what we mean. When you arrive at Electric Library, you see a screen similar to the one shown in Figure 14–2 where we entered the search terms **earthquake in L.A.**

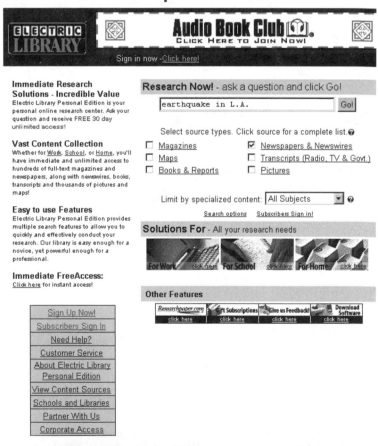

Figure 14–2 Electric Library is a commercial full-text database that offers free index searching.

Electric Library enables you to select source types. For example, in the search we ran on earthquakes in L.A., we limited our format to newspapers and newswires. We did this by placing a check mark in the box next to the phrase *Newspapers & Newswires*. When we ran our search, we got 30 hits. Each citation provided a title, score (relevancy rating with 100 being the highest score), source, author, date, size of text file, and the reading level. Once you run a search, Electric Library can provide you with a list of books from Barnes & Noble (*www.barnesandnoble.com*), and a list of related Internet sites.

A News Service for Kids!

KidNews, shown in Figure 14–3, was rated in the top 5 percent of all sites on the Internet by Point Survey, a Web rating service, back when we wrote the first edition of *Connecting Kids and the Internet*. KidNews is still around, but no longer collecting news from kids. Like many of the free Internet services that experienced success, KidNews wasn't able to continue their high quality site and process the large number of submissions they received without some kind of financial support.

What's  : Take an extra look at Sports, News, Reviews, Features, and Creative for a slew of new material. The power of the internet is amazing! This week there was a poem submitted all the way from Saudi Arabia and the kids from Brazil have been flooding my mailbox like crazy. Way to go! Check out the second edition of the Cool Carnegie Kids PenPal Magazine in the Goodies section, they are very excited to hear from you! Just a reminder, when you send an email looking for a penpal ask your parents make sure your email address accepts incoming mail, especially on AOL. Don't forget that KidNews doesn't post e-mail addresses without a permission form. Happy Writing!

Word of the Week!

```
New! Check back each week for a new word!
    Have fun and Happy Writing!
```

[Next] [Previous] [Random]

Welcome to KidNews!

Kids' Writing from practically everywhere

News | Features | Kids Talk | Creative Writing | Profiles and Quick Hellos | Reviews | Sports | Submit Writing | Goodies | Adults Talk | Cool Hangouts | Winners

KidNews Help and Info |Prizes and Awards | The Rules | Finding my writing | About PenPals | Note to Teachers| Sending Mulitple Submissions to KidNews

Copyright 1995, 1996, 1997, 1998, 1999 Elaine Floyd, Publisher, KidNews

Publisher: Elaine Floyd of Newsletter Resources. Elaine is the author of seven books on Newsletters including Creating Family Newsletters.

Managing Editor: Tara Davis,University of Massachusetts Dartmouth

Editorial Consultant and Founder, Dr.Peter Owens, University of Massachusetts Dartmouth

Thanks To: Kurt Cabral
Graphics: Christine Pillsbury

Comments to KidNews

KidNews pages are continuously revised and updated.

KidNews is a member of NESPA, the National Elementary Schools Press Association.

Figure 14–3 KidNews is a collection of kids' writings compiled over a four-year span.

KidNews was a worldwide news service for kids and teachers pioneered by Dr. Peter Owens of the University of Massachusetts Dartmouth English Department. It provided discussion sections for students and teachers to talk about topics concerning gathering the news, teaching, and computers in online publishing. There is something interesting to learn by visiting KidNews at *www.kidnews.com/* where you can still read all of the kids' writings that were collected. If you or your kids have interests similar to Dr. Owens's, KidNews can serve as a model for you in building a similar news site in the future.

Newspaper Archives

The News Division of the Special Libraries Association maintains a Web site called U.S. News Archives on the Web at *sunsite.unc.edu/slanews/internet/ archives.html*. Here kids can browse newspaper archives by state and also non–U.S. newspaper archives. The creators of this Web site tell you where to find the newspaper's home page, its archive site, holdings, and what the cost is to retrieve the full text of articles.

Registering with Highwired.Net

Before leaving the world of online newspapers, we want to introduce young journalists to an online publishing system for high schools. The service is called Highwired.Net and it prides itself on helping kids build the same skills required for traditional newspaper writing. Kids and teachers don't have to learn HTML code or learn special programs. Everything they need is on Highwired.Net's Web site.

To find out how it works, go to *www.highwired.net* and click on the link labeled **Publish a Test Story**. Follow the instructions at the top of each page and take an interactive tour of the process. You can write an article, attach an image, edit your piece, and then publish it and see it online, all in a matter of minutes. One unique feature of Highwired.Net is the ability to select stories from a national pool of other Highwired.Net papers and attach them to your own paper.

Highwired.Net is free and registration is easy. To join the network, you have to fill out an online form providing information about your school, contacts' names, advisor information, and a name for your paper. The paper is supported through sponsors. Because of the nature of this service, sponsors are screened carefully.

THE WORLD OF E-ZINES

E-zines are online magazines that range in scope from the esoteric and bizarre like *Hi-Rez: Electronic Journal for CyberBeatniks* to more mainstream e-zines like *The Amateur Computerist*. *Zines*, which were first introduced back in the '70s, are small, informal pulp publications. Generally they're created by one person and they're distributed free of charge or for a nominal fee. Many thousands of zines currently exist, and each one focuses on a particular area of interest. Some are in print format (zines) and others are in digital form (e-zines).

SPECIAL OFFER: Get the BOZ and a few random zines for $8
Newly updated: How to Publicize Your E-Zine
Newly added: Free-For-All Links page

An Owl Book from Henry Holt and Company, Inc.
Edited by Chip Rowe

One of Amazon.com's Top 10 Pop Culture Books of 1997

-- QuickNav --

[What's a Zine?] [Resource Guide] [Raw Material]
[Roll Your Own] [Contact Chip] [Purchase] [Awards]

LE   35852

Figure 14–4 *The Book of Zines* is a pulp magazine and an online
zine resource guide.

Zine resources on the Net are many and varied. *Unk! E-Zines* at *ccwf.cc.utexas. edu/~meburns/UNK/zine.html* links you to monosyllabic e-zines only. *The Book of Zines: Readings from the Fringe* is both a pulp magazine and a Web site reachable at *www.zinebook.com*. You can buy the book by sending $10 ($13 overseas) to Chip Rose at The Book of Zines, Web Page Offer, P.O. Box 11967, Chicago, IL 60611, or you can purchase it using a credit card at *www.amazon.com*. *The Book of Zines'* companion site on the Web, shown in Figure 14–4, offers a rich source of materials on zine and e-zine culture, history, archives, interviews with more than 60 zine editors, a how to do your own guide, and more.

EZines at *www.dominis.com/Zines/* offers lots of services, including a browsable list of zines organized by subject, the ability to search the database, links to e-zines, e-zine book store, ZINE-TALK, top zine lists, and more. One of the best, longest standing e-zine sites (since 1993!) on the Web is run by John Labovitz.

The Labovitz List

John Labovitz maintains a directory of 2,537 e-zines located around the world that can be accessed via the Web, Gopher, FTP, e-mail (sometimes referred to as low bandwidth zines), and other services. The list is updated monthly.

Each entry provides a short description of the zine, its format, frequency, and how it can be accessed. A complete alphabetical listing by title and keyword index is available for browsing at his Web site *www.meer.net/~johnl/e-zine-list/*.

ONLINE MAGAZINES FOR KIDS

When we first wrote *Connecting Kids and the Internet*, online magazines were a unique class of electronic publications that stood by themselves. Some were original, but most were online counterparts of traditional print publications. Some of the better-known traditional titles include:

- *Sports Illustrated for Kids* at *www.sikids.com/index.html*
- *Time for Kids* at *www.pathfinder.com/@@dnH@ygYA8@POBBGg/TFK/*
- *Owl* magazine's online counterpart *Wired OWL* for kids eight and over at *www.owl.on.ca*
- *Chickadee* magazine's *Chickadee Net* for kids aged 6 to 9 at *www.owl.on.ca/ chick/chick.html*
- *Chirp* for preschoolers 2 to 6 found at *www.owl.on.ca/chirp/crpsub.html*
- *YES Mag: Canada's Science Magazine for Kids* at *www.yesmag.bc.ca*
- *Tomorrow's Morning: News Stories for Kids* publishes an Internet edition at *morning.com*
- *Stone Soup*, the magazine by young writers and artists, has a home on the Web at *www.stonesoup.com* (see Figure 14–5).

Stone Soup
the magazine by young writers and artists

CURIOUS ELEANOR
A young elephant comes of age in the African savanna.

FEELINGS OF LOVE, MIRACLES OF MAGIC
Can a beautiful Aladdin's enchanted bring Jenny and her father together again?

Also: Illustrations by Erik Weinmann and Michael McGovern, Jr.
A review of a book about a famous sheep woman
A poem celebrating spring rain

25th Anniversary 1973–1998

The beautiful magazine by young writers and artists!

Stone Soup is the international magazine for the home, school, and library. Written and illustrated by young people ages 8 to 13, it inspires young readers and writers everywhere. **Stone Soup** is a great reason to use the World Wide Web! Subscribe, read the issues, and follow the ● links!

● See what's in a <u>sample issue</u>!
● Visit the Stone Soup <u>store</u>!
● Read about our <u>philosophy</u>!
● Parenting Magazine <u>gives us an A+</u>!

Figure 14–5 *Stone Soup* is illustrated and written by kids ages 8 to 13 and edited by Gerry Mandel and William Rubel.

As the Internet evolves, the line that distinguishes online magazines from e-zines, and e-zines from "entertainment" sites has blurred. Magazines like *ABC Kids Gazette* at *www.eint.com/abagain/* is a mixture of resources including poems, jokes, reviews, cool links, and stories. They even offer instructions for making fossils.

A kids' magazine called *Colgate's No Cavities Clubhouse* welcomes you with a message, "Hi <your name>! Welcome to Dr. Rabbit's No Cavities Clubhouse! Here are the exciting things waiting for you:" When kids link to *www.colgate.com/Kids-world/index.html*, they can play Connect the Dots, play a jungle game where they search for healthy snacks, visit the tooth fairy, and play Toothman and save the teeth from the Plaque Monster.

One of the best all-around sources for launching an exploration of kids online magazines is Yahoo!'s magazine site at *www.yahoo.com/Society and Culture/Cultures and Groups/Children/Magazines*. Here kids will find links to a wide variety of magazines like *HiPMag Online*, a magazine for deaf and hard-of-hearing kids, and *The Looking Glass Gazette*, which publishes kids' writing and artwork.

CyberKids, *MidLink Magazine*, and *KidzMagazine* are still around. *CyberKids* is a free online magazine for kids created mostly by kids. It contains stories, artwork, puzzles, and more. To view a copy online, go to *www.cyberkids.com*. At the bottom of Cyberkids' home page, there is a link that connects you to Cyberteens, or you can go there directly by pointing your browser to *www.cyberteens.com/ctmain.html*.

MidLink Magazine is an electronic magazine for kids in the middle grades. Features include COOL Schools, Search Tools, Best Web Sites, Teacher Resources and MidLink Archives. You can find *MidLink Magazine* at *longwood.cs.ucf.edu/~MidLink/*. Since we wrote the first edition of this book, MidLink has added a link for kids in the upper grades called *Secondary Roads*. Featured are articles written by older students and introductions to Internet resources for kids ages 16–19.

KidzMagazine, shown in Figure 14–6, was started back in 1995 by 13–year-old home-schooled Zen Zenith. It includes articles, reviews, and stories all written by kids. You can subscribe via e-mail or by going to KidzMagazine Web site at *www.thetemple.com/KidzMagazine/*.

You're at KidzMagazine!

The only web site made **completely** by kids, for kids! You'll find articles, reviews, previews, stories, and more within KidzMagazine and we're adding more all the time! Remember: These pages are best viewed with Netscape 2.0 or higher, so if you don't have it, get it here!

 To Do List

Take a look at KM's "To Do" list. Things coming to KM in the future!

Music Stop

Another brand new section to KidzMagazine run by, KM's Assistant Editor, Becca. Reviews and Previews of music and more!

 **DYNAMITE SITE OF THE NITE**

On June 19th, KidzMagazine was chosen as Dynamite Site of the Nite (Also known as DSotN). You can check

Figure 14–6 *KidzMagazine* is an online magazine written by kids for kids.

Notes from the Windowsill (formerly *The WEB Online Review*) reviews new and reprinted children's (all ages) books for parents, educators, and children's literature enthusiasts. To subscribe, send an e-mail message to *kidsbooks@ armory.com* including your full e-mail address in the body of the message. Back issues are available via FTP *ftp.armory.com* in the directory */pub/user/web* and on the Web at *www.armory.com/~web/notes.html*.

E-TEXTS

The term *e-texts* is short for electronic texts or books. Generally speaking, e-texts are books that have been converted from print format to digital format. Sometimes this term is used more broadly to describe any electronic publication ranging from zines to essays and mailing list archives to books. In this section we introduce you to Project Gutenberg and The On-Line Books Page, two of the better-known electronic text archives on the Net.

Project Gutenberg

Michael Hart's Project Gutenberg is an online database that contains hundreds of full-text e-texts. Many of the works included in this collection are books written prior to 1920. Titles already released by Project Gutenberg include classics like *A Christmas Carol, Red Badge of Courage, Alice's Adventures in Wonderland, The Scarlet Letter, The War of the Worlds*, and *Aladdin and the Wonderful Lamp*. To view these and more, point your browser to the official Project Gutenberg Web site at *www.promo.net/pg/*.

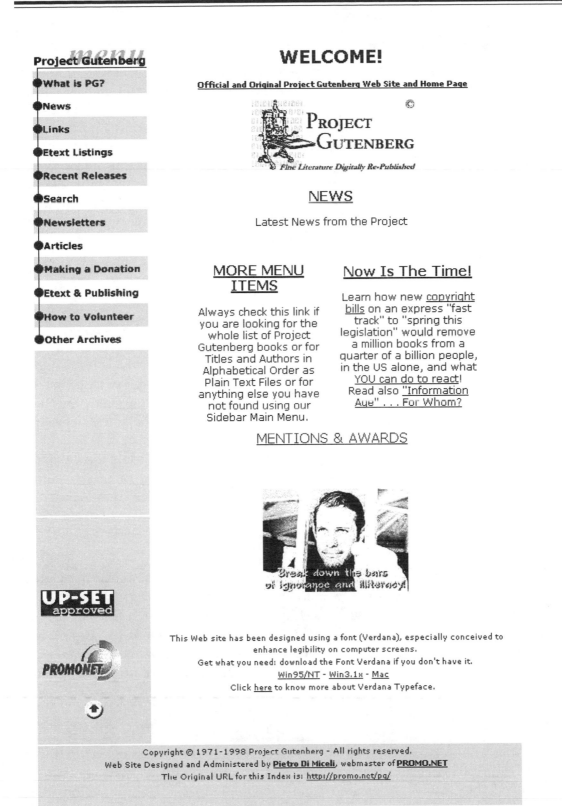

Project Gutenberg

- What is PG?
- News
- Links
- Etext Listings
- Recent Releases
- Search
- Newsletters
- Articles
- Making a Donation
- Etext & Publishing
- How to Volunteer
- Other Archives

UP-SET approved

PROMONET

WELCOME!

Official and Original Project Gutenberg Web Site and Home Page

PROJECT GUTENBERG
© Fine Literature Digitally Re-Published

NEWS

Latest News from the Project

MORE MENU ITEMS

Always check this link if you are looking for the whole list of Project Gutenberg books or for Titles and Authors in Alphabetical Order as Plain Text Files or for anything else you have not found using our Sidebar Main Menu.

Now Is The Time!

Learn how new copyright bills on an express "fast track" to "spring this legislation" would remove a million books from a quarter of a billion people, in the US alone, and what YOU can do to react! Read also "Information Age" . . . For Whom?

MENTIONS & AWARDS

Break down the bars of ignorance and illiteracy!

This Web site has been designed using a font (Verdana), especially conceived to enhance legibility on computer screens.
Get what you need: download the Font Verdana if you don't have it.
Win95/NT - Win3.1x - Mac
Click here to know more about Verdana Typeface.

Figure 14–7 Project Gutenberg began when Michael Hart entered the *Declaration of Independence* into a computer and posted it as electronic text.

The On-Line Books Page

The On-Line Books Page at *www.cs.cmu.edu/People/spok/aboutolbp.html* provides access to thousands of books that can be read right on the Internet. Founded by John Mark Ockerbloom in 1993, The On-Line Books Page only indexes books that are free to read, written in English, and preferably stored in a portable format, such as HTML or plain ASCII text.

Beginning in 1988, The On-Line Books Page started indexing major serials archives. Listings in this index follow these criteria: The collections must be accessible at no charge; they must be significant titles carried by major libraries; they must be high-quality, easily readable transcriptions; they must be permanent collections; and they must include the text of all articles in an issue, not just the tables of contents.

BOOKSTORES

Hundreds of booksellers are currently on the Internet. One of the more complete lists organized by subject is maintained by BookWire at *www.bookwire.com/index/booksellers.html*. Acses at *www.acses.com* offers a search engine that enables you to search out the best book prices, availability, shipping times, and shipping costs at over 25 online bookstores. You can search by title, author, keyword, or ISBN (International Standard Book Number).

Most online bookstores offer the same basic services, including a database of book listings, some interesting links, and the means for making purchases online. Some online bookstores, like amazon.com, offer special services that make them unique among the rest.

AMAZON.COM

Amazon.com at *www.amazon.com* is a bookseller that's a cut above the rest. It not only sells books, it offers tools for browsing and searching its collection of over three million titles. Their Kids! Link enables you to search titles by age: 0–3, 4–8, 9–12, and young adult. The Amazing Gift Gadget helps you explore gift ideas for kids. When you sign up for Amazon.com Delivers, you receive e-mail with recommendations for children's books, young adult, parenting and families, and children's music.

INTERTAIN.COM

Intertain.com is a general bookstore with a large children's catalog. It also offers a list of bestsellers and new releases that are updated weekly. When we last checked their home page, their catalog contained 62,431 adult fiction titles, 244,432 adult nonfiction titles, and 69,098 titles for children. Users can browse the Intertain.com catalog by subject or search by author, title, or keyword. You can explore this Web-based bookstore by connecting to *intertain.com/store/welcome.html*.

EXPLORING CHILDREN'S LITERATURE ON THE NET

Show your kids how exciting the world of literature can be when explored through a multimedia environment like the Net.

- By connecting to Yahoo! at *www.yahoo.com*, teachers and parents can enjoy exploring with their kids home pages that focus on authors such as C. S. Lewis, Mark Twain, and Dr. Seuss and fairy tales and folktales like Cinderella Stories and Aesop's Fables. You can begin your explorations by following this path beginning at the home page: **Arts & Humanities|Humanities| Literature|Genres|Children's**.
- Older kids might enjoy checking out Alan Liu's home page *Voice of the Shuttle*, which links to an extensive page of English literature resources. Point the kids in the direction of *humanitas.ucsb.edu/shuttle/english.html*.
- David K. Brown has put together a Web page at *www.acs.ucalgary.ca/ ~dkbrown/index.html* called *Children's Literature Web Guide* that includes the following resources and services:
  —What's New!
  —What We're Reading: Commentary on Children's Books
  —Web-Traveller's Toolkit: Essential Kid Lit Websites
  —Two discussion boards: Readers Helping Readers and Conference Bulletin Board
  —Children's Book Awards
  —Children's Bestsellers
  —Teaching ideas for children's books
  —Lots of Lists: Recommended Books and Bestsellers
  —Journals and Book Reviews
  —Resources for Parents
  —Resources for Teachers
  —Resources for Storytellers
  —Resources for Writers and Illustrators
  —Digging Deeper: Research Guides and Indexes
  —Children's Literature Associations on the Internet
  —Children's Publishers and Booksellers on the Internet
- Bestselling children's books from *Publishers Weekly* are updated every month at Web site *www.bookwire.com/pw/bsl/bestseller-index.html*, and Dial-A-Book at *dab.psi.net/* offers a link to the American Library Association Children's Newbery Award Winners. Here kids can read the first chapter of selected titles.
- The Dr. Seuss home page at *klinzhai.iuma.com/~drseuss/seuss/* offers a biography of Theodor Seuss Geisel, a list of Dr. Seuss books and videos and where to buy them, a link called *Dr. Seuss goes to the movies*, and other Dr. Seuss links.

RESOURCES

The Electronic Newsstand at *www.enews.com* is one of the largest collections of commercial magazines on the Web. It provides you with links of over 2,000 magazine sites and enables you to place online orders for many titles. The collection can be accessed by browsing or searching. Check out their *Kids and Family* section.

The Association of Research Libraries at *arl.cni.org/scomm/edir/* publishes *The Directory of Electronic Journals, Newsletters and Academic Discussion Lists* in both print format and digital format. The electronic version, currently in its seventh edition, offers access to over 7,000 listings of journals, newsletters, zines, and professional e-conferences accessible via the Internet.

The E-text Archive at the Well (Whole Earth Lectronic Link) offers links to information on authors, book sellers, poetry, zines, and much more. Point your browser to their Gopher server at *gopher://gopher.well.sf.ca.us/*, and at the main menu choose the item that reads **Authors, Books, Periodicals, Zines (Factsheet Five lives here!).** The Well is a commercial conferencing system headquartered in Sausalito, California.

Chapter 15

Serious Research Sites

In Chapter 15 we introduce you to some of the best, time-tested information resources on the Internet. Each resource meets certain, basic criteria. It must be free, searchable, and selective and include abstract or full-text information. By selective we mean that a human has had to go through and do some research, hand selecting, and filtering rather than indiscriminately stringing together Web site addresses with nothing but interesting titles.

Chapter 15 also includes self-study guides that teach valuable Internet lessons that cover how to download, install, and run telnet programs that enable kids to visit online libraries; how to capture images and create help sheets; how to research Medscape's medical database; how to find and download files on the Internet; and how to view images using Gopher.

Chapter 15 concludes with information on how to cite electronic resources in research papers.

The list in Table 15–1 provides you with a summary of the resources and their corresponding addresses described in this chapter. Resource descriptions include the following information:

- resource name
- cost
- location
- description
- when to use
- search strategies
- sample searches

> **Table 15–1** Serious Research Sites
>
> | Resource Name | Resource Address |
> | --- | --- |
> | Alex Catalog of Electronic Texts | www.lib.ncsu.edu/staff/morgan/alex alex-index.html |
> | Atlantic Unbound | www.theatlantic.com/ |
> | CancerNet | cancernet.nci.nih.gov/ |
> | eBlast | www.ebig.com/index.html |
> | Inference | www.inference.com/infind/ |
> | Infomine | lib-www.ucr.edu/Main.html |
> | Information Please | www.infoplease.com/ |
> | The Librarian's Index to the Internet | sunsite.berkeley.edu/InternetIndex/ex/ |
> | The Librarian's Guide to the Internet | www.star-host.com/library/ |
> | Medscape | www.medscape.com |
> | My Virtual Reference Desk | www.refdesk.com/ |
> | National Geographic | www.nationalgeographic.com/kids/ |
> | Researchpaper.com | www.researchpaper.com |
> | Thomas Register of American Manufacturers | www.thomasregister.com/ |
> | ZDNet | www.zdnet.com/ |

RESOURCE NAME: Alex Catalog of Electronic Texts (see Figure 15–1)

RESOURCE LOCATION: *www.lib.ncsu.edu/staff/morgan/alex/alex-index.html*
ABOUT: Alex is a catalog of electronic texts that contains about 2,000 entries. Originally conceived by Hunter Monroe in 1993–94, the collection includes English literature, American literature, and Western philosophy.
WHEN TO USE: When you desire the full text of a particular piece of English literature, American literature, or Western philosophy. Kids should plan ahead and do their searching when they have extra time to spare. The Gopher server has lots of problems retrieving files and running searches.
SEARCH STRATEGIES: You can run searches from the first screen, but this does not link you directly to the full text documents. You can also link to the Gopher server from this first screen and browse Author, Date, Host, Language, Subject, and Title indexes. (The Host index consists of a list of electronic archives where works are housed on the Internet.) Click on the link labeled *sunsite.berkeley.edu/alex/* to do your searching. Search results are linked to the full-text files.
TRY THIS: Go to the search screen at *sunsite.berkeley.edu/alex/* and search on the keywords **tom sawyer**. In the Search Results screen, look for the title: The Adventures of Tom Sawyer. In the **Locations:** field, click on the link labeled **Original** to download the full-text document.

Home | About | Search the catalogue | Downloads | Comments

Catalogue of
Electronic Texts

WELCOME!

*This is the Alex Catalogue of Electronic texts, a collection of digital documents collected in the subject areas of English literature, American literature, and Western philosophy. Please read the **about statement** to learn more about the scope, purpose, and unique features of the Catalogue.*

SEARCH
OR
BROWSE

Search for documents in the Catalogue with the form below or use the full-featured interface:

[   ] [Search]

Context-sensitive help

Alternatively, you can browse the collection via the following links:

- authors
- titles
- file name

A list of other electronic text collections is also available.

The older version of the Alex Catalogue, now called Alex Classic, is still available.

Home | About | Search the catalogue | Downloads | Comments

Version: 1.0 (See the release notes.)
Author: Eric Lease Morgan (eric_morgan@ncsu.edu)
URL: http://sunsite.berkeley.edu/alex/

Figure 15–1 Alex Catalog of Electronic Texts

RESOURCE NAME: Atlantic Unbound (see Figure 15–2)
RESOURCE LOCATION: *www.theatlantic.com/*
ABOUT: Atlantic Unbound is an offspring of *The Atlantic Monthly*. It contains full-text articles covering Web-only features, Poetry Pages, and Flashbacks.
WHEN TO USE: If kids are looking for collections of full-text articles on social issues, this is a worthwhile site to explore. Go to *www.theatlantic.com/election/ connection/index.htm* and browse articles from *The Atlantic Monthly's* archive and related links on these topics:

Abortion|Budget|Congress|Crime|Defense|Economics|
Education|Environment|Family|Foreign Policy|Health Care
|Immigration|Politics|Poverty|Race|Religion

SEARCH STRATEGIES: Hits are ranked according to relevancy. Three databases are searched, including select articles from *The Atlantic Monthly*, *Atlantic Unbound*, and *Political Resources Index*. The search engine supports Boolean AND, OR, and NOT. Use * for truncation at end of a word. If you include common terms in a phrase, you may yield no results.
TRY THIS: Search for articles on the dangers of space junk; browse through articles pertaining to environment.

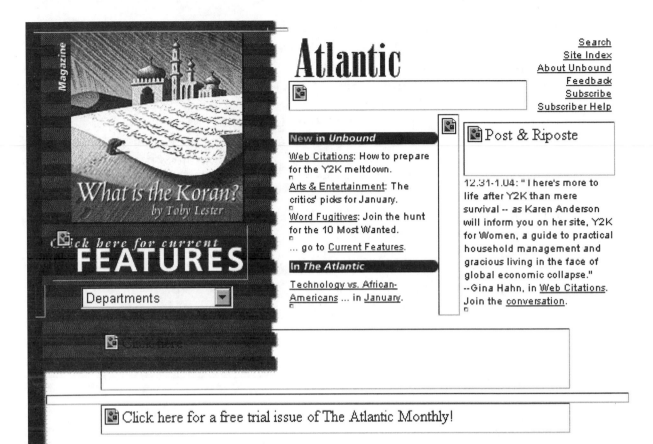

Figure 15–2 Atlantic Unbound

RESOURCE NAME: CancerNet (see Figure 15–3)
RESOURCE LOCATION: *cancernet.nci.nih.gov/*
ABOUT: CancerNet is a prime resource for credible information on cancer from the National Cancer Institute (NCI). Data is reviewed by oncology experts and updated monthly with the latest research. CancerNet provides access to peer-reviewed summaries on cancer treatment, screening, prevention, and supportive care; a registry of about 1,600 open and 9,500 closed cancer clinical trials from around the world; and directories of physicians, genetic counselors, and organizations that provide cancer care.
WHEN TO USE: Kids should search CancerNet when they need summaries on treatments of cancer; information on screening, prevention, or supportive care; or information on ongoing clinical trials.
SEARCH STRATEGIES: CancerNet offers these basic services:

1. A cancer database called PDQ that contains peer-reviewed summaries of treatment, supportive care, screening, and prevention; and a directory of physicians.
2. Fact sheets on cancer treatment, detection, screening, prevention, rehabilitation, and quality of life issues.
3. Information on clinical trials.
4. Selected information from the *Journal of the National Cancer Institute*.
5. Access to CANCERLIT—citations and abstracts from NCI's bibliographical database.
6. Links to other NCI and government home pages.
7. Links to other cancer-related organizations.

TRY THIS: Choose **Patients and Public | Treatment Information | PDQ® Cancer Treatment Information**. Scroll through the alphabetical listing and find the terms **gastric cancer**. Click on the name and link to the document covering this topic. Next, click on the Back button until you come to the Treatment Information screen and click on **Therapy**. See if you can find information on radiotherapy (radiation therapy). Explore what alternative therapies are available.

Go back to the home page and follow the path **Health Professionals | Treatment Information | Cancer Treatment** and scroll the alphabetical listing looking for **gastric cancer**. Compare this information, which is intended for doctors and other health care professionals, to the patient data sheet you looked at earlier.

Go back to the main page and look for the button at the bottom of the page labeled **Search**. Click on this and run your search on **gastric cancer** again. How many hits did you get in your results list?

Starting at the main page, follow this path: **Cancer trials | Finding | Searching | PDQ's Search Screen**. (You can also reach the PDQ® Clinical Trials Search Form for Patients at *cancernet.nci.nih.gov/prot/patsrch.shtml*.) Search on the keywords **gastric cancer**.

CancerNet™

Patients
and the Public

Health
Professionals

Basic
Researchers

To begin your search, choose
from cancer information selected
and organized for your needs as
a patient, health professional, or
basic researcher.

Welcome! You are now connected to a wide range of
accurate, credible cancer information brought to you by the
National Cancer Institute (NCI). CancerNet information is
reviewed regularly by oncology experts and is based on the
latest research.

CancerNet includes a variety of sources to help meet your
cancer information needs:

    • Selected information from PDQ®, NCI's
comprehensive cancer database, including summaries
on cancer treatment, screening, prevention, and
supportive care, and information on ongoing clinical
trials;

    • CANCERLIT®, NCI's bibliographic database;

    • And fact sheets, news, and other resources.

Visit cancerTrials™, NCI's comprehensive clinical trials
information center.

About NCI	About This Site	Useful Links

Figure 15–3 CancerNet

RESOURCE NAME: eBlast (see Figure 15–4)

RESOURCE LOCATION: *www.ebig.com/index.html*

ABOUT: Britannica editors classify, rate, and review over 125,000 Web resources in this Encyclopedia Britannica Internet Guide.

WHEN TO USE: When kids are running subject searches on the Internet at large. eBlast produces more selective results than a general search engine.

SEARCH STRATEGIES: Use "text only" for hard-core searching; site descriptions are indexed and can be keyword searched or browsed by subject. The search engine supports Boolean operators and phrases. Hits are rated with one to five stars, five stars representing the "best of the Web."

TRY THIS: Find information on Aboriginal Culture in Australia by browsing. Find information on Thomas Jefferson's views about slavery using the search engine.

home   about   feedback   **ENCYCLOPÆDIA BRITANNICA'S**®   help   shop   link to us

SITE OF THE DAY
1998 Year in Review

EB QUICK SEARCH
free software

A guide to the Web's top sites, chosen by Britannica's editors

BOOKMARKS
of the smart & famous
James McManus

BRITANNICA ONLINE
what do you want to know today?

31 December 1998 10:03 pm
CST      search   Include AltaVista ☐
more search options

Arts & Literature
performance art, design...

Business, Economy, Employment

Computers & the Internet
censorship, computer science...

Education
study abroad, phys ed...

Entertainment & Leisure
holidays, regional events...

Health & Medicine
death and dying, dentistry...

History
U.S. history, historiography...

Kids
family, style...

Law, Government, Politics
advocacy, ethics...

News & Current Events
environment, welfare...

Philosophy & Religion
theology, hinduism...

Science, Technology, Math
space exploration, acoustics...

Shopping
greeting cards, music...

Society & Social Science
sociology, philanthropy...

Sports & Recreation
college sports, basketball...

Travel & Tourism
online expeditions, cruises...

World Geography & Culture
Australia, Middle East...

ⓐ additional site information provided by
ALEXA

copyright © 1997-1998 Encyclopædia Britannica, Inc.   text-only version

Figure 15–4 eBlast, *Encyclopaedia Britannica*'s Internet Guide

RESOURCE NAME: Inference (see Figure 15–5)
RESOURCE LOCATION: *www.inference.com/infind/*
ABOUT: Inference is a multi-threaded search engine that currently searches in parallel WebCrawler, Yahoo!, Lycos, AltaVista, InfoSeek, and Excite. (Saves you doing eight separate searches by hand.) Eliminates duplicates (dupes) and groups your hits together into categories.
WHEN TO USE: When kids want to search the entire Web by subject or for specific facts.
SEARCH STRATEGIES: You can use Boolean operators and/or quotes to force phrase searching in multi-threaded search engines, but there's no guarantee that all of the search engines will understand or apply these parameters to your search.
TRY THIS: Compare two searches, one on **pro choice** and one on **anti abortion**. Notice how Inference groups your search results.

 Request Info   Send Suggestions   *Inference*®

Helping people work smarter™

The Intelligent and Fast Parallel Web Search

nter Query: [   ]   Search!

MaxTime: [7 ▾] seconds

NEW!
Try *Inference Find* in German!
Try *Inference Find* in French!

Please tell others about us!   Can I do boolean operations?
Please give us feedback!   Can I add Inference Find to my own
What are people saying about   web pages?
Inference Find?   It didn't find my page...How do I add
Yeah, but how does it work?   a link to my page?

Inference Corporation © 1995-98 *webmaster@inference.com*

Figure 15–5 Inference

RESOURCE NAME: Infomine (see Figure 15–6)
RESOURCE LOCATION: *lib-www.ucr.edu/Main.html*
ABOUT: Infomine is a searchable index of annotated links to university-level research and educational tools on the Internet. Resources include over 9,500 links to databases (400 databases in the life sciences alone!), guides to the Internet for most disciplines, textbooks, conference proceedings, and journals.
WHEN TO USE: Older kids can use this tool when they want to access well-organized collections of hand-selected, annotated resources for browsing or searching.
SEARCH STRATEGIES: Infomine offers title, subject, and keyword searching. By default, simple searches search all three fields. Infomine uses subject terms from the Library of Congress Subject Headings (LCSH), and supports nested, boolean searching and truncation (which uses the "#" sign). Result sets include detailed descriptions of resources. Along with descriptions, each resource is linked to a list of related terms that link you to similar resources. Infomine also offers browsing in its ten major collections of resources. In each collection you can browse **What's New**, **Table of Contents**, **Subject**, **Keyword**, and **Title**.
TRY THIS: Choose the category **Government Information** and browse Table of Contents for CODES—UNITED STATES – STATES to see if you can find an online version of the Arkansas Constitution.

Choose the category **Visual and Performing Arts** and then select **Featured Resources—Visual and Performing Arts Reference**. Browse reference information for Musicians. 3) Search for a Web site filled with resources that would be of interest to a teacher of American Literature. (Hint: Run your search and after your search results pages load, use the **Edit|Find** menu feature in your browser to search on keywords.)

About   General   News   E-Journal   Search/Finding
INFOMINE   Reference   Resources   Guides   Tools

Search 14,000+ Academically Valuable Resources In:

Biological, Agricultural & Medical Sciences

Government Information

Instructional Resources: K-12

Instructional Resources: University

Internet Enabling Tools (Help, HTML, Finding Tools...)

Maps & GIS

Physical Sciences, Engineering, Computing & Math

Regional & General Interest

Social Sciences & Humanities (Reference, Business, Literature...)

Visual & Performing Arts

[UC Campuses | UC Phone/Email Directories | MELVYL ® System Databases]
[UC Libraries: Hours, Services, Collections | Featured UC Library Resources | Libraries/Catalogs Worldwide]
[UnCover Journal Articles | Scholarly Societies + | Text Version]

Figure 15–6 Infomine

RESOURCE NAME: Information Please (see Figure 15–7)

RESOURCE LOCATION: *www.infoplease.com/*

ABOUT: Infoplease.com combines the contents of an encyclopedia, a dictionary, and several up-to-the-minute almanacs containing statistics, facts, and historical records.

WHEN TO USE: When kids want an authoritative Internet resource to find factual information.

SEARCH STRATEGIES: You can browse or search infoplease.com. The browsing area is organized by subject on the left edge of the screen. Subjects include world, sports, entertainment, US, people, business and economy, living, society, and science and technology. These links are also available at the bottom of every screen.

To search, enter the words you want to search for in the text box at the top of any page and press return or click on **Go**. This searches all of the almanacs, plus the *Columbia Encyclopedia* and *Random House Webster's College Dictionary* in one click.

For a more focused search, specify a particular reference work by clicking on the pull-down menu next to the search box From. Searches are case insensitive. Different forms of words, such as "computer" and "computers," are considered the same for searching purposes. When you enter more than one search term, pages containing the phrase are listed first, followed by pages that contain the individual words.

TRY THIS: Search for **abacus** in **General Almanac**. Compare your results to a search on **abacus** in the hard copy of *Information Please*. Search for **joint chiefs of staff** in **General Almanac**. Compare your results to a search on **joint chiefs of staff** in the hard copy of *Information Please*. Search on **moldova** in **General Almanac**. Compare your results to a search on **moldova** in the hard copy of *Information Please*.

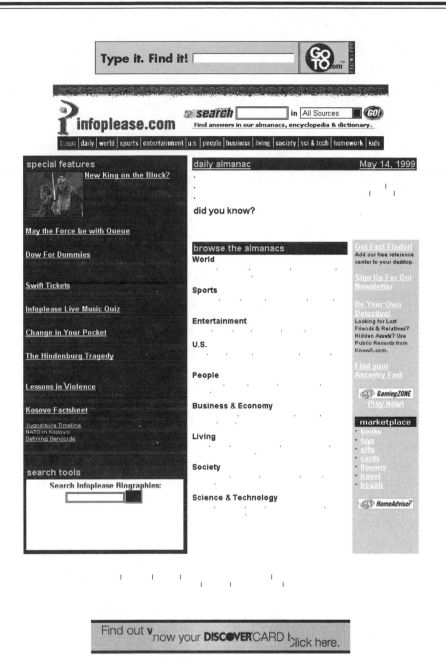

Figure 15–7 Information Please

RESOURCE NAME: The Librarian's Index to the Internet (see Figure 15–8)
RESOURCE LOCATION: *sunsite.berkeley.edu/InternetIndex/*
ABOUT: This index consists of public library resources hand-selected by librarians; includes descriptions.
WHEN TO USE: When kids want to selectively search the Web for information by subject or for specific facts and also have access to resource descriptions. Great for public library settings.
SEARCH STRATEGIES: Supports the Boolean OR operator. In other words, any of the terms you list will be included in the results. The Boolean AND operator is assumed, so documents will contain all of the words you specify. Use an asterisk * at the end of words for truncation.
TRY THIS: Use the search engine to find sites offering images of ticks and RealAudio clips of classical music. Browse the subject index for statistics on crime.

Search word(s): [   ] [Search]

Options: ⦿ ALL ○ Subjects ○ Titles ○ Descriptions   **Search tips**

Browse List of Subjects Used   **Best Search Tools Form**

New This Week - Subscribe! -
more new... - **New Last Week**
Arts - Architecture | Artists |
Decorative | History | Museums |
Performing | more...
Automobiles - Motorcycles
Business - Companies |
Consumers | Investing | Taxes |
more...
California - Politics | Bay Area :
Berkeley | Oakland | San Francisco
| Southern California : Los
Angeles
Computers - Macs | PCs |
Software | Viruses | more...
Cultures (World) - Anthropology
| Languages | Africa | Asia |
Europe | LatA | MidE | NorA
Current Events
Disabilities
Education - K-12 Schools |
Colleges | Distance Learning |
Choosing a College | Financial Aid
| Literacy
Families - Homes | Moving
Food - Recipes | Restaurants |
more...
Gay, Lesbian, Bisexual

Geography - Maps | more...
Government - Local | State | Federal
| International
Health - Alternative | Diseases &
Conditions | Drugs | Nutrition |
more...
History - Genealogy |
Ancient | Medieval | Military |
United States
Images, Graphics, Clip Art
Internet Information -
Censor/Filter | Evaluation | HTML |
Training | WWW | more...
Jobs - Careers | Listings | Resumes
Kids - Fun | Health | Homework |
Internet Safety | Parents | Teachers
Law - Censorship | Copyright |
Crime
Libraries - Public | for Librarians
Literature - Authors | Awards |
Book Reviews | Bookstores |
Fiction Genres | Full-text | Poetry |
Publishers | Writing
Media - News | Magazines |
Newspapers | Radio | TV
Men
Miscellaneous
Music - Classical | Jazz | Lyrics |
Opera | Rock | more...

Organizations
People - Collected Biographies
Philosophy
Politics - Elections
Recreation - Games | Gardening |
Movies | Outdoor | Pets | more...
Reference Desk - Calendars | Census |
Dictionaries | Holidays | Names | Phone
Books | Statistics | Time
Religion - Christianity | Eastern | Islam |
Judaism | Mythology | Paganism
Science - Animals | Astronomy |
Earthquakes | Environment | Math |
Plants | Technology | more...
Searching - About | Best Engines |
Best Indexes | Meta Engines | Others
Seniors
Sports - Baseball | Basketball | Football
| Olympics | Tennis | more...
Surfing the Internet
Travel - Accommodations | Guides |
Places | Transportation
Weather - Tides | more...
Women - History | Politics | Studies

Figure 15–8 The Librarian's Index to the Internet

RESOURCE NAME: The Librarian's Guide to the Internet (see Figure 15–9)
RESOURCE LOCATION: *www.star-host.com/library/*
ABOUT: This is a place at which kids can begin their Internet-based research. Services are grouped according to resource type, (e.g., telnet, gopher, Web, newsgroups, etc.).
WHEN TO USE: Use this guide for general searching and browsing of the Internet including all types of services: Gopher, FTP, Web, Telnet, LISTSERV, USENET News, and so forth. Also a good source for browsing full-text resources.
SEARCH STRATEGIES: First, familiarize yourself with the resource categories available on this page. Most of your searching will be on the Web, so bookmark this page as an entry point Web-based searching and browsing. The first paragraph links you to the major search engines and a little further down you find links to a variety of subject trees.
TRY THIS: Choose a topic and research its several different resource categories. For example, take the subject **gardening** and see what you can find on the Web using search engines, on the Web using an Archie server, searching discussion list databases, searching newsgroups, browsing a subject tree, such as Yahoo!, and searching an online library.

The Librarian's Guide to the Internet

Helping librarians find resources and services on the Net since 1993

Special Services

What's New

Subject Trees for Librarians

Full Text Resources

Security for Libraries

SEARCHING THE WEB

Access dozens of Web Search Engines at William Cross's All-In-One page. For resources relevant to university faculty, students, and research staff, try Infomine. Search UC Berkeley's The Librarians' Index to the Internet for resources of interest to public libraries. For general searching use Metafind or Inference--multi-threaded search engines, or go to eBlast, Encyclopedia Britannica's Internet Guide which classifies, rates, and reviews more than 125,000 sites on the Web. .

FINDING FILES

Search FTP search v3.5, the world's fastest Archie™ server, or link to Nexor which maintains a list of Archie™ gateways worldwide. FILEZ is a huge, incredibly fast search service that indexes 75,000,000 files on 5,000 sites, and WinSite Group, Inc. is "ThePlanet's Largest Software Archive for Windows."

EXPLORING DIGITAL LIBRARIES

Browse or search the American Memory collections at the Library of Congress or visit the Berkeley Digital Library SunSITE™ home page for links to dozens of text and image collections. A list of full text resources links you to Project Gutenberg, Labovitz's E-zine List, and more.

LOOKING FOR PEOPLE

Use Switchboard™ or Whowhere?™ for snail-mail addresses. Other "people finders" can be found on the All-In-One page. Try Four11 for extensive phone listings and the ability to browse through listings for government officials and celebrities.

BROWSING GOPHER SITES

Many Gopher sites are moving their data files to Web servers, but you can still access all of the Gopher servers in the world and launch keyword searches from Washington and Lee University

FINDING MAILING LISTS

The CataList reference site offers access to over 17,000 public LISTSERV lists. LISZToffers a directory of over 84,000 Mailing Lists that can be searched or browsed. Check out TILE.NETif you prefer browsing by mailing list descriptions, names, subjects, host countries, or sponsors. A list of Library-Oriented mailing lists is maintained by Wei Wu at the University of Houston Libraries.

SEARCHING NEWSGROUPS

Use the DejaNews™ Query Form to search through messages posted to thousands of Usenet Newsgroups, or browse FAQs by Title, or search the News.Answers FAQs Archive via WAIS.

VISITING ONLINE LIBRARIES

Visit the Z39.50 Gateway, or link to Peter Scott's HYTELNET for access to library catalogs arranged geographically and by vendor. Peter Scott's and Doug Macdonald's webCATS home page offers access to libraries with Web interfaces.

BROWSING SUBJECT TREES

Visit Yahoo!™, the Web's largest subject tree, LookSmart, or The Mining Company. Kids should check out Yahooligans!™, 700+ Great Sites, KidsClick, or Disney's Internet Guide Dig. You may also visit other general interest subject trees or subject lists for librarians.

EXPLORING WITH TELNET

Access hundreds of Telnet sites using Galaxy. Resources are organized under the topics: Archie Servers, Databases and bibliographies, Distributed File Servers, (Gopher/WAIS/WWW), Electronic books, Fee-Based Services, FREE-NETs & Community Computing Systems, General Bulletin Boards, NASA databases, Network Information Services, and Whois/White Pages/Directory Services.

Figure 15–9 The Librarian's Guide to the Internet

RESOURCE NAME: My Virtual Reference Desk (see Figure 15–10)
RESOURCE LOCATION: *www.refdesk.com/*
ABOUT: My Virtual Reference Desk is considered a "meta" site—a major resource for online information.
WHEN TO USE: Use MVRD when you are running quick searches for facts. It's also a great resource for online newspapers. You can search the archives of the *Arkansas Democrat-Gazette* for free, going back to 1994. To view an entire story, it must be purchased for $1.
SEARCH STRATEGIES: For an overview of MVRD, start with the Table of Contents. The three major categories of resources that will be most useful are **My Virtual Newspaper**, **My Facts Page**, and **My Virtual Encyclopedia**.

For quick information, the "First Things First" page includes links to wire and news services and to current stock quotes.

"My Facts Page" functions as an almanac of the Web, with links to everything from mapping sites to dictionaries of scientific quotations. This section includes dozens of links targeted for librarians, such as indexes of library Web pages, online catalogs, and lists of library vendors.

From the "My Virtual Encyclopedia" page you can explore dozens of topical headings and a wealth of content-based Internet sites.
TRY THIS:
Search on **abacus** in MVRD. How do the results compare with infoplease.com?

Go to **My Virtual Newspaper** and see what online newspapers are available in your home state. Does the *Los Angeles Times* let you search their archives and if so, what are the terms?

The *New York Times* has a 365-day online archive that you can search for free, but you must register online. To view full text, you have to pay a fee. Search on the terms **culinary herbs** and see how many hits you get. You can register to search this archive for free, but to view full text you must pay.

Click on **Internet Help/FAQ** to see what materials are available for library patrons who would like to teach themselves something about the Internet.

Explore **My Facts Page** and see if you can find a link to the **Tiger Map Server**. When you do, see if you can pull up a map of your hometown. (Hint: It takes a while for the Map Server page to load. You can click on the **Stop** button after a few moments pass to proceed with your search. Go to the bottom of the page and look for a text entry box where you can enter your town's name and zip code.)

A student has expressed an interest in writing a paper on crime in the U.S. Browse **My Virtual Encyclopedia** and explore what paths are available. (Hint: Use the **Edit|Find** feature of your browser to zero in on "U.S.")

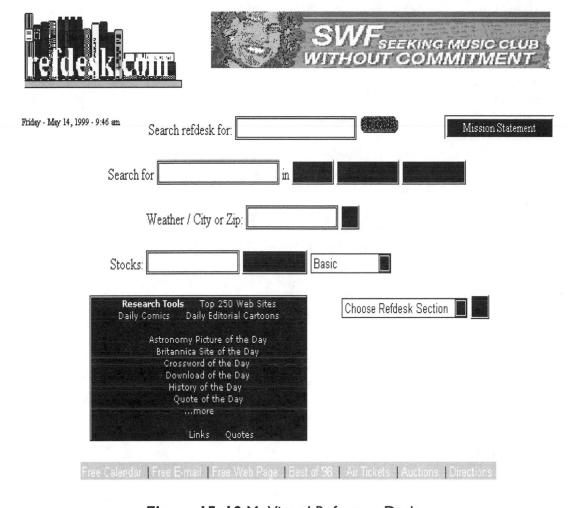

Figure 15–10 My Virtual Reference Desk

RESOURCE NAME: National Geographic
RESOURCE LOCATION: *www.nationalgeographic.com/kids/*
ABOUT: As the name indicates, this amazing Web site is intended to complement the magazine of the same name. In fact, it embellishes the print version by presenting a kid-friendly site that's safe for children of all ages. The site contains several jewels including a feature called Amazing Facts where kids can read about "banana vaccine," "reindeer antifreeze," "bear facts," "why snow stays on mountain tops," and more.

WHEN TO USE: True to the nature of *National Geographic* magazine, this site enables kids to explore world geography online. Kids interested in making new friends can join the National Geographic Pen Pal Network—a pen pal club for English-speaking boys and girls ages 6 through 16.

SEARCH STRATEGIES: The best place to go for launching your searches is *www.nationalgeographic.com/search.html*. This page presents you with three searchable indexes:

1. The nationalgeographic.com Web site
2. An online index of *National Geographic* Magazine
3. The National Geographic Society library catalog

The search engine supports the Boolean operators AND, OR, and NOT. These must be written in ALL CAPITALS. Use parentheses to group search terms (also called "nesting"); for example, **(cows OR pigs) AND farming**. Place quotes around phrases, such as **"south africa"** and use the **?** for truncation. For example, **comput?** finds computer, computing, computation, computed, computers, and so on. Don't hit the RETURN key to run your search, but instead click on the **Seek** button. When you press the RETURN key, you create a return character and this could make it difficult for the system to properly interpret your search statement.

TRY THIS: Click on the pull-down menu labeled "Site Index" at the top of the home page. Scroll down and select the link called **Library (searchable catalog)**. Once the library search screen loads, type in the keyword "shanghai" and then click the **Search** button. How many hits did you get and are they organized? Click on one of the titles to view a complete citation. Now click the Back button until you come to the original results screen. What happens when you click on an author's name?

Return to the home page and click on the Site Index pull-down menu and select the link called **Archives** located at the top of the list. After this page loads, look for the link labeled **Kids Features**. Now select a topic that sounds interesting and explore it further. On the day we checked in there were feature articles on "Shark Surfari," "Cyber Tiger," "Explore the Fantastic Forest," and more.

Just for fun, click on the **Cartoon Factory** link located on the home page. This feature gives you an opportunity to add your very own text to a cartoon image.

Click on the Site Index pull-down menu located on the home page and select **Map Machine**. Click on the link called **Map Machine Atlas** and then select

Index. Scroll down until you find a listing of states in the United States. Can you find your state listed? When you do, click on the name and see what you find written about your state's history. Is there a map of your state that you can enlarge?

RESOURCE NAME: Thomas Register of American Manufacturers (see Figure 15–11)

RESOURCE LOCATION: *www.thomasregister.com/*

ABOUT: The Thomas Register of American Manufacturers publishes a comprehensive buying guide of over 155,000 industrial companies and 124,000 brand name products. Thomas Register also provides you with access to 5,500 online supplier catalogs. Thomas Register on the Internet covers both American and Canadian companies. If you wish, you can receive literature by Fax free of charge and send e-mail to suppliers to receive availability, delivery, and pricing information. The database provides access to over 1,000 Web sites, and users can purchase products through their electronic commerce offering.

WHEN TO USE: Use the Thomas Register online when you need quicker access and more timely information than the print version provides. If your library doesn't subscribe to the print version, make this your primary access point to American manufacturing information.

SEARCH STRATEGIES: Before you can search the database, you must register for a membership ID and password. Registration is free. You can search the Thomas Register database by company, product/services, and brand name. Once you find a list of companies that manufacture the product or service in which you are interested, you can further modify your search by choosing a particular state or province. Multiple states can be selected by pressing the ALT key and clicking left on your mouse.

   Boolean terms that can be used when searching Thomas Register include AND, OR, and NOT.

1. To use the Boolean AND, you can enter: **paint + remover**, **paint AND remover**, or **paint remover** and get the same results list.
2. **cans OR containers** will include records with either the word **cans** or **containers**
3. **cans NOT garbage** will retrieve all records containing the keyword **cans** but not the word **garbage**.

Use keywords to narrow your search results after you run your first search.

TRY THIS: Begin your search with a broad term. For example, if you are looking for a manufacturer of wood moldings, first search on the keyword **wood**. Look at the resulting product heading list and see if you can find keywords that match what you are looking for, for example "wood trim" or "wood molding" or "wood millwork."

   Run a brand name search on **bazooka plumb bob**.

   Run a search on **american national standards institute**.

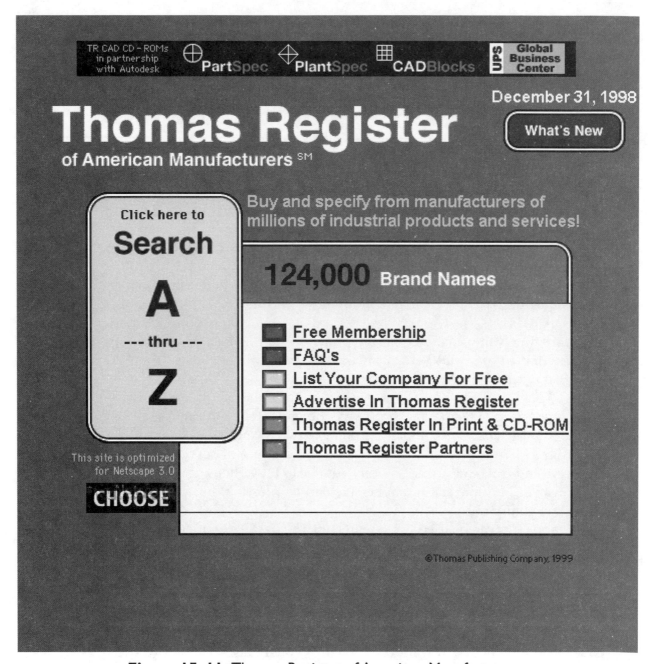

Figure 15–11 Thomas Register of American Manufacturers

RESOURCE NAME: Researchpaper.com
RESOURCE LOCATION: *www.researchpaper.com/*
ABOUT: Researchpaper.com is an online writing and research center developed by Infonautics Corporation in partnership with Macmillan Publishing and Purdue University. Topics presented in the Idea Directory are drawn from *10,000 Ideas for Term Papers, Projects, Reports & Speeches* by Kathryn Lamm and published by Macmillan Publishing USA, Inc. Content in the Writing Center is partly adapted from the Purdue University Online Writing Lab at *owl.english. purdue.edu/*.
WHEN TO USE: Kids should go to Researchpaper.com when they need assistance with school research projects. This site can help get the creative juices flowing with its list of more than 4,000 topics and ideas for term papers and reports. It's a great resource for writing tips and for help with online research techniques.
SEARCH STRATEGIES: There are two ways to find ideas for research papers: 1) by browsing through more than 100 different categories, or 2) by running keyword searches in their idea directory. Each idea in the result list is accompanied by two buttons: one links to Infonautic's Elibrary Web site and the other searches the Internet at large. When you click on the Elibrary button, you launch a comprehensive, simultaneous search through more than 150 full-text newspapers and hundreds of full-text magazines. The result list is just citations, but you may have access to many of these items in your local library. If not, you might consider subscribing to Elibrary or signing up for a free 30-day trial.

When you click on the Net Search button, Elibrary automatically goes out and queries the Internet at large for information relating to your chosen topic.
TRY THIS: Initiate a research project by browsing Researchpaper.com's idea directory. Start on their home page and click on the link labeled **Idea Directory**. Once there, look for a text entry box from which to run your search. Enter a keyword to search on a topic of interest, for example **hobbies**. When the result list appears, go down both paths, first pressing the Elibrary button and then returning and pressing the Net Search button.

Return to the home page and then go to the Writing Center. See if you can find information on how to avoid sexist language, (e.g., words and phrases like mankind, the best man for the job, man-made, the common man, and man-hours). See what you can find on the parts of speech, such as nouns, pronouns, adjectives, adverbs, and so on.

RESOURCE NAME: ZDNet
RESOURCE LOCATION: *www.zdnet.com/*
ABOUT: ZDNet offers kids an opportunity to run full-text searches on material collected from 11 different computer magazines.
WHEN TO USE: Kids can use this resource for searching computer-related news; when they are buying new hardware or software and are looking for reviews; or for staying up-to-date on new computer technologies.

SEARCH STRATEGIES: There are two search modes: Basic Search and Search Options. Search Options allows you to set specific date parameters. You can search all Ziff-Davis publications and channels, or direct your search to a specific publication, such as *Computer Life, Computer Shopper NetBuyer, Family PC, Internet Computing, Mac, MacUser, PC Computing, PC Magazine*, and more.
TRY THIS: Search *Computer Shopper* for information on digital cameras. What kind of information is available? Refine your search to digital video cameras in the price range of $1,000+.

SELF-STUDY GUIDES

The following self-study guides teach some basic lessons that will help you become more familiar with how the Internet works and how to use it to greater advantage. There are six study guides.

Study Guide 1: Downloading and Installing a Telnet Program. The telnet program for Study Guide 1 is called EWAN.

Study Guide 2: Telneting to Arkansas Libraries. Study Guide 2 works with EWAN to access the Arkansas State University Jonesboro online library catalog.

Study Guide 3: Introduction to Medscape's Web Site. Study Guide 3 teaches how to access Medscape, set up an account, and use Medscape resources.

Study Guide 4: Tools for Creating Help Sheets. Study Guide 4 teaches how to download and install a Windows screen capture utility called SnagIt and create help sheets.

Study Guide 5: Viewing Images through Gopher. Although gopher applications are used less and less, there are still some Gophers with valuable information and even a cursory understanding of Gopher sheds light on the early stages of the Internet.

Study Guide 6: Finding and Downloading Files on the Internet. Study Guide 6 teaches the use of a Web browser to find and download files and explains transferring files on the Internet.

Internet Self Study Guide 1

Allen C. Benson   acbenson@star-host.com

-=-Downloading and installing a telnet program-=-

Purpose:
Demonstrate how to download a Windows program, uncompress it, and run it.

Objective:
Learn how to find a telnet program named EWAN, download it, and install it.

Materials:
PC system connected to the Internet; Web browser; and access to a PC's hard drive.

Background:
Telnet is a powerful Internet application that enables librarians to access other library's online catalogs worldwide. Accessing other library catalogs can help you verify information for acquisitions, interlibrary loan, and copy cataloging. Some systems, such as CARL's UnCover (*database.carl.org*), enable you to search magazine article indexes online.

One of the challenges of using telnet to connect to library catalogs is that you have to learn how to use that other library's online catalog, which might be NOTIS, GEAC, SIRSI, VTLS, etc. Telnet is slow and unresponsive at times and this can make using telnet difficult, too.

Procedure:
1. Startup your Web browser and go to this address: *www.filez.com*
2. In the search box, enter the program name **ewan** and press ENTER.
3. FILEZ goes out and searches FTP sites for files with the string "ewan" in their name.
4. When you view the results screen you see many files that contain "ewan" in their name. You can't always be certain which file is the one you are looking for, but here are some general rules: 1) Numbers in file names usually represent versions. The higher the number, the more recent the version. For example, ewan104 is an earlier version than ewan105, and ewan102 is an earlier version than ewan104; 2) The file size of an earlier version is usually smaller than a newer version. As features are added, program sizes increase; and 3) Many search engines show you dates that files were created. This can also give you a clue about which file is the most recent.

5. Select the newest version, probably ewan105.exe, and click on the file name. This action takes you to another window where FILEZ displays a set of download sites that archive this file. Pick one and click on it. You are prompted to save the file to a particular directory. Save it to your C:\TEMP\ directory.

6. Once it is downloaded to your TEMP directory, double-click on the filename and the file self-extracts. A DOS shell opens and you can view the extraction process.

7. Next, look for the file named **INSTALL.EXE** and double-click on it. This starts the install program.

8. First the program tries to create a directory C:\EWAN\. Click **OK** to confirm and proceed with installation. When completed, a program group with this icon will appear:

9. Double-click on the icon to run EWAN. To run EWAN in the future, you can create a shortcut to your desktop, or simply go to the C:\EWAN\ directory and double-click on the Ewan.exe file.

Internet Self Study Guide 2

Allen C. Benson   acbenson@star-host.com

-=-Telneting to Arkansas Libraries-=-

Purpose:
Introduce EWAN telnet program and search online catalogs.

Objective:
Configure EWAN, a windows-based telnet program, to access the ASU Jonesboro online library catalog.

Materials:
PC system connected to the Internet.

Background:
On most systems, opening a telnet URL (*telnet://database.carl.org*, for example) launches an external telnet application. The telnet application is what connects you to the telnet site, not the Web browser. To successfully telnet with Netscape, two things must be done: 1) A telnet client must be installed on your hard drive, and 2) A preference must be set telling Netscape where to find the application on your hard drive. If you are running Windows 95/98, this is already done for you.

If you haven't already done so, download a telnet client and install it on your hard drive. For Windows users, download a copy of *trumptel.exe* or EWAN. (EWAN and other telnet programs are listed at the end of Chapter 17.) In this exercise you will be running EWAN.

Procedure:
1.   Start EWAN. When the window opens, click on **New** to create a new profile as shown in Figure 15–12.

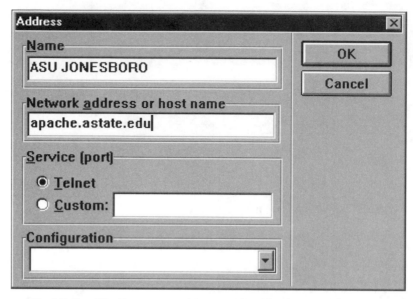

Figure 15–12 Profile for connecting to the library at ASU Jonesboro.

2. After creating the profile, click **OK**.
3. To telnet to the university's library, click on the site's name and then click on **OK**. The screen shown in Figure 15–13 appears.

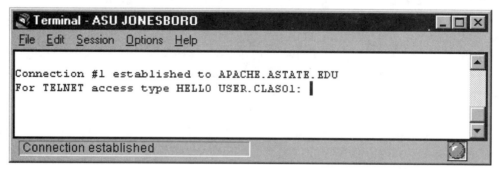

Figure 15–13 Login screen for ASU Jonesboro system. Enter **hello user.clas01**

4. Next, the Welcome screen appears as shown in Figure 15–14.

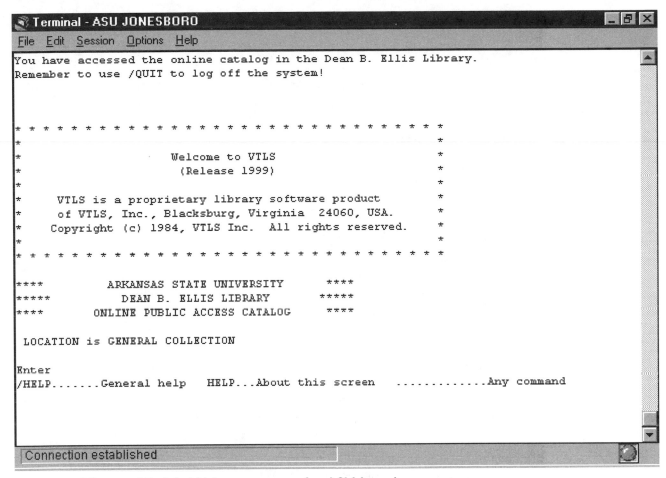

Figure 15–14 Welcome screen for ASU Jonesboro system.

5. The first thing to do when you log into a system you are not familiar with is access help. To access help in this system, which is a VTLS automation system, type **/HELP** at the prompt and press ENTER. This presents you with the screen shown in Figure 15–15.

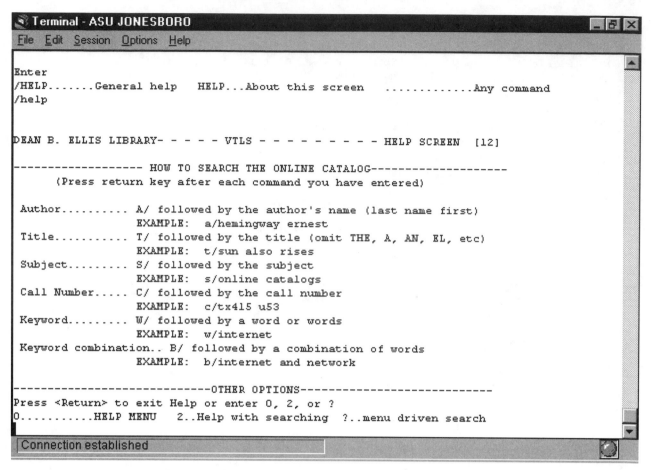

```
Terminal - ASU JONESBORO                                        _ ▢ ✕
 File  Edit  Session  Options  Help

Enter                                                             ▲
/HELP.......General help   HELP...About this screen   .............Any command
/help


DEAN B. ELLIS LIBRARY- - - - - VTLS - - - - - - - - - HELP SCREEN  [12]

------------------- HOW TO SEARCH THE ONLINE CATALOG--------------------
      (Press return key after each command you have entered)

 Author.......... A/ followed by the author's name (last name first)
                  EXAMPLE:  a/hemingway ernest
 Title........... T/ followed by the title (omit THE, A, AN, EL, etc)
                  EXAMPLE:  t/sun also rises
 Subject......... S/ followed by the subject
                  EXAMPLE:  s/online catalogs
 Call Number..... C/ followed by the call number
                  EXAMPLE:  c/tx415 u53
 Keyword......... W/ followed by a word or words
                  EXAMPLE:  w/internet
 Keyword combination.. B/ followed by a combination of words
                  EXAMPLE:  b/internet and network


-------------------------------OTHER OPTIONS--------------------------
Press <Return> to exit Help or enter 0, 2, or ?
0...........HELP MENU   2..Help with searching  ?..menu driven search
                                                                  ▼
 Connection established
```

Figure 15–15 Help screen on ASU's VTLS system.

6. Based on the search options presented to you, try running an author search on William Manchester and see if you can find a book he authored about the life of Winston Churchill.

7. Other libraries in Arkansas that support telnet are shown in Table 15–2. To learn which libraries are located in your home state, explore these online library Web resources: HYTELNET at *moondog.usask.ca/hytelnet/* and WebCATS at *library.usask.ca/hywebcat/*.

Table 15-2 Arkansas Libraries that offer telnet support	
Arkansas State University	TELNET apache.astate.edu To login, type: hello user.clas01 OPAC = VTLS To exit, type QUIT
Harding University	TELNET library.harding.edu Username: OPAC OPAC = DRA Gateway To exit, select QUIT on main menu
Henderson State University (Arkansas)	TELNET aspen.hsu.edu Username: LIBRARY OPAC = DRA Gateway To exit, select QUIT on main menu
Hendrix College	TELNET alpha.hendrix.edu Username: PAC Password: PAC OPAC = DRA To exit, type ex
John Brown University	TELNET library.jbu.edu Username: LIBRARY OPAC = GALAXY To exit, select X on main menu
University of Arkansas—Little Rock	TELNET library.ualr.edu Username: LIBRARY Please enter your 14-digit Library I.D. Number here: (Press RETURN) OPAC = DRA Gateway To exit, select QUIT on main menu
University of Arkansas Medical Sciences Library	TELNET uamslib.uams.edu login: uams Password: libcat OPAC = CLSI To exit, select EXIT on main menu
University of Arkansas at Monticello	TELNET library.uamont.edu Username: PAC OPAC = DRA Gateway To exit, select QUIT on main menu
University of Arkansas, Fayetteville	TELNET library.uark.edu login: library OPAC = INNOPAC To exit, select D on main menu
University of Central Arkansas	TELNET ucark.uca.edu login: library OPAC = INNOPAC To exit, select D on main menu

Internet Self Study Guide 3

Allen C. Benson   acbenson@star-host.com

-=-Introduction to Medscape's Web Site-=-

Purpose:
Introduce the resources and services available through Medscape's Web site.

Objective:
Access Medscape's home page, set up a member account, and become familiar with Medscape's resources and services.

Materials:
PC system connected to the Internet and Web browser.

Background:
Medscape is a multi-specialty, commercial Web service for clinicians and consumers. Librarians can visit this site and search Medscape's database of thousands of free, full-text, peer-reviewed clinical medicine articles. Each article is enhanced with a navigable article outline, "zoomable" graphics, annotated links to Internet resources, and links to related specialty areas on Medscape.

Medscape also offers unrestricted free access to MEDLINE, AIDSLINE, and TOXLINE; DrugSearch, which provides easy searching of the National Drug Data File; the drug database from First DataBank; daily medical news; continuing medical education resources; Merriam Webster's Medical Dictionary online, and more.

Membership is free, but requires one-time membership registration.

Procedure:
1. To register for access to Medscape's databases, go to Medscape's home page at *www.medscape.com/* and click on the **Site Map** tab at the bottom of the page. (see Figure 15–16.)
2. Go to the **"R"** section and look for a link to **Registration**.
3. Take a few minutes to fill out the **Membership Registration Form**.
4. Review Medscape's home page. The primary purpose of their home page is to catch your interest with headlines from today's news stories. You also launch your full-text searches from this page. Go to the bottom of the page and find Medscape's Search dialog box.
5. From here you can search three different databases: 1) Medscape's Full-Text Articles, 2) Medscape's Medical News and Discussion Groups, and

3) Medscape's Patient Information. Use the drop-down menu to make a selection. For this search example choose the default setting **Full Text**.

6. By default, searches from this screen are "simple" searches. In other words, the search engine looks through the database for articles containing the search term just as you typed it. If you enter more than one term, it is treated as a phrase. For example, if you search on the two keywords **children aids**, you will probably get zero hits because these two words are not likely to occur adjacent to each other in that exact order. Articles with the phrase, "children with aids" or "children and aids" will not be found. So, use the simple search only when you think your phrase or keywords will be found exactly as you enter them. Try searching on **children aids** and see how many hits you get.

7. Scroll to the bottom of your results screen and select **Freetext** searching and run your search again. **Freetext** searching results in more hits because it finds documents containing ANY of the terms you specify. Now how many hits do you get on **children aids**?

8. Now go back to the original **Simple** search screen and search on **children and aids**. As you will see, you get far less hits with this search than the earlier search using **Freetext** searching. **Freetext** uses the Boolean **or**, which broadens your search; using the Boolean **and** in the simple search narrows your results.

In the Simple search screen you can use:
*   Boolean operators: AND, OR, and NOT
*   Proximity operators: <NEAR>, <SENTENCE>, <PARAGRAPH> can be placed between words and phrases to limit your results list to those documents where the terms are found near each other. (You must use the angle brackets < and >.)
*   Parentheses may be used for "nesting" to define logical expression order. The search engine examines the words or phrases in parentheses first.
*   Use wildcards in search terms to fill in unknown sections of the word or to find related terms with varied endings. A wildcard is represented by the "*" character.

---

9. At the bottom of the home page, you can focus your searches in any one of the following resources:

Full-Text | MEDLINE | TOXLINE | AIDSLINE | Bookstore | Dictionary | Drugs

10. Select MEDLINE and search on the keywords **cluster headache**. How many hits do you get? MEDLINE is a database of abstracts, not full-text articles. You can order full-text articles from each search page for a fee.

11. Restrict the same search to articles in 1998 only. Did the search set get smaller?

12. Next use **Field abbreviations** to narrow your search further. First restrict your results to English language using the field abbreviation **English:LA** as in **cluster headaches English:LA** Did the results list get smaller? Next try restricting search to a particular journal.

13. Lastly, go back to the **Simple** search screen and run a full-text search on the terms **cluster headaches** and see what results you get. Remember, a **Freetext** search finds articles that contain "cluster" or "headaches" (too many hits!) where a **Simple** search finds articles that find the phrase "cluster headaches" (not enough hits!) and a **Simple** search on **cluster and headache*** yields the best set of results.

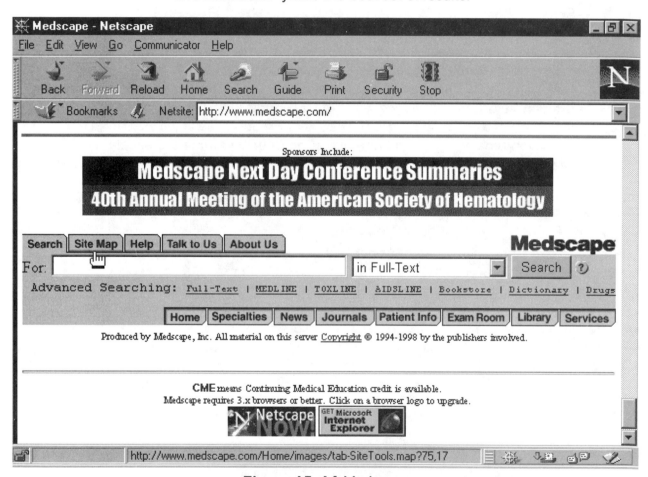

Figure 15–16 Medscape

Internet Self Study Guide 4

Allen C. Benson   acbenson@star-host.com

-=-Tools for creating help sheets-=-

Purpose:
Learn how to utilize a capture tool for making help sheets.

Objective:
Download and install a copy of SnagIt.

Materials:
PC system connected to the Internet; Web browser; ability to save files to PC's hard drive.

Background:
SnagIt is a Windows screen capture utility available as shareware. Capture utilities are programs that help you capture and manipulate images you see on your computer screen. The more sophisticated capture utilities enable you to capture scrolling screens. For example, if you want to capture a picture of a Web page, but it requires paging down to see the full image, the capture program "scrolls" down the screen as it captures the image.

As you prepare help sheets, include images of windows and tool bars to help make instructions easier to understand.

Procedure:
1. Start up your Web browser and go to this address: *www.techsmith.com/*.
2. Click on the **Download Now!** link for SnagIt. An image like the one shown in Figure 15–17 appears. Click on **Save File** and designate where you would like the file saved—for example, C:\TEMP\ directory.

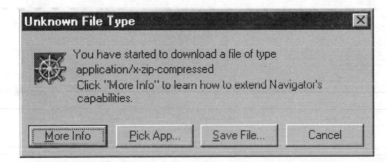

Figure 15–17 This image was captured using SnagIt.

3. After the download has finished, you should have a file named snagit.exe setting on your hard drive. The file size is about 1,705KB (1,705,000 bytes or 1.7MB).

4. Double click on the filename and this starts the installation process. As you proceed, the program installs itself in the C:\Program Files\TechSmith\SnagIt32\ subdirectory. When installation is complete, the screen shown in Figure 15–18 appears.

Figure 15–18 Just before you finish the installation process, SnagIt asks you to choose between different options; for example, creating a shortcut on your desktop and viewing the README.TXT file.

5. If all went as planned, you should have an icon on your desktop that looks like this:

6. Double-click on the icon to run SnagIt. The first window that appears asks you if you want to register or continue your evaluation. Click on the Evaluation button.

7. To set up SnagIt for capturing images, follow these steps:
   A. Click on the Input menu and make your selections as shown in Figure 15–19.

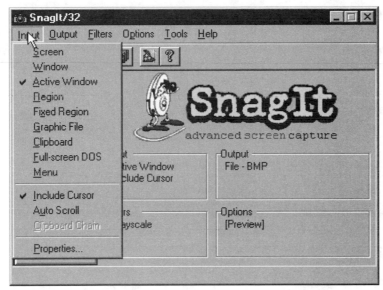

Figure 15–19 The **Input** menu helps you choose which portion of the screen you capture. Choosing **Window** and **Include Cursor** enabled me to create the above image.

   B. Next, click on the Output menu as shown in Figure 15–20. Choose where you would like your image to be placed. When you choose Clipboard, you simply "paste" it into your document as you write by pressing CTRL+V keys.

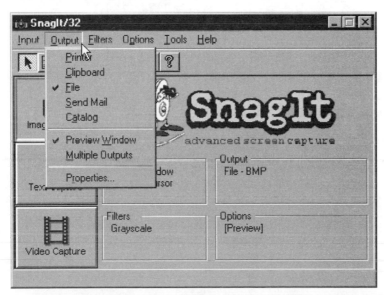

Figure 15–20 The **Output** menu allows you to choose where your image is placed. By checking **Preview Window**, you can preview your captured image before printing it or saving it to the clipboard.

C.   Click on the Filters menu, as shown in Figure 15–21, to choose whether you save your image in color or back & white.

Figure 15–21 For most situations, choose color **Conversion|Grayscale** when making help sheets that will be copied on a black & white photocopier. The file sizes are much smaller than color images.

D.   Clicking on **Options|Program Preferences** enables you to change the capture hot key, which by default is CTRL+SHIFT+P.

Instructions for registering SnagIt32 can be found online at *www.techsmith.com*.

Internet Self Study Guide 5

Allen C. Benson   acbenson@star-host.com

-=-Viewing images through Gopher-=-

Purpose:
View images using Gopher.

Objective:
Use Web browser to connect to the Gopher server at the Library of Congress; view and download images.

Materials:
PC system connected to the Internet; Web browser; ability to save files to PC's hard drive.

Background:
Gopher is an early Internet application that helps organize and present information on the Internet. Information on a Gopher server is organized in a hierarchical menu structure (tree structure) with a root menu and submenus. When you select a particular menu item, Gopher automatically links you to other files and other services. For example, one menu item may connect you to another computer by implementing a telnet session. Another menu item may connect you to a text file stored on any one of thousands of Gopher servers located all around the world. Still other menu items connect you to search engines, or more menus further down in the hierarchy.

The Gopher server at the Library of Congress is called Marvel, which stands for Machine-Assisted Realization of the Virtual Electronic Library. This server offers information about the Library, its activities and collection in the form of text files, search engines, images, and sound files.

If you have a direct connection to the Internet that enables you to run your own Gopher client software, you can either access Gopher with a specialized Gopher client such as TurboGOpher for Macs or WSGopher for Windows, or you can use your Web browser. When you access a Gopher site using a Web browser, addresses begin with **gopher://**.

Procedure:
1.   Start up your Web browser and go to the Library of Congress Gopher at *gopher://marvel.loc.gov/*. Most Gopher root menus offer a README file, or some kind of document that tells you about the site. At this site there's

a menu file called **About LC Marvel**. Upon reading this text file, you soon learn that the site is no longer being kept up-to-date and you are directed to the Library's Web site. Still, it's worthwhile exploring because there are many image files here that are difficult to find or not accessible via the Web.

Notice as you look at the Gopher Menu, small yellow folders represent directories. You burrow down through the directories by clicking on the folders. Scroll down through the menu choices by using the down arrow key or by clicking on the scroll bar on the right side of the screen. Click on the folder labeled **Global Electronic Library**.

2. In the next window that appears, find the folder called **The Arts** and click on it.

3. The next window that appears lists several topics such as Art Museums, Ceramics, Dance, and Music. Click on the folder labeled **Architecture**.

4. This brings you to a set of links that connect to architectural journals, Internet resource guides, the Architecture Gopher at the University of Michigan, and image collections at Johns Hopkins University and University of Virginia. Click on the folder called **Renaissance and Baroque Architecture Images from UVA**.

5. Next, you see several folders ranging in topic from Italy in the 15th Century, to England Exploits Classics. The first item listed in this menu is titled, "About the images in this area." This is an interesting file to examine if you're curious about the equipment used to make the images contained in this archive collection. Notice that the icon accompanying this menu item resembles a small sheet of paper with text written on it. These icons represent text files. Click on the folder labeled **Elsewhere in Italy— Alberti; Venice**.

6. The next window that appears lists several images. Click on the image **Arch of Constantine, Rome, 312** and the image shown in Figure 15–22 appears.

Figure 15–22 Image of the Arch of Constantine, Rome, as viewed at Library of Congress Gopher site.

7. You can print this image by clicking on the **Print** button located on the toolbar, or by pulling down the **File** menu and clicking on **Print**.

8. To save this image to disk, place the cursor on the image and click the right mouse button and then click on **Save image as...**When the **Save as...**window pops up, choose a drive, a folder, and assign a file name (or use the default).

9. View other images in the **Elsewhere in Italy** folder by clicking on the **Back** button located on the toolbar.

Internet Self Study Guide 6

Allen C. Benson   acbenson@star-host.com

-=-Finding and Downloading Files on the Internet-=-

Purpose:
Demonstrate how to use a Web browser to find files and download them.

Objective:
Learn terms associated with transferring files on the Internet and learn how to assist others who are looking for a program that compresses and archives files from PKWARE using **Fast FTP Search v4.0** in Trondheim, Norway.

Materials:
PC system connected to the Internet; Web browser; access to a PC's hard drive and DOS shell.

Background:
File transfer is one of the most frequently used Internet applications. It enables you to copy files from over a thousand different archives around the world. You can think of these archives as libraries—electronic libraries housing digitized information. Although information in traditional paper-based libraries is stored in books and magazines, the file is the unit of storage in electronic libraries.

These files hold such things as text, images, sound, and executable programs. Tools like Archie assist you in exploring the staggering number of files that reside in these archives.

The set of conventions that govern how this file transfer process takes place on the Internet is called *File Transfer Protocol* or *FTP*. The FTP protocol enables you to list directories on remote machines and to transfer files in either direction. When a file is transferred, it is not actually moved; rather, the file is copied from one machine to another. The computer from which the file is copied is sometimes referred to as the *source host* and the computer to which the file is copied is called the *destination host*.

Procedure:
1. Start up your Web browser and enter the following address in the **Location** box near the top of the screen: *ftpsearch.lycos.com/*. This connects you to **Fast FTP Search v4.0**—a search engine in Trondheim, Norway.
2. You are given several dialog boxes in which you can enter variables. The default settings work fine for most searches. Make sure **Search Type** is

set to **Case insensitive substring search**. A patron has asked for a copy of PKUNZIP. Enter the filename **PK250W32.EXE** in the **Search for** dialog box located at the top of the window and then click on the **Search** button. (Hint: To learn more about the various search modes—for example, case-insensitive global searching—click on **Search for**.)

3. After running your search, a window similar to the one shown in Figure 15–23 appears.

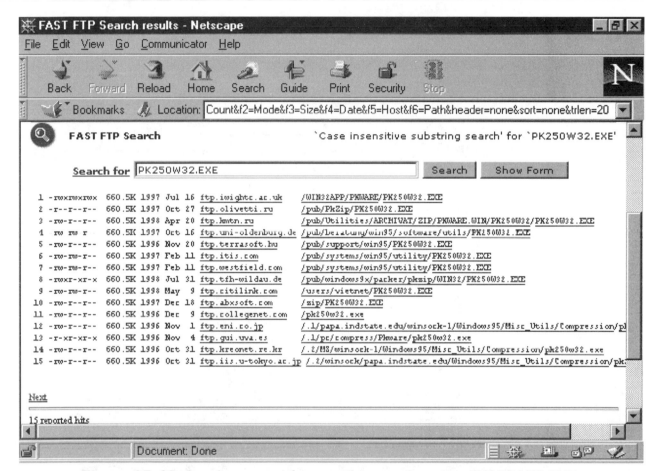

Figure 15–23 Results screen after searching on the string PK250W32.EXE.

4. The results screen presents you with dozens of FTP sites all around the world that archive copies of PK250W32.EXE. Click on the filename **pk250w32.exe** on one of the lines. Theoretically, choosing a site that is in the United States results in a quicker download time, but this isn't always the case. (Hint: If you click on the FTP site name in the left-hand column, you connect to the server's root directory. It's important to click on the filename you want to download and not on one of the directory names in the path statements.)

5. After clicking on the filename, a window appears like the one shown in Figure 15–24.

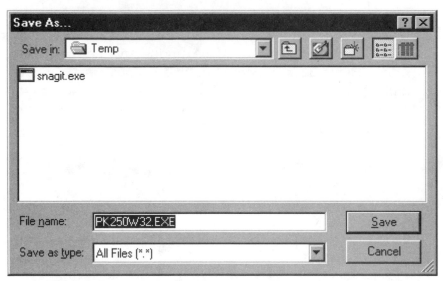

Figure 15–24 The "Unknown file type" window appears when you click on the filename.

6.   Click on the button labeled **Save** and download the file to your C:\TEMP\ directory.

7.   After successfully downloading the file, go to the TEMP directory and double-click on the file name to "unpack" the file. Upon doing so, a window like the one shown in Figure 15–25 appears.

Figure 15–25 Installation window for PKZIP.

8. Click on the button labeled **Extract** to install the program in a directory named C:\Pkware\Pkzipw. The install program asks you to confirm that you want it to create this directory. Click **Yes**. The next window that comes up verifies that the files were authentic. Click **OK**. This completes the extraction process.

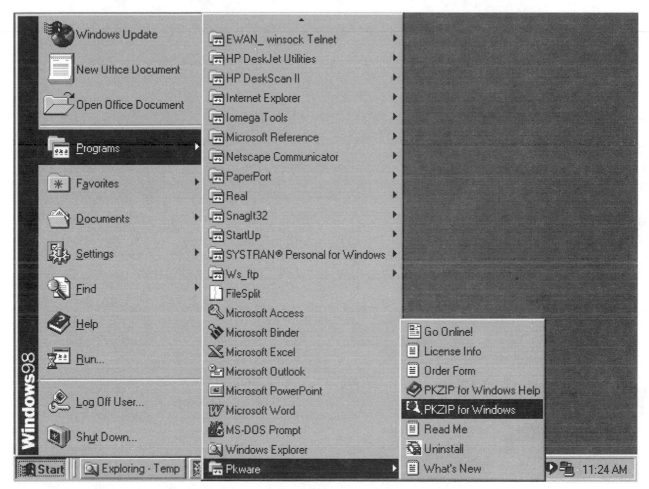

Figure 15–26 Accessing PKZIP for Windows using your START menu in Windows 95.

9. You can access PKZIP for Windows as shown in Figure 15–26.
10. When you run the program, a window like the one shown in Figure 15–27 appears. Click on **HelpIndex** to learn how to compress and uncompress files.

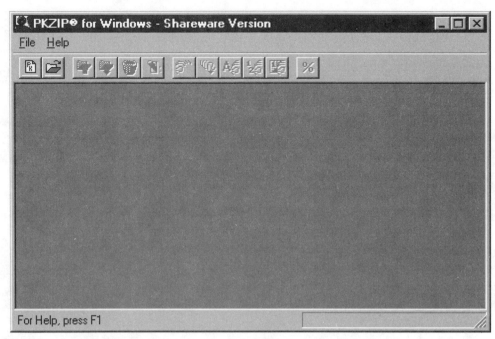

Figure 15–27 Click on **Help** and then **Index** to learn how to compress and uncompress files using PKZIP for Windows. PKZIP is Shareware, so if you'd like to keep using PKZIP, you must register it.

PART V

THE INTERNET
FOR TEENS

In the years we've been observing teens interact with the Internet, two things have become apparent: Teens like communicating with other teens through e-mail and chat and they like interacting with computers in an exploratory manner, learning as much as they can about a system. If your teenagers are interested in the latter—hunkering down with a computer and finding out what makes it tick—Part V is for them.

In Part V we show kids different ways to view and utilize the Internet. If your kids use computers at local libraries and schools, chances are they view the Net through the eyes of a graphical Web browser. There are other more ancient and in some cases less friendly programs used for working on the Internet, too. And why would these interest teenagers? For starters, these programs are more powerful and can be faster than graphical Web browsers. The programs that run faster generally do so because they don't have to wait for images to download, only characters. They are more powerful because you issue commands at a system prompt instead of dragging little pictures around on a Windows or Macintosh screen. Some programs, such as telnet, aren't even supported by a Web browser. You need to run a separate application for this service.

Part V introduces you to these services that go beyond the realm of Web surfing. Part V consists of four chapters that cover UNIX shell accounts and three major Internet services. In Chapter 16, "Diving into Shell Accounts," you learn all about UNIX shell accounts, what they are, where to find them, and how to use them.

In Chapter 17, "Telnet Adventures," you learn about a program called *telnet* that allows you to connect to a remote computer and run applications on that computer.

In Chapter 18, "Newsgroups Galore," we introduce you to the world's largest bulletin board system, Usenet News, and offer suggestions on how your teens might utilize it effectively as a research and communication tool.

Part V ends with Chapter 19, "FTP Fun." FTP is an Internet application that enables you to manage files in electronic libraries and to transfer those files from one computer to another all around the globe. In Chapter 19 we show you basic commands for running FTP, where to find the best FTP sites, and how to set up your own FTP archive that other Internet users can access.

Chapter 16

Diving into
Shell Accounts

Accessing the Internet through shell accounts is a lot of fun. This chapter was written to help you introduce kids to shell accounts and to make the experience both fun and rewarding.

When we talk about a shell account, we are talking about a tool used to access the Internet. If you are willing to stretch your imagination a bit, you could compare a shell account to a Web browser. They both provide you with a means of interacting with the Internet. Both enable you to use your PC to probe the vast resources of the Internet.

There are dissimilarities, too. The interface that a shell account presents—that is, the picture you see on your screen—is quite different from a Web browser. Your computer screen is usually black and you don't see any images, only text. You accomplish tasks by typing commands at your keyboard, not by clicking on pictures with your mouse.

As we show you later, shell accounts also have the ability to go beyond the mere "surfing" capabilities Web browsers offer. In this chapter we introduce you to UNIX shell accounts and explain where to find them and how to use them. We show you how to issue commands in a shell account and what these commands can do. There are some very interesting commands, such as **traceroute**, that enable you to see the path your information follows as it jumps from one computer to the next, heading towards its destination out on the Internet.

Once you have a basic understanding of what a shell account is and how to set it up, you can move on to other services introduced in Part V, including Telnet and FTP.

WHAT IS A UNIX SHELL ACCOUNT, ANYWAY?

To understand fully what a UNIX shell account is, you must first know something about UNIX. UNIX is a computer operating system that began its development back in 1969 in Bell Labs. It functions much like any other operating system, for example Windows 98 or MS-DOS. When you create a document using a word processor and save that document to a floppy disk, you may think that your word processor is saving the file to your disk. It's not. The operating system, which sits between your word processing program and the floppy disk drive, provides a set of rules that enables your program to "talk" to the hardware. An operating system, OS for short, is a layer of software that enables your applications to access your computer's hardware.

When you log into a computer running UNIX, you are generally placed in a program called the shell. A *shell* is a utility program that enables you to interact with the UNIX operating system by typing commands at a prompt. The UNIX prompt is located in the bottom left of your screen and usually looks like a dollar sign ($) or percent sign (%). The prompt may also include the name of your service provider or any other name for that matter.

Shell accounts are character-based interfaces, not GUIs (Graphical User Interfaces). In other words, kids don't point and click with their mouse in a shell account. They run programs by typing commands. They send mail by pressing special key combinations. Some kids look at all of this as unnecessary torture. Others find it interesting and challenging.

HOW DO YOU GET A SHELL ACCOUNT?

If you dial up to the Internet from home, a shell account may already be part of your services. If you are not certain, call your service provider and find out. If you don't already have a shell account, you will have to subscribe to a service that offers shell accounts. Some organizations offer shell accounts for free while others charge a monthly fee. It's not likely that any of our readers dial straight into a UNIX shell account for their primary Internet connection, but it is possible to do so. Table 16–1 presents you with some alternatives for getting your own UNIX shell account.

The services that offer free UNIX shell accounts seem to come and go with great regularity. The two we listed below, Grex and Nyx, may or may not be operational by the time you read this. To stay up-to-date on the availability of free UNIX shell accounts, use a search engine such as NorthernLight (*www.northernlight.com*) and search on the phrase "free unix shell." We recommend that you finish reading the rest of this chapter before signing up with any services.

	Table 16–1 Where to Get UNIX Shell Accounts	
Name	**Where to get**	**Description**
Concentric Network	*www.concentric.net/*	Example of a large Internet Service Provider that offers access to UNIX shell accounts along with their regular dial-up services. Concentric Network has over 350 local call-in points in the United States and Canada.
FreeShells.Net	*www.freeshells.net/*	At the time of this writing, FreeShells.Net was under construction and supported by volunteers only.
Grex Shell Accounts	*telnet://cyberspace.org/*	To sign up, telnet to *cyberspace.org* and log in as **newuser**. You won't have access to a shell account unless you pay, but there is a good menu system available at no charge. To learn more, see descriptions of free Grex services at *www.cyber space.org/*.
Nyx	*telnet://nyx.net/*	To sign up, telnet to *nyx.net* and log in as **new**. Services are somewhat limited unless you pay a small fee. To learn more about setting up a new account, go to *www.nyx.net/newacct.htm*.
WestHost	*www.westhost.com/*	WestHost is one of many Web hosting services that give you access to a UNIX shell account for less than $9.00/month. Web hosting services enable you to set up and run your own "virtual" Web sites.

How to Log into Your UNIX Shell Account

You can log into your UNIX shell account one of two ways:

1. You can dial into the UNIX system using a computer with a modem and any terminal program, such as ProComm Plus or HyperTerminal, which comes with Windows 95/98. (Other terminals are listed in Table 16–2 and described later in this chapter.)
2. You can dial into your Internet service provider using SLIP or PPP and then use telnet to access the UNIX system. You can use the telnet program that comes with Microsoft Windows 95 and 98, or any one of many commercial and freeware telnet applications that are available.

In this chapter we focus on dial-up connections. Telneting to your UNIX shell account is covered in Chapter 17.

Dialing into a UNIX Computer

When you dial into a shell account you are not directly connecting your PC to the Internet as you are with a PPP type connection. Instead you are connecting to an intermediate computer—the UNIX system—which in turn is connected to the Internet. Of all the various methods of connecting, shell accounts are the least expensive and simplest to set up.

General-purpose communication software is computer software that enables you to connect to shell accounts. It's also useful for kids who are interested in interacting with other online services and any of the thousands of active bulletin board systems.

Communication software helps control the modem and helps you send and receive data to and from another modem. The computers that connect to each other don't have to be the same. A Mac can connect to a PC, minicomputer, or mainframe. Any combination of computers can link to each other, but each must be able to communicate with a modem. A modem alone will not allow you to communicate with another computer. You must also run communication software. Communication software is available for DOS, Windows, and Macs.

Name	Where to get	Description
NetTerm	ftp://www.newosoft.com/pub/ users/z/zkrr01/nt32429i.exe	Provides you with a dialer and telnet client for Win95/98/NT; Shareware $20.00.
Com	www.tglmicro.com/com-6.zip	Terminal for Win95/98/NT dial-up connection; Shareware $25.00.
HyperTerminal Private Edition	ftp://ftp.hilgraeve.com/ htpe/htpe4.exe	More powerful than Hilgraeve's HyperTerminal communications program that comes with Win95/ 98/NT 4.x; Freeware.
STerm	ftp://eot.student.utwente.nl/ pub/sterm/st32v20.exe	Windows terminal server with telnet service for Win95/98/NT; Freeware.
TN3270 Plus	www.sdisw.com/sdi/tn3270/ download/TN327032.EXE	Connects your Windows PC to an IBM Mainframe.

Table 16–2 Terminal Emulation Software for Dial-in Accounts

MAKE BELIEVE YOU'RE A TERMINAL

One feature most communication programs offer is the capability of emulating different terminals. *Terminal emulation* is the feature that enables a personal computer to link with minicomputers and mainframes around the world.

The word *terminal* refers to the keyboard and monitor used with multi-user systems such as those used in large corporations and universities. When kids use a personal computer to connect to other computers, there are times when they will use it as a terminal, not a full-fledged computer like a PC or Mac. This means they will mainly be using their keyboard and monitor, not the full processing power of their machine's microprocessor. Using terminal emulation, communication software can transform a PC or Mac into a terminal for the purpose of communicating with other computers.

WHAT TYPE OF TERMINAL ARE YOU?

Depending upon what type of computer kids connect to, their computer will need to emulate, or act like, a certain type of terminal—whatever type the computer on the other end understands.

All the various computers they'll be connecting to on the Internet recognize a limited set of terminal types. The most common one is VT100, which stands for *VAX Terminal, Model 100*. When you purchase your communication software, make sure that VT100 is included among the list of terminals it emulates. You should also be able to emulate an *ANSI terminal*, which will aid you in communicating with Bulletin Board Systems.

The basic goal is to make sure that your terminal emulation is set to the same terminal type as the computer to which you're connecting. VT100 is the default setting on most hosts and it is a good one to choose if you are in doubt.

Transferring Files

File transfer is another common feature supported by most communication software. This feature will help kids send and receive files between their personal computers and a remote computer.

File transfer protocols are sets of rules that regulate how personal computers communicate with the remote host when sending or receiving these files. The communication program you choose should support the most common protocols, which are Kermit, ZModem, YModem, and XModem.

Other Communications Software Features

Some communication programs offer ways to store one or more telephone numbers in a dialing directory. When your kids want to contact a particular service, the program retrieves the desired number and dials it automatically, making the connection for them.

Most communication programs enable kids to capture information so that they can save it to a disk or send it to a printer. When the capture feature is turned on, the characters they type and receive during a session are saved to a disk. If kids are being charged by the minute for online time, this is an economical way to retrieve data quickly and then disconnect. Once they're offline, they can pull their file into a word processor for reading, editing, and printing at their convenience.

Some communication programs support *scripting*. A *script* is a list of instructions that you write in such a way that a program can understand them. Scripting is typically used to write programs that automate routine tasks. For example, if your kids log onto a particular BBS on a regular basis, they can write a login script to do the connecting and logging-in process automatically. Instructions for writing and compiling scripts are usually included in the user manual that accompanies the communication software.

Lastly, a communication program may have a review feature, sometimes called *scroll back* or *replay*, that will enable kids to go back and view data that has already scrolled off the screen. More sophisticated programs offer other features like *automatic dialing, cut and paste editing, scripting,* and *bulletin board functions.*

Choosing Communication Software

You can choose from among several communication programs. Some were listed in Table 16–2. This section provides you with ordering information for a few of the more polished and powerful general-purpose programs.

Kermit 95 for Windows 95, Windows NT, and OS/2, and MS-DOS Kermit for DOS and Windows 3.x are communication software programs developed by the Kermit Project at Columbia University in New York City. Kermit is known for its ability to transfer files even under the worst of conditions—for example, bad connections with lots of line noise. You can order Kermit direct from Columbia University. Single copy price is $54. Write to The Kermit Project, Columbia University, 612 West 115th Street, New York, NY 10025–7799, or call 212–854–3703. You can order Kermit 95 on the Web by pointing your browser to *www.columbia.edu/kermit/k95order.html*. MS-DOS Kermit 3.14 is available for download at *www.columbia.edu/kermit/mskermit.html*.

CrossTalk for Windows is one of the long-established communication packages with a list price of around $179. Setting up CrossTalk is simple and straightforward. It is designed for more experienced users and comes with prewritten scripts for logging into the Internet, bulletin board systems, and other online services like CompuServe. For additional information, contact Digital Communications Associates Inc., 1000 Alderman Dr., Alpharetta, GA 30202–4199; 800–348–3221; FAX 404–442–4358.

Procomm Plus from Quarterdeck is a popular communication program that offers such features as remote control, faxing capabilities, terminal emulation, and many different ways to transfer files. As an added bonus, Procomm Plus includes Microsoft Internet Explorer, Internet e-mail, News Reader, FTP, and telnet. It will handle the needs of kids just starting out and also work for advanced online users. The list price is about $145. You can order Procomm Plus from Microwarehouse, 535 Connecticut Ave., Norwalk, CT 06854; 800–367–7080; *www.microwarehouse.com*. To find out more about Procomm Plus and where it can be purchased, go to Quarterdeck's home page at *www.datastorm.com/* and click on **Products.**

Zterm for Windows operates on Windows 3.1, Windows 95, Windows 98, and Windows NT Workstation and Server. You can use Zterm to connect to your Internet host through a dial-up connection or direct Internet connection using TCP/IP and telnet. Zterm is a simple-to-use communication program that you can download and try for 14 days at no charge. If you like it, contact Zterm or one of their distributors to receive an installation code. For additional information, go to Zterm's Web site at *www.zterm.com/*.

Setting Up a Shell Account

To set up a dial-up connection to a shell account, kids need the following items:

1. A personal computer
2. A telephone line
3. A modem
4. Communications software
5. An agreement with an Internet service provider

Dialing In

Once you successfully install the communication software on your computer and properly configure it to work with your modem, you're then ready to dial into the service provider's computer and link to the Internet.

The service provider will tell you what phone number to dial and will assign you a *userid* and password. Userid stands for user identification and it is a word that usually consists of the first letter of your first name and the first seven letters of your last name. After you login in for the first time, you'll be asked to change your password.

Remember, in a bare bones shell account, you'll see nothing but a system prompt when you first login. To access all of the various Internet services discussed in this book, you'll have to issue a command at this prompt to initiate a session.

If you can't make the dial-up connection work, double-check the phone number you're dialing and the settings in the communication software. Service providers are usually ready and willing to help in any way that they can, so don't hesitate calling them for assistance.

Where to Begin

One of the best places for kids to begin learning how to use a shell account to explore the Internet is by running a program called *Gopher*. Usually with a simple command, **Gopher**, you will be on your way and your kids will be able to navigate dozens of Gopher sites all around the world by simply browsing through menus.

It's also fun to telnet from your shell account to any one of hundreds of online libraries all around the world. Visiting online libraries via telnet was first introduced in Chapter 13. Chapter 17 explains in more detail how to use telnet and shows kids how to access other types of remote computer systems besides online library catalogs. Popular Internet-related UNIX commands are also introduced in the next chapter, including **ping** and **whois**.

We close Chapter 16 with an explanation of some basic UNIX commands used for performing simple housekeeping tasks, such as listing files and directories, deleting files, and running an e-mail program called *Pine*.

Diving into UNIX

Table 16–3 describes basic UNIX commands that can help kids manage their UNIX shell accounts.

Command	Purpose	Example
^Z (ctrl-Z)	suspends the current process	^Z
cd	change directories	cd/pub
cp	copies files	cp .plan plan.copy (The .plan file remains and a new copy named plan.copy is created.)
date	displays date and time of day	date
ls	lists files in a directory	ls
ls -l	lists files along with their size, dates, and other information	ls -l
man	displays online help information	man pico
more	display data one screen at a time	ls -l / more
mv	moves files and renames files (To move a file named logo.gif to a directory named public_html)	mv logo.gif public_html
pico	starts Pico, a simple text editor	pico
pine	starts Pine mail program	pine
pwd	tells you what directory you're currently in	pwd
passwd	change password	passwd
rm	deletes a file	rm.signature
rmdir	removes a directory (directory must be empty)	rmdir Mail/
rmdir -r	removes a directory and all files and subdirectories it contains	rmdir -r News/
touch	creates new file (contains 0 bytes)	touch resume.htm

Table 16–3 Basic UNIX Commands for Shell Account Users

The traceroute Command

Kids may find it interesting to look at the route their computer takes on the Internet to get to another computer with the **traceroute** command. It's easy to use. Just enter the command **traceroute** followed by the address of another computer. For example, to see what route your computer follows when it connects to a computer at Purdue University, enter **traceroute ecn.purdue.edu** at the system prompt.

Your computer traces all the steps it takes to get to the other computer and prints it to your screen. Note how fast connections are made and how indirect the route can be. Routes will vary depending on the time of day and other circumstances. If you start in California, it may look something like the output shown in Figure 16–1.

Figure 16–1 The **traceroute** command lets you see what route your
computer takes when linking to another computer on the Internet.

```
% traceroute ecn.purdue.edu
traceroute to ecn.purdue.edu (128.46.128.76), 30 hops max, 40 byte packets
  1  wfbcn1–fddi.cris.com (199.3.12.188) 2 ms 1 ms 2 ms
  2  199.3.98.22 (199.3.98.22) 30 ms 44 ms 43 ms
  3  aads.agis.net (198.32.130.19) 27 ms 48 ms 103 ms
  4  washington.agis.net (204.130.243.36) 66 ms 57 ms 52 ms
  5  mae-east.ans.net (192.41.177.140) 86 ms 108 ms 101 ms
  6  t3–3.cnss56.Washington-DC.t3.ans.net (140.222.56.4) 106 ms 70 ms 91 ms
  7  t3–0.cnss32.New-York.t3.ans.net (140.222.32.1) 78 ms 92 ms 115 ms
  8  t3–0.cnss48.Hartford.t3.ans.net (140.222.48.1) 74 ms 96 ms 86 ms
  9  t3–2.cnss43.Cleveland.t3.ans.net (140.222.43.3) 90 ms 113 ms 118 ms
 10  t3–1.cnss27.Chicago.t3.ans.net (140.222.27.3) 119 ms 107 ms 96 ms
 11  cnss29.Chicago.t3.ans.net (140.222.27.194) 116 ms 238 ms 203 ms
 12  enss152–2.t3.ans.net (199.221.97.70) 250 ms 193 ms 289 ms
 13  cisco1–oc.gw.purdue.edu (192.5.102.3) 275 ms 280 ms 201 ms
 14  nscmsee.ecn.purdue.edu (128.46.201.99) 208 ms 178 ms 218 ms
 15  harbor.ecn.purdue.edu (128.46.129.76) 229 ms * 177 ms
```

As you trace the path shown in Figure 16–1, it's interesting to see all of the
stops one packet of information makes before it finally reaches its destination—
Washington, New York, Hartford, Cleveland, Chicago, and so on.

Pine is not Elm

UNIX systems are the most widely used systems on the Internet and many of
the more popular mail programs are found on UNIX systems. They include Pine,
Elm, Rmail, Mush, and others. Pine is designed for inexperienced users and offers a simple and straightforward menu as the screen in Figure 16–2 reveals.

To learn more about a particular e-mail program, Elm for example, you could
enter the UNIX command **man elm** at your system prompt. UNIX displays a
manual describing the program and its command line options. In many cases,
the online help screens in the mail program constitute your main source of documentation.

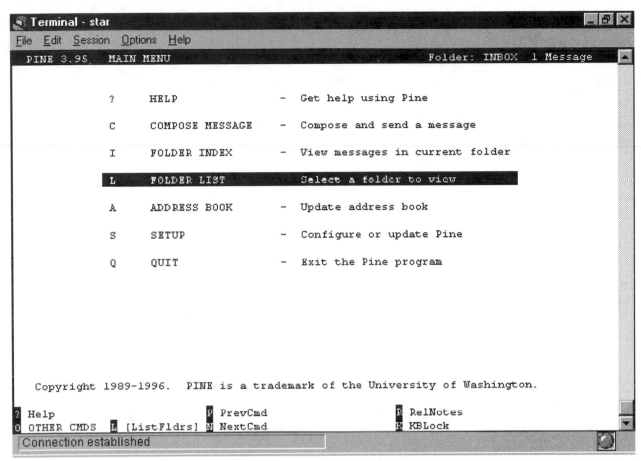

Figure 16–2 The Pine mail program comes with UNIX shell accounts.

How to Start Pine

The nice thing about Pine is that you can use it without ever reading a manual. There are just a few simple commands to remember in order to achieve basic goals. To send a message, enter the command **pine <recipient's address>** at the system prompt; for example, **pine jdeer@farm.org**. This will start the Pine program and provide you with a screen where you can begin composing your message. If you'd like to start Pine and go to the main menu first, type **pine** at the system prompt and press ENTER.

Only the very basic features of Pine are covered here. If you'd like to learn more about things like forwarding messages, replying to messages, and using the address book, type **?** (a question mark) at the main menu for additional help.

Composing a Message

In Pine, the message header is located at the top as shown in Figure 16–3. Here you indicate the recipient's address, whether you want to send a copy to anyone or attach a file, and what the subject of the message is. After you fill in the first line, press ENTER or ARROW DOWN to the next line.

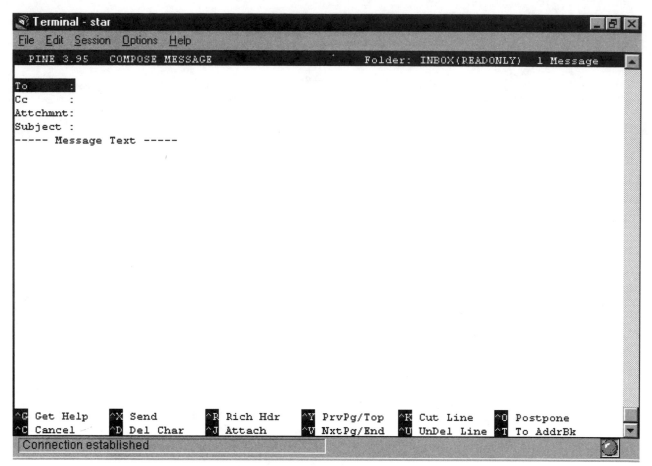

Figure 16–3 Pine displays this screen for composing a message.

At the bottom of the screen are several commands. All of them use the CTRL key which is designated with the caret symbol ^. For example, ^X Send means press the CTRL key while pressing X to send a message. When in doubt, press ^G for help. For additional help on composing messages, move the cursor to the body of the message and press ^G.

Typing the Message

After you fill in the header, move the cursor to the message body and just begin typing your message. The display presented in Figure 16–3 illustrates Pine's header and message area. To move the cursor, you can use the up, down, left, and right arrow keys. To move down one screen, press ^V. To move up one screen, press ^Y. The ^K command can be used to delete an entire line. Place the cursor on the line you would like to delete and press ^K.

When you want to delete a character after you type it, press the BACKSPACE or DELETE key, whichever key is set up to "erase" on your terminal. You can also use the ^H character to do the same thing. These key strokes delete to the left of the cursor. To delete to the right of the cursor, press ^D.

Sending a Message

When you're finished composing your message, send it by pressing ^X. You'll be asked to confirm that you want to send the message. At this point, pressing y will send the message, pressing n will take you back into the composition screen. You can cancel the message by pressing ^C.

You can postpone sending your message until a later time by pressing ^O. Pine will save it to a file automatically, at which point you can stop Pine and do something else. You can come back at a later date and Pine will give you an opportunity to resume writing the message.

For your reference, we've listed the basic commands for composing and sending a message in Table 16–4.

Table 16–4 Pine Commands for Composing and Sending Messages	
Press This Key Combination:	**To Do This:**
^K	Delete current line
^V	Move down one screen
^Y	Move up one screen
^H	Delete to the left of the cursor
^D	Delete to the right of the cursor
^A	Move cursor to start of current line
^E	Move cursor to end of current line
^X	Send message
^C	Cancel message
^O	Postpone message

Attaching Files to a Message

The *Attchmnt:* line in the header is where you indicate whether you want to attach one or more files to the message. The files you are attaching are files that reside on your host computer, not on your own personal computer. If you have a Microsoft Word, WordPerfect, or Excel spreadsheet stored on your personal computer, for example, and would like to attach them to an e-mail message, follow these steps:

1. Upload the file(s) to your host computer using one of the file transfer protocols available to you through your communications program.
2. Once the file(s) are in your directory on the host computer, go to the message composition screen and place your cursor on the *Attchmnt:* line in the header. Press ^T to tell Pine you want to attach a file to the message. Pine will ask you to select the name of the file(s) you want to attach and present you with two quote signs "" between which you can enter any comment. (The recipient will see the comment upon receiving the file.)

3. Use your up, down, right, and left arrow keys to select which file you want to attach and then press ENTER. Directory names will also be listed. When you highlight one of these and press enter, the files within that directory will be listed and you can select one of those. Multiple files should be separated by commas once their names are placed in the *Attchmnt:* field. For example, a child may want to attach a picture of her dog Sparky and a copy of a report she wrote on germinating lima beans when writing to Grandma. The header would specify the two files to be attached as follows:

```
To : grandma@house.in.woods.org
Cc:
Attchmnt: /U/A/sparky.gif (120KB) "My Dog Sparky",
/U/A/beans.txt (4 KB) "Germinating Lima Beans"
Subject: Got an A in science today!
```

This illustrates one of Pine's more notable features, which is its MIME capability (Multipurpose Internet Mail Extensions). This allows it to send and receive multimedia e-mail. By multimedia we mean it has the ability to include graphics, video, and sound in a message. The "U/A/" and "(120KB)" in the preceding example are automatically inserted by Pine. The former is part of the pathname (pathnames are discussed in Chapter 19) and the latter is the size of the file measured in kilobytes.

Reading Your Mail

The simplest way to read messages is to type **pine** at the system prompt and press ENTER. This will bring you to Pine's main menu. From the main menu, press I to display the Index. The Index is a list of all the messages stored in the inbox folder of your mailbox. To display a message, move the cursor to the message you would like to view, using either the up or down arrow keys, and then press ENTER. Pine then displays the message one screen at a time.

For your reference, Table 16–5 shows you Pine's main menu screen commands, and Table 16–6 shows the commands that are available to you while you are viewing a message.

Table 16–5 Pine's Main Menu Commands

Press This Key:	To Do This:
?	Show help text
O	Show all Other available commands
C	Compose a message
P	Select Previous command up on menu
I	FOLDER INDEX screen
N	Select Next command down on menu
L	FOLDER LIST screen
R	Display Pine Release Notes
A	ADDRESS BOOK screen
K	Lock Keyboard
S	SETUP functions
G	Goto a specified folder
Q	Quit Pine

Table 16–6 Pine Commands Available When Viewing a Message

Press This Key:	To Do This:
i	Take you to index from main menu
+ or SPACEBAR	Move forward one screen
- or ^Y	Move back one screen
up- and down-arrow keys	Move up and down one line at a time
m	Return to main menu
d	Deletes message
u	Undelete message
i	Return to index
p	Move to the previous message
n	Go to the next message

Chapter 17

Telnet Adventures

Would you like to be able to browse the online card catalog of a library in a city you are going to visit? How can you find out the weather conditions of a particular city? Would you like to find out the payload of the next NASA mission? How do you have a "discussion" online with several people at once? How do you learn about an imaginary world made of words? You can discover all this and more with an Internet tool called *telnet*!

In this chapter, we introduce you to communitywide information systems, bulletin board systems, and special Internet services where participants chat in real time by typing messages at their computers. These are all Internet services that can be accessed using telnet and will be of special interest to kids.

WHAT IS TELNET?

Telnet is a powerful Internet application that enables you to login to remote computers and—through your keyboard—run programs on that remote computer. Telnet is also called *remote login* for this reason. With telnet, you can access computers all over the world, as long as they are connected to the Internet and you are authorized to use the remote system. You can gain access to a remote system by giving your telnet program a specific computer address to contact. Once connected, the remote system prompts you for a login and password.

How Does Telnet Work?

You can run telnet from your UNIX shell account or from your PC. In order to run it on your UNIX shell account, you must first connect to your shell account either by dialing in with your modem, or connecting by running telnet on your

PC. You might wonder, why would anyone use telnet to connect to another computer just to run telnet from *that* computer? In other words, if you have a telnet program on your PC, why not just launch your telnet session from your own PC?

In our own work, we do it both ways. If we are working in Windows and need to telnet to a remote computer to access a resource, we launch a Windows-based telnet program and connect in that manner. If we are logged into a UNIX shell account checking mail or managing a bulletin board system, we simply do our telneting from that system.

Telnet, whether run on your PC or a UNIX shell account, is based on the client/server model. The client program initiates the connection with a server program usually running on a remote machine. Keystrokes are passed from your keyboard directly to the remote computer just as though they were being typed at a keyboard on the remote computer. Output from the remote computer is sent back and displayed on your monitor. One important exchange that takes place between the server and the client is agreeing on the *terminal type*.

The telnet client software on your personal computer provides terminal emulation and you should be aware of what kind of terminal it is emulating. There should be an option in one of the pull-down menus in your program that lists terminal preferences. Look for an "emulation" setting and make sure it is VT100. The remote host may ask you what type of terminal emulation you are using or give you a number of choices from which to pick. The most common type of terminal emulation is VT100, and most hosts accept VT100 emulation or something similar.

Why Use Telnet?

Telnet is especially useful for accessing changing information, the type of information commonly found in databases. The most widely accessible databases are bibliographic databases (better known as electronic catalogs) maintained by libraries. As the Web evolves, more and more of these databases will become available directly through your Web browser.

Running Telnet on a UNIX Shell Account

In UNIX you use the command **telnet** followed by a computer's address to run the telnet software and open the connection. You login to the remote host using an account number, password, or special username. For example, to connect to NEWTON: Educational Electronic Bulletin Board System at Argonne National Laboratory, you would enter the following at your system prompt: **telnet newton.dep.anl.gov**. (The dot at the end of the preceding sentence is a period, not part of the telnet address.) A few moments later, the message shown in Figure 17–1 appears on your screen:

Figure 17–1 When you first connect to NEWTON, you must set up
a new user account.

Auto-sensing...

Welcome to NEWTON BBS

Welcome to NEWTON BBS! NEWTON is operated by the Division of Educational Programs at Argonne National Laboratory. NEWTON functions to serve math, science, and computer education interests.

Web address: http://newton.dep.anl.gov

If you already have a User-ID on this
system, type it in and press ENTER.
Otherwise type "new":

The Login

Once you are connected, the next step is to login to the system. This requires entering a user ID at the system's *login:* prompt and a password. If you are a new user, you must answer this system's questions before it issues you an account. The application process only takes a couple of minutes and asks you your name and address, telephone number, date of birth, and the name and address of your workplace. The name you give yourself becomes your NEWTON user ID.

Sometimes you connect to a system where a login name is not necessary. You know this because you won't be prompted for a login name. You are just given a list of command options.

Once you establish your account with NEWTON, the Welcome screen shown in Figure 17–2 appears.

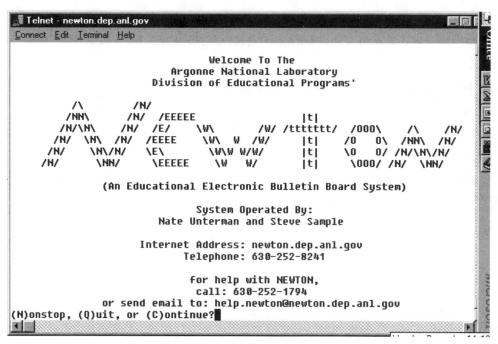

Figure 17–2 The Welcome screen at Argonne National Laboratory's electronic bulletin board system known as NEWTON.

Press C to continue. The main menu shown in Figure 17–3 gives you several options.

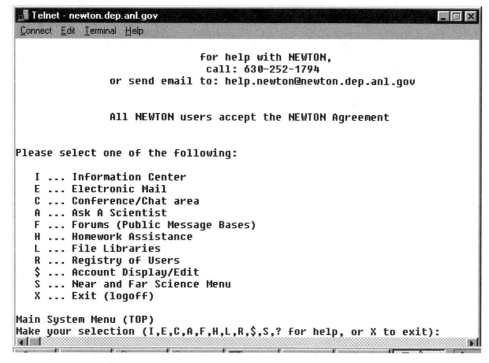

Figure 17–3 NEWTON's main menu offers several options ranging from online forums to homework assistance.

The Telnet Command Mode

If you enter the **telnet** command by itself without a target host's address, a *telnet>* client prompt appears and you are placed in what is called *telnet command mode*. You can type a question mark (**?**) at the *telnet>* prompt to display a list of valid telnet client commands. Among the various telnet commands, you'll probably use **open**, **quit**, **close**, **set**, **carriage return**, and **display** most often.

The **open** command allows you to initiate a session from the *telnet>* prompt by typing **open <domain name>**. For example, if the *telnet>* prompt is displayed on your screen, which means you are in command mode, you initiate a telnet connection by entering **ohionet.org** to telnet to the regional library network called OHIONET. If command mode is not active and the only thing displayed on your screen is the system prompt, you initiate this session by entering **telnet ohionet.org**.

The **set** command allows you to set various operating parameters. Entering **set?** (the word *set* and a question mark) at the *telnet>* prompt provides you with a complete listing of these parameters. The **display** command displays the operating parameters in use for the current telnet session.

Exiting a Telnet Session

Exiting a telnet session is fairly simple. If you are using the menu, just choose Quit. If you are in command mode, use the **quit** command to exit telnet. If you are currently connected to a remote machine, use the **close** command to disconnect from the remote machine without stopping the telnet program.

If you get stuck in the session, however, and it appears that things are locked up, try using the *telnet escape character* to quit. On UNIX systems, the telnet escape character is CTRL]. Press the CTRL key and hold it down while pressing the right square bracket (]): This moves you into command mode. Press ENTER without entering a command to get out of command mode and get back into the telnet session with the remote computer. (Note: In some documentation, you will see the CTRL key indicated with the caret (^). In these cases, CTRL Z is written as ^Z.)

Sometimes it may appear that the escape character doesn't work. Although the remote host acts immediately on the input it receives from your keyboard, the information it sends back to you is buffered. A little time may pass before the information appears on your screen.

Port Numbers

Occasionally, you will be asked to specify a port number when you make a telnet connection. *Port numbers* are positive integers that represent different destinations within a given host computer. Each destination provides a different service, and these services are kept separate by giving each one a different port assignment.

Some ports are always reserved for certain standard services such as electronic mail. Other numbers are used for special services. A host computer called *um-weather.sprl.umich.edu* at the University of Michigan provides weather reports for the United States and Canada. In order to connect to this special service, you must specify a port number of 3000. The command **telnet um-weather.sprl.umich.edu 3000** tells the host that you want to use the weather service.

If the above format for specifying the port number doesn't work at your site, check your local documentation on using telnet. On some systems, such as a VAX/VMS system, it is necessary to specify the port number in the following manner:

telnet um-weather.sprl.umich.edu /port=3000

Recording Information

Telnet is not a service that makes it easy to move information from the remote computer to your own. If you want to record what occurs during a session, it's best to capture a log file of your session. If available, check with your computer department or the manual accompanying the communication software you use to learn just how this can be done on your system. PROCOMM PLUS for Windows, for example, gives the option of capturing to a file or directly to the printer during a telnet session. Both methods are initiated by clicking on the appropriate toolbar button.

Internet Sonar: The *ping* Command

Sometimes, you may experience problems trying to connect to a remote host. If you fail to connect to a host using telnet, an error message appears on your screen, stating something like *UnKnown INTERNET host*.

There are different reasons this may occur. One reason may be that you mistyped the domain name or IP address. Another reason you may be unable to connect is because all the connections that the remote host supports are already in use. When this happens, you get a *time out* message saying something like *Connection refused* or *There are too many interactive users at the moment*.

Another cause may be that the host you are trying to reach is down. At times some part of the network may be down or too congested. A program called *ping* can help in testing this kind of problem. You may have to find out how to do this on your particular system, but you can begin by simply typing the word **ping** at your system prompt, followed by the host address. Then press ENTER. When you enter the command **ping ua1vm.ua.edu**, you may see output as simple as *ua1vm.ua.edu is alive*, or it may look something like this:

comp$ **ping whitehouse.gov**
PING whitehouse.gov (198.137.241.30): 56 data bytes
64 bytes from 198.137.241.30: icmp_seq=0 ttl=244 time=884.6 ms
64 bytes from 198.137.241.30: icmp_seq=1 ttl=244 time=700.5 ms
64 bytes from 198.137.241.30: icmp_seq=2 ttl=244 time=775.7 ms
64 bytes from 198.137.241.30: icmp_seq=3 ttl=244 time=600.7 ms
64 bytes from 198.137.241.30: icmp_seq=4 ttl=244 time=817.7 ms
64 bytes from 198.137.241.30: icmp_seq=5 ttl=244 time=676.6 ms
64 bytes from 198.137.241.30: icmp_seq=6 ttl=244 time=603.2 ms
64 bytes from 198.137.241.30: icmp_seq=7 ttl=244 time=691.5 ms
64 bytes from 198.137.241.30: icmp_seq=8 ttl=244 time=666.5 ms
64 bytes from 198.137.241.30: icmp_seq=9 ttl=244 time=584.1 ms
64 bytes from 198.137.241.30: icmp_seq=10 ttl=244 time=520.7 ms
64 bytes from 198.137.241.30: icmp_seq=11 ttl=244 time=431.3 ms
64 bytes from 198.137.241.30: icmp_seq=12 ttl=244 time=509.8 ms
64 bytes from 198.137.241.30: icmp_seq=13 ttl=244 time=609.3 ms
64 bytes from 198.137.241.30: icmp_seq=14 ttl=244 time=543.4 ms
64 bytes from 198.137.241.30: icmp_seq=15 ttl=244 time=736.3 ms
64 bytes from 198.137.241.30: icmp_seq=16 ttl=244 time=920.1 ms

—- whitehouse.gov ping statistics—-
18 packets transmitted, 17 packets received, 5% packet loss
round-trip min/avg/max = 431.3/663.0/920.1 ms

The ping program sends data packets to the host, which in turn should echo them back if a connection is made. The IP address from which it is echoed back, the time it takes in milliseconds, and sometimes the size of the packet are presented in the screen output.

If you receive a message that says no such host exists, there may be a problem with the domain network software and its attempt to translate the corresponding IP address. If you know the IP address (198.137.241.30), try using it to contact the host. If this works, the problem was the domain name.

Whose Domain Address Is It?

If you'd like to find something out about a particular domain name, telnet to *rs.internic.net* and at the system prompt (which in this case looks like *[dec-vt100] InterNIC >*), type **whois** and press ENTER. Once you connect to InterNIC's whois database, type a domain name and press ENTER. In the following example, the name *ua1vm.ua.edu* was entered:

Whois: ua1vm.ua.edu
University of Alabama (UA1VM-HST)
Seebeck Computer Center
P.O. Box 870346
Tuscaloosa, AL 35487–0346
Hostname: UA1VM.UA.EDU
Address: 130.160.4.100
System: ? running ?
Coordinator: Reese, Danny (DR4) DREESE@UA1VM.UA.EDU
(205) 348–8718

Notice that just under the hostname, the IP address is given. Once the system presents the data, the connection should close automatically. If it doesn't, enter **quit** at the *whois:* prompt and then enter **quit** at the *[vt100] InterNIC >* prompt.

Telneting to an OPAC

OPAC stands for Online Public Access Catalog. This is the online form of a library's card catalog. Online catalogs are powerful tools because they make searching library catalogs easy. Rather than thumbing through author, title, and subject cards, computers enable users to search for any keyword or combination of words in not only the author, title, and subject fields but also fields like publisher and notes fields. Most searches are performed in a few seconds even if the library has hundreds of thousands of records.

Telnet enables you to access libraries' online systems. Are you asking yourself why you or students would want to browse the card catalog of a library you or they cannot physically go to? Many people have asked us that same question. Here are some reasons why you may want to access an OPAC via the Internet:

- OPACs greatly simplify researching. It would be extremely difficult, if not impossible, to find a book in a card catalog if you didn't know the exact spelling of the title or author's name. An OPAC enables you to verify author/title information through keyword searching. Some systems even enable users to access indexes. When you're not exactly sure how to spell an author's name, you can view where you are in the author index as you explore variations in spelling. Once you have verified the correct author and title, then you can see whether your library has the item in their local holdings and what its call number is.
- Another reason for accessing OPACs is so you can learn about a particular library's strengths. Understanding that one university is strong in history and another is strong in films can be useful when choosing a college or writing a bibliography for a research paper or report.
- Most OPACs offer more than just the ability to search the library's hold-

ings. Many offer access to other databases, specialized services, or other Internet resources such as Gopher, Archie, telnet, WAIS databases, and the Web.

Gateway Systems

Gateway systems are sites you telnet to that provide access to several other systems and services. You telnet to reach machine A, and then invoke telnet on machine A to reach machine B. The following example, which connects you to *library.wustl.edu* at Washington University, is a good example of what you see when you access other services through a gateway system.

```
comp% telnet library.wustl.edu
Trying 128.252.173.4...
Connected to library.wustl.edu.
Escape character is '^]'.
UNIX(r) System V Release 4.0 (library)
Please enter your terminal type,
or press RETURN to choose the
default.
TERM = (dcc-vt100)
```

Upon pressing RETURN to default to the vt100 terminal, the screen shown in Figure 17–4 appears. Simply press ENTER to access the WorldWindow as a public user.

```
WorldWindow    Washington University Libraries, St. Louis, MO        12/14/98 14:3

    Welcome to WorldWindow, the WU Libraries' Electronic Information Gateway!  Some
    services are only available to authorized users and require that you log in
    with a username and password.  If you do not have a username and password,
    just press RETURN and you will receive access to all public services.


                          Username [            ]
                          Password [            ]
```

Figure 17–4 WorldWindow at Washington University asks unauthorized users to press RETURN to access their services.

The WorldWindow menu gives you access to other systems. For example, one system you can access is Washington University's library by choosing menu item 2 *Library Catalog*. Menu item *4 Subject Guides* gives you access to both local resources and resources located around the world. You view the subject guides through a Web browser called Lynx as shown in Figure 17–5.

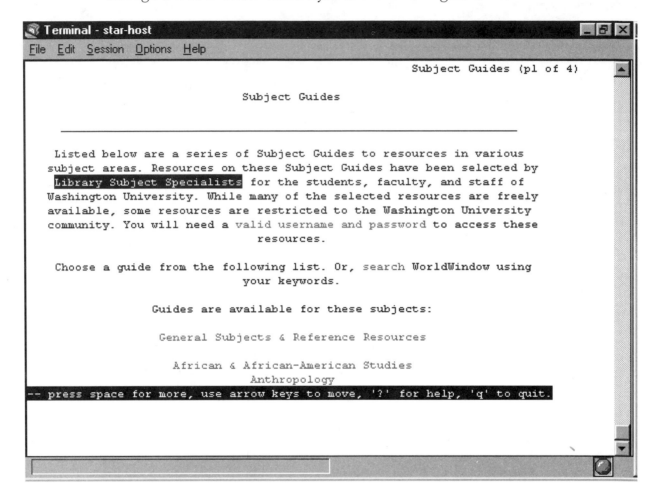

Figure 17–5 Washington University library's subject guides viewed in Lynx.

Lynx is a predecessor of graphical browsers—the Netscape Navigator and Internet Explorer varieties. Some of the subject guides at Washington University link to resources via telnet, but most of the services are themselves running on Web servers. The screen view shown in Figure 17–5 is also presented in Figure 17–6, but this time it is viewed through Netscape Navigator. The speed at which Web pages load is generally faster with text-based browsers, but then you lose some time trying to navigate text-only views of the Web that aren't always as intuitive as graphical views.

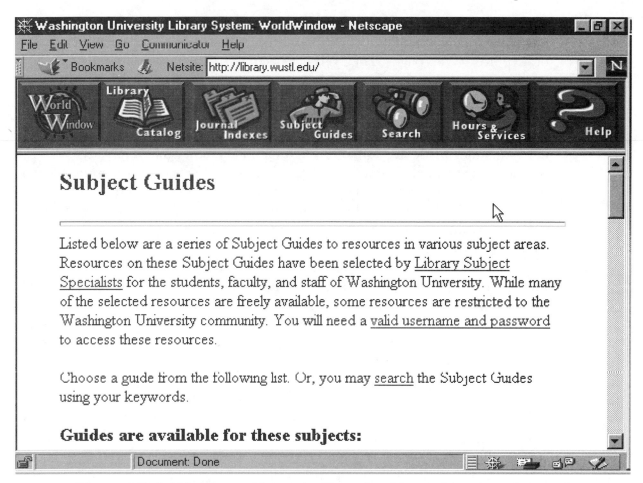

Figure 17–6 Washington University library's subject guides viewed through Netscape Navigator.

COMMUNITY INFORMATION SYSTEMS

A Free-Net is a computerized civic information system following the standards and principles of the National Public Telecommunications Network (NPTN) based in Cleveland, Ohio. NPTN is a nonprofit corporation with an established network of computerized community information systems. NPTN represents the most organized of the community information networks. We regret that during the writing of this latest edition of *Connecting Kids and the Internet* NPTN filed for bankruptcy and was in the process of winding down its operations. At some point in the future their server at *www.nptn.org/* will be shutting down. Community networks are still going strong, however, and new systems come into existence often.

To stay up-to-date with the latest listing of Free-Nets and Community Network Systems, point your browser to the Organization For Community Network's (OFCN) Web site at *ofcn.org*. OFCN is a new organization that provides many of the services that were associated with NPTN.

There are many ways to build a community information network. Some are based on standard BBS (Bulletin Board System) software and others are based on hypertext Web pages. The Web has become the platform of choice for most community information systems, but some can still be accessed by dialing into or telneting to a UNIX system.

Regardless of their method of delivering information, community information networks share common elements. They organize their information in a hierarchical manner made accessible through menu choices. Some offer access to Internet services such as e-mail; however, their main focus is information relevant to the local community or region. Often a "city" metaphor is used—for example, a homework hotline may be located in a menu item called *schoolhouse* and local voters registration sites may be listed under the menu choice called *Government Building* or *City Hall*.

Community networks are predominantly maintained by volunteers organized into committees. As with other telnet services, Free-Nets are limited to a maximum number of simultaneous logins. Often you are also given a maximum amount of time to use the system when logged in as a guest—generally between 15 minutes and an hour. Users are given the option of browsing as a guest or becoming a registered member.

Connecting

You can connect to community information networks using Web browsers, telnet, or by calling directly using a phone number and modem. The simplest way to connect is to surf on in on your Web browser if possible, but since this chapter is promoting the use of telnet, that's what we'll talk about here.

To telnet to a community information system, at your system prompt type **telnet <community information network address>** and press ENTER. Sometimes you will be required to login or give a password or both. For example, to reach the Cleveland Free-Net, at your system prompt, type **telnet freenet-in-a.cwru.edu** and press ENTER. Once connected, you will be asked whether you are a registered user or visitor. Say you are a visitor. Next you are asked why you are there. Choose *2. Explore the system*.

If you do want to dial in using a modem, use your communications software to dial the modem number 216–368–3888 and then wait to be connected. Once connected, you will be asked to follow a login procedure just as when you used telnet.

What's There?

Community information systems offer much useful information pertinent to a local community or region. For example, you may find information on arts and crafts fairs and classes, program guides and services offered by the community access television station, homework hotlines, e-mail to local government agencies, city council agendas and public meeting schedules, social services information, and much more. The main menu for Cleveland Free-Net is shown in Figure 17–7. If you take a journey down through the menu and wish to get back to the main menu, type **m** and then press ENTER.

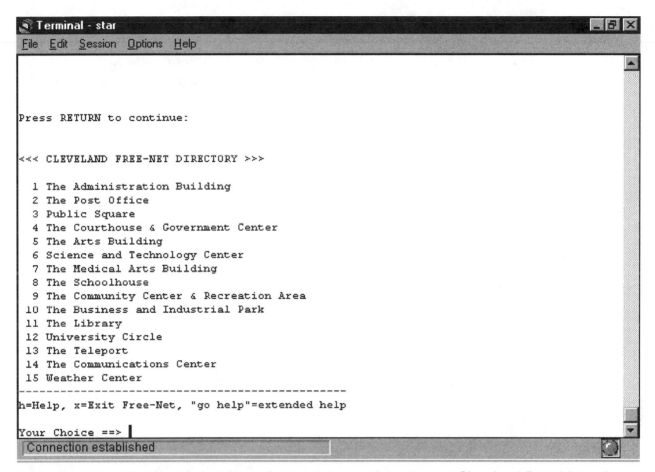

Figure 17–7 To learn more about the resources and services at Cleveland Free-Net, select menu item *1. The Administration Building* and then *10. Free-Net Menu Outline.*

From NPTN Free-Nets you can access Academy One, an international online educational resource for students, educators, parents and administrators of grades K-12. It is one of the main interactive services offered by NPTN Free-Nets. For additional information on how to participate in Academy One, go to *ofcn.org/.* This site also offers a current listing of Free-Nets and Community Networks along with other information concerning Free-Nets and Community Network Systems.

Precautions with Kids

As with other Internet services, check out a telnet site before you let your kids explore. Perhaps the teachers in your school may want to select a few particularly mature or responsible students from upper grades to check out a site for you. This could be a good project for student teachers or observers assigned to your classroom.

A Free-Net and Community Information Sampler

The Internet impacts communities and whole regions by changing the way people communicate with one another. Following are examples of information systems that make it possible for individuals to interact on a large scale by providing access to information anytime, anywhere.

Akron Community Online Resource Network
telnet: *freenet.akron.oh.us* (login **visitor**, hit RETURN when prompted for
      password)

Alabama Community Access Network (ACAN)
telnet: *ns1.maf.mobile.al.us*

Boulder Community Network
telnet: *bcn.boulder.co.us* (login **bcn** password **bcn**)

Buffalo Free-Net
telnet: *freenet.buffalo.edu* (login **freeport**)

Cleveland Free-Net
telnet: *freenet-in-c.cwru.edu*

Eugene Free-Net
telnet: *telnet.efn.org* (login **guest**, hit RETURN when prompted for password)

Heartland Free-Net
telnet: *hrn.bradley.edu* (login **bbguest**, hit RETURN when prompted for
      password)

Prairienet
telnet: *prairienet.org* (login **visitor** password **guest)**

Seattle Community Network (Seattle, Oregon)
telnet: *scn.org* (login **visitor)**

The Well
telnet: *well.sf.ca.us*

Bulletin Board Systems

A bulletin board system, better known as a *BBS*, is a kind of private telecommunications service typically set up by a computer hobbyist, but also by large corporations and government institutions. A hobbyist generally sets up a BBS for his or her own enjoyment and for the enjoyment of others in the same region with similar interests. Corporations and government institutions set up BBSs that reach a much larger audience.

Usually, a BBS enthusiast dialing up to a local BBS reads messages already posted, posts new messages, uploads or downloads some software, does some conferencing (real-time chatting), and then plays a little Trade Wars 2002 (a BBS game). Online users who access corporate and governmental BBSs are usually seeking resources to satisfy specific information needs.

Some BBSs have no links to the Internet at all. Others have connections ranging from e-mail service only to full-fledged Internet access. Some BBSs, even those that are inaccessible via the Internet, play a very significant role in the area of online information service. Anyone with a computer, modem, telephone, and communications software can reach them.

A BBS has traditionally been a personal computer that runs bulletin board software—specialized software that provides an interface for performing various tasks such as answering the phone and logging callers into the system. With the advent of the Internet, BBSs are also found on Internet hosts that can be accessed via telnet. Figure 17–8 illustrates a typical BBS screen design commonly found on government operated BBSs—in this case the Texas State Government BBS.

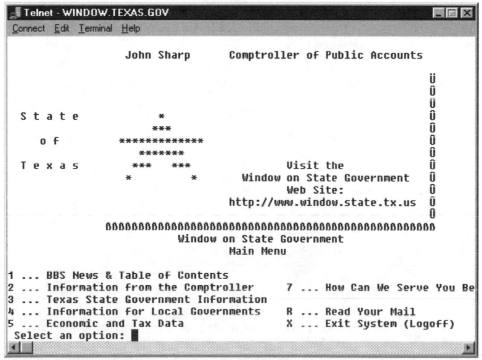

Figure 17–8 The Window on State Government at *window.texas.gov* connects to other systems including the University of Texas Library (UTCAT).

What Can You Find on BBSs?

Many BBSs are specialized and focus on a variety of topics from aviation and Zmodem to exotic bird raising and home renovation. Most dial-up BBSs offer basic services including reading and posting messages, uploading and downloading files, doors (a link to programs that are separate from the BBS software), chat (a service that enables two or more callers to carry on a conversation with each other in real time), and e-mail.

How Do You Connect to a BBS?

There are different ways you can connect to a BBS. When we wrote the first edition of this book the most common connection methods were calling in on a modem using a phone number and your communications software, or by telneting to a BBS via the Internet. Today, software companies have designed BBS software to run on Web servers, providing the same services that BBSs have always offered.

Dialing Up to a BBS

Using whatever communications software you have, you can dial a BBS number and wait for the remote computer to answer. When you access BBSs in this manner, you'll find that some are free (except for long distance telephone charges if they apply); others have modest monthly or annual membership fees. When you first connect, the BBS prompts you for your name and password. If this is your first login, be prepared to answer a lot of questions as part of the registration process. The next time you call in, you can just enter your name and password.

A good place to begin looking for BBS lists is in *Computer Shopper*, a monthly periodical that's available at most libraries and newsstands. You can find out about subscription information by calling 800–274–6384. Each month this magazine publishes a nationwide listing of bulletin boards and online services.

You should also explore what BBSs are available locally by talking to local computer dealers and campus computing departments. If you aren't able to find any within your local calling area, here are some government BBSs that are free and can be accessed via 800 numbers:

- SBA BBS   800–697–4636
- FDA BBS   800–222–0185

BBSs on the Internet

Accessing BBSs via the Internet is easy. To telnet, you need to know a particular BBS's Internet address. Eden Prairie Schools BBS can be reached by telneting to *epbbs.edenpr.k12.mn.us*. As a new user, you will have to fill out a questionnaire before you can login.

For a big list of Internet BBSs, check out Diamond Mine's Telnet BBS Guide at *www.thedirectory.org/telnet/*.

SUPERVISING KIDS ON BBSs

Bulletin boards come and go, so when calling, you may want to test the number on a telephone first to make sure it's really connected to a modem and not to a human being who knows nothing about BBSs. Beware, too, that some bulletin boards require users to be at least 21 years old to login.

MUDs AND MUSEs

If you haven't already heard, you sure will—there are MUDs, MOOs, MUSEs, CHATS, and IRCs on the Internet. These are all referred to as multi-user systems. A *multi-user system* enables more than one person to use the system at the same time and interact with anyone else using the system. This is all done in real time.

These *interactive multi-user virtual realities* were originally known as MUDs or Multi User Dungeons; however, they are now commonly called *muds* (lower-case) or multi-user dimensions/dialogs/domains, in an effort to reflect that some of these virtual reality environments have educational and research purposes also. The biggest difference between the different types of muds—MUSHes, MUCKs, MOOs, and MUSEs—is the underlying programming language. Another difference is the type of players they tend to attract. MUSEs, or multi-user simulated environments, tend to be favored by educators because of the ease of use of the language and the "social structure" inherent in these games.

These systems are text-based electronic adventure games. These games can be combat-oriented or social-oriented. You login and interact with others who are logged in at the same time. Players interact by typing commands and questions. The games are built around a "rooms" theme, where you enter a room and type in commands to discover who and what is in that room. Each game has its own commands allowing users to move around in the game and participate. You can explore your environment, talk to other players, fight monsters, role play, solve puzzles, gather treasures to win points, become a wizard, work with other players or kill them, depending on the theme of the MUD itself, all in a text-based environment.

The imaginary worlds are created entirely from words, although graphics are currently being explored. Some of these games are based on fantasy worlds or mystical places from science fiction stories; others are more conversational in nature. It is easy to lose track of time once connected to a MUD, so you may want to set an alarm clock when your kids login to monitor their time spent mudding. Naturally, you will want to either explore a MUD first before giving your child free use of it or explore it with him or her the first few times to see what it is all about.

Not all MUDs are simply action or violence-filled games. Some are research or educational environments. MicroMUSE, based at MIT's Artificial Intelligence Lab, features explorations and adventures in Cyberion City, an orbiting cylinder high above the earth.

The Land of Oz was created by an eight-year-old as an attraction in the Entertainment Section of Cyberion City. MicroMUSE also offers Missions to Mars, jobs with the Cyberion City Enews, an Exploratorium and Mathematica Exhibit with interactive exhibits from actual science museums plus puzzles in the Narnia Adventures and much, much more.

An explanatory document prepared for MicroMuse participants called *Cyberion City II—Inside and Outside: the Physics, Geography, and Astronomy of Tin Can Cities* is available at the FTP site *ftp.micromuse.org/micromuse/*. To connect to MicroMuse, telnet to *michael.ai.mit.edu* and login as **guest**.

IRCs

You can use telnet to send messages to others who are online and receive messages back, instantly, as though you were talking or "chatting" to them. IRC (Internet Relay Chat) enables you to do this. *Chats*, *Chat lines*, or *IRCs* are conversation-oriented multi-user systems. After logging into an IRC server, you can join a particular group or channel. A *channel* is just another name for the online meeting place, which is organized by topic. Once you have joined a channel, you type what you have to say and then press ENTER. Anyone else who is logged on to that channel can read what you wrote. You can either join an existing group or create your own. When you create your own, you can designate it as private or by invitation only.

What Are the Benefits?

IRC can be a useful tool or a waste of time, depending on how you use it. Choose your chat groups wisely. Perhaps you will want to login to one and "listen" to the dialog taking place, before putting your kids online there. If you are in a home environment, you may want to sit down with your child the first few times they login to a new chat group so you can discover what type of conversations are taking place. There are chat groups set up specifically for kids, such as the KIDLINK chat group at *kids.ccit.duq.edu*.

Connecting to IRCs

First, check to see whether your UNIX shell account service provider has an IRC client running. After logging on to your account, type **irc** at your system prompt. If there is a client running, you will see something similar to the following:

comp% irc
*** Connecting to port 6667 of server irc.uoknor.edu
*** Welcome to the Internet Relay Network lfodemsk (from irc.ecn.uoknor.edu)
*** You have new e-mail.
*** If you have not already done so, please read the new user information with
+/HELP NEWUSER
*** Your host is irc.ecn.uoknor.edu, running version 2.8.21+CSr14+nobots
*** This server was created Thu Oct 12 1995 at 09: 52:32 CDT
*** umodes available oiwsfrcuk, channel modes available biklmnopstv
*** There are 5360 users and 4856 invisible on 99 servers
*** There are 123 operators online
*** 2633 channels have been formed
*** This server has 51 clients and 1 servers connected
*** Highest connection count: 178 (177 clients)
*** - irc.ecn.uoknor.edu Message of the Day -
*** - 22/8/1995 22:49
*** - _ _ _ _ _ _ _ _ _ _
*** - `)//`_///)/`)`)))/`
*** - ////—////////—
*** - (_(_/(___,/___(_/(_//`(_(___,
*** -
*** - TO THE UNIVERSITY OF OKLAHOMA—ALPHA SERVER
*** - RUNNING ON DEC 3000/ALPHA—SOONER THAN THE REST!
*** -
*** - For information concerning IRC at OU, please contact:
*** - ircadmin@mailhost.ecn.uoknor.edu (Wildthang, Mmmm, DaveMan)
*** _____
*** - This server has a very simple bot policy. NO BOTS!
*** - We prefer to provide this service as a means of Chatting with others
*** - not as a bot outpost. Any user running bots on this server will most
*** - likely be Banned from using this server.
*** -—nothing personal just business—
*** - _____
*** - To connect quickly to uoknor, try our other IRC ports—6665, 6668,
*** - 7000,7777,8000,8888,9000,9999
*** - _____
*** - Disclaimer: This IRC server is provided as a service.
*** - The IRC admins and the University of Oklahoma's Engineering Computer
*** - Network take no responsibility and explicitly disclaim any legal
*** - liability for the content of any messages that pass through this
*** - server and the results of running any commands which you do as a result
*** - of being on irc.
*** - Anyone interested in Unix based IRC access, or a UNIX account send

*** - mail to info-request@murc.undernet.org Please specify EFnet as
*** - the Subject.
*** - For information concerning IRC at OU, please contact:
*** - ircadmin@mailhost.ecn.uoknor.edu (Wildthang, Mmmm, DaveMan)

To connect to an IRC server other than what your host is running, at your system prompt, type the command **irc <server address>** and press ENTER. For example, to connect to the KIDLINK chatline, type the command **irc kids.ccit.duq.edu**

IRC Commands

Once connected, your prompt is simply the bottom line of your screen. All IRC commands begin with a forward slash (/). Commands are not case-sensitive. Anything you type without preceding it with a forward slash is considered to be part of a message and will appear on the screen as a message from you; it will be read by everyone logged into that channel. The following commands will enable you to participate on an IRC.

/list lists all the active channels
/join # <channel name> adds you to an active channel
/who returns a list of names of people using that channel
/whois <name> get more information about any name
/msg <screen nickname> send a private message to only one person on that channel
/help provides a list of all the commands available to your client application
/bye or **/exit** or **/quit** closes your connection with the IRC and returns you to your local prompt
/leave closes your connection with that channel

The **/list** command will return a list of channels currently running. There may be hundreds of them, however, so it is a good idea to modify this command. To limit the number of channels listed, use the options -**min nn** and -**max nn**, where **nn** stands for any number. For example, to retrieve a list of channels that only have five or less users, type **/list -max 5** and press ENTER.

To join a channel so that you can participate in the discussion, type the command **/join # <channel name>**. After you join a channel, it is announced that you have joined; then you are given the topic of discussion and finally you are given a list of who else is on this channel by their nickname. Joining a particular channel does not disconnect you from any previous channel you have joined. To leave a channel, you must issue the **/leave** or **/part** commands.

Chatting in Class

A word of caution to the beginner: never type commands that someone else on a channel asks you to type or send any files to anyone on a chat line, unless you know exactly what you are doing. Hackers can gain access to your machine simply by having you type in a command. Hackers are individuals, many times malicious, who try to break into a computer system without having the authority to do so.

There are more commands available for IRC that enable you to create your own chat line and become the channel operator; this gives you the ability to privatize your channel, remove someone annoying from your channel, and much more. Read through the tutorials mentioned in the resource section of this chapter to learn more about becoming a channel operator. These tutorials also describe ways to keep up with the ever-changing world of IRC.

LESSON PLAN IDEAS

Telnet enables you to connect to another computer and use its system. Once you have connected to a site using telnet, you will need to learn whatever commands that system uses. Because this entails learning dozens of different systems, lesson plans like those presented in earlier chapters aren't really applicable here. Instead, we offer telnet sites for you to visit and explore along with your kids.

You may still want to make a Telnet Command Guide Card and guide cards for specific sites you telnet to frequently.

Telnet Sites for Kids

1. Create your own IRC channel and become the channel operator, also called the *chop* or *ops*. As the channel operator, you set the channel's attributes, such as private or by invitation only. Read about how to do this in the Usenet newsgroup *alt.irc*. To retrieve IRC tutorials, FTP to site *cs-ftp.bu.edu* and change to the directory *irc/support*. IRC FAQs are available via FTP at *rtfm.mit.edu* in the directory */pub/usenet-by-hierarchy/alt/irc/questions/*. Look for the files named:

   IRC_Frequently_Asked_Questions_(FAQ)_(Part_1_of_2)
   IRC_Frequently_ Asked_Questions_(FAQ)_(Part_2_of_2)

2. The University of Michigan maintains the Weather Underground, which contains weather and climatic data. Telnet to *um-weather.sprl.umich. edu:3000*.

3. The Environmental Protection Agency maintains a database of documents and reports plus access to regional databases: *epaibm.rtpnc.epa.gov* menu selections: *public access/OLS*.

4. FedWorld Information Network offers a huge amount of information about scientific and technical subjects, business issues, and consumer information: *fedworld.gov* login **new**.

Telnet Sites for Teachers

1. Newton Education BBS (for math and science teachers and students): *newton.dep.anl.gov* login **new**.

2. PENpages is a database of agricultural information provided by the College of Agricultural Sciences at Pennsylvania State University: *psupen.psu.edu*. To login, enter your two-letter state abbreviation.

RESOURCES

Several RFC documents pertaining to telnet are available. Two that may be of particular interest are *#854 Telnet Protocol Specification. 5/83* and *#855 Telnet Option Specifications. 5.83*. To obtain copies of these and other documents, FTP to site *nic.ddn.mil* and go to the */rfc/rfc directory*.

Access hundreds of telnet sites using GALAXY at *galaxy.einet.ent/hetelnet/SITES2.html*. Resources are organized under the topics: Archie Servers, Databases and Bibliographies, Distributed File Servers, Electronic Books, Fee-Based Services, FREE-NETs & Community Computing Systems, General Bulletin Boards, NASA Databases, Network Information Services, and Whois/White Pages/Directory Services.

BBSs

- Another online source for bulletin board lists besides those mentioned earlier is the Small Business Administration's BBS, which can be reached at 800–697–4636. This bulletin board offers a list of Federal Government Bulletin Board Systems. You can capture this file to a disk for future reference. Dial up to the SBA's bulletin board, log in, and choose *[7]Talk to Your Government* at the top menu and *[2]Listing of Federal Bulletin Boards* at the next menu.

- To learn more about BBSs, read the Usenet newsgroup called *compo.bbs. misc* or *alt.bbs.internet*. The topic of BBSs is also covered in a FAQ with the file name *inet-bbs-faq* available at FTP site *ftp.isnet.is* in the */usenet/answers/* directory.

MUDs, MOOs, and MUSEs

If you are interested in learning more about MUDs, MOOs, and MUSEs, here are some resources that will provide additional information:

- There are several Usenet newsgroups where you can find information about a specific type of MUD. For more information on starting a MUD, check out the Usenet newsgroup *rec.games.mud.admin*. For information about the social-oriented MUDs (MUSEs, MUCKs, and MUSHes), try the Usenet newsgroup *rec.games.mud.tiny*.
- You can find a copy of *Frequently Asked Questions: Basic Information about MUDs and MUDDing* at *mdstud.chalmers.se/~md5bern/mudfaq.html*.

Here are some sources for IRC client software and addresses for connecting to IRC servers in the United States:

- If you have a SLIP/PPP connection, note that there are many IRC software clients available for both the PC and Mac. Some Mac software is IRCle, Talk, and Homer (*support.primenet.com/html/irc_software_0.html*). For Windows there is Telecafe, Virc Virc96, and Wintalk all available at *aldebaran.na-cp.rnp.br/packages/irc_talk/clients/*. One of the more popular IRC programs for Windows is mIRC. To learn more, go to Web site *rtfm.ml.org/mirc/*.
- For a list of IRC servers around the world, check out *www.moonbeam.co.za/irclist.htm*.

Chapter 18

Newsgroups Galore

Usenet newsgroups (also called *Network News* and *Internet News*) are electronic bulletin boards on which millions of people exchange ideas by leaving messages. Newsgroups are the coffee houses, meeting halls, bulletin boards, and post-it notes of the Internet.

Usenet is divided by subject into discussion groups called *newsgroups*. By using *news reader* programs, you can read messages (also called *articles*) that have been posted by other users and you can participate in discussions by posting your own articles. These articles are stored on a central machine called a *news server*.

Storing newsgroup messages on a central server makes this form of communication more efficient than mailing lists for large group discussions. It enables you to choose when you want to read newsgroup articles rather than having large volumes of unsought electronic mail sent to your mailbox, as with mailing lists.

In this chapter, we explain what Usenet newsgroups are all about, how they're organized, and how to access them. We share with you which newsgroups may be of interest to parents, teachers, and kids and give you helpful tips on newsgroup etiquette. Access through the Web will be the easiest, most user-friendly method for kids to interact with Usenet news.

WHAT IS USENET?

Usenet (an acronym for *User's Network*) is a large collection of computers carrying something called *Usenet news*—a distributed conferencing system consisting of more than 9,000 discussion groups. Some of these discussion groups are on Internet computers; others are not. Internet service providers decide how much of their disk space they'll devote to newsgroups by choosing which ones they'll subscribe to and which ones they'll ignore. One host may carry 3,395 newsgroups, while another may carry only 2,500.

How Are Newsgroups Organized?

Each newsgroup specializes in a particular subject. They're organized in a tree structure, or hierarchy, with various levels of topics and subtopics. For instance, one newsgroup hierarchy called *soc* posts articles relating to social issues. The newsgroup *soc.culture.indian.telugu* is a social newsgroup concentrating on the culture of the Telugu people of India.

The World Newsgroups

One collection of newsgroups, termed *World* newsgroups, are usually distributed around the entire Usenet worldwide. World newsgroups are divided into the following seven broad classifications: *rec* (recreation), *sci* (science), *comp* (computers), *soc* (social), *talk*, *news* (newsgroups), and *misc* (miscellaneous). Each of these classifications is organized into groups and subgroups according to topic.

For example, under the classification of *rec* (groups oriented towards the arts, hobbies, and recreational activities), there are a number of music groups which are further divided into subgroups such as classical, folk, and afro-latin. Following are three examples of music newsgroups in the *rec* hierarchy: The column on the left is the electronic name of the newsgroup and a brief description of what they are about is on the right.

rec.music.classical	Discussion about classical music
rec.music.folk	Folks discussing folk music
rec.music.afro-latin	Music with African and Latin influences

Other broad topics in the *rec* classification include arts, audio, aviation, food, games, sport, travel, and so forth. As with music, these groups are broken down into more specialized subgroups.

Under the classification *sci* (discussions relating to research in or applications of the established sciences) are groups like engineering, space, medicine, philosophy, astronomy, chemistry, and so on. Subgroups under the topic space include:

sci.space	Space, programs, related research, etc.
sci.space.news	Space-related announcement
sci.space.shuttle	The space shuttle and the STS program

The *comp* newsgroups discuss topics of interest to both computer professionals and hobbyists, including topics in programming language, software, hardware, and operating systems.

The *soc* groups address social issues; for example, religion, politics, and culture.

The *talk* classification consists of groups that are debate-oriented and contain very little useful information.

The *news* groups discuss issues relating to newsgroups (network and software).

The *misc* groups address subjects that can't easily be classified under any of the other headings.

Specialized Newsgroups

You will notice several other newsgroup classifications listed on the main menu that are not part of the traditional or mainstream hierarchy of newsgroups. These are classified as *alternative* newsgroups hierarchies. Alternative newsgroups are organized into groups and subgroups similar to the traditional newsgroups. They are called alternative because they don't conform to Usenet standards.

The formation of a new mainstream newsgroup is strictly controlled. An announcement must be made, followed by a discussion and a request for people to vote. The alternative newsgroups are less strict. Anyone who knows how to start one can do so.

Some of the classifications that are included in the alternative hierarchy include *alt*, *bionet*, *bit*, and *biz*. Examples of newsgroups in the *alt* classification include these:

alt.alien.visitors	Space alien topics
alt.appalachian	Appalachian region culture
alt.banjo	Banjo playing
alt.culture.alaska	Alaskan culture
alt.fan.bill-gates	Fans of Microsoft's Bill Gates
alt.folklore.ghost-stories	Ghost stories

There are many hundreds more; parents and teachers may find a number of these newsgroups to be objectionable for kids such as those subgroups that come under *alt.sex*.

Bionet is a newsgroup hierarchy for topics of interest to biologists.

Bit newsgroups are redistributions of the Bitnet Listserv mailing lists. Before you subscribe to a mailing list, you might want to see whether it's echoed (duplicated) on Usenet news to avoid having to manage the large volumes of e-mail associated with joining a mailing list.

Biz carries information about business products, especially computer products and services. The *Clari* hierarchy of newsgroups is gatewayed from Clarinet News, a commercial electronic publishing service that provides UPI, AP, and satellite news services. Groups under this classification include:

clari.biz.market	General stock market news
clari.canada.briefs	Canadian news briefs
clari.news.almana	Daily almanac, quotes, etc.

Newsgroup Descriptions

Because many newsgroup participants possess a very high level of expertise in their respective fields, Usenet news can serve as a useful resource tool for kids writing reports. Kids can direct their questions to the newsgroup that specializes in the particular field in which they're interested. Subjects range from geophysical fluid dynamics to baking with sourdough.

To find a newsgroup that might be interesting to your kids, jump over to the Ohio State University Computer and Information Science Web site at *www.cis.ohio-state.edu/*. Click on the link labeled **Internet Services**. Next look for the **Usenet FAQs** link. On this page you can browse newsgroup FAQs (Frequently Asked Questions) by subject. Topics are arranged alphabetically. Take for example the topic Coin Collecting. Linking to this FAQ takes you to a table of contents that includes the charter for the newsgroup *rec.collecting.paper-money*. Wondering what this newsgroup is all about and who the specialists are? The charter explains the group's purpose and scope. If your kids are interested in any aspect of paper money collecting, this group should interest them. Many times the author of a FAQ is a specialist in the field about which she or he writes, so see if you can track down the author's name. Usually the author's name and e-mail address are listed on the first page of the FAQ where the credits and copyright notice are listed. You might also consider writing to the authors and requesting information on known authorities in the field and what their e-mail addresses are.

What's Out There for Parents and Kids?

As we stated, FAQs are a great place to start your search. At the Ohio State University site listed earlier, we found an interesting FAQ under Misc Kids called *Children's Software FAQ*. This FAQ is a summary of the ideas readers have shared on the *misc.kids.computers* newsgroup. This FAQ provides information on shareware, demos, reviews, and print and electronic resources.

Other subgroups you might want to explore in the *misc-kids* newsgroup include:

misc-kids/allergy+asthma/*...
misc-kids/babyproofing/*...
misc-kids/books
misc-kids/books/female-chars misc.kids FAQ on Children's Books/Central
    Female Characters
misc-kids/books/recs
misc-kids/books/recs/part1 misc.kids FAQ on Children's Books Recs. Part1/2
misc-kids/books/recs/part2 misc.kids FAQ on Children's Books Recs. Part2/2
misc-kids/breastfeeding/*...
misc-kids/chicken-pox Chicken Pox FAQ
misc-kids/colic misc.kids FAQ on Colic
misc-kids/crib-safety-faq FAQ: Crib and Cradle Safety Regulations
misc-kids/crib-to-bed-transition misc.kids FAQ on Crib to Bed Transition
misc-kids/eczema misc.kids FAQ on Eczema
misc-kids/faq
misc-kids/faq/part1 Welcome to misc.kids/FAQ File Index Part 1/2
misc-kids/faq/part2 Welcome to misc.kids/FAQ File Index Part 2/2
misc-kids/faq Welcome to Misc.kids/FAQ File Index
misc-kids/firearms-safety misc.kids FAQ on Firearms Safety & Children
misc-kids/good-things misc.kids FAQ on Good things about having kids
misc-kids/joggers
misc-kids/joggers/part1 Misc.kids FAQ on Jogging Strollers, Part 1/2
misc-kids/joggers/part2 Misc.kids FAQ on Jogging Strollers, Part 2/2
misc-kids/misc-kids-info-faq Welcome to misc.kids.info!
misc-kids/miscarriage/*...
misc-kids/outdoor-activities/*...
misc-kids/pediatrician-questions Misc.kids FAQ-Potential Pediatrician Questions
misc-kids/pregnancy/*...
misc-kids/sids Sudden Infant Death Syndrome (SIDS) misc.kids FAQ
misc-kids/starting-solids misc.kids FAQ on Starting Solid Foods
misc-kids/temper-tantrum misc.kids FAQ on Temper Tantrums
misc-kids/travel-tips misc.kids FAQ on Traveling with Kids
misc-kids/vaccinations/*...

Back to the Ohio State University site, under the heading Music, topics range from Amy Grant and Smashing Pumpkins to Celtic Music and Squeezebox (slang for accordion, in this case the concertina). We found an interesting music FAQ under the heading Performing called *rec.music.classical.performing—FAQ*. This newsgroup is for individuals who like performing classical music at all levels of ability. While classical music may seem like a safe subject to let your kids loose in, you should still exercise caution. Read the FAQ and see what topics are being discussed. Serious musicians—kids and adults alike—may have problems with performance anxiety or suffer from different kinds of overuse problems, such as carpal tunnel syndrome. On topics like this, help your kids discern what information is based on personal experience and what is based on professional medical advice.

Reading through the messages in this newsgroup, we saw readers sharing concert information and asking questions about performers and recordings. This newsgroup wasn't too active last time we checked, but all it takes is one or two kids with a passion for their hobbies to get things going! The newsgroups *rec.music.industrial* and *rec.music.beatles* seemed to be where most of the action was taking place.

Anyone who knows a young rocketeer should explore the Model Rockets FAQ. This FAQ is quite extensive, covering 13 parts. The *rec.models.rockets* newsgroup covers topics such as amateur rocketry, international rocketry, model rockets, scale modeling, and more.

The *rec.puzzles* newsgroup should interest most kids who like solving problems. The FAQ for this newsgroup explains various kinds of puzzles shared by readers. Categories include situation puzzles, sequence puzzles, paradoxes, and the equation analysis test.

Teachers and school media specialists will find the newsgroup classification *K12* interesting and packed full of information. The *K12* hierarchy is a collection of school-based or school-oriented newsgroups including:

> *k12.chat.elementary*
> *k12.chat.junior*
> *k12.chat.senior*
> *k12.chat.special*
> *k12.chat.teacher*

Table 18–1 lists all of the newsgroup classifications covered so far.

Table 18–1 Usenet Categories	
alt (alternative)	Everything from soup to nuts
bit (Bitnet)	Mailing lists for academic institutions
bionet (biologists)	Biology topics
biz (business)	Business, marketing, advertising
clari (Clarinet News)	Live feed from AP and UPI news services
comp (computers)	Computers
k12 (education)	Kindergarten through high school
news (newsgroups)	Network and software discussions
misc (miscellaneous)	Items not easily categorized
rec (recreation)	Recreation, hobbies, the arts
sci (science)	Research and the sciences
soc (social)	Social issues
talk (idle chatter)	Debate, arguments, sharing

READING THE NEWS

News articles look like e-mail messages, but they're delivered in a very different way. With Usenet, messages are not sent to individuals the way they are in the mailing lists. Instead, a user sends, or *posts*, an article to a newsgroup on one site, and the local system collects its articles and sends them as a file to adjoining Usenet sites. In a mailing list, a subscriber mails a message to the mailing-list manager (a piece of software), and all subscribers to that list receive the same mail message. Rather than sending many copies of one message, Usenet provides a single central copy that all subscribers can read.

Like most of the Internet services described in this book, Usenet news also makes use of a client/server model. The server program manages the "news feed." The client program, called a *news reader*, provides you with your interface to Usenet.

Getting on Board

A connection to the Internet does not automatically give you access to news-groups. In the case of dial-up connections, your service provider must make arrangements to receive Usenet files or get a news feed from another site that already receives them.

If your connection to the Internet is through a shell account, you can access newsgroups through your service provider's client program.

Using Your Provider's Client Program

Find out whether there's a client program available on your Internet service provider's computer. If so, ask your provider what command to type at the system prompt to get it running. The following section provides a simple reference guide for a popular news reader that shell account users might have available to them called *trn*. For more detailed information on this program or other news readers, consult the online help services at your site.

It will become clear as you look through the commands noted in this section that operating a text-based news reader on a UNIX machine is not that simple. If your kids have access to a SLIP/PPP account, we would recommend setting up a graphical program like Trumpet Newsreader instead. Sources for this application and others are explained later. Web browsers like Netscape Navigator also come with their own built-in news readers.

trn Quick Reference Guide

Here's a quick reference guide for **trn**, a Usenet news reader that runs on UNIX platforms. Note that these commands are case sensitive.

- Type the letter **h** to bring up help at any point.
- Type **trn** and press ENTER to start the newsreader.
- Type **q** to quit the program.
- The program creates a file called *.newsrc* in which all of the newsgroups you subscribe to are placed. This file also keeps track of the messages you have read.
- The program begins by going through all of the new newsgroups fed to your site. You have four choices for each newsgroup as it is listed: type **y** to subscribe to the newsgroup currently listed on the screen; type **Y** to subscribe to the newsgroup currently listed and all remaining new groups; type **n** to skip the current newsgroup and move on to the next; and type **N** to leave all remaining new groups unsubscribed.
- If you pressed **y**, trn asks you where you would like to put the newsgroup. Respond in one of the following ways:

Type **.** to put it before the current newsgroup (Position 0).

Type **-<newsgroup name>** to put it before the named newsgroup.

Type **+<newsgroup name>** to put it after the named newsgroup.

Type **L** for a listing of newsgroups and their positions.

Type **q** to abort the current operation.

- To save an article, press **s** followed by the name of the file in which you want the article saved.
- Press **^** (caret) to go to the first newsgroup with unread news.
- Press **p** to go to the previous newsgroup with unread news.
- Press **P** to go to the previous newsgroup.
- Press **1** to go to the first newsgroup.
- Press **$** to go to the end of the newsgroups.
- Type **g <name>** to go to the named newsgroup. Subscribe to new newsgroups this way, too.
- Type **/<pattern>**, where **<pattern>** is the name of a newsgroup you would like to match.
- Typing **?<pattern>** searches backward for a newsgroup matching the pattern.

Using SLIP/PPP Accounts to Access Newsgroups

If you have a SLIP/PPP account, you can access Usenet News through a news reader running on your own computer. John Norstad's *NewsWatcher* is a Macintosh news reader that's pretty well designed and easy to use. NewsWatcher requires a Mac running System 7.0 or later with 2.5 megabytes or more of memory on a hard drive. It's free and you can find a copy at Web site *ftp:// ftp.acns.nwu.edu/pub/newswatcher/*.

Trumpet Newsreader for Windows can be downloaded for the Web at *ftp:// jazz.trumpet.com.au/pub/wintrump/*. The latest version at the time of this writing was *wtwsk10a.zip*. After you've downloaded it and unpacked the file (see Chapter 19 for more details on what to do with *.zip* files), you will find a useful user's manual in the *wtdoc.doc* file and the latest information about the program in the *readme.txt* file.

Searching and Filtering Services

With the advent of the Web, different services are becoming available that can help kids sort through the thousands of messages that are posted to Usenet newsgroups daily. Two of these services are described here: Deja News and Reference.COM.

DEJA NEWS

Deja News is a newsgroup service on the Web that offers several features:

- The ability to post messages to Usenet newsgroups
- Browse Usenet news by subject and newsgroup hierarchy
- Read and bookmark Usenet news articles
- Run keyword searches on all newsgroups or just those in which you're interested
- Access lots of online hints and useful information relating to newsgroups

To explore Deja News further, connect to their home page shown in Figure 18–1 at *www.dejanews.com/*.

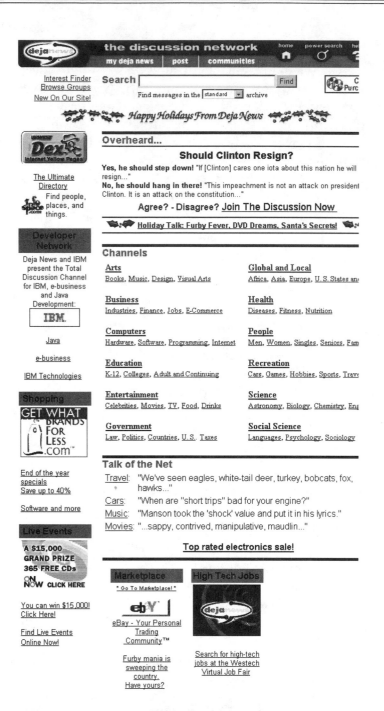

Figure 18–1 Deja News Home Page

THE STANFORD INFORMATION FILTERING TOOL

Back when we wrote the first edition of this book, we told you about the Stanford Information Filtering Tool, or SIFT for short. This was a service designed by Tak Yan of Stanford University that automatically sorted through Usenet News articles looking for messages that matched your interests.

InReference, Inc. had joined Stanford University in making this service available through their Web home page at *www.reference.com*. Today, Sift, Inc. manages this site (see Figure 18–2), and the filtering tool, called *Active Queries*, lets you store questions on the Reference.COM computer, where they are posted daily for a number of days. You can interactively refine your search using message header fields such as author, organization, and thread. You must first create an account with Reference.COM, before you can store queries in their database.

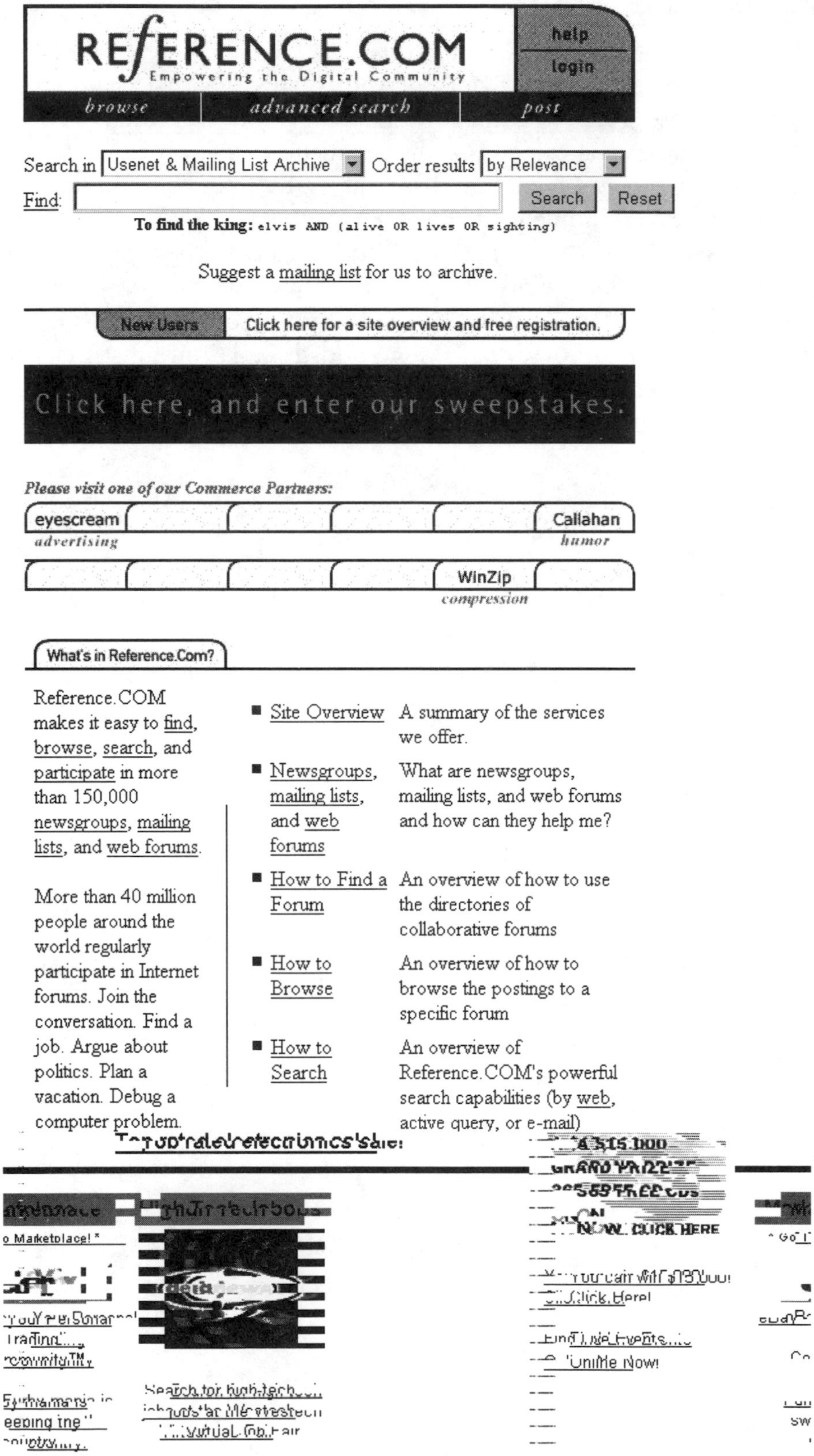

REFERENCE.COM
Empowering the Digital Community

help | login

browse | advanced search | post

Search in Usenet & Mailing List Archive ▾ Order results by Relevance ▾

Find: [_____] Search | Reset

To find the king: `elvis AND (alive OR lives OR sighting)`

Suggest a mailing list for us to archive.

New Users | Click here for a site overview and free registration.

Click here, and enter our sweepstakes.

Please visit one of our Commerce Partners:

eyescream | | | | | Callahan
advertising | | | | | *humor*

| | | WinZip |
compression

What's in Reference.Com?

Reference.COM makes it easy to find, browse, search, and participate in more than 150,000 newsgroups, mailing lists, and web forums.

More than 40 million people around the world regularly participate in Internet forums. Join the conversation. Find a job. Argue about politics. Plan a vacation. Debug a computer problem.

■ Site Overview — A summary of the services we offer.

■ Newsgroups, mailing lists, and web forums — What are newsgroups, mailing lists, and web forums and how can they help me?

■ How to Find a Forum — An overview of how to use the directories of collaborative forums

■ How to Browse — An overview of how to browse the postings to a specific forum

■ How to Search — An overview of Reference.COM's powerful search capabilities (by web, active query, or e-mail)

Figure 18–2 Reference.COM Home Page

USEFUL TIPS FOR WORKING WITH USENET NEWSGROUPS

Rules and manners are important when interacting with others on Usenet. Remember that the ideas being exchanged in newsgroups are coming from a wide variety of people from all around the world—from kids in K–12 who are just experimenting to scientists who are collaborating with one another on important research projects. As you introduce Usenet to your students, teach them to follow these rules and everyone should get along fine:

- When you first discover a newsgroup, lurk—hang loose for a while. Don't post any message in the newsgroup until you've followed it for a few weeks. Learn what subjects are being discussed and what kind of people participate. Read the newsgroup's FAQ if one is available.
- Read the messages posted to a newsgroup called *news.announce.newusers*. This newsgroup posts documents that are of particular interest to users that are new to Usenet.
- When responding to a message, quote the relevant portions of the note to which you're responding. The other readers will find it easier to follow the meaning of your response.
- Messages in newsgroups are much like any other e-mail message, consisting of a header with sender's address and subject line, the body of the message, and a signature at the end. Keep the text of your message concise and to the point. Restrict your signature to three or four lines and don't include graphics.
- Be careful where you use capital letters because they represent SHOUTING.
- Avoid sarcasm. Flag your jokes so people understand when you're trying to be funny. Use *emoticons* like smiley faces, such as :-) (read sideways).
- Don't advertise or do any self-promotion. Announcing a new product that you might find interesting is permissible.
- Before exploring the picture files residing on the various *alt.binaries.pictures* newsgroups, download a copy of the FAQ that explains all of the idiosyncrasies of posting and downloading files in this format. FTP to site *bongo.cc.utexas.edu* and **get** the files called *FAQ.abp.1* and *FAQ.abp.2* residing in the */gifstuff* directory.
- Lastly, to help you understand what newsgroup readers are talking about, here is a guide to some of their jargon:
  blathering—going on and on without making a point
  newbie—a newcomer to Usenet News
  spamming—posting a message to dozens or thousands of newsgroups
  B1FF-speak—an unorthodox typography found in the newsgroups that uses ALL CAPS, I=1, O=0, E=3, and so on, plus surfer-type slang: HEY D00DZ!1!! B1FF IZ A K()()L D00D!!@!!
  flame—an angry response to a message. People get "flamed" when they

say something that upsets another, or break one of the Internet taboos such as advertising over the network.

flamebait—old, tired topics that invoke arguments

RESOURCES

The Usenet Info Center at *metalab.unc.edu/usenet-i/* is a source for information on Usenet and all of the newsgroups. Here you can browse the Usenet newsgroups, search for a Usenet newsgroup, and read Usenet FAQs. You can also link from this site to DejaNews and other indexing and archiving services.

Chapter 19

FTP Fun

FTP stands for *File Transfer Protocol*. It is one of the most frequently used Internet applications. FTP enables you to upload and download files from archives around the world. You can think of these archives as libraries—electronic libraries housing digitized information. While information in traditional paper-based libraries is stored in books and magazines, the *digital file* is the unit of storage in electronic libraries. These files hold text, images, sound, and executable programs. They come in the form of historical documents, pictures of country flags and postage stamps, summaries of TV news shows, sound files of speeches, and software programs for drawing, solving math problems, and much more.

WHAT IS FTP?

FTP is a set of rules, called *protocols*, which govern data transfer. The FTP protocol enables you to look at lists of directories and files on remote machines and transfer those files to or from remote machines. When a file is transferred, it is not actually moved; rather, the file is copied from one machine to another. The computer from which the file is copied is sometimes referred to as the *source host* and the computer to which the file is copied is called the *destination host*.

FTP is based on a client/server model. You run a program on your local machine called an *FTP client*, which in turn connects to another program running on a remote machine called an *FTP server*.

As with other Internet protocol names, FTP is sometimes used as a verb. For example, you may see a sentence like, "You can obtain a copy of Helen Cody Wetmore's *Last of the Great Scouts* by FTPing to *ftp.cdrom.com/pub/gutenberg/etext98/*."

FTP sites limit the number of users that can login at any one time. When one site is busy, there are usually one or more archives around the world that can provide the same files. These archives are referred to as *mirror* sites. How do you know where to find a mirror site? When you first login to an FTP site, the opening text that scrolls across the screen will usually mention mirror sites if they exist.

Directories and Subdirectories

Each FTP site you connect to is organized under the same hierarchical structure. This structure can be compared to a contractor's office containing file cabinets. Suppose that you are this contractor. You organize your carpentry information in a four-drawer file cabinet. The cabinet itself is labeled **carpentry**. The four drawers are labeled **building codes**, **framing**, **roofs**, and **siding**.

Within each of these drawers, you keep various files containing engineering reports, construction techniques, suppliers' addresses, government regulations, and other text documents.

There are three other file cabinets in your office organizing other information you store. These are labeled: **electrical**, **plumbing**, and **heating**. Each of these cabinets contain four drawers and within each drawer there are several files. These are all empty for the time being.

Now let's look at this in terms of directories and subdirectories. In Figure 19–1, the carpentry file cabinet is a *parent directory*. Parent directories contain other directories—in this case, four *subdirectories*: **building codes**, **framing**, **roofs**, and **siding**. We might say that the **building codes** subdirectory contains three files: **local building codes**, **state building codes**, and **federal building codes**. The **framing** subdirectory contains two subdirectories: **floors** and **walls**. The **walls** subdirectory contains two files: **sheet rock** and **paneling**.

The *root directory* is the single main directory. The root directory is the parent of all other directories in the system. When you first connect to an FTP server, you land in the root directory. Thus, you might imagine that the contractor's office containing the four file cabinets is the root directory.

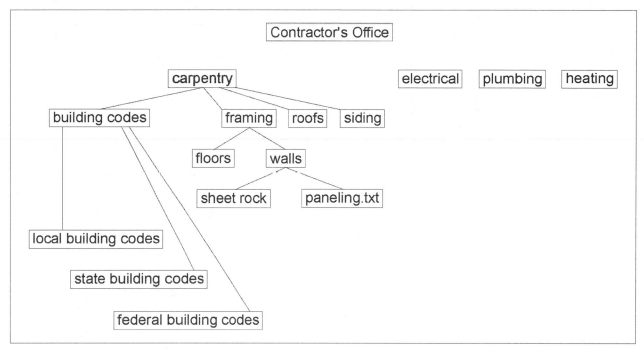

Figure 19–1 A Sample Directory Tree

Pathnames

Each file in an FTP archive has a *pathname*. The pathname tells you the path you must follow to find the file you want.

When you specify a directory that lies within the root, you type a slash (/) followed by the directory name. In our earlier example, the directory *carpentry* (the carpentry file cabinet) lies within the / root directory (the contractor's office) and would be written */carpentry*.

To indicate a directory or file within a directory, write the names and separate them with a /. To indicate the subdirectory *building codes*, you would write */carpentry/building codes*. The formal name for the file named *federal building codes* is */carpentry/building codes/federal building codes*.

When you are directed to get the file */carpentry/framing/walls/paneling.txt*, you will be getting a file called *paneling.txt* located in a directory called *walls*, which is a subdirectory of *framing*, which is a subdirectory of *carpentry*, all of which is located in the root directory.

Touring a Directory

UNIX operating systems are the most prevalent operating systems on the Internet. When you connect to a site using FTP, it's likely you'll be connecting to a UNIX system. When you connect to a UNIX system, the first place you arrive after logging in will be the root directory. To list what's in the root, type the "list" command **ls** and press ENTER. When you login to the University of North Texas FTP server at site *ftp.unt.edu* and enter **ls**, you'll see something like this:

```
ftp> ls
200 PORT command successful.
150 Opening ASCII mode data connection for file list.
lost+found
EJDE
Electronic Journal of Differential Equations
README
articles
dev
cdrom
cutcp
bin
dma
ejde
etc
ian
incoming
library
localhosts
micro
ncd243
operator
pub
EMDE
temp
usr
.acastro
.testing
emde
ls-lr
space
Electronic Monographs in Differential Equations
unt_ppp
lib
test.message
.message
2.5.1_Recommended.tar.Z
226 Transfer complete.
357 bytes received in 0.012 seconds (29 Kbytes/s)
ftp>
```

When you enter the **ls** command with the **-l** option, you're presented with a "long listing" of the directory's contents. If you enter the command **ls -l** at the site we just visited, the output will look something like this:

```
ftp> ls -l
200 PORT command successful.
150 Opening ASCII mode data connection for /bin/ls.
total 52972
drwxr-xr-x   16 root     root         1024     Oct 31 16:21 .
drwxr-xr-x   16 root     root         1024     Oct 31 16:21 ..
drwxr-sr-x6  1113        1570          512     Jan 9 1996 .acastro
-rw-r—r—      2 root     uucp         2058     Jul 6 1994 .message
drwx———       2 root     other        1024     Mar 11 1996 .testing
-rw———        1 root     other    26684017     Oct 10 1997 2.5.1_Recommended.tar.Z
lrwxrwxrwx    1 root     other          13     Mar 11 1996 EJDE -> .acastro/EJDE
lrwxrwxrwx    1 root     other          13     Mar 11 1996 EMDE -> .acastro/EMDE
lrwxrwxrwx    1 root     other          13     Mar 11 1996 Electronic Journal of Differential
                                                            Equations -> .acastro/EJDE
lrwxrwxrwx    1 root     other          13     Mar 11 1996 Electronic Monographs in Differential
                                                            Equations -> .acastro/EMDE
-rw-r—r—      2 root     uucp         2058     Jul 6 1994 README
lrwxrwxrwx    1 root     other          12     Mar 11 1996 articles -> pub/articles
lrwxrwxrwx    1 root     other           9     Mar 11 1996 bin -> ./usr/bin
lrwxrwxrwx    1 root     other           9     Mar 11 1996 cdrom -> pub/cdrom
lrwxrwxrwx    1 root     other           9     Mar 11 1996 cutcp -> pub/cutcp
d—x—x—x       2 root     other         512     Mar 11 1996 dev
drwxr-xr-x    2 root     other         512     Sep 29 1994 dma
lrwxrwxrwx    1 root     other          13     Mar 11 1996 ejde -> .acastro/EJDE
lrwxrwxrwx    1 root     other          13     Mar 11 1996 emde -> .acastro/EMDE
d—x—x—x       2 root     other         512     Mar 11 1996 etc
drwxr-xr-x14 1191        1190          512     Oct 8 1996 ian
drwx-ws-wx    2 root     uucp         2048     Apr 16 20:16 incoming
lrwxrwxrwx    1 root     other           9     Mar 11 1996 lib -> ./usr/lib
lrwxrwxrwx    1 root     other          11     Mar 11 1996 library -> pub/library
-rw-r—r—      1 root     other      191017     Sep 5 1995 localhosts
drwx———       2 root     root         8192     Dec 19 22:35 lost+found
-rw-r—r—      1 root     other      141694     Oct 12 1995 ls-lr
lrwxrwxrwx    1 root     other           9     Mar 11 1996 micro -> pub/micro
drwx———       7 root     uucp          512     Mar 11 1996 ncd243
drwx———       2 uucp     uucp          512     Sep 29 1994 operator
drwxr-xr-x   26 root     uucp          512     Feb 15 08:43 pub
-rw-r—r—      1 root     other         127     Nov 17 1995 space
drwx———       3 root     operator      512     Sep 5 1996 temp
-rw———        1 root     other        1093     Nov 30 1995 test.message
drwxr-x—      2 root     untlocal      512     Mar 11 1996 unt_ppp
d—x—x—x       4 root     other         512     Apr 24 1996 usr
226 Transfer complete.
```

The information in the left-hand column displays the *file permissions*, something you won't really need to know too much about. Permissions simply refer to who can get to a particular file and in what way. There is one character, however, that is of special interest. It is the character at the far left. Regular files are designated with a hyphen (-). Directories are designated with a letter d. This means that lines starting with a hyphen are ordinary files—something you can download, like a text file or picture file. Lines starting with a *d*, like the last line in the listing, are directories and cannot be downloaded.

The columns on the far right side also contain some interesting information that will be useful to you. If you look at the first line in the preceding example above, you'll see the word README on the far right side. This is the name of a file. You can tell it's a file because the first character on that line on the far left side is a hyphen (-).

Just to the left of README is the date July 6 1994. This is the date the file was created. The number to the left of that, 2058, is the file's size. The size of this README file is 2058 bytes—not quite a single-typed written page of text.

Keep in mind that UNIX file and directory names are case sensitive. This means that when you type a command to change directories or download a file, you must type the name of the directory or file just as it is shown, paying careful attention to upper- and lowercase letters. For example, you cannot download the file called *README* if you ask for *readme*, nor can you change to the directory called *usr* if you type *USR*.

Anonymous FTP

The sites you will most often be connecting to allow *anonymous FTP*, which provides unrestricted access to public files. This means that anyone can login, browse, and download files from specified areas of an archive without registering. Some sites require authorization and prohibit you from accessing files until you register. Sites are called anonymous because you use the name *anonymous* to login and then you give your e-mail address as the password.

Starting To Play

No matter what type of computer you have, the basic login procedure is the same:

1. Start your FTP software program
2. Enter the address you want to connect to
3. Identify yourself and give a password
4. Move through the directories
5. Grab the file(s) you're interested in
6. Log off

On Your Mark, Get Set, Go!

To connect to an FTP site using a shell account, type **ftp <site address>** at your system prompt and press ENTER. The **<site address>** is the FTP archive to which you want to connect.

When running a graphical FTP program such as *Fetch* for Macs or *WS-FTP* for Windows, you'll see a screen with labeled boxes, like the one shown in Figure 19–2. Note that the information you see is the same, regardless of whether you use graphical software or text-based software. First we show you how to login to an FTP site.

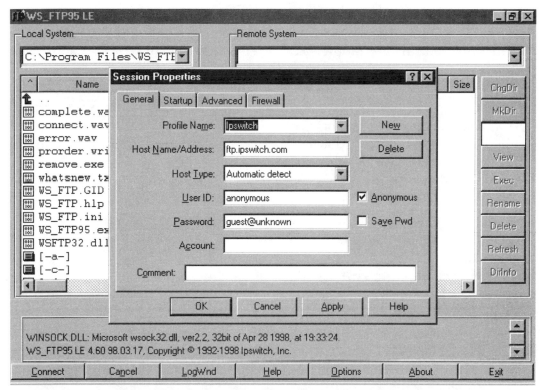

Figure 19–2 WS_FTP95 LE (Limited Edition) is a popular Windows 3.x, 95/98, NT application for viewing and downloading files on the Internet. It is free with no expiration date to noncommercial users. There is a Pro version of WS_FTP that offers additional functionality. Both versions are available for download from Ipswitch's Web site at *www.ipswitch.com* and their FTP site at *ftp1.ipswitch.com*.

Address, Please!

Before you can login to a remote FTP site, you'll need an FTP address. *FTP addresses* look the same as many other Internet addresses. They consist of a series of names and abbreviations, separated by dots (what people would normally refer to as "periods"). Sometimes, *ftp* is part of the address itself, as in *ftp.eff.org*, the home of the Electronic Frontier Foundation.

Site names are the names of the organizations or institutions that maintain the files. Following are some examples of FTP addresses and their corresponding site names.

> Internet Address: *garbo.uwasa.fi* (You can log to Garbo also by *http:// garbo.uwasa.fi/*)
> FTP Site Name: FTP archives at the University of Vaasa, Finland
> Internet Address: *ftp.monash.edu.au*
> FTP Site Name: Monash University FTP Server. Melbourne, Australia.

If you want to connect to the University of Vaasa's FTP server named Garbo, you would type **ftp garbo.uwasa.fi** at your system prompt and then press ENTER. If you are using a Windows-based FTP program, enter Garbo's address in the appropriate box and proceed from there. Be prepared to wait a few seconds while the computer contacts the host and requests access.

If the system you are trying to access is busy, you receive a message explaining the connection could not be made. Sometimes you may need to try more than once. Often it's useful to have more than one address ready in case one site is busy. Many FTP sites are busy during working hours, especially in the afternoon. If you don't need to schedule computer time during the day, as public school teachers must do, try using FTP after 5 p.m. in the evening.

Following are examples of what you might experience if a site doesn't respond. The first type of error message results from too many individuals being logged in. It usually says something like "Connection timed out." There is a limit to how many users can access a given FTP server simultaneously. For example, if the maximum number is 250 and you are the 251st individual to login, your connection will be timed out and you will have to try again later.

In other instances you may attempt connecting to a site that was active at one time, but is no longer operational. The following screen output shows you what happens when you try to login into Mississippi State University's FTP site, a site that no longer exists.

```
CRCINET 12> ftp ra.msstate.edu
Connected to ra.msstate.edu.
220 Ra.MsState.Edu FTP server (UNIX(r) System V Release 4.0) ready.
Name (ra.msstate.edu:anonymous): anonymous
530 User anonymous unknown.
Login failed.
ftp>
```

Who Goes There?

Once the connection is made using a shell account, you will be prompted to identify yourself and give a password. With anonymous FTP, you login to the remote system by entering the word **anonymous** as your ID. When prompted for a password, your e-mail address is considered common courtesy. When you connect to an FTP server using a Windows-based application, such as WS_FTP95 shown in Figure 19–2, the login sequence is automated. Notice in Figure 19–2 that the *Session Properties* screen includes the host name, user ID, and password. All you need to do is click the **OK** button and WS_FTP95 automatically connects and logs you in.

The following is an example of a complete login sequence to the Freie Universit%ot Berlin (Germany). In this example, *comp%* is the system prompt. On your Internet service provider's computer, the prompt might be a dollar sign ($) or something else. Note also that, in the example, there is no e-mail address typed after the word *Password:*. When you do this yourself and enter your own password, nothing will show up. Passwords are "secret" and no one else should see them, so the characters don't *echo* as you type. That is to say, they don't appear on the screen as you type. Remember, characters in FTP addresses are case sensitive, so type in the upper- and lowercase letters just as they are presented here.

```
comp% ftp FTP.FU-Berlin.DE
Connected to pascal.zedat.fu-berlin.de.
220 FTP.FU-Berlin.DE ready, please login as user ôftö.
Name (FTP.FU-Berlin.DE:lfodemsk): anonymous
331 Anonymous login ok, send your e-mail address as password.
Password:
230–
230–Welcome at Free University of Berlin (Germany).
230–
230 Anonymous login ok, for special commands see the README.
ftp>
```

Whose Move Is It?

Now that you're connected and authorized to access the information, it's your turn to move. How you move depends on how you're connected.

With a software program running on a SLIP/PPP account, you'll have scroll bars and buttons to click as you move through lists of files and change directories. The display is similar to File Manager in Windows. The commands still mean the same thing, regardless of how you choose them.

With a shell account, you'll simply see a list of file and directory names, much like viewing a directory in DOS. You get to have the fun of typing in cryptic commands, which younger kids can think of as "codes," to access the files into which they have "anonymously" snuck! In all actuality, you're not anonymous at all. You've entered your e-mail address at login and the computers know who requested entry into their system.

How Do You Take Your Turn?

What you do at an FTP site is get files or browse, regardless of whether you point-and-click or type word commands. You're moving through directories and subdirectories, looking at file and directory names. You cannot view or read or hear any of the files themselves; you can only look at the file names or download the files. This changes, however, when you use the World Wide Web.

At this point, you will use the command **cd** to change directories and the command **dir** to list the contents of the directory you're currently in. The **dir** command is a DOS command, not a UNIX command. The reason you can use a DOS command like this is because most UNIX system administrators have mapped the **dir** command to the UNIX **ls –l** command. Administrators understand that many of the users that login to their site are DOS users and unfamiliar with the UNIX command structure.

You use the command **cd ..** to move up one directory level—that is, to return to the directory you were just in. Tell your students that, just like Hansel and Gretel, they always have a bag of "bread crumbs" to help them find their way back home. The command **cd <pathname>** is used to go directly to a certain directory, without having to go step by step. For example, returning for a moment to the contractor example, to get to the directory containing the file named *local_building_codes,* you could do one of the following:

1. Type **cd carpentry** and press ENTER and then type **cd local_building_ codes** and press ENTER, or
2. Type **cd carpentry/local_building_codes** and press ENTER.

Oh No! I'm Lost!

Some directories contain hundreds of files. As they scroll past on your screen after you enter the **dir** command, you might be overwhelmed by the sheer volume. You might see a file name or two that catches your attention, and before you know it, you'll forget what directory you're even in! The **pwd** command can be used to rescue you and your students.

This command prints to the screen the name of the current directory. The command literally means **print working directory**. See whether your kids can guess or figure out what the meaning of **pwd** is on their own. It's both an entertaining and extremely useful command. Your kids will probably like this command a lot because it's like asking, "Where am I?"

How Do I Win?

The files are your goal and reward. Remember, these files can be text, pictures, sound recordings, or software. Software resources on the Internet can be divided into four classifications: public domain, freeware, shareware, and commercial.

Public domain software carries no copyright and is made available by the programmer without any restrictions. No limitations are imposed on its distribution and it can be transformed or modified by anyone without first obtaining permission from the author or paying the author a fee.

Freeware is copyrighted software made available for public use without charge. By retaining the copyright, the author can restrict the redistribution and modification of the software.

Shareware programs are also copyrighted but are made available on a trial basis; if, after you try it out, you decide to keep it and use it, you're required to pay the author a small fee. In return, you become a registered user and receive certain benefits such as a printed manual and technical support. If you decide not to keep the program, you must destroy the copies you have in your possession. Some shareware has a 30–day trial period and when the 30 days are up, the software just quits working.

Commercial software is software that is copyrighted and sold for a price. When you download commercial software from the Internet, you usually fill out an application form and pay for it online using a credit card. The software vendor then sends you a password or registration code via e-mail that enables you to *unlock* the software so you can install and configure it. Some vendors make watered-down versions of their commercial software available for free, but charge for the full-blown professional versions. An example is WS_FTP95, which was introduced earlier in this chapter.

If you looked around your house, you'd recognize the difference between pictures, software, sound recordings, and textual documents by their shape or container. On the Internet, these different items are identified by their file extension—the three characters that come at the end of a file name after the dot.

There are two types of files: ASCII and binary. ASCII is plain text and everything else is binary. The file *extension* usually indicates whether a file is ASCII or binary.

ASCII Text Files

ASCII, pronounced (ass'-kee), is an acronym for American Standard Code for Information Interchange. This is the standard language to transfer files between different types of programs. Don't just tell your kids this, though. Use one of the acronym dictionaries (Kind's glossary or Howe's dictionary) mentioned in Chapter 1 to show them how they can find this information on their own!

ASCII text files contain plain text and are usually given the extension *.txt, .doc,* or in some cases, no extension at all.

BINARY FILES

Any data that is not plain text is binary data and a file that contains any binary data, is referred to as a *binary file*. Some examples of binary files are sound recordings, pictures, and executable programs.

Binary files have file extensions like *.z, .zip, .tar, .hqx, .sea, .sit, .arc, .arj, .bin, .exe, .gif,* and *.jpg*. Binary files are often very large, so they are usually *compressed*. Compressing a file squeezes it so that it takes less space on a disk and less time to download. There are many ways to compress files, such as archiving and zipping. File extensions indicate the type of software that was used for compressing or archiving a file. The extension also tells you what type of program to run to uncompress or unarchive a file. Later in this chapter, we fully discuss this process.

I'm Stuffed! (and BinHexed)

Mac users have their own file types with which to be concerned. If a file ends with the *.sit* extension, that means it has been stuffed (compressed) with the shareware program Stuffit. You can find this program at several different FTP sites, usually in the */Mac/Utilities* directory.

Files with the *.hqx* extension are called *BinHexed* files and must be decoded with a program called *BinHex*. Sometimes files are both stuffed (*.sit* extension) and BinHexed (*.hqx* extension) and will have two extensions such as *checkers.sit.hqx*. This means that when you download the file called *checkers*, first you must decode it and then unstuffit. If you see a file with a *.cpt* extension, it has been compressed with a shareware program called *Compact Pro*.

Another file extension you'll see is *.sea*, which stands for *self-extracting archive*. These files automatically uncompress themselves when you double-click them.

Zippity-Do-Dah, Zippity-Aye!

Files that have been compressed, archived, or zipped must be transformed back into their original state before you can use them. This is done by decompressing, unarchiving, or unzipping them.

Most of the text and data compression programs used for performing these operations are standard public domain software applications.

Compression programs copy individual files to compressed versions of the same files. *Archiving programs* can take several files, compress them, and copy them all into one large file. The programs *zip* and *unzip* not only allow you to compress files, but they also allow you to create a single large file containing several compressed files. Files that have been zipped have the extension *.zip*.

GNU software has more recently come out with the *gzip* and *gunzip* programs. These files have the extension *.gz*. In addition to these programs, there are a variety of public domain programs that are available free of charge at many FTP sites. These include formats like ARC, SQX, and ZOO, among others.

Audio Files

Audio files are yet one more way of communicating ideas on the Internet. They come in the form of music, voice, or simple sound effects like bird calls.

Audio, or sound, files come in stereo and monaural and in various formats depending on whether they're for Macs or PCs. The most common types of sound files are Mac sound files. One reason they're more prevalent than PC sound files is because the hardware necessary for playing sound files on Macs is standard equipment on Macs.

To play sound files on PCs, you need to install a sound card and external speakers. Mac sound files can be played on a PC, but you will need to run some conversion software like WHAM (Waveform Hold and Modify). You can get WHAM for Windows 3.1 from ftp site *ftp.sovam.com*. Go to the */.1/mswindows/* directory and download the file called *wham131.zip*. If this site is no longer operational when you try your download, go to *ftpsearch.lycos.com/* and run a search on the string *wham131.zip* to find other download sites for this file.

Even if you're using a Mac, there may be instances where you need to use a sound-conversion program like Sound Machine to handle certain files. You can get a copy of *sound-machine-255.sit* at ftp site *garbo.uwasa.fi* in the directory */mac/sound/*. You can access this site using your Web browser by entering *ftp:// garbo.uwasa.fi/mac/sound/* in the location box.

Common file extensions for Mac and PC audio files are:

> *.au*—(Mu-Law) standard format for Sun and NeXT
> *.snd*—Macintosh system files
> *.aif, .aiff, .aifc*—(Audio Interchange File Format) developed by Apple for Macintosh
> *.wav*—Wave-form (WAVE or WAV for short) was developed by Microsoft and IBM and is the standard audio format used on PCs.

PCs Picture Files

Two of the most common formats for storing pictures are GIF and JPEG. GIF (Graphics Interchange Format) files were originally developed by CompuServe. These files are usually given the extension *.gif*. JPEG pictures are stored in files with *.jpg* extensions. The name JPEG stands for the Joint Photographic Experts Group, the organization that developed this particular image format.

GIF and JPEG images are stored as binary files, so the same procedure used for downloading compressed or executable files is also used for downloading picture files. The difference comes in how these pictures are displayed. In order to view a GIF or JPEG file, you must run a program called a *viewer*, which transforms the file into an actual image.

Downloading

When you *download* a file, you're moving a copy of the file from a remote computer to a local computer. The command to begin downloading a file is **get <filename>**, where <filename> is the name of the file you want to download. Before issuing this command, however, you must first set the *file type transfer mode*. The file type transfer mode simply means telling the computer whether you are downloading ASCII or binary files. Whatever transfer mode you set will remain in effect for all file transfers until you change it again. You can change it repeatedly just by typing the command **ASCII** or **binary** before typing the **get** command.

Did You Take Out the Garbage?

Sometimes you will download a zipped text file (a text file with the *.zip* extension) and see unrecognizable characters mixed in with the text when you unzip it and view it, or you may not be able to view it at all. The unrecognizable characters are referred to as garbage, colloquially, and as a corrupted file, formally.

What probably caused this is your failure to set the transfer type to binary before you transferred the file from the remote host to your local host. Or, it could have happened when you transferred the .zip file from your local machine to your own personal computer. You must also use the proper commands for transferring a binary file at this stage of the transfer.

Downloading Files Can Take Two Steps

If you are using a shell account, you have two steps for downloading a file. First you must download the file(s) from the remote host to your service provider's computer; then you must download the file from there to your own personal computer. For good file management, delete the file from your workspace on the dial-up host account while it is still clear in your mind what that file's purpose is and that you no longer need it.

Downloading files requires that you run a program designed just for that purpose. You must determine which file transfer protocols are supported by both your communications software and the local host to which you are connecting. Some of the common ones are Kermit, Ymodem, Xmodem, and Zmodem.

Zmodem is supported widely and you can be fairly certain that it will be supported by both your Internet service provider and the communications software you're using. On UNIX shell accounts, you issue the command **sz** to have the Zmodem program send a file from the local computer to your own computer.

If you had a text file in your directory on your local host called *library.txt*, you would enter the command **sz library.txt** at your system prompt and press ENTER to download that file. If you wanted to download a binary file called *library.zip*, you would enter the command **sz -b library.txt** and press ENTER to send. Zmodem has a companion command for uploading files which is **rz**. Uploading a file means you transfer it from your personal computer to the local host. We won't go into that process here, but it's useful if you want to upload a file from your personal computer to your service provider's computer.

Procomm Plus for Windows, a communications program introduced in Chapter 16, displays a status window that tracks the downloading process, showing the number of bytes being transferred per second, the estimated time until completion, and the percentage of the total file that has transferred at any given time. When the download is complete, the program beeps three times and the window disappears.

Most communications programs allow you to switch over to a DOS prompt without quitting the communications program or breaking your connection with the dial-up host. You can use this feature to confirm that the transfer took place successfully. After establishing that the file you downloaded is residing on your disk, you can exit back to the communications program and continue your communications with the dial-up host.

Judging a File by Its Name

Special purpose files located in FTP archives assist you in understanding what things are stored at that particular site. Your kids will probably delight in these file names when they first see them! The most common file is a README file (also named Readme, read.me, AAA_README.1ST, Index, 00README, 00–index.txt, and other similar variations).

Readme files are text files describing the contents of a directory, special instructions, or a brief explanation of the archive's contents and/or purpose. Many times when you first connect to a site, you see a message on the opening screen requesting that users read the file README. It's like Alice in Wonderland reading an "EAT ME" sign on a cake or finding a box with the words "OPEN ME" written on it. You won't grow bigger or find a box of chocolates, but you will find helpful information to attach some meaning to the somewhat cryptic file names in an archive's holdings. FTP directories are, as Forrest Gump says, like a box of chocolates. You never know what you might find or what a file named *xrt_203D.txt* might contain, until you read a *READ.ME* or *INDEX.TXT* file.

FTP COMMANDS

The following list describes the major FTP commands. For a more complete listing online, enter **help** or **?** at the *FTP>* prompt.

ascii	sets the mode to transfer ASCII text files
binary	sets the mode to transfer binary files
cd	changes directories on the remote host
cd ..	changes directories to the directory one level up
cdup	changes the directory to the directory one level up
dir	lists the contents of the current directory
get <filename>	downloads the specified file from the remote host to the local host
get <remote filename> **<local filename>**	downloads a file named one thing on the remote host onto your local host giving it another name
help	prints online user help
ls	lists the contents of the current directory
mget <filenames>	transfers multiple files from the remote host to the local host
pwd	displays the current directory on the remote host
quit	ends your FTP session
statistics	switches the feature that prints file transfer timing statistics on or off

LESSON PLAN IDEAS

Learning how to use FTP requires learning commands and sequences. FTP commands are text-based and less applicable to and appropriate for the young child. Here are some things relevant to FTP that you can do with younger students:

1. Spelling and Typing Skills
   Learn to spell the word *anonymous*. If the children you are working with have no keyboarding skills, let them practice typing just this word, learning where the letters are on a keyboard or typewriter.
2. Command Games
   Help students understand the words and meanings behind cryptic commands and acronyms. Show them that many commands are acronyms or codes for two or three other words; for example, **pwd** literally means **p**rint **w**orking **d**irectory and **cd** means **c**hange **d**irectory.

   Brainstorm with kids to help them create their own acronyms and codes for things said or terms used repeatedly in school, in your classroom, within your family, or with your librarian. They can have fun thinking these up while learning the concept behind something such as setting the file transfer mode.

When starting a discussion, for example, you could have someone set the "ryh" (raise your hand) mode by writing it on the chalk board. You could have a sign in your library saying "The library is in 'st' (story time) mode."

3. Guide Cards

Have your children create Guide Cards that are color coded. On each card, list commands or procedures for logging in and out. Perhaps they can "market" these to students and teachers in upper grades or to the librarian. In this manner, they will become familiar with the terms, even though they are not yet logging in themselves.

Use 3x5 or 4x6 index cards or cards cut from cardstock paper. You can use different color cards or paper to identify FTP and the other applications presented in this book such as Gopher, telnet, and the WWW. The finished cards can be organized in a number of ways, such as in a file box, posted on a board near the computer, laminated, hole punched, and placed on a ring, or placed within plastic protector sheets in a ring binder.

Topics that can be covered with Guide Cards include:

- *A Login/Logoff Guide Card:* Shows how to login and logoff (see section called "Starting to Play")
- *A Commands Guide Card:* Lists common commands such as **pwd**, **cd**, **cd ..**, **dir**, and **help** (see section called "FTP Commands")
- *Binary and ASCII Download Guide Cards:* Shows how to download binary and ASCII files

RESOURCES

In this section, we point you to sources for graphical FTP software, sound files, picture files, and audio players.

Graphical Software

With a SLIP/PPP account, when you transfer files over the Net the files you download come directly to your computer, not an intermediary computer. Your computer is a full-fledged host on the Internet and can run graphical software. Here are some FTP clients you might consider using.

A popular FTP program for Macs is Dartmouth College's Fetch 2.1.2. Fetch is free to educational and nonprofit groups, and $25 for other users. Fetch_2.1.2.sit.hqx is a Macintosh FTP client. Fetch makes it easy to transfer files to and from FTP servers from a Macintosh. Fetch recognizes and interprets Binhex, StuffIt, and MacBinary file formats. You can find Fetch using your Web browser with the address *ftp://ftp.dartmouth.edu*. Go to the */pub/mac/ directory*. You can also copy the file called *Fetch_2.1.2.sit.hqx* by FTPing to site *ftp.dartmouth.edu* and going to the */pub/mac* directory. Their Web site is located at *www.dartmouth.edu/pages/softdev/fetch.html*.

FTPPro2000 is a Windows-based FTP program that looks a lot like Windows Explorer, except you can also transfer files to and from FTP sites. FTPPro2000 enables you to drag and drop files from your local computer to a remote computer and copy entire folders. To learn more, point your browser to *www.ftppro. coml*.

Jackhammer is an FTP client that allows you to keep trying a file until the site is no longer busy and then it will download the file for you. You can download a copy at *www.sausage.com/jackhammer/jackhammer.html*.

CuteFTP is a Windows-based FTP client that, like other Windows-based programs, allows you to utilize the capabilities of FTP without having to know all of the commands described earlier in this chapter. You can use CuteFTP in conjunction with your Web browser. Copy a URL to the clipboard, and CuteFTP will automatically download the file. When you connect to a site, CuteFTP can send a LIST command (**ls**) to the server that displays the files in the current directory. A newer feature enables you to select multiple files from various directories and tag them for later transfer. To learn more, check out *www.cuteftp.com/*.

There are several good shareware FTP programs that you can download and install for use on your own computer. Visit *www.shareware.com* for some examples such as these:

uftp_v10.zip	UltraFTP 1.0: Graphical Win95/98/NT FTP client
ftpcomm.zip	FTP Commander v2.0: Freeware FTP client
aftp15.zip	AbsoluteFTP: FTP client for Windows 95/98/NT
ftpv6004.zip	FTP Voyager v6.0.0.4: Explorer-like FTP client

Running Your Own FTP Server

Even with a dial-up SLIP/PPP connection, you could run your own FTP server as long as you let the world know what your host address is. If your IP number is dynamically assigned by your service provider (a different number is assigned to you each time you dial up), this would be difficult. But if you are on a permanent connection through work or school, then your PC may have a dedicated IP address assigned to it. In either case, one of the best UNIX-style servers built for Windows 95/98/NT computers is *War FTP Daemon* and it is freeware. You can download a copy from *www.jgaa.com/tftpd.htm*. This would give you and your kids an opportunity to build your very own file archive and make its holdings available to anyone with a connection to the Internet.

Tip

You can FTP using Netscape in the same manner as if you were moving from one URL to another. For example, if you want to FTP to Netscape you would type in the following address in the location box: **ftp://ftp.netscape.com**. This will display all the FTP directories in your Netscape window.

If you want to FTP into your shell account and post your Web pages, type **ftp://username@host/** in the location area. You will be asked to supply your password (same as your login password) before you are able to access your shell account. For example, if your username is *acbenson* and your host address is *ftp.visi.com*, you would enter **ftp://acbenson@ftp.visi.com/**.

Netscape Navigator and Internet Explorer (IE) can download files using FTP, however they do not allow files to be uploaded. IE can log into anonymous FTP locations only. IE will not permit logging into your personal FTP directory.

For more information on using Internet Explorer to FTP, visit *www.microsoft.com/support*. For any questions regarding Netscape visit *help.netscape.com*.

If you have access to a private FTP site, one that requires a login ID and password (as opposed to an anonymous FTP site), here's how you might be able to connect using your Web brower. In the location box at the top of your browser's screen, enter this address format: **ftp://user:pass@host:port/path/filename**.

In place of *user*, enter your user name or ID. In the place of *pass*, enter your password. After the @ sign, enter the host address and FTP port number (optional), which is usually port number 21. This will place you in the root directory. You can add a path statement if you like, for example, */pub/*. A sample address might look like this: *ftp://acbenson:cn4268@ftp.ford.com:21/pub/sound/hello.au*.

FTP Sites

Apple Software Updates are posted and available for downloading *ftp://ftp.apple.com*. These updates include all of the latest updates of Apple software, including most printer drivers, updates to utilities, and networking and communication software. Parents should read the posted Apple Software License Agreement before downloading any software. For a complete listing of the best known Apple II WWW and FTP sites, visit Rolf Braun's home page at *www.cstone,net/~rbraun/misc/a2ftp.html*.

Picture Files

For additional information on picture files, consult the frequently asked questions (FAQ) list on viewing pictures. This list consists of three files called *part1*, *part2*, and *part3*. These files reside in the */pub/usenet/news.answers/pictures-faq* directory at FTP site *rtfm.mit.edu*.

AltaVista Photo Finder at *image.altavista.com* is one of the most comprehensive image databases on the Net with excellent search capabilities. This database combines the Corbis photo database with indexed images from the Web. Images include photos, drawings, and artwork, and each search returns up to 12 thumbnails at a time.

PedagoClips is a clip art search engine located at *www.pedagonet.com/*

clipart.eht. Here you find search forms for HotBot, Lycos, Filez, and AltaVista—all optimized to search for graphics.

The Image Finder at *sunsite.berkeley.edu/ImageFinder/* allows you to search 11 image databases including Architectural Images, Digital Library SunSITE, Fort Worth Star-Telegram, Images 1: National Library of Australia, Library of Congress, Library of Virginia, NASA, NAU Cline Library, Smithsonian Institution, and WebSeek.

Image Search Tools at *www.rcls.org/psearch.htm* does the same thing the Image Finder does, but with different indexes. Here you can access the Yahoo Image Surfer, The Amazing Picture Machine, NASA Image Exchange, Scour.net Multimedia Search, Smithsonian Photo Database, and Lycos.

WebSeek at Columbia University *www.ctr.columbia.edu/webseek* links to the visual data stored on the Web. WebSeek makes it possible for you to search by keywords or browse by subject more than 665,000 images and videos.

The North Central Regional Technology in Education Consortium (NCRTEC) helps schools integrate technology into their classrooms. One of their services includes the Amazing Picture Machine Web site at *www.ncrtec.org/picture.htm.* The Amazing Picture Machine is designed to help educators find pictures, diagrams, and maps on the Internet.

Graphics Software

ThingMaker at *www.thingworld.com/tools/tmtmore.asp* enables you to work with "things" like banners and buttons. You'll need to download ThingViewer at *www.thingworld.com/tools/tvmore.asp* to view these files.

Xara Webster at *www.xara.com/* can help you whip up some great Web graphics, animations, clickable image maps, and much more.

PART VI

READY-TO-GO
LESSON PLANS

In addition to links to a wide array of outstanding kid-safe Web sites, the enclosed CD-ROM also contains lesson plans for kids of all ages. There are two types of lesson plans on the CD-ROM. If you click on **Lesson Plans on the Internet**, you will find links to six sites that offer literally hundreds of lesson plans in all subjects from the Civil War to health and physical education. These sites also offer advice on planning lessons and their own links to related Web sites.

The other choice, **Connecting Kids Lesson Plans**, is a set of fourteen lesson plans that we prepared especially for this edition of *Connecting Kids and the Internet*. To make it possible for you to work on the lessons while you are away from your computer, we have included the print version of these lessons in this appendix. In addition to the lesson plans and their accompanying handouts and resource lists, the CD-Rom also features live links to the materials referred to in the plans and to all of the sites in the resource lists. You can, of course, customize the Lesson Plans on the CD-ROM to fit your particular class or your family.

The authors and the publisher invite you to copy the materials contained in the **Connecting Kids Lesson Plans** for nonprofit, individual classroom or library use only. For other Connecting Kids Lesson Plans uses, please contact the publisher: Neal-Schuman Publishers, Inc., 100 Varick Street, New York, NY 10013-1506; Telephone (212) 935-8650; Fax: 1-800-584-2414; e-mail: info@neal-schuman. com.

LESSON PLAN INFORMATION

Please note that these lesson plans were written for an audience that encompasses parents, teachers, and librarians. Our goal was to make each lesson plan flexible enough so that, with minor modifications, a parent, teacher, or librarian could use them. For ease of readability, the term "student" is used, instead of child or patron. Also, the term "classroom" is used, rather than home or library. The grade levels given are only suggestions. If the topic of a lesson plan interests you, read through it first to determine if it would be applicable to the children with whom you work. You may be working with Internet savvy kids or gifted children who would do fine with a plan designated for older students. You may also have kids who are unfamiliar with the Internet. These kids might benefit using a plan designated for younger kids.

Lesson Plan Links on the CD-ROM

Ed's Oasis - *http://www.edsoasis.org/*
> Ed's Oasis is the first stop teachers should make when looking for lesson plans online. They offer much more besides lesson plans, such as evaluation forms for determining the value of a Web site, teacher links, examples of good Web sites, and the Treasure Zone offers Web sites to use in the classroom. They recently sponsored a lesson plan contest and the winners results will be posted at The Gateway - *http://www.thegateway.org/*.

Teachers.Net LESSON BANK - *http://teachers.net/lessons/*
> Net LESSON BANK features over 400 lesson plans and curriculum development ideas with the capability to browse lesson plans by subject matter or search by keyword.

Virtual Field Trips Teacher Page - *http://www.bess.net/~garyg/TeacherPg.htm*
> The Virtual Field Trips Teachers Page has dozens of lesson plans from a variety of sources covering topics such as bird study, biographies, headline news, and graphing coasters.

Learning Page of the Library of Congress Lesson Ideas - *http://memory.loc.gov/ammem/ndlpedu/lesson.html*
> The Learning Page presents strategies and lesson plans developed by education professionals to help integrate primary sources, especially those in the American Memory Web site, into the classroom. Lessons are grouped by topic and include Civil War, Conservation, the Great Depression, Immigration, and the Revolutionary Era.

Lesson Plans Across the Curriculum - *http://members~aol.com/Donnpages/LessonPlans.html* Lesson Plans Across the Curriculum offers lesson plans covering a wide variety of topics such as Special Education, computer skills, critical thinking, world languages, nutrition, and ecology and the environment.

Internet Lesson Links - *http://www.pekin.net/pekin/pilots/lesson_plans.html* Internet Lesson Links are offered by Pilot Program. Lesson plan topics covered are Health and P.E., Art & Music, Science, Social Studies, Math, and Language Arts. Pilot Program involves 40 new teachers each year in a comprehensive four year program that trains teachers to effectively use technology in a restructured classroom environment.

LIST OF LESSON PLANS

Lesson Plan 1: The World Wide Web Addressing System (Grades 3–7)
Teaches the elements of a WWW address.

Lesson Plan 2: Evaluating Web Sites (Grades 4–12)
Teaches the necessity to determine the authenticity and accuracy of a Web site when researching.

Lesson Plan 3: Bookmarking Bookmarks (Grades K–6)
Teaches how to create bookmarks and the value of doing so.

Lesson Plan 4: Copyright Copycats (Grades 3–7)
Teaches awareness of copyrights.

Lesson Plan 5: Creating a Web Page: Basic Tags (Grades 3–7)
Teaches the basic tags required for all HTML documents.

Lesson Plan 6: Creating a Web Page: Formatting Lists (Grades 7 and up)
Teaches the tags necessary for creating lists within an HTML document.

Lesson Plan 7: Creating a Web Page: Making Tables (Grade 7 and up)
Teaches the tags required for building tables in an HTML document and gives examples of tables.

Lesson Plan 8: Understanding E-Mail Addresses (Grades 3–7)
Teaches the parts of an e-mail address.

Lesson Plan 9: E-Mail Signatures (Grades 3–7)
Teaches how to create and use an e-mail signature file.

Lesson Plan 10: Mailing Lists (Grades 5–9)
Teaches how to subscribe, unsubscribe, and participate in a mailing list.

Lesson Plan 11: Online Safety Issues (Grades 3–7)
Teaches the important basic rules of conduct for online interactivity.

Lesson Plan 12: Creating an FTP Archive Source List (Grade 7 and up)
Teaches how to navigate through FTP archives and locate files.

Lesson Plan 13: Downloading PC Compression Programs (Grade 7 and up)
Teaches how to download a program file and install and use it.

Lesson Plan 14: Looking at Pictures (Grade 7 and up)
Teaches how to use a downloaded viewer program file.

Lesson Plan #1: The World Wide Web Addressing System
Grade Level: Grades 3–7

Objectives
In this activity students become familiar with the WWW addressing system as they *travel* to Web sites to gather data.

Overview
Using URLs listed in the Resource List, you visit Web sites and print pages. These pages are mounted on poster board or otherwise displayed in the classroom. Students use mock passports with the URLs to visit the poster board Web sites, familiarizing themselves with WWW addresses. Built into this lesson are typical mistakes or error messages you see when traveling online. Students are required to gather data from the destination page and this feature enables you to customize this activity to fit into a current unit of study.

Activities
1. Divide students up into 5 groups.
    The size of the groups can vary depending on the number of students participating and how many destination posters you have time to prepare.
2. Print a *passport* and photocopy enough so that each student gets one.
3. Using the Resource List, select five sites and visit them. **Your printer must print the URL for this project to work**. Print the page you are directed to in the URL, plus the home page of the site. Also visit some of the links at the site and print at least five other pages.
4. Choose two of the sites you visited and do the following:
    *   For one site, leave out one character from the URL and type this into your Web browser, then print the error message you get.
    *   For the other site, replace one character in the URL, type this into your Web browser, and print the error message.
    If, instead of getting an error message, you pull up another site, print that page (as long as the site is decent).
    When choosing which letter to omit and which to change, try to imitate a common typing error or misspelling. The point of this is to bring attention to the fact that one letter in a URL can make a big difference and by reviewing the URL you typed, you can often see the mistake.
5. Post the printed pages to a poster board, and display on the wall or chalkboard, making sure to place them randomly. Use a sheet, cloth, or paper to cover the displays. For the two sites that you collected *error* pages, place the correct page on the back of the poster board. The erroneous page should be posted on the front of the poster board along with the other pages for that site.

6.	Set up five other poster boards using a plain piece of paper to print the following messages: (one message per paper)
-	This site has moved. Please check with the source of the URL that brought you to this page.
-	We're under construction right now. Please check back with us in a few weeks.
-	Can't find the requested URL.
-	*Graphics alert! There are so many graphics on this page that you'll be here for a long time waiting for them to all download so you can view them.
-	*Either your system or the system you are trying to reach has so many users logged on right now that the page you requested may only be partially viewable or may not load at all. Please try again later.

(*) *These are not error messages per se, but rather situations that occur online from time-to-time. Use the messages as an opportunity to discuss these situations with students.*

7.	Pick five URLs from the Resource List that you did not pick earlier and fill out five passports with these URLs.
8.	Divide up the remaining passports into five groups. For two groups, fill out the passports using the wrong URLs you created in step #4. Use the three other correct URLs to fill out passports for the other three groups. Print one of the following questions on the passport for the students to answer. You could also use your own directed activity for the students to accomplish after reaching their destination.
-	What is this Web site about?
-	List the first link you'd like to explore at this site.
-	If there is an e-mail address for comments, write it down.
-	Describe how this site frustrated you.
-	How could this site help with a topic of study?
-	What did you like best about this site?
9.	Set up a sound device, such as a bell, whistle, kazoo, or bicycle horn that students can use when they are lost. Everyone should stop and listen to the question and answer. Any student already familiar with URLs can work as an agent and answer questions.
-	The students receiving the passports for the sites created in step #6 may need help. After discussing the situation they are in, put them in with another group.
-	The two groups with the error messages may also have questions. They should be encouraged to look more closely at their URL and guess what may be wrong. Once they figure it out, they can then look on the back of the poster for the correct page to get the data they need.
10.	Upon reaching the destination page listed on their passports, students

collect the information requested on their passport. Use this information for hands-on exploring of the site in the computer lab at another time or for use in a class project.

Extending this Topic

- Remember, you can use your own URLs to tailor this lesson plan to a unit of study relevant to your situation.
- Students may want to do it again. Invite a neighboring class or class from another school to "travel" with your seasoned students.
- Create URL puzzles! Use blank puzzles or the back of a 35–50 piece puzzle to create URL puzzles. Write the parts of a URL on consecutive puzzle pieces. Let the kids put them together and then visit the site. After visiting a URL, students can decorate the rest of the puzzle pieces based on what they found at that site. Suggest using graphics from the site they printed out. Use the puzzles again, or glue them together and post them in the classroom, hallway, or library. This allows others to see what students found at the site.

Resource List

Athena, Earth and Space Science for K-12
http://www.athena.ivv.nasa.gov/index.html

The Moonlit Road
http://www.themoonlitroad.com/

InfoUse's PlaneMath Main Page
http://www.planemath.com/planemathmain.html

Home Page: American Memory from the Library of Congress
http://memory.loc.gov/ammem/amhome.html

Kids Center
http://www.townsqr.com/kidspage.html

The Kids on the Web
http://www.zen.org/~brendan/kids.html

CLASSROOM LINKS
http://www.bess.net/~garyg/FTlinks.htm

Aesop's Fables Online Collection
http://www.pacificnet.net/~johnr/aesop/

Goosebumps
http://place.scholastic.com/goosebumps/

Kid's Castle
http://www.kidscastle.si.edu/

Making Friends and other Crafts for Kids
http://www.makingfriends.com/

Voyages
http://www.4kids.org/coolspots/fantasticvoyages/page1.shtml

Timeline from the PBS Series: Life on the Internet
http://www.pbs.org/uti/

My Virtual Reference Desk
http://www.refdesk.com/

IPL—The Internet Public Library
http://www.ipl.org/

My WWW Passport
Name
Destination URL
Question:
Findings:

My WWW Passport
Name
Destination URL
Question:
Findings:

Lesson Plan #2: Evaluating Web Sites
Grade Level: Grades 4–12

Objectives
In this activity students discover the elements that make a Web site useful and appropriate to use for research and enjoyment.

Overview
Students create a checklist of the things they'd look for in a good Web site and then compare their thoughts with a form containing the basic elements of a good Web site. Students discuss whether there is anything they'd remove or include in the basic form. This form then becomes a tool for students when online.

Activities
1. Print the Web site Evaluation Form and photocopy enough for each participating student.
2. Ask each student to make a list of ten things a good Web site should have. If they can't think of ten, encourage them to come up with at least five. If you have students that have never been online or seen a Web site, encourage them to guess what would be the most important things to have on a Web site. Point out what they notice about good newspapers, magazines, or TV and radio stations. If you have too many people without a clue, take your students browsing a few times first.
3. Pass out one Web site Evaluation Form to each student. Have them highlight or color or otherwise mark the items on their sheet that are also on the form.
4. Discuss the results. Is there anything important that went unrecognized? What, if anything, did everyone write down? Note which students recognized most of the points on the form. Ask questions to determine how much time these students spend online or how long they have been using the Internet. Why did other students recognize fewer points on the form? Discuss what the underlying reasons may be, for example, less hands-on computer time. Ask students which points they think are important, or if they think there were important points left out.
5. Collect any changes your students may want to make in the form and retype the form. Distribute a few forms to each student and have a supply of forms available in the classroom. Encourage students to take the form home and test some pages they use regularly at home.

Extending This Topic
- Request that students submit a page that fits certain criteria and then have a discussion. Criteria suggestions: a site they rated as very good, a site they rated as poor, sites that were good but were missing one thing on the list, and sites that only had one good element.

- Publish what you find out! Some of the students may want to publish their findings or assessments once during the year or at regular intervals. Suggest the school newsletter or Web site, unless your class has its own Web site. Other opportunities for publishing would be in the education section of the local paper or on a kids-oriented mailing list. You could also ask your principal to periodically announce over the school's PA system a site the whole class rated as good. Also, try placing an announcement on the local community access television station.

Resource List

Assessment of Student Projects + Build Your Own
http://www.cusd.chico.k12.ca.us/~tgray/Assess.html

PBS Kids: TechKnow
http://www.pbs.org/kids/techknow/

ozline—Learning with the World
http://www.ozline.com/learning/workshop.html

Kathy Schrock's Guide for Educators—Critical Evaluation Surveys
http://discoveryschool.com/schrockguide/eval.html

Ten C's for Evaluating Internet Resources
http://www.uwec.edu/Admin/Library/10cs.html

Web Page Evaluation Criteria
http://www.ozline.com/learning/workshop.html

Evaluating Web Resources | Advertising & Sponsorship
http://www2.widener.edu/Wolfgram-Memorial-Library/adspon.htm

ED's Oasis Evaluation Guidelines: Streamlined Version
http://www.EDsOasis.org/guide3.html

Online Instructional Resource Evaluation Guideline
http://www.EDsOasis.org/guide2.html

Web Site Evaluation Form

YES	Question	NO
	You can tell who created the site, including information about the author or professional credentials.	
	The site offers chat rooms or discussion forums.	
	The site has links to other sites.	
	The site is easy to navigate.	
	You can tell when the site was last updated.	
	The site has interesting graphics.	
	The site is useful for homework or research.	
	The site is just for fun and entertainment.	
	The site loads quickly.	
	The site is respectful to others.	
	People from different ages would enjoy the site.	
	The site is easy to use with a group.	

Lesson Plan #3: Bookmarking Bookmarks
Grade Level: Grades K–6

Objectives

In this activity students practice browsing the Web and learn how to set up bookmarks to create a unique list for the family or class.

Overview

Students browse various Web sites, chosen either from the Resource List or obtained from other sources. As they browse, they'll set the bookmarks. When offline, they will access their bookmark files to edit and print as useful resources.
The instructions given here are for Netscape Navigator, but you can modify the commands to accommodate any browser you use.

Activities

1. Assign students to work in teams of two. Give each team an index card with three URLs from the Resource List or from other sources. It doesn't matter if some or all teams have the same URLs. It would be useful to give the same two URLs to everyone and have one URL different; there are extension activities you can do if you use this method.
2. Students logon to their Internet account and start a Web browser. In the Location Dialog box at the top of Netscape's browser, students type the first URL listed on their card and then press ENTER.
3. Once the site is loaded (check the information box at the bottom of the screen—It should read: document done), click once on Bookmarks and choose Add Bookmark. The URL for this site and its name are now added to your bookmark list.
4. Repeat the previous step for each URL on the list. Encourage students to find and bookmark three other URLs by exploring the sites on their lists. *If you've already done Lesson Plan #2, encourage students to use the Web site Evaluation Form.*
5. After visiting the sites on their cards, have students log off the account.
6. Now students will click on Bookmarks and then choose Edit Bookmarks. A separate window will appear displaying the bookmarks they've just created. Click once on the first entry on this list. It will be called something like Linda's Bookmark List or Ramay Jr. High Computer Lab Bookmarks List. Now click on File, and then choose Add Folder to create a new folder. A Bookmarks Properties box will appear and the Name field will be highlighted. Have students type in their names and press ENTER to create a folder for the bookmarks they've just collected. The new folder with the student's name should now appear as the second item on the Bookmarks List. This folder will have a box with a minus sign in it, meaning that the folder is empty.
7. The students can now click once and hold down the mouse button on the bookmarks just created. While holding down the mouse button, they

drag the item to the folder they just created with their name. When the folders are highlighted, they can release the mouse button.

8.   Once the bookmarks are sorted, you can choose to print the list.

HINTS:

- Clicking twice will prompt Netscape to try to connect to that URL. Your browser will give you a warning message saying there was an error connecting to that site. Click OK to continue.
- The entire folder can also be moved to another location in the list or to another folder in the list.
- Dragging a bookmark item or folder between two other items on the list until a line appears between those two items will move the object you're dragging between those two items.
- Clicking on a plus sign next to a folder expands the folder so you can view all the items in that folder. Clicking on a minus sign collapses the folder so you can only view the name of the folder.

WARNING: The print option will print the entire file.

You may want to save printing until all the teams that will be using this computer have completed the previous steps.

Extending this Topic

- Use the printed list as an in-class resource or provide a copy as a resource in the library for students to browse for good Web sites before they get online.
- Students can photocopy just their part of the list to keep with them or take home.
- Suggest that other classes post their bookmark lists in the hall outside the door for others to browse, or copies can be stored in the library or computer lab.
- If many of your students used the same URLs, start discussing the findings!

Suggested Topics

- How many people liked the site and how many didn't? Why?
- What is most attractive about this site? The reason people didn't like it?
- How many people found the same link or an additional resource from the same site?
- Why did so many people find this same link?
- Why didn't anyone or very few people pick the same links?
- Did anyone find a megasite with dozens or hundreds of links?
- Did anyone find a dead end?
- Incorporate math and social studies skills by conducting surveys of other classes' findings, either locally or online. Charts, graphs, and comparisons are a good place to start.

Resource List
Yahooligans!
http://www.travlang.com/languages/

Discovery Channel Online
http://http://www.yahooligans.com/

United States Information
http://www.usia.gov/regional/posts/posts.htm

Geography World
http://members.aol.com/bowermanb/101.html

KIDS Report
http://scout.cs.wisc.edu/scout/KIDS/index.html

Weekly Reader Galaxy
http://www.weeklyreader.com/

mamamedia.com
http://www.mamamedia.com/

KidsCom
http://www.kidscom.com/

Little Explorers Picture Dictionary with Links
http://www.EnchantedLearning.com/Dictionary.html

Young Writer's Clubhouse
http://www.realkids.com/club.shtml

School House Rock
http://www.genxtvland.simplenet.com/SchoolHouseRock/

Skylight's Kids Graphics
http://members.xoom.com/Sky_Light/

World Surfari
http://www.supersurf.com/

The Franklin Institute
http://sln.fi.edu/tfi/jump.html

Lesson Plan #4 : Copyright Copycats
Grade Level: Grades 3–7

Objectives
In this activity students practice the skills of storyboarding to create Web sites on paper. They practice playing the roles of thief and victim concerning copyright issues and discuss their feelings and how copyright laws may have been broken.

Overview
Students use their creativity to create Web sites on paper. You don't need to know HTML. Each paper Web site is created with various levels of copyright usage and infringement, including one team that steals from the other sites. Discussion is a big part of this lesson plan as students become attached to their work and experience what happens when they see their work without proper credit.

Activities
1. Divide students into four groups. Each group uses regular paper to create a three-page Web site. (*This step is called storyboarding and is the first step in creating a real Web site*.) You can let the students decide the topic of their Web sites or you can give them a topic relevant to class studies. Start three groups earlier than the last group. Give one of the following criteria to each of the three early groups:
   - Content must all be completely original, including graphics, text, and design. (This group should use a copyright statement on all their pages.)
   - Content should be a mixture of original work and material from other sources, such as magazines, newspaper, flyers, etc. (Credit must be given on all copyrighted material that allows reprint with the copyright statement.)
   - Content should be a mixture of original work and material from other sources. (The copyright statement on all pages should grant free use of material without permission.)
2. Display two copies of each of the three sites, with one copy on top of the other. Students then visit each other's sites and see what the others have done.
3. During this time, the fourth group creates a Web site by using material from the other three. The duplicate pages are available for them to use to cut and paste. This will demonstrate the ability to download or copy information from the Web without disturbing the original site. This group should use elements from all three other sites.
4. Display the last group's Web site and start discussing copyright issues! Point out how one group used copyrighted material without permission and then another person stole it from them because it did not have a

copyright statement. Which sites could actually be published legally? What group could turn their Web site into a flyer without penalty?

Extending this Topic
- Explore the copyright statements on the various clip art sites listed in The Link Farm. Each one is a little different and provides many opportunities to discuss copyright issues.
- Visit The Copyright Website listed in the Resource List. All aspects of copyright issues are covered here. They also list real infringement cases with examples. Explore these with students. Let the students make guesses about how the cases will be resolved.

Resource List

Web Diner Inc.
http://www.webdiner.com/

The Copyright Website
http://www.benedict.com/index.html

HTML Writer's Guild
http://www.hwg.org/

ZooNet Image Archives
http://www.mindspring.com/~zoonet/gallery.html

Link Farm Clip Art Page
clip.htm

Lesson Plan #5: Creating a Web Page: Basic Tags
Grade Level: Grades 3–7

Objectives
In this activity students learn the basic tags required in every Web page and the preliminary steps necessary before typing any HTML code.

Overview
Students go through the preliminary steps necessary to create a Web page—thinking of what content to put on their Web page, what graphics they want to use, and what format to use to present the information. They use a template that includes the basic tags every HTML document must contain.

Activities
1. Print and photocopy enough Webmaster Forms so that each student has one form.
   - You may want to use teams instead of individuals.
   - You many want to use Lesson Plan #4 before attempting this project to give students experience with storyboarding.
2. Each student or team chooses a topic for their Web page or you can assign topics based on a current unit of study. Students write a title and three headings for their topic. After each heading they should write a paragraph about the heading topic.
3. The students now know what will be on their Web site and now they can design the placement of these elements on their Web page. For this project students are limited to horizontal format. That means that data and images can be placed right, left, or center and are separated by horizontal lines. Students will probably go through several sheets of paper arranging the elements of their Web page.
4. After they decide on a design, students are ready to type their Web pages. They can use an HTML editor or a word processor. They use the Webmaster Form for the HTML codes and add their text where it is designated in the form.
5. To effectively view students' pages, create an index page with links to each student's page using the Index Page Form. Students save their documents with their first names and the extension html, for example, john.html. Students with the same first name use initials. Now upload all student files and the index file to your Web server using FTP file transfer or an FTP program such as WS_FTP.
6. Have students view their pages in pairs and critique them, taking note of errors so they can fix them later.

Extending this Topic

- Students can scan drawings, pictures or photos to place on their Web pages. They can also use image files they may already have. Refer to Chapter 19 for descriptions of image tags, or visit one of the sites in the Resource List for more information about using image files.
- Visit the Web color Web sites in the Resource List and experiment with background color, background images, and text color.

Resource List

Dr. Watson's - Web Page Analyzer
http://watson.addy.com

Web Diner Inc.
http://www.webdiner.com/

A Beginner's Guide to HTML
http://www.ncsa.uiuc.edu/General/Internet/WWW/HTMLPrimer.html

Help Desk
http://web.canlink.com/helpdesk/

ColorIndex
http://www.infi.net/wwwimages/colorindex.html

VisiBone Webmaster's Color Lab
http://www.visibone.com/colorlab/

Super Color Chart
http://www.zspc.com/color/index-e.html

The Palette Man
http://www.paletteman.com/

Basic HTML Tags

```
<html>
<head>
<title> Type the name or title here.
</title>
</head>
<body>

<h1> Type the name or title here, also.</h1>

<h2> Type your first heading here.</h2>
<P> Type a paragraph about your heading here.

<h2> Type your second heading here.</h2>
<P> Type a paragraph about your heading here.

<h2> Type your third heading here.</h2>
<P> Type a paragraph about your heading here.

</body>
</html>
```

Lesson Plan #6: Creating a Web Page: Formatting Lists
Grade Level: Grade 7 and up

Objectives

In this activity students reinforce their understanding of basic HTML tags and learn three commonly used tags for creating lists on a Web page.

Overview

Lesson Plan #5 is a prerequisite for this lesson plan. Students use the basic document they created in that project and add lists. The lesson can be repeated until all students have created one of each type of list.

Activities

1. Copy the page in Chapter 11 that contains examples of the list tags. Make enough copies for each student to have one.
2. Using the Web page students created in Lesson Plan #5, have students choose one heading from that Web page and modify the descriptive paragraph so that there are at least three elements about their heading or from the paragraph that they can put into list form. Students can entirely replace the descriptive paragraph with their list or add the list before, after, or in the middle of the paragraph.
3. Have students choose one of the following three list formats to use:

Ordered—this is a numbered list.

My Favorite Things

1. My favorite activity is playing the piano.
2. My favorite subject is History.
3. My favorite movie is *Toy Story*.

Unordered—this is a bulleted list.

What I did on vacation in Tennessee.

*   I went horseback riding.
*   I built a campfire every night.
*   I visited the Sunsphere from the 1982 World's Fair.

**Directory—this list includes a heading with an indented
line for a description.**

My Photos

My Friends

    From left to right: Tommy, Ashley, Karen, Zach, and Paul.

Sparky

    Sparky is my pet fish and he lives in a bowl on the counter top next to the refrigerator.

My School
> This is what the ball field at my school looks like when you lie across the seats and hold the camera sideways!

4. Students use the page with the list tags to type in the tags for the lists they are going to use. They can either type in all the tags first and then fill in the information, or they can type in the information as they go. Have students check off or circle the type of list they use. Repeat this lesson until all students have created one of each type of list.

Extending this Topic

- Create a test by printing this Lesson Plan. Students then fill in the correct tags in each of the examples listed in step #2.

- Once students have created the basic lists, let them experiment with the concept of *nesting*. Nesting tags enable you to create lists that meet the specific needs of your particular list. They also enable you to incorporate some creativity in the list. Try putting an ordered list as a descriptive element in a directory tag. Use the paired directory list tags more often in your list to create an outline.

- Have students play with icons in their lists. Students can find buttons and bars (or rules, as they are sometimes called) and other icons from Web sites for free. Then they can use a little red ball or an arrow or a NEW! icon, in before, or after the <LI> tag to add more creativity and individualism to their lists.

Resource List

IPL—The Internet Public Library
http://www.ipl.org/
Look up HTML Help Guides.

Web Diner Inc.
http://www.webdiner.com/
Find lots of help on writing Web pages here.

Dr. Watson's—Web Page Analyzer
http://watson.addy.com/
Check your Web page for spelling and code errors.

Skylight's Kids Graphics
http://members.xoom.com/Sky_Light/
Free graphics, including backgrounds, ABC borders, pets, and more.

Icons & Images
http://www.uncg.edu:80/~bucknall/uncg/icons/
Dots, flowers, stars, arrows, pointer, and various other icons and gizmos.

Lesson Plan #7: Creating a Web Page: Making Tables
Grade Level: Grade 7 and up

Objectives
In this activity students strengthen their understanding of basic HTML tags and learn the tags used to create tables in HTML documents.

Overview
Lesson Plan #5 is a prerequisite for this lesson plan. Students use the basic document they created in that project and add at least one table. Tables can be frustrating and fun. It is recommended that students use an HTML editor for this project, mainly for the ability to switch easily from viewing code to viewing the code as it appears online.

Activities
1. Print and photocopy enough Table Tags Guides for each student to have one.
2. Students use the previously created Web page and choose one heading topic for their tables. Require students to have at least three rows and three columns plus a heading row for their table.
3. Students draw a grid on paper and write down what will be in each box of their table. They should number the rows and columns outside of the boxes. This will help them keep track of their data and tags.
4. Using the Table Tags Guide, students type in the tags and their information to create their table.

Extending this Topic
- Try some of the tag attributes, such as rowspan and colspan, to create interesting and unique tables.
- Try inserting images into some of the boxes of the table.
- Experiment with color and font tags.

Resource List
Web Diner Inc.
http://www.webdiner.com/

Dr. Watson's—Web Page Analyzer
http://watson.addy.com/

A Beginner's Guide to HTML
http://www.ncsa.uiuc.edu/General/Internet/WWW/HTMLPrimer.html

Table Tags Guide

Code for Sample Table 1

```
<TABLE BORDER=1>
<TR>
<TH> Cities </TH>
<TH></TH>
<TH></TH>
</TR>
<TR>
<TD> Minneapolis </TD>
<TD> Ithaca </TD>
<TD> San Antonio </TD>
</TR>
</TABLE>
```

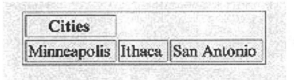

Sample Table 1
Basic table with a heading that spans
only the first column.

Code for Sample Table 2

```
<TABLE BORDER=1>
<TR>
<TH> Cities </TH>
<TH></TH>
<TH></TH>
</TR>
<TR>
<TD> Minneapolis </TD>
<TD> Ithaca </TD>
<TD> San Antonio </TD>
</TR>
<TR>
<TH> States </TH>
<TH></TH>
<TH></TH>
</TR>
<TR>
<TD> Wyoming </TD>
<TD> Oregon </TD>
<TD> New Mexico </TD>
</TR>
</TABLE>
```

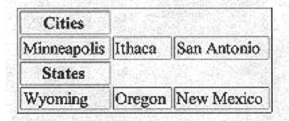

Sample Table 2
An extended example of the above table.

Code for Sample Table 3

```
<TABLE BORDER=1>
<TR>
<TH COLSPAN=3> Cities </TH>
</TR>
<TR>
<TD> Minneapolis </TD>
<TD> Ithaca </TD>
<TD> San Antonio </TD>
</TR>
</TABLE>
```

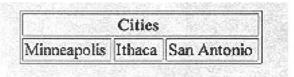

Sample Table 3
Basic table with a heading that spans
all three columns.
Note the *colspan* attribute in the code.

Code for Sample Table 4

```
<TABLE BORDER=1>
<TR>
<TH> classes </TH>
<TH> Teacher Name </TH>
<TH> Grade </TH>
</TR>
<TR>
<TD> French </TD>
<TD> Mrs. O'Donnel </TD>
<TD> C </TD>
</TR>
<TR>
<TD> Honors Algebra </TD>
<TD> Mr. Reeves </TD>
<TD> B </TD>
</TR>
<TR>
<TD> English Composition </TD>
<TD> Miss Gallen </TD>
<TD> B </TD>
</TR>
</TABLE>
```

Classes	Teacher Name	Grade
French	Mrs. O'Donnel	C
Honors Algebra	Mr. Reeves	A
English Composition	Miss Gallen	B

Sample Table 4
Basic table with a heading for **each** column.

Code for Sample Table 5

```
<TABLE BORDER=1>
 <TR>
  <TD></TD>
  <TH> Type </TH>
  <TH> Name </TH>
  <TH> Color </TH>
 </TR>
 <TR>
  <TH ROWSPAN=2> My Pets </TH>
  <TD>cat</TD>
  <TD>Timmy</TD>
  <TD>black and white</TD>
 </TR>
 <TR>
  <TD> rat </TD>
  <TD> Mathias </TD>
  <TD> brown </TD>
 </TR>
</TABLE>
```

Sample Table 5
A more complicated table
using the *rowspan* attribute.

Lesson Plan #8: Understanding E-Mail Addresses
Grade Level: Grades 3–7

Objectives
In this activity students learn the components of e-mail addresses.

Overview
Students set up a mock postal system and deliver e-mail in paper form to others. The project is self-checking, since mail with invalid addresses cannot be delivered.

Activities
1. Ask students to collect e-mail addresses from friends, family, or teachers. Collect some yourself in case some students don't have any. You should make a list of the domain names in the addresses, such as ipq.net, comcenter.com, aol.com, or gte.net

2. Divide students into groups to decorate or label mailboxes. You will need one box to use as a regular mailbox, including a slot to drop mail into. You will also need several individual mailboxes for each domain name you have collected from the addresses. Make the individual mailboxes out of shoeboxes, the lid of a box, or plastic, stacking desktop file baskets. The individual mailboxes don't need to be decorated. Students can write nametags for each one using your domain name list or you can prepare this in advance.

3. Give each student three or four envelopes. You can use plain sheets of paper folded over and stapled or taped closed.

4. On the front of one envelope each student should write the form of all e-mail addresses:
    username@domain name.extension
    Example: Linda@myplace.com

5. On the front of the other envelopes, students write one other address. Now all envelopes are dropped into the mailbox.

6. Let students take turns being postmasters. They take the envelopes out of the mailbox and attempt to deliver it to mailboxes. Students check if there is a username, @ "at" sign, and domain name, including extension. If the address is complete, it can go in the corresponding mailbox for that domain name. Create a dud letter box where all undeliverable mail can be stored. One group can go through the dud letters and determine what is wrong or missing in the addresses. They should write the corrected address on the back of the envelope. The postmasters should check spellings carefully. In the real world, one typing error will prevent an e-mail message from being sent.

Extending this Topic

- Extend this project by asking another class from your school or another school to exchange e-mail.
- Have your students join a mailing list to practice sending and receiving e-mail. See Chapter 9 for help and suggested mailing lists or try Lesson Plan 10.
- Help your students find penpals in town or across the country. See Chapter 10 for details and suggestions or use a site from the Resource List.

Resource List

Finding E-Mail Addresses
http://babel.its.utas.edu.au/docs/comlaw/email_addresses.html

Inter-Links E-Mail Guide
http://albanza.com/kabacoff/Inter-Links/e-mail/e-mail.htmlv

E-mail for Everyone
http://www.emailhelp.com/

Lesson Plan #9: E-Mail Signatures
Grade Level: Grades 3–7

Objectives

In this activity students learn the important elements of an e-mail signature file as they become familiar with ASCII art and keys on the keyboard. They may not use signature files very often, but they will know how they are used and how to create them.

Overview

Students create a signature file that they can use when responding to others via e-mail. They sketch their idea, then use a text editor or word processor to create the file.

Activities

1.   Explain the elements students should (and should not) include in an e-mail signature. Refer to Chapter 8 for more information. Point out how adults will provide much more information and that the purpose of a signature is to contact someone who sent an e-mail note easily or in a way other than e-mail.

Two basic rules for signature files:

1.   For the most part, children should not give out their last names, phone numbers, or mailing addresses. Just as in everyday life, children must exercise caution when giving out personal information in the form of a signature file.

2.   Limit the signature to four or five lines. Many people use the signature block to express their creativity by including small pictures they have drawn with keyboard characters and famous quotes from their favorite authors. People who include extravagant drawings along with 10 or 15 lines of text are considered annoying.

Have at least one keyboard available in the room for students to use for reference. If possible, obtain a picture of a keyboard with all the keys marked. Photocopy enough so each student gets one. Have the class work in small groups during the initial creation stage of this project. Students can get ideas from each other.

2.   Using a plain sheet of paper and the keyboard picture or a keyboard itself, students sketch their signature. They may need a few sheets of paper until they get a design they like. Require each student to include at least five characters that are not alphabetic or numerical.

3.   As soon as someone has an idea they like they can go to the computer and type it in using any word processor. This could take a little time.

Some characters may not appear on screen the way the students drew them. Also, it may take the student some time to figure out how to use spaces with the non-numeric and non-alphabetic characters to get the design they want.

4.   Students should save their files as a text documents and name them with their initials followed by sig.txt. Example: lmfsig.txt

NOTE: *To use this file when sending e-mail, you must tell the e-mail program what file to use and where the file is located. If students are using the same computer, you may want to create a signature file folder and keep all the signature files there. If each student always uses the same computer and they are the only person using it, they can move the file into the proper folder and configure a three-mail program one time. You will need to research how to set the signature function in your e-mail program.*

Even if you do not want students to use their signature files when sending e-mail, this exercise makes them aware of what signature files are and teaches them how to create one to use when they are older. They can also use this file for fun activities. See the section on Extending this Topic for details.

Extending this Topic
- Students can print their signature files and decorate them with borders or themes and use them as business cards or as name tags when you have visitors or a substitute. They could also use them in their lockers or book jackets or binders.

Resource List
Safety Tips for Kids on the Internet
http://www.fbi.gov/kids/internet/internet.htm

Surfing the Net WITH KIDS
http://www.surfnetkids.com/

Lesson Plan #10: Mailing Lists
Grade Level: Grades 5–9

Objectives

In this activity students practice commands for participating on mailing lists.

Overview

Students join mailing lists and discuss what they find useful and what they don't like about them.

Activities

1. Divide students into groups and give each group one of the sites listed in the Resource List. They search their site to find a mailing list to join. You may want to give them criteria for the type of list to look for. They could find a list about a topic they find interesting or a topic the class is currently studying.

2. Each group subscribes to the mailing list they find. Students will check their e-mail daily for two weeks. The students in the group can take turns checking the e-mail received. Students should keep a tally of how many messages they receive each day. Decide in advance if students will print all messages or only some.

3. Each group meets once a day for a set amount of time to read and discuss the e-mail received. They should keep a log, noting if they found anything interesting, if there were too many messages to read them all, if the list got off topic, etc.

4. At the end of two weeks, each group writes a review of their mailing list, presenting some of the following information:
   - Was the list useful?
   - Did they make any new friends?
   - Were there a lot or a few people writing to this list?
   - Would they recommend this list? If not, why?
   - Did they have any trouble subscribing or unsubscribing?

Extending this Topic

- Encourage students to try some of the other commands available for mailing lists. See Chapter 9 for additional commands, such as setting vacation mode and getting the list in digest form.
- Team students up with another student in your school or another school. Both students join the same list and discuss what they find out about the list. You could also encourage students to find a penpal who would like to join the same mailing list and discuss it. Use the sources listed in either The Link Farm or Chapter 10 to find a penpal.

Resource List
Liszt
http://www.liszt.com/

Publicly Accessible Mailing Lists
http://www.neosoft.com/internet/paml/indexes.html

Tile.net
http://www.neosoft.com/internet/paml/indexes.html

Pitsco
http://www.pitsco.com/p/Respages/listinfo.html

Command Guide Card	
ascii	sets the mode to transfer ASCII text files
binary	sets the mode to transfer binary files
cd	changes directories on the remote host
cd ..	changes directories to the directory one level up
cdup	changes the directory to the directory one level up
dir {local filename}	downloads a file named one thing on the remote host onto your local host giving it another name
help	prints online user help
ls	list the contents of the current directory
mget {filenames}	transfers multiple files from the remote host to the local host
pwd	displays the current directory on the remote host
quit	ends your FTP session
statistics	switches the feature that prints file

Get That File!

1. Logon to your Internet account.
2. Type the command **cd** to change directories until you are in the directory containing the file pk204g.exe.
3. Set the file transfer mode to binary by typing **binary** and then pressing ENTER.
4. Type **get pk204g.exe** or the name of the file you want to download.
5. When you see **File transfer complete** printed on the screen and you see the **FTP >** prompt, type **quit** and press ENTER.
6. To download the file to your personal computer using Zmodem: Type **sz -b pk204g.exe** at the system prompt and press ENTER.
7. Logoff your Internet account.
8. From DOS, File Manager, or Windows Explorer, create a separate directory on your own computer.
9. Copy the file named pk204g.exe into that directory.
10. At the DOS prompt for the directory where you placed the file, type **pk204g** and press ENTER. After a few moments, the directory displays more than a dozen normal files.

Safely@the.keyboard—Rules for Kids

1. Kids should never give out personal information such as telephone numbers, addresses, school names, or last names in e-mail messages or in public online forums. Be very cautious about this, unless both you and your child know with whom you are communicating.
2. Encourage your kids to confide in you. If something doesn't seem right, for example, if they are being asked to respond to something in an e-mail message that makes them feel uncomfortable, ask them to bring it to your attention.
3. Kids should never arrange to meet with someone in person without adult permission. If your child does become friends with someone on the Internet and would like to meet them in person, go with them and arrange the meeting in a public place.
4. Point out that they cannot believe everything they read on the Net.
5. Kids should never send photographs of themselves to e-mail buddies without checking with you first.
6. Point out to your kids that some people may portray themselves to be someone they're not.
7. Set up rules about what time of day your kids can go online, how much time they can spend online, and which services they can access.

Lesson Plan #11: Online Safety Issues
Grade Level: Grades 3–7

Objectives
In this activity students learn the important rules for safe conduct while online by creating posters.

Activities
1. Print and photocopy enough Safety@the.keyboard handouts so each student gets one. Divide students into seven groups. On seven small pieces of paper, write rule #1, rule #2, rule #3, and so on. Put the papers into a box and have one person from each group pick a paper and their group will design a poster for that rule.
2. Each group designs a picture or graphic representation of their rule. They will put the *Don't do this!* symbol (circle with a slash across it) on top of their final design.
3. Students must also write the rule they are representing at the bottom of the poster. You can use construction paper and laminate it when the poster is done or cut a poster board in half or quarters for the final posters. Each poster should be the same size.
4. Places you may want to post the signs:
    *   In the classroom near the computer.
    *   In the library. Ask the librarian to create a display for them.
    *   Randomly in the hallways.
    *   In the media center.
    *   In the computer lab or the hallway near the computer lab.
    *   On loan to another school! Invite a class from another school to visit your school and view the posters. You can loan the posters to them for a month and let them display them in their school.

Extending This Topic
*   Students who have mastered the Safety@the.keyboard rules can volunteer to be Peer Helpers for other students or classes who have questions about interacting online.
*   Create a Safety@the.keyboard game. You'll need to gather examples of both appropriate and inappropriate e-mail. Collect these from the kids, parents, friends, and faculty. You could also make up examples. An older student or volunteer parent or friend of the class may want to use a simple template to create dummy e-mail for the game. The level of inappropriateness will depend on your situation, school, and community; however, these examples should not be sexually explicit or vulgar. Spamming, junk mail, fake virus warnings, calls for action with no signature file, chain letters, and e-mail that asks for name, street address, phone number, or other identifying information are all good examples to

be used. Also consider e-mail that has no content but a revealing sub-ject line, such as XXX-free video. (E-mail with no content and a subject line containing "XXX" should not be opened.) Another type of e-mail with no content would be e-mail with attached files that contain viruses. (Never open an attachment from someone you don't know.)

Game Rules

The game board should consist of an image of a keyboard with another piece that can be propped up and decorated to look like a monitor. This piece should be able to hold several sheets. Create or find dice with the alphabet. Use anything available for player's pieces. With a role of the die, move to the letter on the keyboard. Each student keeps track of how many letters they visit. If they've already landed on the letter, roll again. Landing on a letter requires the person to the left to take an "e-mail" note from a special folder, place it on the monitor, and read it out loud. The player takes a guess as to whether anything in the message might be considered inappropriate. All players are invited to give their opinions, just take a stab at it or otherwise discuss the letter with the player who read it out loud (after the player has spoken). If all players are in agreement, everyone can write down that letter. If everyone disagrees with the original player, the player goes to the space bar and waits for his or her next turn. If the opinion is split, the letter should be set aside and discussed with an adult. Any response is considered valuable; kids can just hazard a guess as to the appropriateness of the message. The important thing is to get them talking.

Resource List

Safety Tips for Kids on the Internet
http://www.fbi.gov/kids/internet/internet.htm

Surfing the Net WITH KIDS
http://www.surfnetkids.com/

Lesson Plan #12: Creating an FTP Archive Source List
Grade Level: Grade 7 and up

Objectives

In this activity students explore FTP archives, discovering games, documents, and software. They create a list of resources to use again and share with others. They also become familiar with logging in and out procedures, site addresses, file names and pathnames, opening screen messages, and FTP commands.

Overview

Students work in pairs and use Guide Cards to help navigate through FTP archives. They use an Information Form that contains two addresses to look for interesting files and answer questions. The completed Information Forms are compiled to form the Source List.

For the Information Sheets you can use full sheets of paper (to keep in a binder for later) or index cards (to keep in a file box). Decide ahead of time which format suits your situation best. In this example we refer to index cards to keep things simple. Encourage the students to decorate the pages or card with borders or themes for the types of files found at these sites.

Activities

1. Print and photocopy enough Command Guide Cards and Login/Logoff Guide Cards to give each pair of students one of each card.

2. Using blank index cards, prepare Information Forms as follows: On one side of the card print two addresses from the Resource List or addresses you already have. One address should contain a file name and one address should not have a file name. On the back of this card, print at least one of the following questions. You can use more questions, depending on the time available and how many students you are working with.
   - List the oldest date in one of the directories you visited.
   - List the most recent date in one of the directories you visited.
   - How many directories you visited contained more than 25 files?
   - How many directories you visited contained fewer than 5 files?
   - In the directories you visited, what directory had the most files and how many files were in that directory?

   It does not matter if some students get the same addresses, but don't give everyone the same address. You will have a larger source list if you use more addresses and you'll have more topics for later discussions.

3. Divide students into pairs. Give each pair a Command Guide Card, a Login/Logoff Guide Card, and an Information Form.

4. Students log onto their Internet account and use the guide cards to change directories one by one to find the first file listed on their Information Form. While changing directories to get to that file, they should browse the files listed and find one other file that sounds interesting or that they are curious about and write this down on their Information Form.

5. After finding the file named in the first address and finding one other file, students type the command **quit** to close the connection with this FTP host. Then they start FTP again to connect to the next address—the one without a file name. Following the paths listed on their Information Form, they search for a file in the last directory listed and write the complete path for this file on their Information Forms.

6. Students turn over their Information Forms and browse through directories to answer the question(s) on the back of the card. This does not have to be a separate step, and some students may want to look for these answers while searching for their file names.

7. Create the Source List by compiling the Information Forms in a box or ring binder, depending on which method you chose. The first page or first card in the file can be reserved for unexplored sites. Whenever anyone finds an address of interest, list it there. Once a site has been explored, cross it off the unexplored sites list.

Extending This Topic
- This activity may work well for some people in larger groups.
- Later, when you have exposed them to downloading, they can explore these sites further by downloading the index and read.me files. If anything useful is found, the student can write a more detailed or descriptive summary about what is at that site.
- You may have a student or parent who would like to compile the cards another way, for example, on/in a spreadsheet or database.
- Follow-up steps to this lesson are to use the Source List and download one of the files share with everyone else. Is it a document, software, game?
- If a library class does this activity, the Source List can be available as a library resource for other classes to check out.
- Encourage students to find sites on their own in print sources such as computer books, magazines about computers, magazines for kids or teachers, the newspaper, parents, or the computer lab or library of the local university.
- Extend this project by conducting surveys incorporating math, social studies, and language skills into analyzing where the most useful information was obtained and what types of information are provided by various organizations.
  - Share your Source List by publishing it in a variety of ways:
  - Create a flyer to distribute in the school, community, or other schools.
  - Create a FAQ to post to the schools' Web site.
  - Exchange the list via e-mail with penpals or in a global classroom project.

Resource List

FTP files

ftp://mthvax.cs.miami.edu/pub/recipes/lacto/caramel-popcorn

ftp://ftp.books.com/eBooks/NonFiction/History/Speeches/JEFFERSON/
JEFFER.TXT

ftp://ftp.books.com/eBooks/NonFiction/Aviation/tmota.txt

FTP archives to explore
ftp://ftp.winsite.com/pub/pc/

ftp://ftp.honors.unr.edu/pub/

ftp://ftp.vt.edu/pub/k12/

Login / Logoff Guide Card

1. Start your FTP software program

2. Enter the address you want to connect to

3. Identify yourself and give a password

4. Move through the directories

5. Grab the file(s) you're interested in

6. Log off

Lesson Plan #13: Downloading PC Compression Programs
Age/Grade Level: Grade 7 and up

Objectives
In this activity students find and download a compression program file and install it. They will practice FTP commands, learn how to download a file, learn the concepts of compressed files and installation procedures.

Overview
Students use Guide Cards and a step-by-step handout to download a decompression program called PKUNZIP. They install the program by opening the file—it decompresses itself. They then use the program to decompress another file.

Activities
1. Divide students into pairs. Print and photocopy enough of the following items so that each pair gets one of each.
   - Command Guide Card
   - Login/Logoff Guide Card
   - Get That File! handout
2. Give each group the following address:
   Site Address: ftp.pkware.com
   File name: pkz204g.exe
3. The students log onto their Internet accounts and follow the steps in the handout using the Guide Cards when necessary. The Get That File! handout directs the students through the whole process, from the login onto their account to installing the program they downloaded.
4. Discuss the meaning of self-extracting files. PKUNZIP.EXE is a self-extracting MS-DOS executable file. (Self-extracting files decompress themselves on disk when you run them.) Compare this with other files that aren't self-extracting and explain how the students will use the program they installed to decompress the file before they can use any of the files it contains.
5. Students can now use this program to decompress any file with the .zip extension. Students are working in a DOS environment still. They place a copy of the file they want to unzip into the directory containing PKUNZIP. The DOS prompt should contain the name of the directory that contains PKUNZIP. At this prompt, students type PKUNZIP [file name] and then press ENTER.

Three zip files and their locations:
ftp://ftp.winsite.com/pub/pc/win95/games/cross99.zip:
Crossword puzzles that can be printed out.

ftp://ftp.winsite.com/pub/pc/win95/games/quark.zip:
This is a game, the object of which is to eliminate all the charged particles (quarks) by forcing them into a containment chamber.

ftp://ftp.island.net/pub/win95/toilet.zip:
This file changes the recycle bin icon to make it look like a toilet.

Extending this Topic

- PKZIP and PKUNZIP are the most commonly used DOS programs for compressing and decompressing files. Discuss what other compression programs are available.
- PKZIP and PKUNZIP are shareware programs produced by PKWARE, Inc. Discuss what shareware is and copyright issues concerning shareware.
- Discuss the importance of looking at the file date. If you get the most recent version of this program, it will unzip all previous versions
- Use this lesson plan again to download and install PKZIP. After downloading that file, students can make their own compressed files.

Lesson Plan #14: Looking at Pictures
Grade Level: Grade 7 and up

Objectives
In this activity students practice all the FTP commands covered in Chapters 19 and 20 and obtain an image viewer program. They also become familiar with the process of downloading image files from FTP archives and they install and learn to use VPIC.

Overview
Students download a shareware viewer program called VPIC. VPIC version 6.0 is a DOS image viewer for GIF images. They also download image files from FTP archives and install VPIC. VPIC enables students to look at the image files and create a slide show to display several pictures in sequence on the Internet.

Activities
1. Divide students into groups of three and give each group a Command Guide Card and a Login/Logoff Guide Card.
2. Make an image file source card for each group using addresses from the Resource List or use your own. Write two FTP addresses on each source card: one address is for the vpic60.zip file and the other address is for a site with graphics files.
3. The students log onto their Internet accounts and use the Guide Cards to locate the directory with the vpic60 file and then download it. They could also download another viewer program in this directory called DVPEG. It is a DOS program for viewing both JPEG and GIF files. Both programs include documentation on how to set them up on your system and run the programs.

   After downloading the viewer, students close that FTP connection and connect to the second address on their source card and download graphics files. Image files can be identified by directory names such as graphics, pictures, GIFS, and images. The files themselves are identified by their extensions: .gif and .jpg. *You can remind students at this point to set the file transfer mode to binary before downloading a picture file or you can leave students on their own as a self-check. Students who forget this step will be unable to view their pictures and will have to download their files again.*
4. After downloading all their files, students download one more time to move all of the files onto their personal computer. Follow the procedures listed on the Download Guide Card.
5. Students now logoff their Internet account and move the vpic60.zip file to its own directory. Students use PKUNZIP to extract all of the compressed files. If the directory that contains PKUNZIP.EXE is in the DOS PATH, go to the directory containing vpic60.zip, type **pkunzip vpic60**,

and press ENTER. Students then type **dir/p** to page through all of the file names.

6. After the students are sure all of the files are properly extracted from the archive, they can delete the original zip-formatted files or save them to a disk. Remind students to notice the files called readme.1st, config.doc, and vpic.doc. These are text documents that provide information on how to configure VPIC and VPIC's general features. This information can be printed ahead of time or at this point. You may want to have one group of students print one file and photocopy the printed files so that all groups get a copy of each file.

7. Now students move the .gif files they collected to the same directory where the VPIC viewer program resides. Type **vpic** and press ENTER. The names of the GIF files are displayed on the screen. Students select the file they want to view by moving the highlight bar to the appropriate line and pressing ENTER.

Resource List
ftp.fc.net/pub/astro/vpic60e.zip

ftp.wellesley.edu/pub/msdos/vpic60.zip

Graphics File Sources
ftp.umbc.edu/geog/daniel/mast/RSCC/USC/IMAGES/

ftp.seds.org/pub/images/

ftp.sunet.se/pub/pictures/

Index

About the Authors

Allen C. Benson is the director of Library Services at Arkansas State University Mountain Home. He earned his Master of Library Science degree from the University of Alabama where he was also awarded the Faculty Scholar Award in 1993. Benson is known throughout the U.S. for his pioneering work in integrating Internet services into traditional library practices. He has published three other books with Neal-Schuman: *The Complete Internet Companion for Librarians* (1995); the second edition, titled *Neal-Schuman Complete Internet Companion for Librarians* (1997); and *Securing PCs and Data in Libraries and Schools* (1998). Benson works closely with K–12 teachers and students developing the South Shore Memory Project—a digital library project recording the history of the Ozark Mountains.

Linda M. Fodemski is actively involved with helping K–12 children use the Internet as a publishing medium and resource for information. Her experience is hands-on and starts at home. She helps her teenage sons and their school friends create Web sites for various activities. She promotes young children's use of the Internet in grade schools by working with her daughter and other children and their parents in after-school sessions. Linda also works as coordinator of online ordering and Webmaster for Ozark Cooperative Warehouse, a natural foods distributor. She provides technical support for all electronic ordering systems, writes user manuals and help guides for the company's software, and maintains the company's Web site.

CD-ROM Instructions

TO ACCESS THE LINK FARM

1. Place the CD-ROM in the CD-ROM drive on your computer. Open your Web browser; click on <u>File</u> and then <u>Open</u>.
2. Open the appropriate drive.
3. An alphabetical list of files will appear on the screen.
4. From this list, select **index**.
5. The index will give you a menu of the subjects you can explore with the Link Farm. If your computer is connected to the Internet, you can then visit the selected sites by just clicking on the name of the Web site you want to visit.

TO ACCESS THE LESSON PLANS

1. Follow steps 1-4 for accessing the Link Farm.
2. Select **<u>LESSON PLANS</u>** from the Link Farm menu. (It's the last choice in the right hand column.)
3. The screen that comes up will give you two choices: **<u>Connecting Kids Lesson Plans</u>** and **<u>Lesson Plans on the Internet</u>**.
4. If you select **<u>Connecting Kids Lesson Plans</u>** you will get a list of 14 lesson plans from which to select. The text of the plans matches the text of the plans in the Appendix, but the CD-ROM has complete materials, including links to handouts and Web sites. If you select <u>Lesson Plans on the Internet</u>, you will get a list of specifically chosen Web sites with even more lesson plans and information on planning lessons.
5. If you want to save a step, when you first open the CD-ROM instead of selecting **index**, select **lesson**.